THE GREAT BIG
COOKIE
BOOK

THE GREAT BIG
COOKIE
BOOK

Over 200 recipes for cookies, brownies,
scones, bars and biscuits

HILAIRE WALDEN

LORENZ BOOKS

This edition is published by Lorenz Books, an imprint of Anness Publishing Ltd,
Blaby Road, Wigston, Leicestershire LE18 4SE

Email: info@anness.com

Web: www.lorenzbooks.com; www.annesspublishing.com

If you like the images in this book and would like to investigate using them for publishing, promotions or advertising,
please visit our website www.practicalpictures.com for more information.

Publisher: Joanna Lorenz
Project Editor: Joanne Rippin
Recipes supplied by: Liz Trigg, Patricia Lousada, Carla Capalbo, Laura Washburn, Frances Cleary, Norma MacMillan,
Christine France, Pamela Westland, Hilaire Walden, Elizabeth Wolf-Cohen, Janice Murfitt, Carole Handslip,
Steven Wheeler, Katherine Richmond, Joanna Farrow, Judy Williams, Sue Maggs, Carole Clements, Jacqueline Clark,
Sarah Maxwell, Sallie Morris, Lesley Mackley, Roz Denny, Sarah Gates, Norma Miller, Maxine Clark, Shirley Gill,
Judy Jackson, Gilly Love, Janet Brinkworth, Ruby Le Bois, Elisabeth Lambert Ortiz, Sohelia Kimberley
Photographers: Karl Adamson, Edward Allright, Steve Baxter, James Duncan, John Freeman, Michelle Garrett,
Nelson Hargreaves, Amanda Heywood, David Jordan, Patrick McLeavey, Michael Michaels, Polly Wreford
Designer: Siân Keogh, Axis Design
Illustrator: Christos Chrysanthou, Axis Design

ETHICAL TRADING POLICY
Because of our ongoing ecological investment programme, you, as our customer, can have the pleasure and reassurance of knowing
that a tree is being cultivated on your behalf to naturally replace the materials used to make the book you are holding.
For further information about this scheme, go to www.annesspublishing.com/trees

PUBLISHER'S NOTE
Although the advice and information in this book are believed to be accurate and true at the time of going to press, neither the authors nor the
publisher can accept any legal responsibility or liability for any errors or omissions that may have been made nor for any inaccuracies nor for
any loss, harm or injury that comes about from following instructions or advice in this book.

NOTES
For all recipes, quantities are given in both metric and imperial measures and, where appropriate, in standard cups and spoons.
Follow one set of measures, but not a mixture, because they are not interchangeable.
Standard spoon and cup measures are level. 1 tsp = 5ml, 1 tbsp = 15ml, 1 cup = 250ml/8fl oz.
Australian standard tablespoons are 20ml. Australian readers should use 3 tsp in place of 1 tbsp for measuring small quantities.
American pints are 16fl oz/2 cups. American readers should use 20fl oz/2.5 cups in place of 1 pint when measuring liquids.
Electric oven temperatures in this book are for conventional ovens. When using a fan oven, the temperature will probably need to be reduced
by about 10–20°C/20–40°F. Since ovens vary, you should check with your manufacturer's instruction book for guidance.
Medium (US large) eggs are used unless otherwise stated.

Contents

Introduction

Americans call them cookies and the British traditionally use the term biscuits, although now the word cookie has become quite common all over the world.

Whichever name is used, cookies and biscuits are individual, small, crisp, baked sweet and savoury cakes that are good to nibble: the sweet ones with a cup of coffee or tea or other drink, or to serve with ice cream or other light dessert; the savoury ones with a drink or soup.

The American word 'cookie' is of Dutch origin, from the word *koekje* meaning little cake. The origins of the biscuit are to be found in the word itself: it comes from the French *bis cuit,* meaning twice cooked, and goes back to the days when bakers put slices of newly-baked bread back into the cooking oven, so that they dried out completely, becoming something like a rusk. This was really a method of preservation for it enabled the cookies to be kept for a long time; so long, in fact that they could be taken as a basic food item, known as 'ships' biscuits', on long sea voyages.

For many years housewives continued with the practice of drying their biscuits a second time, and it was not until the beginning of the last century that the habit died out. Then both the quality and variety of biscuits that could be made improved dramatically.

A batch of homemade cookies will fill your kitchen with a wonderful aroma when they are ready to come out of the oven. There is a great difference between homemade cookies and the commercial ones sold in shops and supermarkets. Packaged, mass-produced cookies are more concerned with profit and long shelf-life. They are usually too sweet, contain additives and their character and flavour, let alone purity, cannot compare with a tasty cookie from your own store cupboard. Baking your own cookies means you can use only the best ingredients.

There is almost no end to the range of cookies that can be made at home, using recipes that, over the years, have become great favourites the world over, with adults, teenagers and children alike. Many countries of the world have classic recipes and their own traditional favourites, such as Mexican Biscochitos.

This comprehensive collection of recipes suits every occasion and every taste, no matter if the fancy is for something rich and indulgent or traditionally wholesome, delightfully crisp or moist and chewy, satisfyingly chunky or elegantly thin, nutty or chocolatey. This book will inspire you to bake your favourite cookies for high days, holidays and special occasions, delight your friends to a gift-wrapped box of homemade goodies, keep some dough in the freezer for unexpected guests, and determine never again to resort to the supermarket for your cookies, brownies, bars or biscuits.

▶ *Cookies are not only ideal for everyday eating, or special treats at home; they can also be gift-wrapped and given away as a special gift.*

Cookie Tips
and Techniques

Cookies can be made using a wide variety of methods to suit all ranges of ability, and to match the time and ingredients available. Most cookies are easy to make and special skills are rarely required. But, as with most things, once you know exactly the right way to do something, it becomes that much quicker, easier and enjoyable, and the results are far more likely to be successful. The following pages in the Cookie Tips & Techniques section provide all the information you will need to make successful cookies every time, with the minimum amount of effort.

You will find advice on choosing the most appropriate ingredients for the particular cookie you are making, and handy tips on how to carry out simple but vital tasks like measuring accurately. There are detailed instructions for all the methods used for making and shaping cookies, including piping the raw mixture, as well as the various methods of melting chocolate. Ideas for making cookies look really attractive are also included, and the way to make piping bags from greaseproof paper is described.

There are also recommendations on storing the made cookies so they will remain fresh for as long as possible, plus ideas on how to wrap and present your cookies so they become special gifts with a strong personal feel.

Store cupboard

The ingredients for cookie making can be found in most people's store cupboards and fridges.

Chocolate Buy good quality chocolate with at least 50% cocoa solids for baking. Plain chocolate gives a distinctive strong, rich flavour while milk chocolate has a sweeter taste. White chocolate often does not contain any cocoa solids, and lacks the flavour of true chocolate. It is the most difficult chocolate to melt and has poor setting qualities.

Eggs Eggs should be at room temperature so, if you keep them in the fridge, move the number you want to room temperature at least 30 minutes before making a recipe.

Flours Flour provides the structure that makes the cookies. Always sift flour. Not only will this remove any lumps, which are rare nowadays, but it also lightens the flour by incorporating air, and makes it easier to mix in.

Self-raising flour has raising agents added and is the type of flour most usually used in straightforward cookies that need to rise.

Plain flour is used when rising is considered a fault, as when making shortbread. Rich or heavy mixtures that should be raised also often call for plain flour plus additional raising agents in the specific proportions required for the particular recipe.

Wholemeal flour adds more flavour than white flour and is the healthier option but does produce denser cookies. When lightness is important extra raising agents should be added. Some recipes work well with a mixture of white and wholemeal flour.

Butter and margarine Butter gives the best flavour to cookies and should be used whenever possible, especially when there is a high fat content, as in shortbread. However, it can be used interchangeably with hard block margarine. Butter or margarine to be used for creaming with sugar needs to be at room temperature and softened. For rubbing in, the fat should be at a cool room temperature, not fridge hard, and chopped quite finely.

Soft margarine is really only suitable for making cookies by the all-in-one method and when the fat has to be melted.

Dried fruits Today, most dried fruits are dried by artificial heat rather than by the sun, and are treated with sulphur dioxide to help their preservation. Oils are sometimes sprayed on to the fruit to give a shiny appearance and to prevent them sticking together. Try to buy fruit which have been coated with vegetable oils not mineral oils.

Cookie Tips & Techniques

Glacé fruits Wash glacé fruits before using them to remove the syrupy coating, then dry thoroughly.

Spices Ground cinnamon, ginger, mixed spice, nutmeg and cloves may be used in cookies. All spices should be as fresh as possible. Buy in small quantities to use within a few months.

Honey Honey adds its own distinctive flavour to cookies. It contains 17% water so you will need to use slightly more honey than sugar, and reduce the amounts of the other liquids used. For easy mixing in, use clear honey.

Sugars Caster sugar is the best sweetener to use for the creaming method because the crystals dissolve easily and quickly when creamed with the fat. Granulated sugar is coarser textured than caster sugar so this is best used for rubbed-in mixtures and when the sugar is heated with the fat or liquid until it dissolves. Icing sugar appears in the ingredients for some cookie recipes where it is important that the sugar dissolves very readily. Demerara sugar can be used when the sugar is dissolved over heat before being added to the dry ingredients. Soft light and dark brown sugars are used when a richer flavour and colour are called for.

Nuts Nuts become rancid if stored for too long, in the light or at too high a temperature, so only buy in amounts that you will use within 1-2 months and keep them in an airtight container in a cool, dark cupboard. Alternatively, freeze them for up to 1 year.

Equipment

A delightful aspect of cookie making is that it requires the minimum of special equipment.

You can make quite a range of cookies with just a mixing bowl, measures or weights, a wooden spoon, a baking sheet and a wire rack. Only a few items are needed to extend the range much further. Many supermarkets now sell all you will need for cookie making.

Baking tins Use good quality sturdy tins; thin, cheap tins will buckle with time. Cheap tins also heat more quickly so cookies are liable to cook quickly, brown and stick to them more readily. Non-stick tins, of course, save greasing, and lining when called for, greatly reduce sticking and cut down on washing up.

Cannelle knife This tool is great for carving stripes in the skin of citrus fruit. Pare off thin strips before slicing the fruit to make an attractive edge.

Cutters Cutters are available in many different shapes and sizes, ranging from simple plain biscuit circles in various sizes, to small cutters for *petits fours* and savoury cocktail nibbles, to animal shapes, hearts and flowers. For best results, the important criterion that applies to all cutters is that they should be sharp, to give a good clear, sharp outline. This really means that they should be made from metal; plastic cutters tend to compress the cut edges.

To use a cutter, press down firmly on the cutter so that it cuts straight down right through the dough. Then lift up the cutter, without twisting it.

If you want to cut out a shape for which you do not have a cutter, the thing to do is to make a template, or pattern. This is very easy.

Trace or draw the design on to greaseproof paper or card and cut it out using scissors. Lay the template on to the rolled out cookie dough. Use the point of a large, sharp knife to carefully cut around the template, taking care not to drag it. With a thin metal pallette knife or fish slice, transfer the shape to the prepared baking sheet, without distorting the shape.

Food processor Although food processors save time, their drawback is their very speed; they work so fast that you must be careful not to overmix a mixture. Food processors combine rather than beat ingredients together, so they are not so useful for recipes where lightness is important. Also, many models cannot whisk egg whites, and even in those designed for whisking, the whites will not become really stiff.

Knives A round-bladed knife can be used for the initial stages of cutting in the fat before it is rubbed in. Large, sharp knives are needed for cutting cleanly and efficiently through rolled-out dough, or refrigerated dough. Palette knives are invaluable for

spreading and smoothing mixtures in cake tins, transferring cut out cookies to baking sheets before baking and then transferring the baked cookies to a wire rack to cool. They can also be used for spreading icing on cookies.

Measures A set of accurate measuring spoons is vital for measuring 15ml/1 tablespoon, 5ml/1 teaspoon and fractions of teaspoons. All the amounts given in recipes are for level spoonfuls unless otherwise stated. For liquids, use a heatproof jug, preferably see-through, that is calibrated for both imperial and metric measures.

Pastry brushes A large pastry brush is very useful for brushing surplus flour from work surfaces and cookie doughs that are being rolled out, and for greasing cake tins. A pastry brush is also needed for brushing on glazes. Buy good quality brushes with firmly-fixed bristles.

Piping bags and nozzles A medium piping bag with a selection of nozzles is very useful to have for piping uncooked cookie dough, and for decorating cookies after baking. Use small disposable piping bags for chocolate or icing, where a fine line is required.

Rolling pin Rolling pins made of wood are the most common, but you can now buy marble or even plastic ones which are considered to be more hygienic.

Scales A good set of scales is essential for successful cookie making. Whether you use spring balance, modern electronic or old-fashioned balanced scales with a set of weights, test them frequently for accuracy by putting something on them which has the weight printed on it.

Sieves If possible have a set of strong sieves in 2 or 3 different sizes.

Skewers and cocktail sticks Either of these can be used for testing whether cookie mixtures are cooked.

Spatulas A flexible rubber spatula is indispensable for scraping every last morsel from the mixing bowl into the cake tin.

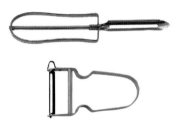

Swivel-blade peelers Both long-handled and broad-handled peelers are the best tools for peeling fruit.

Tea strainer A tea strainer will come in handy for sifting icing sugar over cookies as last-minute decoration.

Whisk Use either a wire balloon whisk or a rotary whisk for beating eggs together. It is a good idea to have two sizes of balloon whisks, to suit the amount of mixture.

Zester Ideal for citrus fruit, a zester has the same function as a cannelle knife but produces a row of thin stripes.

Measuring ingredients

Cooks with years of experience may not need to measure ingredients, but if you are a beginner or are trying a new recipe for the first time, it is best to follow instructions carefully. Also, measuring ingredients precisely will ensure consistent results.

1 For liquids measured in pints or litres: use a glass or clear plastic measuring jug. Put it on a flat surface and pour in the liquid. Bend down and check that the liquid is level with the marking on the jug, as specified in the recipe.

2 For liquids measured in spoons: pour the liquid into the measuring spoon, to the brim, and then pour it into the mixing bowl. Do not hold the spoon over the bowl when measuring because some liquid may overflow.

3 For measuring dry ingredients in a spoon: fill the spoon, scooping up the ingredient. Level the surface with the rim of the spoon, using the straight edge of a knife.

4 For measuring dry ingredients by weight: scoop or pour on to the scales, watching the dial or reading carefully. Balance scales give more accurate readings than spring scales.

5 For measuring syrups: set the mixing bowl on the scales and turn the gauge to zero, or make a note of the weight. Pour in the required weight of syrup.

6 For measuring butter: cut with a sharp knife and weigh, or cut off the specified amount following the markings on the wrapping paper.

Making cookies by the rubbing in method

Plain cookies are usually made by rubbing the fat into the flour. For this, the fat, whether butter, margarine or lard, should be neither rock hard from the fridge, nor too warm. It is first chopped into small pieces, then added to the dry ingredients in a bowl. The mixture is lifted high and the lumps of fat rubbed between the fingertips as the mixture is allowed to fall back into the bowl.

1 Sift the flour into a bowl, adding the raising agents, salt and any sugar or spices and mix them evenly.

2 Stir in any other dry ingredients; combine the oats or other cereal, or coconut. Add the butter or margarine, cut into pieces.

3 Sprinkle the liquid ingredients (water, cream, milk, buttermilk or beaten egg) over the mixture.

4 Mix with your fingers or stir with a fork until the dry ingredients are thoroughly moistened and will come together in a ball of fairly soft dough in the centre of the bowl.

5 Press the dough into a ball. If it is too dry to form a dough, add some extra water.

6 Turn the dough on to a lightly floured surface. Knead very lightly, folding and pressing, to mix evenly – about 30 seconds. Wrap the ball of dough in clear film or greaseproof paper and chill it for at least 30 minutes.

Making cookies by the creaming method

To make cookies by the creaming method, the fat and sugar are 'creamed' – or beaten – together before the eggs and dry ingredients are added. The fat (usually butter or margarine) should be soft enough to be beaten so, if necessary, remove it from the refrigerator and leave for at least 30 minutes. For best results, the eggs should be at room temperature.

1 Sift the flour with the salt, raising agent(s) and any other dry ingredients, such as spices or cocoa powder, into a bowl. Set aside.

2 Put the fat in a large, deep bowl and beat with an electric mixer at medium speed, or a wooden spoon, until the texture is soft and pliable.

3 Add the sugar to the creamed fat gradually. With the mixer at medium-high speed, or using the wooden spoon, beat it into the fat until the mixture is pale and very fluffy. The sugar should be completely incorporated.

5 Add the dry ingredients to the mixture. Beat at low speed just until smoothly combined, or fold in with a large metal spoon.

6 If the recipe calls for any liquid, add it in small portions alternately with portions of the dry ingredients.

7 If the recipe specifies, whisk egg whites separately until frothy, add sugar and continue whisking until stiff peaks form. Fold into the mixture.

Making cookies by the all-in-one method

Some cookies are made by an easy all-in-one method where all the ingredients are combined in a bowl and beaten thoroughly. The mixture can also be made in a food processor, but take care not to over-process. A refinement on the all-in-one method is to separate the eggs and make the mixture with the yolks. The whites are whisked separately and then folded in. Soft margarine has to be used.

1 Sift the flour and any other dry ingredients such as salt, raising agents and spices, into a bowl.

2 Add the liquid ingredients, such as eggs, melted or soft fat, milk or fruit juices, and beat until smooth, with an electric mixer for speed. Pour into the prepared tins and bake as specified in the recipe.

4 Add the eggs or egg yolks, one at a time, beating well after each addition. Scrape the bowl often so all the ingredients are evenly combined. If the mixture curdles, add 15ml/1 tbsp of the measured flour.

8 Pour the mixture into a prepared cake tin and bake as specified.

Rolling and cutting cookies

A cookie dough that is to be rolled and cut must have the right consistency; if it is too dry it will crumble, crack and be difficult to roll neatly, whereas if it is too wet it will stick when rolled out and will spread during baking.

1 After mixing, knead the cookie dough lightly so it holds together, then wrap it in clear film or greaseproof paper and chill it for at least 1 hour. To speed the chilling, put the dough in the freezer for 30 minutes. Tap over the dough with a rolling pin to flatten it, then gently roll out the dough with short, light strokes in one direction to the required thickness.

2 Doughs that are stiff enough to roll may be cut with a knife into squares, rectangles, triangles or fingers, or they can be stamped into rounds or fancy shapes using cutters. To prevent sticking, sprinkle the work surface generously with flour or sugar, according to the recipe, before rolling out the dough, and use a floured or sugared rolling pin.

3 Position the floured cutter near the outside edge of the dough and cut out the shape. Continue cutting out shapes, each time placing the cutter close to the cut out holes, to minimize trimmings. Carefully transfer to the prepared baking sheet. Glaze with beaten egg and sprinkle with nuts, seeds or cheese, if used.

Shaping drop cookies

1 Drop cookies are made from a number of different mixtures, but they invite the use of coarse-textured oats, nuts and dried fruits that cannot be piped. Drop cookies are very easy to shape; spoonfuls of mixture are simply dropped on to the prepared baking sheet.

2 Leave plenty of space between the cookies because they spread during cooking. If a mixture is quite stiff it will have to be spread with the back of a teaspoon or fork, but this is not usually necessary. Drop teaspoons of the mixture on to the prepared baking sheet, spacing them well apart.

Shaping tuiles & cigarettes

Delicate drop cookies, such as Tuiles d'amandes and Brandy Snaps, can be a challenge to the cook. The mixture is particularly thin and a tablespoon or more of flour or liquid can make the difference between success and failure.

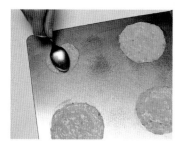

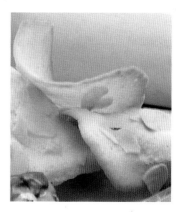

1 Roll spoonfuls of the dough into balls and place 2.5–5cm/1–2in apart on the prepared baking sheets. Press down with a spoon to flatten.

2 Bake until golden brown, 8–10 minutes. Curve tuiles over a rolling pin and roll cigarettes around a wooden spoon handle.

Moulding cookies

Doughs that are too rich to roll out can be shaped by hand. Some recipes call for moistening your hands with water before handling the dough, others recommend lightly flouring your hands, or using cocoa powder or sugar.

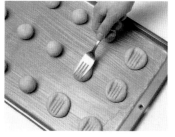

1 Take walnut-size pieces of dough and roll into smooth balls between the palms of your hands. Set them spaced well apart on the prepared baking sheet.

2 Flatten the balls with the back of the tines of a wetted fork to give an attractive lined effect. Alternatively, the base of a greased glass dipped in caster or icing sugar can be used.

Making refrigerator cookies

These are so-called because the dough must be thoroughly chilled before it can be cut into slices for baking, or for serving, and also because the dough can be conveniently kept in the refrigerator for up to a week before it is baked. The dough can also be frozen and used straight from the freezer, using a good sharp knife.

Refrigerator cookies are simple to make because the chilled logs are firm and easy to slice. They are also time-saving because you can make the roll ahead and slice off just as many cookies as you need at any time. Use a thin, sharp knife and wet the knife occasionally to help to give a smooth, clean cut.

The thickness of the slices determines the character of baked cookies: very thin slices will bake into thin, crisp cookies; thick slices result in thicker, more chewy cookies. Place 2.5cm/1in apart on the baking sheets, which are usually ungreased.

1 Beat together the butter and sugar until light and fluffy. Add the flour in three batches, folding in well between each addition. Add any other ingredients and stir in gently.

2 Divide the dough in half and shape each half into a log about 5cm/2in in diameter. Wrap in greaseproof paper and chill overnight. Preheat the oven to 190°C/375°F/Gas 5. Lightly grease two baking sheets.

3 Cut the dough logs across into slices about 3mm/⅛in thick. Place on the prepared baking sheets. Bake for about 10 minutes, until just golden around the edges. Transfer to a wire rack to cool.

Piping cookies

The mixture for piped cookies needs to be soft enough to pipe, but it should not be too loose or it will spread and lose its shape during baking. You will need a piping bag of an appropriate size and a large nozzle, either plain or star-shaped, depending on the effect you want to produce (obviously, a star nozzle will give a more decorative appearance). Drop the piping nozzle into the piping bag and twist, tucking the bag into the nozzle. This will prevent any filling from leaking out at the bottom.

1 Fold the top of the bag over your hand to form a collar, or stand the bag in a tall glass. Add the mixture, scraping the spoon or spatula against your hand or the side of the glass. When the bag is one-half to two-thirds full, twist the top until there is no air left.

2 Hold the twisted end of the bag firmly in one hand. Use the other hand to lightly guide the nozzle. Exert a very firm, steady pressure and start to pipe. The trick is to keep the pressure steady until the design is finished. A sudden squeeze will produce a large blob rather than an even flow.

3 As soon as the shape is complete, stop applying pressure, push down slightly and quickly lift up the nozzle.

4 The bag is kept upright for piping swirls, stars or rosettes, but to make straight lines it is held at an angle.

Making a greaseproof-paper icing bag

Greaseproof-paper icing bags are particularly ideal for piping small quantities

of icing or when two or more colours of icing are being used at once.

They are also easy to use for any type of icing. The bag can be used without

a piping nozzle for making simple, plain lines, or it can be fitted with any size of nozzle.

It is a good idea to make several of these bags at a time.

1 Cut a piece of good quality greaseproof paper to a 25cm/10in square. Fold in half to form a triangle.

2 Fold the short side of the triangle over to the right-angled corner to form a cone.

3 Holding the cone together with one hand, wrap the long point of the triangle around the paper cone.

Tip To use the bag for piping, do not overfill it; instead, open it carefully and refill it when necessary, taking care not to split it or let it unfold. The filled bag can be kept in a plastic bag for a few hours.

4 Tuck the point of paper inside the cone to secure it. For extra security, clear sticky tape can be used to hold the paper together. Add the icing, then cut a small, straight piece off the end of the bag.

5 For using with a nozzle, cut off the pointed end of the bag and position the nozzle so that it fits snugly into the point before adding the icing.

Decorating cookies with icing

It is very easy to turn plain cookies into special-looking treats, whether for a children's birthday party or to give as a present to an adult. All that is needed is some icing – you don't even have to do any piping. However, it is a very simple matter to add a little piped icing. There's no need to be adept at icing – the surfaces you will be covering are small so it won't matter if the lines are squiggly.

A very easy way to decorate the tops of cookies is to spread the icing over the top, using a palette knife.

Another very straightforward way to ice or coat cookies is to just dip them in the coating.

Icing glaze This is like glacé icing but is thinned with egg white so that it sets, making a thin, tangy biscuit glaze.

15ml/1 tbsp lightly beaten egg white
15ml/1 tbsp lemon juice
75–115g/3–4oz/³/₄–1 cup icing sugar
Mix the egg white and lemon juice in a bowl. Gradually beat in the icing sugar, until the mixture is smooth and has the consistency of thin cream. The icing should coat the back of a spoon.

Stencilling

A simple yet effective way to decorate cookies is to pipe lines of a contrasting colour backwards and forwards across the top of the baked cookies. With just a few simple, short lines you can add the finishing touches to some spectacular cookies.

A portion of the raw cookie mixture can be coloured then piped over the shaped, but still unbaked cookies, so the design is cooked in the cookies.

Stencilling is a fun way to liven up cookies. There are no hard and fast rules – experiment with different templates. Cut a small design or initial out of card and place it over a cookie. Dust the cookie with icing sugar or cocoa before carefully removing the card.

Melting chocolate

Melt chocolate slowly, as overheating will spoil both the flavour and texture. Dark chocolate should not be heated above 49°C/120°F; milk and white chocolate should not go above 43°C/110°F. Do not allow water or steam to come into contact with melting chocolate as this may cause it to stiffen. Leave chocolate uncovered, after melting, as condensation could also cause it to stiffen.

Using a double boiler

1 Fill the base of a double boiler or saucepan about a quarter full. Fit the top pan or place a heatproof bowl over the saucepan. The water should not touch the top container. Bring the water to just below boiling point, then turn down the heat to the lowest possible setting.

2 Chop the chocolate or break it into squares and place in the top pan or bowl. Leave to melt completely. Stir until smooth. Keep the water at a very low simmer all the time.

▲ **Using the microwave** Chop the chocolate or break it into squares and place it in a bowl suitable for use in the microwave. Heat until just softened – chocolate burns easily in the microwave, so check often, remembering that chocolate retains its shape when melted in this way.

Approximate times for melting plain or milk chocolate in a 650–700 watt microwave oven are: 115g/4oz, 2 minutes on High (100% power), 200–225g/7–8oz 3 minutes on High (100% power), 115g/4oz white chocolate, 2 minutes on Medium (50% power).

◀ **Using direct heat** This is only suitable for recipes where the chocolate is melted in plenty of other liquid, such as milk or cream. Chop the chocolate or break it into a saucepan. Add the liquid, then heat gently, stirring occasionally, until the chocolate has melted and the mixture is smooth.

Cookie Tips & Techniques

Storing cookies

Cookies should always be cooled completely before storing. When stored, crisp cookies tend to go soft, and soft ones can harden and dry out. The key to storing cookies is to choose an airtight container. This could be a jar or tin with a tight-fitting lid, or a rigid plastic box with a close-fitting lid. If you are not quite sure about the fit of a lid, put the cookies in a sealed plastic bag first. Alternatively, cover the top of the tin, jar or container with clear film before putting on the lid.

▲ **Glass jars** Glass jars with airtight stoppers or corks, or screw-topped lids, allow the cookies to be seen. Found mostly in kitchen departments or shops, some jars come in wonderful shapes and colours.

▶ **Tins** Tins make excellent airtight containers for cookies and come in all shapes and sizes. Look for the more unconventional shapes and designs in large stores, kitchen shops and stationers.

Gift-wrapping cookies

Cookies make wonderful gifts, and you can easily make the wrapping as special as the contents for an irresistible present.

▶ **Gift-wrapping materials** The emphasis on attractive gift-wrap has increased considerably in recent years. It is relatively simple to make small gifts at home and package them beautifully. Personalized gifts are as much a joy to give as to receive.

There are many shops that specialize in gift-wrapping materials. Papers, ribbons, different types of boxes, containers, labels and cards are all available. When making your own gifts, look out for unusual accessories with which to enhance the packaging of the fruits of your labours. Keep an eye open for innovative containers in second-hand, bric-a-brac and antique shops and markets.

▲ **Boxes** These make wonderful containers for cookies. You will find many different designs, colours and sizes in stationers, paper specialists or large stores. If your gift will be given, and eaten, quickly, a pretty box lined with tissue paper may be the answer.

▲ **Bags** Paper and fabric bags can be used for cookies that are given and eaten quickly. They come in a variety of sizes and often have a matching gift label attached. A utilitarian brown paper bag undergoes a complete transformation when it is spatter-sprayed with gold and silver paint. Here it is decorated with a trio of candies wired to the ribbon and with gilded hydrangea heads stuck onto one side.

▲ **Cellophane** For a simple yet stylish presentation, wrap neat piles of cookies in cellophane and tie with string or a pretty ribbon.

Many different shapes and types of container make the gift seem that little bit extra special. For a very special gift, choose a fine porcelain dish, cover with cellophane or clear wrap, and tie with a co-ordinating ribbon.

▲ Many different shapes and types of container make the gift seem that little bit extra special.

▶ **Gift cards and tags** These are often available to co-ordinate with your chosen paper, box or container. You can easily make your own tags by sticking your chosen paper on to a plain piece of card before making a hole in the corner and adding a ribbon. The choice of ribbons is overwhelming; even the simplest ribbons can transform a gift more than any other packaging.

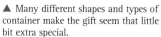

Traditional
Cookies

Snickerdoodles, Tollhouse Cookies, Melting Moments, Ginger Cookies, Scottish Shortbread – these are not just cookies but an integral part of a country's national cuisine, even its national heritage. Such cookies are foods we have known, eaten and loved all our lives, so making them can easily result in a trip along memory lane.

Traditional cookies have been made by generations of family and country cooks, usually using local produce, as in Brittany Butter Cookies which come from the rich dairy-land of western France, and Oatmeal Wedges from Scotland. The ingredients are inexpensive, available, everyday items and the methods straightforward.

Cookies will usually keep well; if they lose their freshness or crispness, they can be refreshed in a low oven, about 160°C/325°F/Gas 3 for about three minutes.

It is a good idea to make a large batch of cookie dough and keep some in the freezer, either as a ball of dough, or ready-shaped, depending on the amount of room available, so you can quickly cook some cookies when you need them. Cookies can also be frozen after baking, but after defrosting will need to be refreshed in a low oven for about three minutes before serving.

Granola Cookies

Makes 18

INGREDIENTS

115g/4oz/½ cup butter or
margarine
75g/3oz/½ cup light brown sugar
75g/3oz/⅓ cup crunchy
peanut butter
1 egg
50g/2oz/½ cup plain flour
2.5ml/½ tsp baking powder
2.5ml/½ tsp ground cinnamon
pinch of salt
225g/8oz/2 cups muesli
50g/2oz/⅓ cup raisins
50g/2oz/½ cup walnuts, chopped

1 Preheat the oven to 180°C/350°F/
Gas 4. Grease a baking sheet. Put
the butter or margarine in a bowl.

2 With an electric mixer, cream the
butter or margarine and sugar
until light and fluffy. Beat in the
peanut butter, then beat in the egg.

3 Sift the flour, baking powder,
cinnamon and salt over the
peanut butter mixture and stir to
blend. Stir in the muesli, raisins, and
walnuts. Taste the mixture to see if it
needs more sugar, as mueslis vary in
sweetness.

4 Drop rounded tablespoonfuls of
the batter on to the prepared
baking sheet about 2.5cm/1in apart.
Press gently with the back of a spoon
to spread each mound into a circle.

5 Bake for about 15 minutes until
lightly coloured. With a metal
spatula, transfer to a wire rack and
leave to cool.

Crunchy Oatmeal Cookies

Makes 14

INGREDIENTS

175g/6oz/¾ cup butter or
margarine
125g/4½oz/¾ cup caster sugar
1 egg yolk
175g/6oz/1½ cups plain flour
5ml/1 tsp bicarbonate of soda
pinch of salt
40g/1½oz/½ cup rolled oats
40g/1½oz/½ cup crunchy
nugget cereal

Variation For Nutty Oatmeal Cookies,
substitute an equal quantity of
chopped walnuts or pecans for the
cereal, and prepare as described.

1 With an electric mixer, cream the
butter or margarine and sugar
together until light and fluffy. Mix in
the egg yolk.

2 Sift over the flour, bicarbonate of
soda and salt, then stir into the
butter mixture. Add the oats and
cereal and stir to blend. Chill for at
least 20 minutes.

3 Preheat the oven to 190°C/375°F/
Gas 5. Grease a baking sheet.
Flour the bottom of a glass.

4 Roll the dough into balls. Place
them on the prepared baking
sheet and flatten with the bottom of
the glass.

5 Bake for 10–12 minutes until
golden. With a metal spatula,
transfer to a wire rack to cool
completely.

Coconut Oat Cookies

Makes 18

❧

INGREDIENTS

175g/6oz/2 cups quick-cooking
oats
75g/3oz/1 cup shredded coconut
225g/8oz/1 cup butter or
margarine, at room temperature
115g/4oz/¹⁄₂ cup granulated sugar
40g/1¹⁄₂oz/¹⁄₄ cup firmly packed
dark brown sugar
2 eggs
60ml/4 tbsp milk
7.5ml/1¹⁄₂ tsp vanilla essence
115g/4oz/1 cup plain flour
2.5ml/¹⁄₂ tsp bicarbonate of soda
pinch of salt
5ml/1 tsp ground cinnamon

❧

1 Preheat the oven to 200°C/400°F/
Gas 6. Lightly grease two baking
sheets. Grease the bottom of a glass
and dip in sugar.

2 Spread the oats and coconut on
an ungreased baking sheet. Bake
for 8–10 minutes until golden brown,
stirring occasionally.

3 With an electric mixer, cream the
butter or margarine and both
sugars until light and fluffy. Beat in
the eggs, one at a time, then add the
milk and vanilla essence. Sift over the
dry ingredients and fold in. Stir in
the oats and coconut.

4 Drop spoonfuls of the dough
2.5–5cm/1–2in apart on the
baking sheets and flatten with the
glass. Bake for 8–10 minutes. Transfer
to a wire rack to cool.

Crunchy Jumbles

Makes 36

❧

INGREDIENTS

115g/4oz/¹⁄₂ cup butter or
margarine, at room temperature
225g/8oz/1 cup sugar
1 egg
5ml/1 tsp vanilla essence
175g/6oz/1¹⁄₄ cups plain flour
2.5ml/¹⁄₂ tsp bicarbonate of soda
pinch of salt
115g/4oz/2 cups crisped rice
cereal
1 cup chocolate chips

❧

Variation For even crunchier cookies,
add ¹⁄₂ cup walnuts, coarsely chopped,
with the cereal and chocolate chips.

1 Preheat the oven to 180°C/350°F/
Gas 4. Lightly grease two baking
sheets.

2 With an electric mixer, cream the
butter or margarine and sugar until
light and fluffy. Beat in the egg and
vanilla. Sift over the flour, bicarbonate
of soda, and salt and fold in.

3 Add the cereal and chocolate
chips. Stir to mix thoroughly.

4 Drop spoonfuls of the dough
2.5–5cm/1–2in apart on the
prepared sheets. Bake for 10–12
minutes until golden. Transfer to a
wire rack to cool.

Malted Oaty Crisps

These cookies are very crisp and crunchy – ideal to serve with morning coffee.

Makes 18

❧

INGREDIENTS

175g/6oz/1½ cups rolled oats
75g/3oz/¼ cup light
muscovado sugar
1 egg
60ml/4 tbsp sunflower oil
30ml/2 tbsp malt extract

❧

1 Preheat the oven to 190°C/375°F/ Gas 5. Lightly grease two baking sheets. Mix the rolled oats and brown sugar in a bowl, breaking up any lumps in the sugar. Add the egg, sunflower oil and malt extract, mix well, then leave to soak for 15 minutes.

2 Using a teaspoon, place small heaps of the mixture well apart on the prepared baking sheets. Press the heaps into 7.5cm/3in rounds with the back of a dampened fork.

3 Bake for 10–15 minutes, until golden brown. Leave to cool for 1 minute, then remove with a palette knife and cool on a wire rack.

Variation To give these crisp biscuits a coarser texture, substitute jumbo oats for some or all of the rolled oats.

Shortbread

Makes 8

❦

INGREDIENTS

*175g/6oz/²⁄₃ cup unsalted butter
115g/4oz/½ cup caster sugar
150g/5oz/1¼ cups plain flour
50g/2oz/½ cup rice flour
1.5ml/¼ tsp baking powder
pinch of salt*

❦

1 Preheat the oven to 160°C/325°F/
Gas 3. Grease a shallow 20cm/8in
cake tin.

2 With an electric mixer, cream the
butter and sugar together until
light and fluffy. Sift over the flours,
baking powder and salt and mix well.

3 Press the dough neatly into the
prepared tin, smoothing the
surface with the back of a spoon.
Prick all over with a fork, then score
into eight equal wedges.

4 Bake for 40–45 minutes. Leave in
the tin until cool enough to
handle, then unmould and recut the
wedges while still hot.

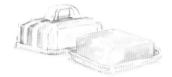

Oatmeal Wedges

Makes 8

❦

INGREDIENTS

*50g/2oz/4 tbsp butter
25ml/1½ tbsp treacle
50g/2oz/⅓ cup dark brown sugar
175g/6oz/1¼ cups rolled oats
pinch of salt*

❦

Variation If wished, add 5ml/1 tsp
ground ginger to the melted butter.

1 Preheat the oven to 180°C/350°F/
Gas 4. Line a 20cm/8in shallow
cake tin with greaseproof paper and
grease the paper.

2 Place the butter, treacle and sugar
in a saucepan over a low heat.
Cook, stirring, until melted and
combined.

3 Remove from the heat and add
the oats and salt. Stir to blend.

4 Spoon into the prepared cake tin
and smooth the surface. Bake for
20–25 minutes until golden brown.
Leave in the tin until cool enough to
handle, then unmould and cut into
eight equal wedges while still hot.

Melting Moments

These cookies are very crisp and light – and they melt in your mouth.

Makes 16–20

INGREDIENTS

40g/1½oz/3 tbsp butter or margarine
65g/2½oz/5 tbsp lard
75g/3oz/½ cup caster sugar
½ egg, beaten
few drops of vanilla or almond essence
150g/5oz/1¼ cups self-raising flour
rolled oats for coating
4–5 glacé cherries, quartered

1 Preheat the oven to 180°C/350°F/ Gas 4. Grease two baking sheets. Cream together the butter or margarine, lard and sugar, then gradually beat in the egg and vanilla or almond essence.

2 Stir the flour into the beaten mixture, then roll into 16–20 small balls in your hands.

3 Spread the rolled oats on a sheet of greaseproof paper and toss the balls in them to coat evenly.

4 Place the balls, spaced slightly apart, on the prepared baking sheets, place a piece of cherry on top of each and bake for 15–20 minutes, until lightly browned. Allow the cookies to cool for a few minutes before transferring to a wire rack.

Apricot Yogurt Cookies

These soft cookies are very quick to make and are useful for lunch boxes.

Makes 16

INGREDIENTS

175g/6oz/1½ cups plain flour
5ml/1 tsp baking powder
5ml/1 tsp ground cinnamon
75g/3oz/1 cup rolled oats
75g/3oz/½ cup light muscovado
sugar
115g/4oz/¾ cup chopped ready-
to-eat dried apricots
15ml/1 tbsp flaked hazelnuts or
almonds
150g/5oz/⅔ cup natural yogurt
45ml/3 tbsp sunflower oil
demerara sugar, for sprinkling

1 Preheat the oven to 190°C/375°F/ Gas 5. Lightly oil a large baking sheet.

2 Sift together the flour, baking powder and cinnamon. Stir in the oats, sugar, apricots and nuts.

Cook's Tip These cookies do not keep well, so it is best to eat them within two days, or to freeze them. Pack into polythene bags and freeze for up to four months.

3 Beat together the yogurt and oil, then stir evenly into the flour mixture to make a firm dough. If necessary, add a little more yogurt. Use your hands to roll the mixture into about 16 small balls.

4 Place the balls on the prepared baking sheet and flatten with a fork. Sprinkle with demerara sugar. Bake for 15–20 minutes, until firm and golden brown. Transfer to a wire rack and leave to cool.

Applesauce Cookies

These fruit-flavoured cookies are a favourite with children.

Makes 36

❧

INGREDIENTS

*450g/1lb cooking apples, peeled,
cored and chopped
45ml/3 tbsp water
115g/4oz/¹/₂ cup caster sugar
115g/4oz/¹/₂ cup butter or margarine
115g/4oz/1 cup plain flour
2.5ml/¹/₂ tsp baking powder
1.5ml/¹/₄ tsp bicarbonate of soda
pinch of salt
2.5ml/¹/₂ tsp ground cinnamon
50g/2oz/¹/₂ cup chopped walnuts*

❧

1 Cook the apple with the water in a covered saucepan over a low heat until the apple is tender. Cool slightly then purée in a blender or mash with a fork Measure out 175ml/6fl oz/³/₄ cup.

2 Preheat the oven to 190°C/375°F/ Gas 5. Grease a baking sheet. In a medium-size bowl, cream together the sugar and butter or margarine until well mixed. Beat in the apple sauce.

Cook's Tip If the apple sauce is too runny, put it in a strainer over a bowl and let it drain for 10 minutes before measuring it out.

3 Sift the flour, baking powder, bicarbonate of soda, salt and cinnamon into the mixture, and stir to blend. Fold in the chopped walnuts.

4 Drop teaspoonfuls of the dough on to the prepared baking sheet, spacing them about 5cm/2in apart.

5 Bake the cookies for 8–10 minutes until they are golden brown. Transfer to a wire rack and leave to cool.

Chocolate Chip Hazelnut Cookies

Chocolate chip cookies, with a delicious nutty flavour.

Makes 36

INGREDIENTS

115g/4oz/1 cup plain flour
5ml/1 tsp baking powder
pinch of salt
75g/3oz/1/3 cup butter or
margarine
115g/4oz/1 1/2 cups caster sugar
50g/2oz/1/3 cup light brown sugar
1 egg
5ml/1 tsp vanilla essence
125g/4 1/2oz/2/3 cup chocolate chips
50g/2oz/1/2 cup hazelnuts,
chopped

3 Stir in the chocolate chips and half of the hazelnuts, using a wooden spoon.

4 Drop teaspoonfuls of the mixture on to the prepared baking sheets, to form 2cm/3/4in mounds. Space the cookies 2.5–5cm/1–2in apart.

5 Flatten each cookie lightly with a wet fork. Sprinkle the remaining hazelnuts on top of the cookies and press lightly into the surface.

6 Bake for 10–12 minutes until golden. Transfer the biscuits to a wire rack and leave to cool.

1 Preheat the oven to 180°C/350°F/ Gas 4. Grease 2–3 baking sheets. Sift the flour, baking powder and salt into a small bowl. Set aside.

2 With an electric mixer, cream together the butter or margarine and the sugars. Beat in the egg and vanilla essence. Add the flour mixture and beat well with the mixer on low speed.

Chocolate Chip Oat Biscuits

Makes 60

INGREDIENTS

115g/4oz/1 cup plain flour
2.5ml/½ tsp bicarbonate of soda
1.5ml/¼ tsp baking powder
pinch of salt
115g/4oz/½ cup butter or
margarine
115g/4oz/½ cup caster sugar
90g/3½oz/generous ½ cup light
brown sugar
1 egg
½ tsp vanilla essence
75g/3oz/¾ cup rolled oats
175g/6oz/1 cup plain chocolate
chips

1 Preheat the oven to 180°C/350°F/
Gas 4. Grease 3–4 baking sheets.

2 Sift the flour, bicarbonate of
soda, baking powder and salt into
a mixing bowl. Set aside.

3 With an electric mixer, cream
together the butter or margarine
and the sugars. Add the egg and
vanilla essence and beat until light
and fluffy.

4 Add the flour mixture and beat
on a low speed until thoroughly
blended. Stir in the rolled oats and
chocolate chips. The dough should be
crumbly. Drop heaped teaspoonfuls on
to the prepared baking sheets, spacing
the dough about 2.5cm/1in apart.

5 Bake for about 15 minutes until
just firm around the edge but still
soft to the touch in the centre. With a
slotted spatula, transfer the biscuits to
a wire rack and leave to cool.

Mexican Almond Cookies

Light and crisp, these biscuits are perfect with a cup of strong coffee.

Makes 24

INGREDIENTS

115g/4oz/1 cup plain flour
175g/6oz/1¹/₃ cups icing sugar
pinch of salt
*50g/2oz/¹/₂ cup almonds, finely
chopped*
2.5ml/¹/₂ tsp vanilla essence
*115g/4oz/¹/₂ cup unsalted butter
icing sugar for dusting*

Variation Try using other nuts such as walnuts, peanuts or pecans.

3 Roll out the dough on a lightly floured surface until it is 3mm/¹/₈in thick. Using a round cutter, stamp out into about 24 biscuits, re-rolling the trimmings as necessary.

4 Transfer the biscuits to non-stick baking sheets and bake for 30 minutes, until browned. Transfer to wire racks to cool, then dust thickly with icing sugar.

1 Preheat the oven to 180°C/350°F/ Gas 4. Sift the flour, icing sugar and salt into a bowl. Add the almonds and mix well. Stir in the vanilla essence.

2 Using your fingertips, work the butter into the mixture to make a dough. Form it into a ball.

Peanut Butter Cookies

For extra crunch add 50g/2oz/¹/₂ cup chopped peanuts with the peanut butter.

Makes 24

❦

INGREDIENTS

*115g/4oz/1 cup plain flour
2.5ml/¹/₂ tsp bicarbonate of soda
pinch of salt
115g/4oz/¹/₂ cup butter
125g/4¹/₂oz/³/₄ cup firmly packed
light brown sugar
1 egg
5ml/1 tsp vanilla essence
225g/8oz/1 cup crunchy peanut
butter*

❦

1 Sift together the flour, bicarbonate of soda and salt and set aside.

2 With an electric mixer, cream together the butter and sugar until light and fluffy.

3 In another bowl, mix the egg and vanilla essence, then gradually beat into the butter mixture.

4 Stir in the peanut butter and blend thoroughly. Stir in the dry ingredients. Chill for at least 30 minutes, until firm.

5 Preheat the oven to 180°C/350°F/ Gas 4. Grease two baking sheets.

6 Spoon out rounded teaspoonfuls of the dough and roll into balls.

7 Place the balls on the prepared baking sheets and press flat with a fork into circles about 6cm/2¹/₂in diameter, making a criss-cross pattern. Bake for 12–15 minutes, until lightly coloured. Transfer to a wire rack to cool.

Tollhouse Cookies

Makes 24

❦

INGREDIENTS

*115g/4oz/¹/₂ cup butter or
margarine
50g/2oz/¹/₄ cup granulated sugar
75g/3oz/¹/₂ cup dark brown sugar
1 egg
2.5ml/¹/₂ tsp vanilla essence
125g/4¹/₂oz/1¹/₈ cups flour
2.5ml/¹/₂ tsp bicarbonate of soda
pinch of salt
175g/6oz/1 cup chocolate chips
50g/2oz/¹/₂ cup walnuts, chopped*

❦

1 Preheat the oven to 180°C/350°F/ Gas 4. Grease two baking sheets.

2 With an electric mixer, cream together the butter or margarine and the two sugars until the mixture is light and fluffy.

3 In another bowl, mix the egg and vanilla essence, then gradually beat into the butter mixture. Sift over the flour, bicarbonate of soda and salt. Stir to blend.

4 Add the chocolate chips and walnuts, and mix to combine thoroughly.

5 Place heaped teaspoonfuls of the dough 5cm/2in apart on the prepared baking sheets. Bake for 10–15 minutes until lightly coloured. With a metal spatula, transfer to a wire rack to cool.

Snickerdoodles

Makes 30

INGREDIENTS

115g/4oz/¹/₂ cup butter
115g/4oz/1¹/₂ cups caster sugar
5ml/1 tsp vanilla essence
2 eggs
50ml/2fl oz/¹/₄ cup milk
400g/14oz/3¹/₂ cups plain flour
1 tsp bicarbonate of soda
50g/2oz/¹/₂ cup walnuts or pecans,
finely chopped
For the coating
75ml/5 tbsp sugar
30ml/2 tbsp ground cinnamon

1 With an electric mixer, beat the butter until light and creamy. Add the sugar and vanilla essence and continue until fluffy. Beat in the eggs, then the milk.

2 Sift the flour and bicarbonate of soda over the butter mixture and stir to blend. Stir in the nuts. Refrigerate for 15 minutes. Preheat the oven to 190°C/375°F/Gas 5. Grease two baking sheets.

3 To make the coating, mix the sugar and cinnamon. Roll tablespoonfuls of the dough into walnut-size balls. Roll the balls in the sugar mixture. You may need to work in batches.

4 Place the balls 5cm/2in apart on the prepared baking sheets and flatten slightly. Bake for about 10 minutes until golden. Transfer to a wire rack to cool.

Chewy Chocolate Cookies

Makes 18

INGREDIENTS

4 egg whites
300g/11oz/2¹/₂ cups icing sugar
115g/4oz/1 cup cocoa powder
30ml/2 tbsp plain flour
5ml/1 tsp instant coffee powder
15ml/1 tbsp water
115g/4oz/1 cup walnuts, finely
chopped

1 Preheat the oven to 180°C/350°F/Gas 4. Line two baking sheets with greaseproof paper and then grease the paper well.

2 With an electric mixer, beat the egg whites until frothy.

3 Sift the sugar, cocoa, flour and coffee into the whites. Add the water and continue beating on low speed to blend, then on high for a few minutes until the mixture thickens. With a rubber spatula, fold in the walnuts.

4 Place generous spoonfuls of the mixture 2.5cm/1in apart on the prepared baking sheets. Bake for 12–15 minutes until firm and cracked on top but soft on the inside. With a metal spatula, transfer to a wire rack to cool.

Variation Add 75g/3oz/¹/₂ cup chocolate chips to the dough with the chopped walnuts.

Buttermilk Cookies

Makes 15

❦

INGREDIENTS

175g/6oz/1½ cups plain flour
pinch of salt
5ml/1 tsp baking powder
2.5ml/½ tsp bicarbonate of soda
50g/2oz/4 tbsp cold butter or
margarine
175ml/6fl oz/¾ cup buttermilk

❦

1 Preheat the oven to 220°C/425°F/ Gas 7. Grease a baking sheet.

2 Sift the dry ingredients into a bowl. Rub in the butter or margarine until the mixture resembles coarse crumbs.

3 Gradually pour in the buttermilk, stirring with a fork until the mixture forms a soft dough.

4 Roll out to about 1cm/½in thick. Stamp out 15 5cm/2in circles with a biscuit cutter.

5 Place on the prepared baking sheet and bake for 12–15 minutes until golden. Serve warm or at room temperature.

Baking Powder Cookies

These make a simple accompaniment to meals, or a snack with fruit preserves.

Makes 8

❦

INGREDIENTS

165g/5½oz/1⅓ cups plain flour
30ml/2 tbsp sugar
15ml/1 tbsp baking powder
pinch of salt
40g/1½oz/5 tbsp cold butter,
chopped
120ml/4fl oz/½ cup milk

❦

Variation For Berry Shortcake, split the cookies in half while still warm. Butter one half, top with lightly sugared fresh berries, such as strawberries, raspberries or blueberries, and sandwich with the other half. Serve with dollops of whipped cream.

1 Preheat the oven to 220°C/425°F/ Gas 7. Grease a baking sheet. Sift the flour, sugar, baking powder and salt into a bowl.

2 Rub in the butter until the mixture resembles coarse crumbs. Pour in the milk and stir with a fork to form a soft dough.

3 Roll out the dough to about 5mm/¼in thick. Stamp out circles with a 6cm/2½in biscuit cutter.

4 Place on the prepared baking sheet and bake for about 12 minutes, until golden. Serve these soft biscuits hot or warm, spread with butter for meals. To accompany tea or coffee, serve with butter and jam or honey.

Traditional Sugar Cookies

Makes 36

❦

INGREDIENTS

350g/12oz/3 cups plain flour
5ml/1 tsp bicarbonate of soda
10ml/2 tsp baking powder
2.5ml/^{1}/$_2$ tsp grated nutmeg
115g/4oz/^{1}/$_2$ cup butter or
margarine
225g/8oz/1 cup caster sugar
2.5ml/^{1}/$_2$ tsp vanilla essence
1 egg
115g/4oz/^{1}/$_2$ cup milk
coloured or demerara sugar for
sprinkling

❦

1 Sift the flour, bicarbonate of soda, baking powder and nutmeg into a small bowl. Set aside.

2 With an electric mixer, cream together the butter or margarine, caster sugar and vanilla essence until the mixture is light and fluffy. Add the egg and beat to mix well.

3 Add the flour mixture alternately with the milk to make a soft dough. Wrap in clear film and chill for at least 30 minutes.

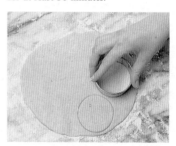

4 Preheat the oven to 180°C/350°F/ Gas 4. Roll out the dough on a lightly floured surface to 3mm/^{1}/$_8$in thick. Cut into rounds or other shapes with floured biscuit cutters.

5 Transfer to ungreased baking sheets. Sprinkle with sugar. Bake for 10–12 minutes until golden brown. Transfer the cookies to a wire rack to cool.

Brittany Butter Cookies

These little biscuits are similar to shortbread, but richer. Traditionally, they
are made with lightly salted butter.

Makes 18–20

INGREDIENTS

6 egg yolks, lightly beaten
15ml/1 tbsp milk
250g/9 oz/2¼ cups plain flour
175g/6oz/¾ cup caster sugar
200g/7oz/scant 1 cup butter

1 Preheat the oven to 180°C/350°F/
Gas 4. Butter a heavy baking
sheet. Mix 15ml/1 tbsp of the egg
yolks with the milk to make a glaze.

2 Sift the flour into a bowl. Add the
egg yolks, sugar and butter, and
work them together until creamy.

3 Gradually bring in a little flour at
a time until it forms a slightly
sticky dough.

4 Using floured hands, pat out the
dough to about 5mm/¼in thick
and cut out rounds using a 7.5cm/3in
cutter. Transfer the rounds to the
prepared baking sheet, brush each
with a little egg glaze, then, using the
back of a knife, score with lines to
create a lattice pattern.

5 Bake for about 12–15 minutes,
until golden. Cool in the tin on a
wire rack for 15 minutes, then
carefully remove the biscuits and
leave to cool completely on the rack.

Cook's Tip To make a large Brittany
Butter Cake, pat the dough with well-
floured hands into a 23cm/9in loose-
based cake tin or springform tin. Brush
with egg glaze and score the lattice
pattern on top. Bake for 45 minutes–
1 hour, until firm to the touch and
golden brown.

Toffee Cookies

Makes 36

INGREDIENTS

175g/6oz/³/₄ cup unsalted butter, melted
200g/7oz/1³/₄ cups instant porridge oats
115g/4oz/packed ¹/₂ cup soft light brown sugar
120ml/4fl oz/¹/₂ cup corn syrup
30ml/2 tbsp vanilla essence
large pinch of salt
175g/6oz/³/₄ cup plain chocolate, grated
40g/1¹/₂oz/¹/₃ cup chopped walnuts

1 Preheat the oven to 200°C/400°F/ Gas 6. Grease a 37.5 x 25cm/15 x 10in baking tin.

2 Mix together the butter, oats, sugar, syrup, vanilla essence and salt and press into the prepared tin. Bake for about 15–18 minutes, until the mixture is brown and bubbly.

3 Remove from the oven and immediately sprinkle on the chocolate. Set aside for 10 minutes, then spread the chocolate over the base. Sprinkle on the nuts. Transfer to a wire rack to cool. Cut into squares.

Rosewater Thins

These light, crunchy biscuits are easy to make and bake in minutes.

Makes 60

INGREDIENTS

225g/8oz/1 cup slightly salted butter
225g/8oz/1 cup caster sugar
1 egg
15ml/1 tbsp single cream
300g/11oz/2¹/₂ cups plain flour
pinch of salt
5ml/1 tsp baking powder
15ml/1 tbsp rosewater
caster sugar for sprinkling

1 Preheat the oven to 190°C/375°F/ Gas 5. Line two baking sheets with non-stick baking paper.

2 Soften the butter and mix with all the other ingredients until you have a firm dough. Mould the mixture into an even roll and wrap in greaseproof paper. Chill until it is firm enough to slice very thinly. This will take 1–1¹/₂ hours.

3 Arrange the cookies on the prepared baking sheets with enough space for them to spread. Sprinkle with a little caster sugar and bake for about 10 minutes until they are just turning brown at the edges.

Scottish Shortbread

Light, crisp shortbread looks very professional when shaped in a mould,
although you could also shape it by hand.

Makes 2 large or
8 individual shortbreads

INGREDIENTS

175g/6oz/³/₄ cup plain flour
50g/2oz/¹/₂ cup cornflour
50g/2oz/¹/₄ cup caster sugar, plus
extra for sprinkling
115g/4oz/¹/₂ cup unsalted butter,
chopped

1 Preheat the oven to 160°C/325°F/
Gas 3. Lightly flour the mould
and line a baking sheet with non-
stick baking paper. Sift the flour,
cornflour and sugar into a mixing
bowl. Rub the butter into the flour
mixture until it binds together and
you can knead it into a soft dough.

2 Place the dough into the mould
and press to fit neatly. Invert the
mould on to the baking sheet and tap
firmly to release the dough shape.
Bake for 35–40 minutes, until pale
golden in colour.

3 Sprinkle the top of the shortbread
with a little caster sugar and cool
on the baking sheet. Wrap in
cellophane paper or place in a box
tied with ribbon to make a delicious
hogmanay gift.

Spanish Churros

INGREDIENTS

250ml/8fl oz/1 cup water
15ml/1 tbsp granulated sugar,
plus extra for coating
pinch of salt
175g/6oz/1½ cups plain flour
1 egg
oil for deep frying
½ lime or lemon

Cook's Tip A funnel can be used to shape the churros. Close the end with a finger, add the batter, then release into the oil in small columns.

1 Bring the water, sugar and salt to the boil. Remove from the heat and beat in the flour until smooth.

2 Beat in the egg, using a wooden spoon, until the mixture is smooth and satiny. Set the batter aside.

3 Pour the oil into a deep frying pan to a depth of about 5cm/2in. Add the lime or lemon, then heat the oil to 190°C/375°F, until a cube of day-old bread added to the oil browns in 30–60 seconds.

4 Pour the batter into a piping bag fitted with a fluted nozzle. Pipe 7.5cm/3in strips of batter and then add to the oil, a few at a time. Fry for 3–4 minutes, until golden brown.

5 Using a slotted spoon, remove the churros from the pan and drain on kitchen paper. Roll the hot churros in granulated sugar before serving with a cup of thick hot chocolate.

Golden Pillows

INGREDIENTS

225g/8oz/2 cups plain flour,
sifted
15ml/1 tbsp baking powder
pinch of salt
30ml/2 tbsp lard or margarine
175ml/6fl oz/¾ cup water
corn oil for frying
syrup or honey, to serve

Cook's Tip Use your imagination when deciding what to serve with the pillows. Sprinkle them with cinnamon and sugar, or syrup flavoured with rum.

1 Put the flour, baking powder and salt into a large bowl. Lightly rub in the lard or margarine, using your fingertips, until the mixture resembles coarse breadcrumbs.

2 Gradually stir in the water, using a fork, until the mixture clings together to form a soft dough.

3 Shape the dough into a ball, then turn on to a lightly floured surface and knead very gently until smooth. Roll out thinly to a rectangle measuring about 46 x 35cm/18 x 15in. Using a sharp knife, carefully cut about 30 7.5cm/3in squares. For a decorative edge, use a pastry wheel to cut out the squares.

4 Heat the oil to 190°C/375°F, until a cube of day-old bread browns in 30–60 seconds.

5 Fry the squares, a few at a time, in the oil. As they brown and puff up, turn over to cook the other side. Remove with a slotted spoon and drain on kitchen paper. It is important that the temperature of the oil remains constant during the cooking process. Serve warm, with syrup or honey.

Chunky Chocolate Drops

Do not allow these cookies to cool completely on the baking sheet or they will become too crisp and will break when you try to lift them.

Makes 18

INGREDIENTS

175g/6oz plain chocolate, chopped
115g/4oz/½ cup unsalted butter, chopped
2 eggs
90g/3½oz/½ cup granulated sugar
50g/2oz/⅓ cup light brown sugar
40g/1½oz/⅓ cup plain flour
25g/1oz/¼ cup cocoa powder
5ml/1 tsp baking powder
10ml/2 tsp vanilla essence
pinch of salt
115g/4oz/1 cup pecans, toasted and coarsely chopped
175g/6oz/1 cup plain chocolate chips
115g/4oz fine quality white chocolate, chopped into 5mm/¼in pieces
115g/4oz fine quality milk chocolate, chopped into 5mm/¼in pieces

1 Preheat the oven to 160°C/325°F/ Gas 3. Grease two large baking sheets. In a medium saucepan over a low heat, melt the plain chocolate and butter, stirring until smooth. Remove from the heat and set aside to cool slightly.

2 In a large mixing bowl, using an electric mixer, beat the eggs and sugars for 2–3 minutes, until pale and creamy. Gradually pour in the melted chocolate mixture, beating until well blended. Beat in the flour, cocoa powder, baking powder, vanilla essence and salt until just blended. Stir in the nuts, chocolate chips and chocolate pieces.

3 Drop heaped tablespoons of the mixture on to the prepared baking sheets 10cm/4in apart. Flatten each to 7.5cm/3in rounds. Bake for 8–10 minutes, until the tops are shiny and cracked and the edges look crisp; do not over-bake or the cookies will become fragile.

4 Remove the baking sheets to a wire rack to cool for 2 minutes, then transfer to the rack to cool completely.

Chocolate Marzipan Cookies

These crisp little cookies satisfy a sweet tooth and have a little almond surprise inside.

Makes 36

INGREDIENTS

200g/7oz/scant 1 cup unsalted butter
200g/7oz/generous 1 cup light muscovado sugar
1 egg
300g/11oz/2½ cups plain flour
60ml/4 tbsp cocoa powder
200g/7oz white almond paste
115g/4oz white chocolate, chopped

1 Preheat the oven to 190°C/375°F/ Gas 5. Lightly grease two large baking sheets. Cream the butter with the sugar in a bowl until pale and fluffy. Add the egg and beat well.

2 Sift the flour and cocoa over the mixture. Stir in, first with a wooden spoon, then with clean hands, pressing the mixture together to make a fairly soft dough.

3 Roll out about half the dough on a lightly floured surface to a thickness of about 5mm/¼in. Using a 5cm/2in biscuit cutter, cut out rounds, re-rolling the dough as required until you have about 36 rounds.

4 Cut the almond paste into about 36 equal pieces. Roll into balls, flatten slightly and place one on each round of dough. Roll out the remaining dough, cut out more rounds, then place on top of the almond paste. Press the dough edges to seal. Bake for 10–12 minutes until the cookies have risen well. Cool completely. Melt the white chocolate, spoon into a paper piping bag and pipe on to the biscuits.

Cook's Tip If the dough is too sticky to roll, chill it for about 30 minutes, then try again.

Double Chocolate Cookies

Keep these luscious treats under lock and key unless you're feeling generous.

Makes 18–20

❧

INGREDIENTS

115g/4oz/½ cup unsalted butter
115g/4oz/⅔ cup light muscovado
sugar
1 egg
5ml/1 tsp vanilla essence
150g/5oz/1¼ cups self-raising
flour
75g/3oz/¾ cup porridge oats
115g/4oz plain chocolate, roughly
chopped
115g/4oz white chocolate, roughly
chopped

❧

Cook's Tip If you're short of time when making the cookies, substitute chocolate chips for the chopped chocolate. Chopped stem ginger would make a delicious addition as well.

1 Preheat the oven to 190°C/375°F/ Gas 5. Lightly grease two baking sheets. Cream the butter with the sugar in a bowl until pale and fluffy. Add the egg and vanilla essence and beat well.

2 Sift the flour over the mixture and fold in lightly with a metal spoon, then add the oats and chopped plain and white chocolate and stir until evenly mixed.

3 Place small spoonfuls of the mixture in 18–20 rocky heaps on the prepared baking sheets, leaving space for spreading.

4 Bake for 15–20 minutes, until beginning to turn pale golden. Cool for 2–3 minutes on the baking sheets, then transfer to wire racks to cool completely.

Chocolate and Nut Refrigerator Cookies

The dough must be chilled thoroughly before it can be sliced and baked.

Makes 50

INGREDIENTS

225g/8oz/2 cups plain flour
pinch of salt
50g/2oz plain chocolate, chopped
225g/8oz/1 cup unsalted butter
225g/8oz/1 cup caster sugar
2 eggs
5ml/1 tsp vanilla essence
115g/4oz/1 cup walnuts, finely chopped

Variation For two-tone cookies, melt only 25g/1oz chocolate. Combine all the ingredients, except the chocolate, as above. Divide the dough in half. Add the chocolate to one half. Roll out the plain dough on to a flat sheet. Roll out the chocolate dough, place on top of the plain dough and roll up. Wrap, slice and bake as described.

1 In a small bowl, sift together the flour and salt. Set aside. Melt the chocolate in the top of a double boiler, or in a heatproof bowl set over a saucepan of hot water. Set aside.

2 With an electric mixer, cream the butter until soft. Add the sugar and continue beating until the mixture is light and fluffy.

3 Mix the eggs with the vanilla essence, then gradually stir into the butter mixture.

4 Stir in the chocolate, then the flour followed by the nuts.

5 Divide the dough into four parts, and roll each into 5cm/2in diameter logs. Wrap tightly in foil and chill or freeze until firm.

6 Preheat the oven to 190°C/375°F/ Gas 5. Grease two baking sheets. Cut the dough into 5mm/¼in slices. Place on the prepared sheets and bake for about 10 minutes. Transfer to wire rack to cool.

Chocolate Kisses

These rich little cookies look attractive mixed together on a plate and dusted with icing sugar. Serve them with ice cream or simply with coffee.

Makes 24

❦

INGREDIENTS

75g/3oz plain chocolate, chopped
75g/3oz white chocolate, chopped
115g/4oz/¹⁄₂ cup butter
115g/4oz/¹⁄₂ cup caster sugar
2 eggs
225g/8oz/2 cups plain flour
icing sugar, to decorate

❦

1 Put each chocolate into a small bowl and melt it over a saucepan of hot, but not boiling, water, stirring until smooth. Set aside to cool.

2 Whisk together the butter and caster sugar until pale and fluffy. Beat in the eggs, one at a time.

3 Sift the flour over the butter, sugar and egg mixture and mix in thoroughly.

4 Halve the mixture and divide it between the two bowls of chocolate. Mix each chocolate in well. Knead the doughs until smooth, wrap them in clear film and chill for 1 hour. Preheat the oven to 190°C/375°F/ Gas 5. Grease two baking sheets.

5 Shape slightly rounded teaspoonfuls of both doughs roughly into balls. Roll the balls in the palms of your hands to make neater ball shapes. Arrange the balls on the prepared baking sheets and bake for 10–12 minutes. Dust with sifted icing sugar and then transfer to a wire rack to cool.

Chocolate Pretzels

Makes 28

INGREDIENTS

115g/4oz/1 cup plain flour
pinch of salt
45ml/3 tbsp cocoa powder
115g/4oz/¹/₂ cup butter
150g/5oz/²/₃ cup caster sugar
1 egg
1 egg white, lightly beaten, for
glazing
sugar crystals for sprinkling

1 Sift together the flour, salt and cocoa powder. Set aside. Grease two baking sheets.

2 With an electric mixer, cream the butter until light. Add the sugar and continue beating until light and fluffy. Beat in the egg. Add the dry ingredients and stir to blend. Gather the dough into a ball, wrap in greaseproof paper, and chill for 1 hour, or freeze for 30 minutes.

3 Roll the dough into 28 small balls. If the dough is sticky, flour your hands. Chill the balls until needed. Preheat the oven to 190°C/375°F/Gas 5.

4 Roll each ball into a rope about 25cm/10in long. With each rope, form a loop with the two ends facing you. Twist the ends and fold back on to the circle, pressing in to make a pretzel shape. Place on the prepared baking sheets.

5 Brush the pretzels with the egg white. Sprinkle sugar crystals over the tops and bake for 10–12 minutes until firm. Transfer to a wire rack to cool.

Chocolate, Maple and Walnut Swirls

Makes 12

❦

INGREDIENTS

*450g/1lb/4 cups strong white
flour
2.5ml/¹/₂ tsp ground cinnamon
50g/2oz/4 tbsp unsalted butter,
chopped
50g/2oz/¹/₄ cup caster sugar
1 sachet easy-blend dried yeast
1 egg yolk
120g/4fl oz/¹/₂ cup water
60ml/4 tbsp milk
45ml/3 tbsp maple syrup, to
finish
For the filling
40g/1¹/₂oz/3 tbsp unsalted butter,
melted
50g/2oz/¹/₄ packed cup light
muscovado sugar
175g/6oz/1 cup plain chocolate
chips
75g/3oz/³/₄ cup chopped walnuts*

❦

1 Grease a deep 23cm/9in springform cake tin. Sift the flour and cinnamon into a bowl, then rub in the butter until the mixture resembles coarse breadcrumbs.

2 Stir in the sugar and yeast. In a jug, beat the egg yolk, with the water and milk, then stir into the dry ingredients to make a soft dough.

3 Knead until smooth, then roll out to about 40 x 30cm/16 x 12in. Brush with melted butter.

4 To make the filling, sprinkle with the muscovado sugar, plain chocolate chips and chopped walnuts.

5 Roll up the dough from a long side like a Swiss roll, then cut into 12 thick even-size slices.

6 Pack the slices closely together in the prepared cake tin. Cover and leave in a warm place for 1¹/₂ hours, until well risen and springy to the touch. Preheat the oven to 220°C/425°F/Gas 7.

7 Bake for 30–35 minutes, until well risen, golden brown and firm. Remove from the tin and transfer to a wire rack. To finish, spoon the maple syrup over the cake. Pull the pieces apart to serve.

Cook's Tip The amount of liquid added to the dry ingredients may have to be adjusted slightly as some flours absorb more liquid than others.

Old-fashioned Ginger Cookies

Makes 60

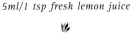

INGREDIENTS

300g/11oz/2¹/₂ cups plain flour
5ml/1 tsp bicarbonate of soda
7.5ml/1¹/₂ tsp ground ginger
1.5ml/¹/₄ tsp ground cinnamon
1.5ml/¹/₄ tsp ground cloves
115g/4oz/¹/₂ cup butter or
margarine
350g/12oz/1¹/₂ cups caster sugar
1 egg, beaten
60ml/4 tbsp black treacle
5ml/1 tsp fresh lemon juice

1 Preheat the oven to 160°C/325°F/ Gas 3. Grease 3–4 baking trays.

2 Sift the flour, bicarbonate of soda and spices into a small bowl. Set aside.

3 With an electric mixer, cream together the butter or margarine and two-thirds of the sugar.

4 Stir in the egg, treacle and lemon juice. Add the flour mixture and mix in thoroughly with a wooden spoon to make a soft dough.

5 Shape the dough into 2cm/³/₄ in balls. Roll the balls in the remaining sugar and place them about 5cm/2in apart on the prepared baking trays.

6 Bake for about 12 minutes until the biscuits are just firm to the touch. With a slotted spatula, transfer the biscuits to a wire rack and leave to cool.

Double Gingerbread Cookies

Packed in little bags or into a gingerbread box, these pretty cookies would make a lovely gift.

They are easy to make, but will have everyone wondering how you did it!

Makes 25

INGREDIENTS

For the golden gingerbread
mixture
175g/6oz plain flour
1.5ml/¹/₄ tsp bicarbonate of soda
pinch of salt
5ml/1 tsp ground cinnamon
*65g/2¹/₂oz unsalted butter, cut
in pieces*
75g/3oz caster sugar
*30ml/2 tbsp maple or
golden syrup*
1 egg yolk, beaten
For the chocolate gingerbread
mixture
175g/6oz/1¹/₂ cups plain flour
pinch of salt
10ml/2 tsp ground mixed spice
2.5ml/¹/₂ tsp bicarbonate of soda
25g/1oz/4 tbsp cocoa powder
*75g/3oz/¹/₃ cup unsalted butter,
chopped*
*75g/3oz/¹/₃ cup light muscovado
sugar*
1 egg, beaten

1 To make the golden gingerbread
mixture, sift together the flour,
bicarbonate of soda, salt and spices.
Rub the butter into the flour in a
large bowl, until the mixture resembles
fine breadcrumbs. Add the sugar, syrup
and egg yolk and mix to a firm dough.
Knead lightly. Wrap in clear film and
chill for 30 minutes before shaping.

2 To make the chocolate gingerbread
mixture, sift together the flour,
salt, spice, bicarbonate of soda and
cocoa powder. Knead the butter into
the flour in a large bowl. Add the
sugar and egg and mix to a firm
dough. Knead lightly. Wrap in clear
film and chill for 30 minutes.

3 Roll out half of the chocolate
dough on a floured surface to a 28
x 4cm/11 x 1¹/₂in rectangle, 1cm/
¹/₂in thick. Repeat with half of the
golden gingerbread dough. Using a
knife, cut both lengths into seven long,
thin strips. Lay the strips together, side
by side, alternating the colours.

4 Roll out the remaining golden
gingerbread dough with your
hands to a long sausage, 2cm/³/₄in
wide and the length of the strips. Lay
the sausage of dough down the centre
of the striped dough.

5 Carefully bring the striped dough
up around the sausage and press
it gently in position, to enclose the
sausage completely. Roll the
remaining chocolate dough to a thin
rectangle measuring approximately
28 x 13cm/11 x 5in.

6 Bring the chocolate dough up
around the striped dough, to
enclose it. Press gently into place.
Wrap and chill for 30 minutes.

7 Preheat the oven to 180°C/350°F/
Gas 4. Grease a large baking
sheet. Cut the gingerbread roll into
thin slices and place them, slightly
apart, on the prepared baking sheet.

8 Bake for about 12–15 minutes,
until just beginning to colour
around the edges. Leave on the
baking sheet for 3 minutes and
transfer to a wire rack to cool
completely.

Chocolate Cinnamon Tuiles

Makes 12

❦

INGREDIENTS

1 egg white
50g/2oz/¼ cup caster sugar
30ml/2 tbsp plain flour
40g/1½oz/3 tbsp butter, melted
15ml/1 tbsp cocoa powder
2.5ml/½ tsp ground cinnamon

❦

Cook's Tip Work as quickly as possible when removing the tuiles from the baking sheets – if they firm up too quickly, pop the baking sheet back in the oven for a minute and try again.

1 Preheat the oven to 200°C/400°F/ Gas 6. Lightly grease two large baking sheets. Whisk the egg white in a clean, grease-free bowl until it forms soft peaks. Gradually whisk in the sugar to make a smooth, glossy mixture.

2 Sift the flour over the mixture and fold in evenly. Stir in the butter. Transfer about 45ml/3 tbsp of the mixture to a small bowl and set aside.

3 In a separate bowl, mix together the cocoa and cinnamon. Stir into the larger quantity of mixture.

4 Leaving room for spreading, drop spoonfuls of the chocolate-flavoured mixture on to the prepared baking sheets, then spread each gently with a palette knife to make a neat round.

6 Bake for 4–6 minutes, until just set. Using a palette knife, lift each biscuit carefully and quickly drape it over a rolling pin, to give a curved shape as it hardens.

7 Leave the tuiles to cool until set, then remove them gently and finish cooling on a wire rack. Serve on the same day.

5 Using a small spoon, drizzle the reserved plain mixture over the rounds to give a marbled effect.

Spiced-nut Palmiers

Makes 40

INGREDIENTS

*75g/3oz/²/₃ cup chopped
almonds, walnuts or hazelnuts
30ml/2 tbsp caster sugar, plus
extra for sprinkling
2.5ml/¹/₂ tsp ground cinnamon
225g/8oz rough-puff or puff
pastry, defrosted if frozen
1 egg, lightly beaten*

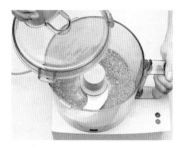

1 Lightly butter two large baking
sheets, preferably non-stick. In a
food processor fitted with a metal
blade, process the nuts, sugar and
cinnamon until finely ground.

2 Sprinkle the work surface with
sugar and roll out the pastry to a
50 x 20cm/20 x 8in rectangle about
3mm/¹/₈in thick. Brush the pastry
lightly with beaten egg and sprinkle
evenly with half of the nut mixture.

3 Fold in the long edges of the
pastry to meet in the centre and
flatten with the rolling pin. Brush
with egg and sprinkle with most of
the nut mixture. Fold in the edges
again to meet in the centre, brush
with egg and sprinkle with the
remaining nut mixture. Fold one side
of the pastry over the other.

4 Cut the pastry crossways into
8mm/³/₈in thick slices and place
about 2.5cm/1in apart on the baking
sheets.

5 Spread the pastry edges apart to
form a wedge shape. Chill the
palmiers for at least 15 minutes.
Preheat the oven to 220°C/425°F/
Gas 7.

6 Bake for about 8–10 minutes,
until golden. Carefully turn them
over halfway through the cooking
time. Keep an eye on them as the
sugar can easily scorch. Transfer to a
wire rack to cool.

Cinnamon and Treacle Cookies

These cookies are slightly moist, spicy and nutty.

Makes 24

INGREDIENTS

30ml/2 tbsp black treacle
*50g/2oz/4 tbsp butter or
margarine*
115g/4oz/1 cup plain flour
1.5ml/¼ tsp bicarbonate of soda
2.5ml/½ tsp ground ginger
5ml/1 tsp ground cinnamon
*40g/1½oz packed cup soft brown
sugar*
*15ml/1 tbsp ground almonds or
hazelnuts*
1 egg yolk
115g/4oz/1 cup icing sugar, sifted

1 Lightly grease a baking sheet. Heat the treacle and butter or margarine gently until just beginning to melt.

2 Sift the flour into a large bowl with the bicarbonate of soda and spices, then stir in the sugar and almonds or hazelnuts.

3 Beat the treacle mixture and egg yolk briskly into the bowl, drawing the ingredients together to form a firm but soft dough.

4 Roll out the dough on a lightly floured surface to 5mm/¼in thick and stamp out shapes, such as stars, hearts or circles. Re-roll the trimmings and cut more shapes. Place on the prepared baking sheet and chill for 15 minutes.

5 Preheat the oven to 190°C/375°F/ Gas 5. Prick the cookies lightly with a fork and bake for 12–15 minutes, until just firm. Transfer to wire racks to become crisp.

6 Mix the icing sugar with a little lukewarm water to make it slightly runny, then drizzle it over the biscuits on the wire racks.

Cinnamon Refrigerator Cookies

Makes 50

❦

INGREDIENTS

225g/8oz/2 cups flour
pinch of salt
10ml/2 tsp ground cinnamon
225g/8oz/1 cup unsalted butter
225g/8oz/1 cup caster sugar
2 eggs
5ml/1 tsp vanilla essence

❦

1 In a bowl, sift together the flour, salt and cinnamon. Set aside.

2 With an electric mixer, cream the butter until soft. Add the sugar and continue beating until the mixture is light and fluffy.

3 Beat together the eggs and vanilla essence, then gradually stir into the butter mixture.

4 Add the dry ingredients to the butter mixture and stir together until evenly combined.

5 Divide the dough into four parts, then roll each into 5cm/2in diameter logs. Wrap tightly in foil and chill or freeze until firm.

6 Preheat the oven to 190°C/375°F/Gas 5. Grease two baking sheets.

7 With a sharp knife, cut the dough into 5mm/¼in slices. Place the rounds on the prepared baking sheets and bake for about 10 minutes until lightly coloured. With a metal spatula, transfer to a wire rack to cool completely.

Spicy Pepper Biscuits

Makes 48

INGREDIENTS

200g/7oz/1³/₄ cups plain flour
50g/2oz/¹/₂ cup cornflour
10ml/2 tsp baking powder
2.5ml/¹/₂ tsp ground cardamom
2.5ml/¹/₂ tsp ground cinnamon
2.5ml/¹/₂ tsp grated nutmeg
2.5ml/¹/₂ tsp ground ginger
2.5ml/¹/₂ tsp ground allspice
pinch of salt
2.5ml/¹/₂ tsp freshly ground black pepper
225g/8oz/1 cup butter or margarine
90g/3¹/₂oz/1¹/₃ cups light brown sugar
2.5ml/¹/₂ tsp vanilla essence
5ml/1 tsp finely grated lemon rind
50ml/2fl oz/¹/₄ cup whipping cream
75g/3oz/³/₄ cup finely ground almonds
30ml/2 tbsp icing sugar

1 Preheat the oven to 180°C/350°F/ Gas 4.

2 Sift the flour, cornflour, baking powder, spices, salt and pepper into a bowl. Set aside.

3 With an electric mixer, cream the butter or margarine and brown sugar together until light and fluffy. Beat in the vanilla essence and grated lemon rind.

4 With the mixer on low speed, add the flour mixture alternately with the whipping cream, beginning and ending with flour. Stir in the ground almonds.

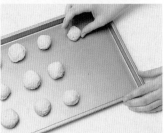

5 Shape the dough into 2cm/³/₄in balls. Place them on ungreased baking sheets, about 2.5cm/1in apart. Bake for 15–20 minutes until golden brown underneath.

6 Leave to cool on the baking sheets for about 1 minute before transferring to a wire rack to cool completely. Before serving, sprinkle lightly with icing sugar.

Lavender Heart Cookies

In folklore, lavender has always been linked with love, as has food, so make some heart-shaped cookies and serve them on Valentine's Day or any other romantic anniversary.

Makes 16–18

INGREDIENTS

115g/4oz/¹/₂ cup unsalted butter
50g/2oz/¹/₄ cup caster sugar
175g/6oz/1¹/₂ cups plain flour
30ml/2 tbsp fresh lavender florets
or 15ml/1 tbsp dried culinary
lavender, roughly chopped
30ml/2 tbsp superfine sugar for
sprinkling

1 Cream together the butter and sugar until fluffy. Stir in the flour and lavender and bring the mixture together in a soft ball. Cover and chill for 15 minutes.

2 Preheat the oven to 200°C/400°F/ Gas 6. Roll out the dough on a lightly floured surface and stamp out about 18 biscuits, using a 5cm/2in heart-shaped cutter. Place on a heavy baking sheet and bake for about 10 minutes, until golden.

3 Leave the biscuits standing for 5 minutes to set. Using a metal spatula, transfer carefully from the baking sheet on to a wire rack to cool completely. The biscuits can be stored in an airtight container for up to one week.

Vanilla Crescents

These attractively shaped cookies are sweet and delicate, ideal for an elegant afternoon tea.

Makes 36

❦

INGREDIENTS

175g/6oz/1¼ cups unblanched almonds
115g/4oz/1 cup plain flour
pinch of salt
225g/8oz/1 cup unsalted butter
115g/4oz/½ cup granulated sugar
5ml/1 tsp vanilla essence
icing sugar for dusting

❦

1 Grind the almonds with a few tablespoons of the flour in a food processor, blender or nut grinder.

2 Sift the remaining flour with the salt into a bowl. Set aside.

3 With an electric mixer, cream together the butter and sugar until light and fluffy.

4 Add the almonds, vanilla essence and the flour mixture. Stir to mix well. Gather the dough into a ball, wrap in greaseproof paper, and chill for at least 30 minutes.

5 Preheat the oven to 160°C/325°F/ Gas 3. Lightly grease two baking sheets.

6 Break off walnut-size pieces of dough and roll into small cylinders about 1cm/½in in diameter. Bend into small crescents and place on the prepared baking sheets.

7 Bake for about 20 minutes until dry but not brown. Transfer to a wire rack to cool only slightly. Set the rack over a baking sheet and dust with an even layer of icing sugar. Leave to cool completely.

Mexican Aniseed Cookies

Makes 24

INGREDIENTS

175g/6oz/1½ cups plain flour
5ml/1 tsp baking powder
pinch of salt
115g/4oz/½ cup unsalted butter
115g/4oz/½ cup caster sugar
1 egg
5ml/1 tsp whole aniseed
15ml/1 tbsp brandy
50g/2oz/¼ cup caster sugar mixed
with 2.5ml/½ tsp ground
cinnamon for sprinkling

1 Sift together the flour, baking powder and salt. Set aside.

2 Beat the butter with the sugar until soft and fluffy. Add the egg, aniseed and brandy and beat until incorporated. Fold in the dry ingredients until just blended to a dough. Chill for 30 minutes.

3 Preheat the oven to 180°C/350°F/ Gas 4. Grease two baking sheets.

4 On a lightly floured surface, roll out the chilled dough to about 3mm/⅛in thick.

5 With a floured cutter, pastry wheel or knife, cut out the biscuits into squares, diamonds or other shapes. The traditional shape for biscochitos is a fleur-de-lis but you might find this a bit too ambitious.

6 Place on the prepared baking sheets and sprinkle lightly with the cinnamon sugar.

7 Bake for about 10 minutes, until just barely golden. Cool on the baking sheet for 5 minutes before transferring to a wire rack to cool completely. The biscuits can be kept in an airtight container for up to one week.

Festive and Fancy Cookies

Over the years, some cookies have become associated with certain festivals – Jewelled Christmas Trees dangle jauntily from the tree at Christmas, Easter Cookies always find their way into the cookie jar at that time of the year, and at carnival time Italians would feel deprived if Italian Pastry Twists did not make an appearance. Other cookies are festive just because they are fancy. Chocolate-dipped Hazelnut Crescents or Black-and-White Ginger Florentines immediately perk up the spirits and make you feel something special is happening.

If you are making cookies for a holiday period such as school holidays, try to select recipes that keep well so you can make them a week or so in advance. Alternatively, freeze them, either raw or baked. Don't forget to make a note of how long they need to thaw, plus the baking time for raw cookies, and remember that cooked ones will benefit from being refreshed in the oven.

Baklava

This, the queen of all pastries, is enjoyed all year but is specially associated with the Persian New Year on 21st March, celebrating the first day of spring.

Makes 30

INGREDIENTS

350g/12oz/3 cups ground
pistachios
150g/5oz/1¼ cups icing sugar
15ml/1 tbsp ground cardamom
150g/5oz/⅔ cup unsalted butter,
melted
450g/1lb filo pastry
For the syrup
450g/1lb/2 cups granulated sugar
300ml/½ pint/1¼ cups water
30ml/2 tbsp rosewater

1 Place the sugar and water in a saucepan, bring to the boil and simmer for 10 minutes, until syrupy. Stir in the rosewater. Mix together the nuts, icing sugar and cardamom. Preheat the oven to 160°C/325°F/Gas 3. Brush a baking tin with butter.

2 Taking one sheet of filo pastry at a time, and keeping the remainder covered with a damp cloth, brush with melted butter and lay on the bottom of the tin. Continue until you have six buttered layers in the tin. Spread half of the nut mixture over, pressing down with a spoon.

3 Take another six sheets of filo pastry, brush with butter and lay over the nut mixture. Sprinkle over the remaining nuts and top with a final layer of six filo sheets. Cut the pastry into small lozenge shapes. Pour the remaining butter over the top. Bake for 20 minutes then increase the heat to 200°C/400°F/Gas 6 and bake for 15 minutes, until light golden in colour and puffed.

4 Remove from the oven and drizzle most of the syrup over the pastry, reserving the remainder for serving.

Cinnamon Balls

These almond balls should be soft inside, with a very strong cinnamon flavour. They harden
with keeping, so it is a good idea to freeze some and only use them when required.

Makes 15

❦

INGREDIENTS

175g/6oz/1½ cups ground almonds
75g/3oz/⅓ cup caster sugar
15ml/1 tbsp ground cinnamon
2 egg whites
oil for greasing
icing sugar for dredging

❦

3 Bake for about 15 minutes, so they remain slightly soft inside – too much cooking will make them hard and tough. Slide a palette knife under the balls to release them from the baking sheet and leave to cool.

4 Sift a few tablespoons of icing sugar on to a plate. When the cinnamon balls are cold slide them on to the plate. Shake gently to completely cover the cinnamon balls in sugar. Store in an airtight container or in the freezer.

1 Preheat the oven to 180°C/350°F/ Gas 4. Oil a large baking sheet. Mix together the ground almonds, sugar and cinnamon. Whisk the egg whites until they begin to stiffen and fold enough into the almonds to make a fairly firm mixture.

2 Wet your hands with cold water and roll small spoonfuls of the mixture into balls. Place these on the prepared baking sheet.

Coconut Pyramids

Coconut biscuits are sold in Israeli street markets during Passover.

Makes 15

INGREDIENTS

*225g/8oz/1 cup desiccated
coconut
115g/4oz/½ cup caster sugar
2 egg whites*

Cook's Tip The heat in ovens tends to be uneven, so, if necessary, turn the sheets round during baking for the pyramids to brown evenly.

1 Preheat the oven to 190°C/375°F/ Gas 5. Grease a large baking sheet with a little oil.

2 Mix together the desiccated coconut and sugar. Lightly whisk the egg whites. Fold enough egg white into the coconut to make a fairly firm mixture. You may not need quite all the egg whites.

3 Form the mixture into pyramid shapes by taking a teaspoonful and rolling it first into a ball. Flatten the base and press the top into a point. Arrange the pyramids on the prepared baking sheet.

4 Bake for 12–15 minutes on a low shelf. The tips should begin to turn golden and the pyramids should be just firm, but still soft inside.

5 Slide a palette knife under the pyramids and leave to cool before transferring to a wire rack.

Easter Cookies

These are enjoyed as a traditional part of the Christian festival of Easter.

Makes 16–18

INGREDIENTS

115g/4oz/¹/₂ cup butter, chopped
75g/3oz/¹/₃ cup caster sugar, plus
extra for sprinkling
1 egg, separated
200g/7oz/1¹/₄ cups plain four
2.5ml/¹/₂ tsp ground mixed spice
2.5ml/¹/₂ tsp ground cinnamon
50g/2oz/scant ¹/₃ cup currants
15ml/1 tbsp chopped mixed peel
15–30ml/1–2 tbsp milk

3 Turn the dough on to a floured surface, knead lightly until just smooth, then roll out using a floured rolling pin, to about 5mm/¹/₄in thick. Cut the dough into rounds using a 5cm/2in fluted biscuit cutter. Transfer the rounds to the prepared baking sheets and bake for 10 minutes.

4 Beat the egg white, then brush over the biscuits. Sprinkle with caster sugar and return to the oven for a further 10 minutes, until golden. Transfer to a wire rack to cool.

1 Preheat the oven to 200°C/400°F/ Gas 6. Lightly grease two baking sheets. Beat together the butter and sugar, then beat in the egg yolk.

2 Sift the flour and spices over the egg mixture, then fold in with the currants and peel, adding sufficient milk to mix to a fairly soft dough.

Italian Pastry Twists

Deep-fried pastry twists, hearts or knots, traditionally flavoured with vin santo, *a sherry-like Italian wine, are served hot, dusted with icing sugar, at Italian carnival time.*

Makes 40

❧

INGREDIENTS

250g/9oz/2¼ cups plain flour
1 egg
pinch of salt
25g/1oz/2 tbsp granulated sugar
2.5ml/½ tsp vanilla essence
25g/1oz/2 tbsp butter, melted
45–60ml/3–4 tbsp sherry
oil for deep-frying
icing sugar for sprinkling

❧

1 Sift the flour into a large mixing bowl and make a well in the centre. Add the egg, salt, sugar, vanilla essence and melted butter.

2 Mix with your hands until the mixture starts to come together. When the dough becomes stiff, add enough sherry to make the dough soft and pliable. Knead until smooth and then wrap and chill for about 1 hour.

3 Roll out the pastry thinly and cut into 40 18 x 1cm/7 x ½in strips. Tie each strip loosely into a knot.

4 Heat the oil in a pan to 190°C/375°F and deep-fry the knots in batches for 2–3 minutes, until puffed up and golden.

5 Drain the pastry twists on kitchen paper, sprinkle generously with icing sugar and serve either hot or cold with coffee.

Apricot Meringue Bars

Makes 16

❦

INGREDIENTS

50g/2oz/¹/₂ cup plain flour
50g/2oz/¹/₂ cup butter
2.5ml/¹/₂ tsp vanilla essence
large pinch of salt
1 large egg, separated
115g/4oz/¹/₂ cup caster sugar
50g/2oz/¹/₃ cup chopped walnuts
50g/2oz/¹/₃ cup chopped pecans
115g/4oz/¹/₂ cup apricot jam

❦

1 Preheat the oven to 180°C/350°F/ Gas 4. Grease a 20cm/9in square baking tin. Beat together the flour, butter, vanilla essence, salt, egg yolk and 50g/2oz/¹/₄ cup of the sugar. Spread the mixture evenly over the base of the baking tin, prick it all over with a fork and bake in the oven for 10 minutes.

2 Beat the egg white until stiff. Gradually beat in the remaining 50g/2oz/¹/₄ cup sugar until the mixture is smooth and glossy. Gently fold in the chopped walnuts and pecans, but do not over-mix.

3 Remove the tin from the oven, spread the apricot jam over the base and spread the meringue mixture to cover it evenly.

4 Bake in the oven for 20 minutes, until the meringue is crisp and light brown. Cool on a wire rack, then cut into 10 x 2.5cm/4 x 1in bars for serving.

Cook's Tip Apricot Meringue Bars may be stored in an airtight container for up to 3 days.

Moravian Tarts

Makes 35

❦

INGREDIENTS

115g/4oz/¹/₂ cup unsalted butter
2.5ml/¹/₂ tsp vanilla essence
large pinch of salt
150g/5oz/scant ²/₃ cup caster sugar
1 egg, beaten
115g/4oz/1 cup plain flour
1.5ml/¹/₄ tsp bicarbonate of soda
7.5ml/1¹/₂ tsp ground cinnamon
1 egg white, lightly beaten
35 pecan halves

❦

1 Cream the butter, vanilla essence, salt and 115g/4oz/¹/₂ cup of the sugar until light and fluffy. Gradually add the egg, beating constantly.

2 Sift together the flour, bicarbonate of soda and 2.5ml/ ¹/₂ tsp of the cinnamon and stir a little at a time into the butter mixture. Form the mixture into a dough and chill overnight. Remove from the refrigerator 30 minutes before using.

3 Preheat the oven to 180°C/350°F/ Gas 4. Lightly grease a baking sheet. Roll out the dough until it is about 3mm/¹/₈in thick. Cut into rounds with a 5cm/2in cutter.

4 Place the rounds on the prepared baking sheet and brush the tops with the egg white. Mix the remaining ground cinnamon with the remaining caster sugar. Sprinkle over the rounds and press a pecan half into each centre. Bake for 8–10 minutes, until golden brown.

Glazed Ginger Cookies

These also make good hanging biscuits for decorating trees and garlands. For this, make a
hole in each biscuit with a skewer, and thread with fine ribbon.

Makes about 20

INGREDIENTS

1 quantity Golden Gingerbread
mixture
2 quantities Icing Glaze
red and green food colourings
175g/6oz white almond paste

1 Preheat the oven to 180°C/350°F/
Gas 4. Grease a large baking
sheet. Roll out the gingerbread dough
on a floured surface and, using a
selection of floured cookie cutters, cut
out a variety of shapes, such as trees,
stars, crescents and bells. Transfer to
the prepared baking sheet and bake
for 8–10 minutes, until just beginning
to colour around the edges. Leave the
cookies on the baking sheet for
3 minutes.

2 Transfer the cookies to a wire
rack and leave to cool. Place the
wire rack over a large tray or plate.
Using a dessertspoon, spoon the icing
glaze over the cookies until they are
completely covered. Leave in a cool
place to dry for several hours.

3 Knead red food colouring into
half of the almond paste and
green into the other half. Roll a thin
length of each coloured paste and
then twist the two together into a
rope.

4 Secure a rope of paste around a
biscuit, dampening the icing with
a little water, if necessary, to hold it
in place. Repeat on about half of the
cookies. Dilute a little of each food
colouring with water. Using a fine
paintbrush, paint festive decorations
over the plain cookies. Leave to dry
and then wrap in tissue paper.

Christmas Cookies

Makes 30

INGREDIENTS

175g/6oz/³/₄ cup unsalted butter
300g/11oz/1¹/₄ cups caster sugar
1 egg
1 egg yolk
5ml/1 tsp vanilla essence
grated rind of 1 lemon
pinch of salt
300g/11oz/2¹/₂ cups plain flour
For the decoration (optional)
coloured icing and small sweets
such as silver balls, coloured
sugar crystals

3 Sift the flour over the mixture and stir to blend. Gather the dough into a ball, wrap, and chill for 30 minutes.

4 Preheat the oven to 190°C/375°F/ Gas 5. On a floured surface, roll out until about 3mm/¹/₈in thick.

5 Stamp out shapes or rounds with floured cookie cutters.

6 Bake for about 8 minutes until lightly coloured. Transfer to a wire rack and leave to cool completely before decorating, if wished, with icing and sweets.

1 With an electric mixer, cream the butter until soft. Add the sugar gradually and continue beating until light and fluffy.

2 Using a wooden spoon, slowly mix in the whole egg and the egg yolk. Add the vanilla essence, lemon rind and salt. Stir to mix well.

Jewelled Christmas Trees

These cookies make an appealing gift. They look wonderful hung on a
Christmas tree or in front of a window to catch the light.

Makes 12

INGREDIENTS

175g/6oz/1¹/₂ cups plain flour
75g/3oz/¹/₃ cup butter, chopped
40g/1¹/₂oz/3 tbsp caster sugar
1 egg white
30ml/2 tbsp orange juice
225g/8oz coloured fruit sweets
coloured ribbons, to decorate

1 Preheat the oven to 180°C/350°F/ Gas 4. Line two baking sheets with non-stick baking paper. Sift the flour into a mixing bowl.

2 Rub the butter into the flour until the mixture resembles fine breadcrumbs. Stir in the sugar, egg white and enough orange juice to form a soft dough. Knead on a lightly floured surface until smooth.

3 Roll out thinly and stamp out as many shapes as possible using a floured Christmas tree cutter. Transfer the shapes to the prepared baking sheets, spacing them well apart. Knead the trimmings together.

4 Using a 1cm/¹/₂in round cutter or the end of a large plain piping nozzle, stamp out and remove six rounds from each tree shape. Cut each sweet into three and place a piece in each hole. Make a small hole at the top of each tree to thread through the ribbon.

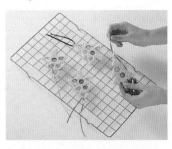

5 Bake for 15–20 minutes, until the biscuits are slightly gold in colour and the sweets have melted and filled the holes. Cool on the baking sheets. Repeat until you have used up the remaining cookie dough and sweets. Thread short lengths of ribbon through the holes so that the biscuits can be hung up.

Cranberry and Chocolate Squares

Made for each other – that's the contrasting flavours of tangy-sharp cranberries and sweet chocolate.

Makes 12

INGREDIENTS

115g/4oz/½ cup unsalted butter
60ml/4 tbsp cocoa powder
215g/7½oz/1¼ cups light muscovado sugar
150g/5oz/1¼ cups self-raising flour
2 eggs, beaten
115g/4oz/1 cup fresh or thawed frozen cranberries
For the topping
150ml/¼ pint/⅔ cup soured cream
75g/3oz/6 tbsp caster sugar
30ml/2 tbsp self-raising flour
50g/2oz/4 tbsp soft margarine
1 egg, beaten
2.5ml/½ tsp vanilla essence
75ml/5 tbsp coarsely grated plain chocolate for sprinkling

1 Preheat the oven to 180°C/350°F/ Gas 4. Grease an 18 x 25cm/7 x 10in cake tin and dust lightly with flour. Combine the butter, cocoa and sugar in a saucepan and stir over a low heat until melted and smooth.

2 Remove from the heat and stir in the flour and eggs. Stir in the cranberries, then spread the mixture in the prepared cake tin.

3 To make the topping, mix all the ingredients, except the chocolate, in a bowl. Beat until smooth, then spread over the base.

4 Sprinkle with the grated chocolate and bake for 40–45 minutes, until risen and firm. Cool in the tin, then cut into 12 squares.

Festive and Fancy Cookies

Biscotti

These lovely Italian biscuits are part-baked, sliced to reveal a feast of mixed nuts and then baked again until crisp and golden. Traditionally they're served dipped in vin santo, *a sweet dessert wine.*

Makes 24

❦

INGREDIENTS

50g/2oz/¼ cup unsalted butter
115g/4oz/½ cup caster sugar
175g/6oz/1½ cups self-raising
flour
pinch of salt
10ml/2 tsp baking powder
5ml/1 tsp ground coriander
finely grated rind of 1 lemon
50g/2oz/½ cup polenta
1 egg, lightly beaten
10ml/2 tsp brandy or orange-
flavoured liqueur
50g/2oz/½ cup unblanched
almonds
50g/2oz/½ cup pistachios

❦

1 Preheat the oven to 160°C/325°F/ Gas 3. Lightly grease a baking sheet. Cream together the butter and sugar in a bowl.

2 Sift the flour, salt, baking powder and coriander into the bowl. Add the lemon rind, polenta, egg and brandy or liqueur and mix together to make a soft dough.

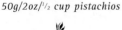

3 Stir in the nuts until evenly combined. Halve the mixture. Shape each half into a flat sausage about 23cm/9in long and 6cm/2½in wide. Bake for about 30 minutes, until risen and firm. Remove from the oven.

4 When cool, cut each sausage diagonally into 12 thin slices. Return to the baking sheet and cook for a further 10 minutes, until crisp.

5 Transfer to a wire rack to cool completely. Store in an airtight container for up to one week.

Cook's Tip Use a sharp, serrated knife to slice the cooled biscuits, otherwise they will crumble.

Sultana Cornmeal Cookies

These little yellow biscuits come from the Veneto region of Italy.

Makes 48

INGREDIENTS

75g/3oz/¹/₂ cup sultanas
115g/4oz/1 cup finely ground
yellow cornmeal
175g/6oz/1¹/₂ cups plain flour
7.5ml/1¹/₂ tsp baking powder
pinch of salt
225g/8oz/1 cup butter
225g/8oz/1 cup granulated sugar
2 eggs
15ml/1 tbsp marsala or 5ml/1 tsp
vanilla essence

1 Soak the sultanas in a small bowl of warm water for 15 minutes. Drain. Preheat the oven to 180°C/350°F/Gas 4. Grease a baking sheet.

2 Sift the cornmeal, flour, baking powder and salt together into a mixing bowl. Set aside.

3 Cream the butter and sugar until light and fluffy. Beat in the eggs, one at a time. Beat in the marsala or vanilla essence.

4 Add the dry ingredients to the butter mixture, beating until well blended. Stir in the sultanas.

5 Drop heaped teaspoons of the mixture on to the prepared baking sheet in rows about 5cm/2in apart. Bake for 7–8 minutes, until the cookies are golden brown at the edges. Transfer to a wire rack to cool.

Amaretti

If bitter almonds are not available, make up the weight with sweet almonds.

Makes 36

INGREDIENTS

150g/5oz/1¹/₄ cups sweet almonds
50g/2oz/¹/₂ cup bitter almonds
225g/8oz/1 cup caster sugar
2 egg whites
2.5ml/¹/₂ tsp almond essence or
5ml/1 tsp vanilla essence
icing sugar for dusting

1 Preheat the oven to 160°C/325°F/Gas 3. Peel the almonds by dropping them into a saucepan of boiling water for 1–2 minutes. Drain. Rub the almonds in a cloth to remove the skins.

2 Place the almonds on a baking tray and let them dry out in the oven for 10–15 minutes without browning. Remove from the oven and allow to cool. Turn the oven off. Dust with flour.

3 Grind the almonds with half of the sugar in a food processor. Use an electric beater or wire whisk to beat the egg whites until they form soft peaks.

4 Sprinkle over half the remaining sugar and continue beating until stiff peaks are formed. Gently fold in the remaining sugar, the almond or vanilla essence and the almonds.

5 Spoon the almond mixture into a piping bag fitted with a smooth nozzle. Pipe out the mixture in rounds the size of a walnut. Sprinkle lightly with the icing sugar, and leave to stand for 2 hours. Near the end of this time, turn the oven on again and preheat to 180°C/350°F/Gas 4.

6 Bake for 15 minutes, until pale gold. Remove from the oven and cool on a wire rack.

Macaroons

Freshly ground almonds, lightly toasted beforehand to intensify the flavour,

give these biscuits their rich taste and texture so, for best results,

avoid using ready-ground almonds as a shortcut.

Makes 12

INGREDIENTS

*115g/4oz/1½ cup blanched
almonds, toasted
165g/5½oz/¾ cup caster sugar
2 egg whites
2.5ml/½ tsp almond or vanilla
essence
icing sugar for dusting*

1 Preheat the oven to 180°C/350°F/
Gas 4. Line a large baking sheet
with non-stick baking paper. Reserve
12 almonds for decorating. In a food
processor grind the rest of the
almonds with the sugar.

2 With the machine running, slowly
pour in enough of the egg whites
to form a soft dough. Add the almond
or vanilla essence and pulse to mix.

3 With moistened hands, shape the
mixture into walnut-size balls
and arrange on the baking sheet.

4 Press one of the reserved almonds
on to each ball, flattening them
slightly, and dust lightly with icing
sugar. Bake for about 10–12 minutes,
until the tops are golden and feel
slightly firm. Transfer to a wire rack,
cool slightly, then peel the biscuits off
the paper and leave to cool
completely.

Cook's Tip To toast the almonds,
spread them on a baking sheet and
bake in the preheated oven for 10–
15 minutes, until golden. Leave to cool
before grinding.

Madeleines

These little tea cakes, baked in a special tin with shell-shaped cups,

were made famous by Marcel Proust, who referred to them in his novel.

They are best eaten on the day they are made.

Makes 12

INGREDIENTS

*165g/5½oz/1¼ cups plain flour
5ml/1 tsp baking powder
2 eggs
75g/3oz/¾ cup icing sugar, plus
extra for dusting
grated rind of 1 lemon or orange
15ml/1 tbsp lemon or orange juice
75g/3oz/6 tbsp unsalted butter,
melted and slightly cooled*

1 Preheat the oven to 190°C/375°F/
Gas 5. Generously butter a 12-
cup madeleine tin. Sift together the
flour and baking powder.

2 Using an electric mixer, beat the
eggs and icing sugar for 5–7
minutes until thick and creamy and
the mixture forms a ribbon when the
beaters are lifted. Gently fold in the
lemon or orange rind and juice.

3 Beginning with the flour mixture,
alternately fold in the flour and
melted butter in four batches. Leave
the mixture to stand for 10 minutes,
then carefully spoon into the tin. Tap
gently to release any air bubbles.

4 Bake for 12–15 minutes, rotating
the tin halfway through cooking,
until a skewer or cake tester inserted
in the centre comes out clean. Tip on
to a wire rack to cool completely and
dust with icing sugar before serving.

Cook's Tip If you don't have a special
tin for making madeleines, you can use
a bun tin, preferably with a non-stick
coating. The cakes won't have the
characteristic ridges and shell shape,
but they are quite pretty dusted with a
little icing sugar.

Chocolate Macaroons

Makes 20

INGREDIENTS

*50g/2oz plain chocolate chopped
into small pieces
115g/4oz/1 cup blanched almonds
2 egg whites
200g/7oz/1 cup caster sugar
2.5ml/¹/₂ tsp vanilla essence
1.5ml/¹/₄ tsp almond essence
icing sugar for dusting*

1 Preheat the oven to 150°C/300°F/
Gas 2. Line two baking sheets
with non-stick baking paper.

2 Melt the chocolate in the top of
a double boiler, or in a heatproof
bowl placed over a saucepan of
barely simmering water.

3 Grind the almonds finely in a food
processor, blender or nut grinder.

4 In a mixing bowl, whisk the egg
whites until they form soft peaks.
Fold in the sugar, vanilla and almond
essence, ground almonds and cooled
melted chocolate. The mixture should
just hold its shape. If it is too soft,
chill it in the fridge for 15 minutes.

5 Place heaped teaspoonfuls of the
mixture, spaced well apart, on
the prepared baking sheets and
flatten slightly. Brush each ball with
a little water and sift over a thin
layer of icing sugar.

6 Bake for 20-25 minutes until
just firm. With a metal spatula,
transfer to a wire rack and allow to
cool completely.

Variation For Chocolate Pine Nut
Macaroons, spread 75g/3oz/³/₄ cup pine
nuts in a shallow dish. Press the balls
of chocolate macaroon dough into the
nuts to cover one side and bake as
described, nut-side up.

Coconut Macaroons

Makes 24

INGREDIENTS

*40g/1¹/₂oz/¹/₃ cup plain flour
pinch of salt
215g/7¹/₂oz/2¹/₂ cups desiccated
coconut
150ml/¹/₂ pint/²/₃ cup sweetened
condensed milk
5ml/1 tsp vanilla essence*

1 Preheat the oven to 180°C/350°F/
Gas 4. Line two baking sheets
with greaseproof paper and grease
the paper.

2 Sift the flour and salt into
a large bowl. Stir in the
dessicated coconut.

3 Pour in the sweetened condensed
milk. Add the vanilla essence and
stir together from the centre.
Continue stirring until a very thick
batter is formed.

4 Drop heaped tablespoonfuls of
batter 2.5cm/1in apart on the
prepared baking sheets. Bake the
macaroons for about 20 minutes,
until golden brown. Transfer to a
wire rack to cool.

Variation For a very rich, sweet and
tempting *petits four*, make the
macaroons smaller, and when cooked
coat them in melted plain chocolate.
Place on greaseproof paper and leave
until the chocolate is hard. Serve with
small cups of strong, black coffee after
a dinner party.

Festive and Fancy Cookies

Brandy Snaps

Eat these on high days

and holidays as an

indulgent treat.

Makes 18

INGREDIENTS

50g/2oz/4 tbsp butter
150g/5oz/²⁄₃ cup caster sugar
7.5ml/1 rounded tbsp golden
syrup
40g/1¹⁄₂oz/¹⁄₃ cup plain flour
2.5ml/¹⁄₂ tsp ground ginger
For the filling
250ml/8fl oz/1 cup whipping
cream
30ml/2 tbsp brandy

1 With an electric mixer, cream together the butter and sugar until light and fluffy, then beat in the golden syrup. Sift over the flour and ginger and mix to a rough dough.

2 Transfer the dough to a work surface and knead until smooth. Cover and chill for 30 minutes.

3 Preheat the oven to 190°C/375°F/ Gas 5. Grease a baking sheet.

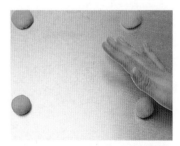

4 Working in batches of four, form walnut-size balls of dough. Place well apart on the prepared baking sheet and flatten slightly. Bake for about 10 minutes, until golden.

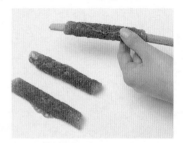

5 Remove from the oven and leave to cool for a few moments. Working quickly, slide a metal spatula under each biscuit, turn over, and wrap around the handle of a wooden spoon. When firm, slide off the snaps and place on a wire rack to cool.

6 To make the filling, whip the cream and brandy until soft peaks form. Fill a piping bag and pipe into each end of the brandy snaps just before serving.

Chocolate-dipped Hazelnut Crescents

Walnuts or pecans can be used instead of hazelnuts, but they must be finely ground.

Makes 35

INGREDIENTS

*300g/11oz/2½ cups plain flour
pinch of salt
225g/8oz/1 cup unsalted butter
50g/2oz/¼ cup caster sugar
15ml/1 tbsp hazelnut liqueur or
water
5ml/1 tsp vanilla essence
75g/3oz plain chocolate, finely
grated
65g/2½oz/½ cup hazelnuts,
toasted and finely chopped
icing sugar for dusting
350g/12oz plain chocolate,
melted, for dipping*

1 Preheat the oven to 160°C/325°F/
Gas 3. Grease two large baking
sheets. Sift the flour and salt into a
small bowl.

2 In a large bowl, using an electric
mixer, beat the butter until
creamy. Add the sugar and beat
until fluffy, beat in the hazelnut
liqueur or water and vanilla essence.
Gently stir in the flour, until just
blended, then fold in the grated
chocolate and hazelnuts.

3 With floured hands, shape the
dough into 5 x 1cm/2 x ½in
crescent shapes. Place on the
prepared baking sheets, 5cm/2in
apart. Bake for 20–25 minutes, until
the edges are set and the cookies
slightly golden. Remove the baking
sheets to a wire rack to cool for 10
minutes. Transfer the biscuits from
the baking sheets to wire racks to
cool completely.

4 Line the baking sheets with non-
stick baking paper. Dust the
cookies with icing sugar. Using a pair
of kitchen tongs, or fingers, dip half
of each crescent into melted
chocolate. Place on the prepared
baking sheets. Chill until the
chocolate has set.

Black-and-White Ginger Florentines

These florentines can be refrigerated in an airtight container for one week.

Makes 30

❧

INGREDIENTS

120ml/4fl oz/½ cup double cream
50g/2oz/¼ cup unsalted butter
90g/3½oz/½ cup granulated sugar
30ml/2 tbsp honey
150g/5oz/1⅓ cups flaked almonds
40g/1½oz/⅓ cup plain flour
2.5ml/½ tsp ground ginger
50g/2oz/⅓ cup diced candied
orange peel
65g/2½oz/½ cup diced stem
ginger
200g/7oz plain chocolate,
chopped
150g/5oz fine quality white
chocolate, chopped

❧

1 Preheat the oven to 180°C/350°F/
Gas 4. Lightly grease two large
baking sheets. In a medium saucepan
over a medium heat, stir the cream,
butter, sugar and honey until the
sugar dissolves. Bring the mixture to
the boil, stirring constantly.

2 Remove from the heat and stir in
the almonds, flour and ground
ginger until well blended. Stir in the
orange peel, stem ginger and
50g/2oz/⅓ cup chopped plain
chocolate.

3 Drop teaspoons of the mixture on
to the prepared baking sheets at
least 7.5cm/3in apart. Spread each
round as thinly as possible with the
back of the spoon. (Dip the spoon in
water to prevent sticking.)

4 Bake in batches for 8–10 minutes,
until the edges are golden brown
and the biscuits are bubbling. Do not
under-bake or they will be sticky, but
be careful not to over-bake as they
burn easily. If you wish, use a
7.5cm/3in biscuit cutter to neaten the
edges of the florentines while on the
baking sheet.

5 Remove the baking sheet to the
wire rack to cool for 10 minutes
until firm. Using a metal palette
knife, carefully transfer the
florentines to a wire rack to cool
completely.

6 In a small saucepan over a very
low heat, melt the remaining
chocolate, stirring frequently, until
smooth. Cool slightly. In the top of a
double boiler over a low heat, melt
the white chocolate until smooth,
stirring frequently. Remove the top of
double boiler from the bottom and
cool for about 5 minutes, stirring
occasionally until slightly thickened.

7 Using a small metal palette knife,
spread half the florentines with
the plain chocolate on the flat side of
each biscuit, swirling to create a
decorative surface, and place on a
wire rack, chocolate side up. Spread
the remaining florentines with the
melted white chocolate and place on
the rack, chocolate side up. Chill for
10–15 minutes to set completely.

Tuiles d'Amandes

These biscuits are named after the French roof tiles they so resemble. Making them is a little fiddly, so bake only four at a time until you get the knack. With a little practice you will find them easy.

Makes 24

INGREDIENTS

65g/2¹/₂oz/generous ¹/₂ cup whole blanched almonds, lightly toasted
65g/2¹/₂oz/¹/₃ cup caster sugar
40g/1¹/₂oz/3 tbsp unsalted butter
2 egg whites
2.5ml/¹/₂ tsp almond essence
30g/1¹/₄oz/scant ¹/₄ cup plain flour, sifted
50g/2oz/¹/₂ cup flaked almonds

Cook's Tip If the biscuits flatten or lose their crispness, reheat them on a baking sheet in a moderate oven, until completely flat, then reshape.

1 Preheat the oven to 200°C/400°F/ Gas 6. Generously butter two heavy baking sheets.

2 Place the almonds and about 30ml/2 tbsp of the sugar in a food processor fitted with the metal blade and process until finely ground.

3 Beat the butter until creamy, then add the remaining sugar and beat until light and fluffy. Gradually beat in the egg whites, then add the almond essence. Sift the flour over the butter mixture, fold in, then fold in the ground almond mixture.

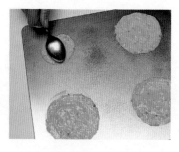

4 Drop tablespoonfuls of the mixture on to the prepared baking sheets about 15cm/6in apart. With the back of a wet spoon, spread each mound into a paper-thin 7.5cm/3in round. (Don't worry if holes appear, they will fill in.) Sprinkle with flaked almonds.

5 Bake the cookies, one sheet at a time, for 5–6 minutes, until the edges are golden and the centres still pale. Working quickly, use a thin palette knife to loosen the edges of one cookie. Lift the cookie on the palette knife and place over a rolling pin, then press down the sides of the biscuit to curve it.

6 Continue shaping the cookies, transferring them to a wire rack as they cool. If they become too crisp to shape, return the baking sheet to the hot oven for 15–30 seconds, then continue as above.

Flaked Almond Biscuits

Makes 30

INGREDIENTS

175g/6oz/³/₄ cup butter or
margarine, chopped
225g/8oz/2 cups self-raising flour
150g/5oz/²/₃ cup caster sugar
2.5ml/¹/₂ tsp ground cinnamon
1 egg, separated
30ml/2 tbsp cold water
50g/2oz/¹/₂ cup flaked almonds

1 Preheat the oven to 180°C/350°F/
Gas 4. Rub the butter or
margarine into the flour. Reserve
15ml/1 tbsp of the sugar and mix the
rest with the cinnamon. Stir into the
flour and then add the egg yolk and
cold water and mix to a firm dough.

2 Roll out the dough on a lightly
floured board to 1cm/¹/₂in thick.
Sprinkle over the almonds. Continue
rolling until the dough is
approximately 5mm/¹/₄in thick.

3 Using a floured fluted round
cutter, cut the dough into rounds.
Use a palette knife to lift them on to
an ungreased baking sheet. Re-form
the dough and cut more rounds to
use all the dough. Whisk the egg
white lightly, brush it over the
cookies, and sprinkle over the
remaining sugar.

4 Bake for about 10–15 minutes,
until golden. To remove, slide a
palette knife under the cookies, which
will still seem a bit soft, but they
harden as they cool. Leave on a wire
rack until quite cold.

Nut Lace Cookies

Makes 18

❦

INGREDIENTS

50g/2oz/¹/₂ cup blanched almonds
50g/2oz/4 tbsp butter
45ml/3 tbsp plain flour
115g/4oz/¹/₂ cup granulated sugar
30ml/2 tbsp double cream
2.5ml/¹/₂ tsp vanilla essence

❦

Variation Add 40g/1¹/₂oz/¹/₄ cup finely chopped candied orange peel to the mixture.

1 Preheat the oven to 190°C/375°F/ Gas 5. Grease 1–2 baking sheets.

2 With a sharp knife, chop the almonds as finely as possible. Alternatively, use a food processor, blender or nut grinder to chop the nuts very finely.

3 Melt the butter in a small saucepan over a low heat. Remove from the heat and stir in the remaining ingredients, including the almonds.

4 Drop teaspoonfuls of the mixture 6cm/2¹/₂in apart on the prepared baking sheets. Bake for about 5 minutes until golden. Cool on the sheets briefly, until the cookies are just stiff enough to lift off.

5 With a metal spatula, transfer the cookies to a wire rack to cool completely.

Oatmeal Lace Cookies

Makes 36

❦

INGREDIENTS

165g/5¹/₂oz/²/₃ cup butter or margarine
175g/6oz/1¹/₂ cups rolled oats
175g/6oz/³/₄ cup firmly packed dark brown sugar
175g/6oz/³/₄ cup granulated sugar
45ml/3 tbsp plain flour
pinch of salt
1 egg, lightly beaten
5ml/1 tsp vanilla essence
50g/2oz/¹/₂ cup pecans or walnuts, finely chopped

❦

1 Preheat the oven to 180°C/350°F/ Gas 4. Grease two baking sheets.

2 Melt the butter or margarine in a small saucepan over a low heat. Set aside.

3 In a mixing bowl, combine the oats, brown sugar, granulated sugar, flour and salt.

4 Add the butter or margarine, the egg and vanilla essence.

5 Mix until blended, then stir in the chopped nuts.

6 Drop rounded teaspoonfuls of the batter about 5cm/2in apart on the prepared baking sheets. Bake for 5–8 minutes until lightly browned on the edges and bubbling. Leave to cool for 2 minutes, then transfer to a wire rack to cool completely.

Strawberry Shortcakes

A favourite American summer dessert.

Makes 6

INGREDIENTS

*450g/1lb strawberries, hulled and
halved or quartered, depending on
size
45ml/3 tbsp icing sugar
250ml/8fl oz/1 cup whipping
cream
mint leaves to decorate
For the shortcakes
250g/8oz/2 cups plain flour
75g/3oz/⅓ cup caster sugar
15ml/1 tbsp baking powder
pinch of salt
225ml/8fl oz/1 cup whipping
cream*

Cook's Tip To achieve the best results
when whipping cream, chill the bowl
and beaters until thoroughly cold. If
using an electric mixer, increase the
speed gradually, and turn the bowl
while beating to incorporate as much
air as possible.

1 Preheat the oven to 200°C/400°F/
Gas 6. Lightly grease a baking
sheet.

2 To make the shortcakes, sift the
flour into a mixing bowl. Add
50g/2oz/¼ cup of the caster sugar,
the baking powder and salt. Stir well.

3 Gradually add the cream, tossing
lightly with a fork until the
mixture forms clumps.

4 Gather the clumps together, but
do not knead the dough. Shape
the dough into a 15cm/6in log. Cut
into six slices and place them on the
prepared baking sheet.

5 Sprinkle with the remaining
caster sugar. Bake for about
15 minutes until light golden brown.
Leave to cool on a wire rack.

6 Meanwhile, mash a quarter of the
strawberries with the icing sugar.
Stir in the remaining strawberries.
Leave to stand for 1 hour at room
temperature.

7 Just before serving, whip the
cream until soft peaks form.

8 Slice each shortcake in half. Put
the bottom halves on individual
plates and top with some of the cream.
Divide the strawberries among the six.
Replace the tops and decorate with
mint. Serve with the remaining cream.

Orange Shortbread Fingers

These are a real tea-time treat. The fingers will keep in an airtight container for up to 2 weeks.

Makes 18

❦

INGREDIENTS

115g/4oz/¹/₂ cup unsalted butter
50g/2oz/4 tbsp caster sugar, plus
extra for sprinkling
finely grated rind of 2 oranges
175g/6oz/1¹/₂ cups plain flour

❦

1 Preheat the oven to 190°C/375°F/ Gas 5. Grease a large baking sheet. Beat together the butter and sugar until soft and creamy. Beat in the orange rind.

2 Gradually add the flour and gently pull the dough together to form a soft ball. Roll out the dough on a lightly floured surface to about 1cm/¹/₂in thick. Cut into fingers, sprinkle over a little extra caster sugar and put on the baking sheet. Prick the fingers with a fork and bake for about 20 minutes, until the fingers are a light golden colour.

Raspberry Sandwich Cookies

Children will love these sweet, sticky treats.

Makes 32

❧

INGREDIENTS

115g/4oz/1 cup blanched almonds
175g/6oz/1½ cups plain flour
175g/6oz/¾ cup butter
115g/4oz/½ cup caster sugar
grated rind of 1 lemon
5ml/1 tsp vanilla essence
1 egg white
pinch of salt
40g/1½oz/⅓ cup slivered
almonds, chopped
350g/12oz/1 cup raspberry jam
15ml/1 tbsp lemon juice

❧

1 Finely grind the almonds and 45ml/3 tbsp of the flour.

2 Cream together the butter and sugar until light and fluffy. Stir in the lemon rind and vanilla essence. Add the ground almonds and remaining flour and mix well to form a dough. Gather into a ball, wrap in greaseproof paper, and chill for 1 hour. Preheat the oven to 160°C/325°F/Gas 3. Line two baking sheets with greaseproof paper.

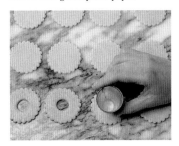

3 Divide the dough into four. Roll each piece out on a lightly floured surface to a thickness of 3mm/⅛in. With a floured 6cm/2½in pastry cutter, stamp out circles, then stamp out the centres from half the circles.

4 When all the dough has been used, check you have equal numbers of rings and circles, then place the dough rings and circles 1cm/½in apart on the prepared baking sheets.

5 Whisk the egg white with the salt until just frothy. Brush only the cookie rings with the egg white, then sprinkle over the chopped almonds. Bake for 12–15 minutes until very lightly browned. Leave to cool for a few minutes on the sheets before transferring to a wire rack.

6 In a saucepan, melt the jam with the lemon juice until it comes to a simmer. Brush the jam over the cookie circles and sandwich together with the rings. Store in an airtight container with sheets of greaseproof paper between the layers.

Pecan Tassies

These sweet tarts accompany coffee perfectly.

Makes 24

🍃

INGREDIENTS

115g/4oz/½ cup cream cheese
115g/4oz/½ cup butter
115g/4oz/1 cup plain flour
For the filling
2 eggs
115g/4oz/⅔ cup dark brown sugar
5ml/1 tsp vanilla essence
pinch of salt
25g/1oz/2 tbsp butter, melted
115g/4oz/1 cup pecans

🍃

1 Place a baking sheet in the oven and preheat to 180°C/350°F/ Gas 4. Grease 24 mini-muffin tins.

2 Chop the cream cheese and butter. Put in a mixing bowl. Sift over the flour and mix to form a dough.

3 Roll out the dough thinly. With a floured fluted pastry cutter, stamp out 24 7cm/2½in rounds. Line the muffin tins with the rounds and chill.

4 To make the filling, lightly whisk the eggs in a bowl. Gradually whisk in the brown sugar, a few tablespoons at a time, and add the vanilla essence, salt and butter. Set aside until required.

5 Reserve 24 undamaged pecan halves and chop the rest coarsely with a sharp knife.

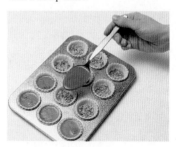

6 Place a spoonful of chopped nuts in each muffin tin and cover with the filling. Set a pecan half on the top of each.

7 Bake on the hot baking sheet for about 20 minutes, until puffed and set. Transfer to a wire rack to cool. Serve at room temperature.

Variation To make Jam Tassies, fill the cream cheese pastry shells with raspberry or blackberry jam, or other fruit jams. Bake as described.

Pecan Puffs

Makes 24

❦

INGREDIENTS

115g/4oz/½ cup unsalted butter
30ml/2 tbsp granulated sugar
pinch of salt
5ml/1 tsp vanilla essence
115g/4oz/1 cup pecans
115g/4oz/1 cup plain flour, sifted
icing sugar for dusting

❦

1 Preheat the oven to 150°C/300°F/ Gas 2. Grease two baking sheets.

2 Cream the butter and sugar until light and fluffy. Stir in the salt and vanilla essence.

3 Grind the nuts in a food processor, blender or nut grinder. Stir several times to prevent nuts becoming oily.

4 Push the ground nuts through a sieve set over a bowl to aerate them. Pieces too large to go through the sieve can be ground again.

5 Stir the nuts and flour into the butter mixture to make a dough. Roll the dough into marble-size balls between the palms of your hands. Place on the prepared baking sheets and bake for 45 minutes.

6 While the puffs are still hot, roll them in icing sugar. Leave to cool completely, then roll once more in icing sugar.

Sablés with Goat's Cheese and Strawberries

Sablés are little French biscuits, made from egg yolk and butter. Crisp and slightly sweet, they contrast perfectly with the tangy goat's cheese and juicy strawberries.

Makes 24

INGREDIENTS

75g/3oz/⅓ cup butter
150g/5oz/1¼ cup plain flour
75g/3oz/¾ cup blanched hazelnuts, lightly toasted and ground
30ml/2 tbsp caster sugar
2 egg yolks beaten with 30–45ml/2–3 tbsp water
115g/4oz goat's cheese
4–6 large strawberries, cut into small pieces
hazelnuts and mint, to decorate

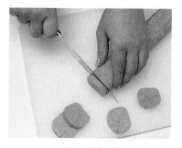

1 Put the butter, flour, ground hazelnuts, sugar and beaten egg yolks into a food processor and process to a smooth dough. Scrape out the dough. Shape into a log about 4cm/1½in thick. Wrap and chill.

2 Preheat the oven to 200°C/400°F/ Gas 6. Line a large baking sheet with non-stick baking paper. With a sharp knife, slice the dough into 5mm/¼in thick rounds and arrange on the prepared baking sheet. Bake for 7–10 minutes, until golden brown. Transfer to a wire rack to cool and crisp slightly.

3 On a plate, crumble the goat's cheese into small pieces. Mound a little goat's cheese on to each sablé, top with a piece of strawberry and sprinkle with a few hazelnuts. Serve warm.

Variation These sablés are ideal served with fruit. Beat 75g/3oz/⅓ cup cream cheese with 15ml/1 tbsp icing sugar and a little lemon or orange rind. Spread a little on the sablés and top with a few pieces of sliced kiwi fruit, peach, nectarine and a few raspberries.

Coffee Sponge Drops

These are delicious on their own, but taste even better with a filling

of low-fat soft cheese and chopped stem ginger.

Makes 12

INGREDIENTS

50g/2oz/¹/₂ cup plain flour
15ml/1 tbsp instant coffee powder
2 eggs
75g/3oz/¹/₃ cup caster sugar
For the filling
115g/4oz/¹/₂ cup low-fat soft cheese
40g/1¹/₂oz/¹/₄ cup chopped stem ginger

1 Preheat the oven to 190°C/375°F/ Gas 5. Sift the flour and instant coffee powder together. To make the filling, beat together the soft cheese and stem ginger. Chill until required.

2 Combine the eggs and caster sugar. Beat with an electric whisk until thick and mousse-like.

3 Carefully add the sieved flour and coffee to the egg mixture and gently fold in with a metal spoon, being careful not to knock out any air.

4 Spoon the mixture into a piping bag fitted with a 1cm/¹/₂in plain nozzle. Pipe 4cm/1¹/₂in rounds on to lined baking sheets. Bake for 12 minutes. Cool on a wire rack. Sandwich together with the filling.

Lady Fingers

Named after the pale, slim fingers of highborn gentlewomen.

Makes 18

INGREDIENTS

90g/3¹/₂oz/²/₃ cup plain flour
pinch of salt
4 eggs, separated
115g/4oz/¹/₂ cup granulated sugar
2.5ml/¹/₂ tsp vanilla essence
icing sugar for sprinkling

1 Preheat the oven to 150°C/300°F/ Gas 2. Grease two baking sheets, then coat lightly with flour, and shake off the excess.

2 Sift the flour and salt together twice.

3 With an electric mixer, beat the egg yolks with half of the sugar until thick enough to leave a ribbon trail when the beaters are lifted.

4 In another bowl, beat the egg whites until stiff. Beat in the remaining sugar until glossy.

5 Sift the flour over the yolks and spoon a large dollop of egg whites over the flour. Carefully fold in with a large metal spoon, adding the vanilla essence. Gently fold in the remaining whites.

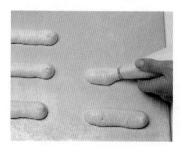

6 Spoon the mixture into a piping bag fitted with a large plain nozzle. Pipe 10cm/4in long lines on the prepared baking sheets about 2.5cm/1in apart. Sift over a layer of icing sugar. Turn the sheet upside down to dislodge any excess sugar.

7 Bake for about 20 minutes until crusty on the outside but soft in the centre. Cool slightly on the baking sheets before transferring to a wire rack.

Walnut Cookies

Makes 60

INGREDIENTS

115g/4oz/¹/₂ cup butter or
margarine
175g/6oz/³/₄ cup caster sugar
115g/4oz/1 cup plain flour
10ml/2 tsp vanilla essence
115g/4oz/1 cup walnuts, finely
chopped

1 Preheat the oven to 150°C/300°F/ Gas 2. Grease two baking sheets.

2 With an electric mixer, cream the butter or margarine until soft. Add 50g/2oz/¹/₄ cup of the sugar and continue beating until light and fluffy. Stir in the flour, vanilla essence and walnuts. Drop teaspoonfuls of the batter 2.5–5cm/1–2in apart on the prepared baking sheets and flatten slightly. Bake for about 25 minutes.

3 Transfer to a wire rack set over a baking sheet and sprinkle with the remaining sugar.

Variation To make Almond Cookies, use an equal amount of finely chopped unblanched almonds instead of walnuts. Replace half the vanilla with 2.5ml/¹/₂ tsp almond essence.

Mocha Viennese Swirls

Makes 20

INGREDIENTS

250g/9oz plain chocolate,
chopped
200g/7oz/scant 1 cup unsalted
butter
50g/2oz/½ cup icing sugar
30ml/2 tbsp strong black coffee
200g/7oz/1¾ cups plain flour
50g/2oz/½ cup cornflour
about 20 blanched almonds

Cook's Tip If the mixture is too stiff
to pipe, soften it with a little more
black coffee.

1 Preheat the oven to 190°C/375°F/
Gas 5. Lightly grease two large
baking sheets. Melt 115g/4oz of the
chocolate in a heatproof bowl over a
saucepan of hot water. Cream the
butter with the icing sugar in a bowl
until smooth and pale. Beat in the
melted chocolate, then the strong
black coffee.

2 Sift the flour and cornflour over
the mixture. Fold in lightly and
evenly to make a soft mixture.

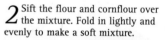

3 Spoon the mixture into a piping
bag fitted with a large star nozzle
and pipe 20 swirls on the prepared
baking sheets, allowing room for
spreading during baking.

4 Press an almond into the centre
of each swirl. Bake for about
15 minutes, until the biscuits are firm
and just beginning to brown. Leave
to cool for about 10 minutes on the
baking sheets, then lift carefully on
to a wire rack to cool completely.

5 Melt the remaining chocolate and
dip the base of each swirl to coat.
Place on a sheet of non-stick baking
paper and leave to set.

Festive and Fancy Cookies

Chocolate Amaretti

Makes 24

INGREDIENTS

150g/5oz/1¼ cups blanched whole
almonds
90g/3½oz/scant ½ cup caster
sugar
15ml/1 tbsp cocoa powder
30ml/2 tbsp icing sugar
2 egg whites
pinch of cream of tartar
5ml/1 tsp almond essence
flaked almonds, to decorate

1 Preheat the oven to 180°C/350°F/
Gas 4. Place the almonds on a
baking sheet and bake for 10–
12 minutes until golden brown. Leave
to cool. Reduce the oven temperature
to 160°C/325°F/Gas 3. Line a large
baking sheet with non-stick baking
paper. In a food processor, process the
almonds with half the sugar until
they are finely ground but not oily.
Transfer to a bowl and sift in the
cocoa and icing sugar. Set aside.

2 In a mixing bowl with an electric
mixer, beat the egg whites and
cream of tartar until stiff peaks form.
Sprinkle in the remaining sugar a
tablespoon at a time, beating well
after each addition, and continue
beating until the whites are glossy
and stiff. Beat in the almond essence.

3 Sprinkle over the almond-sugar
mixture and gently fold into the
beaten egg whites until just blended.
Spoon the mixture into a large piping
bag fitted with a plain 1cm/½in
nozzle. Pipe 4cm/1½in rounds about
2.5cm/1in apart on the prepared
baking sheet. Press a flaked almond
into the centre of each.

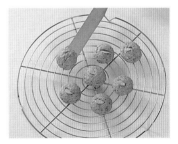

4 Bake the cookies for 12–15
minutes, or until crisp. Remove
the baking sheets to a wire rack to
cool for 10 minutes. With a metal
palette knife, remove the amarettis to
a wire rack to cool completely.

Decorated Chocolate Lebkuchen

Wrapped in paper or cellophane, or beautifully boxed, these decorated cookies make a lovely present. Don't make them too far in advance as the chocolate will gradually discolour.

Makes 40

INGREDIENTS

*1 quantity Lebkuchen mixture
115g/4oz plain chocolate, chopped
115g/4oz milk chocolate, chopped
115g/4oz white chocolate, chopped
chocolate vermicelli, for sprinkling
cocoa powder or icing sugar for dusting*

3 Melt the plain chocolate in a heatproof bowl over a small saucepan of hot water. Melt the milk and white chocolate in separate bowls.

4 Make three small paper piping bags out of greaseproof paper. Spoon a little of each chocolate into the three paper piping bags and reserve. Spoon a little plain chocolate over one third of the biscuits, spreading it slightly to cover them completely. (Tapping the rack gently will help the chocolate to run down the sides.)

5 Snip the merest tip from the bag of white chocolate and drizzle it over some of the coated biscuits, to give a decorative finish.

6 Sprinkle the chocolate vermicelli over the plain chocolate-coated biscuits that haven't been decorated. Coat the remaining biscuits with the milk and white chocolate and decorate some of these with more chocolate from the piping bags, contrasting the colours. Scatter more undecorated biscuits with vermicelli. Leave the biscuits to set.

7 Transfer the undecorated biscuits to a plate or tray and dust lightly with cocoa powder or icing sugar.

Cook's Tip If the chocolate in the bowls starts to set before you have finished decorating, put the bowls back over the heat for 1–2 minutes. If the chocolate in the piping bags starts to harden, microwave briefly or put in a clean bowl over a pan of simmering water until soft.

1 Grease two baking sheets. Roll out just over half of the Lebkuchen mixture until 5mm/¼in thick. Cut out heart shapes, using a 4.5cm/1¾in heart-shaped cutter. Transfer to baking sheet. Gather the trimmings together with the remaining dough and cut into 20 pieces. Roll into balls and place on the baking sheet. Flatten each ball slightly with your fingers.

2 Chill both sheets for 30 minutes. Preheat the oven to 180°C/350°F/Gas 4. Bake for 8–10 minutes. Cool on a wire rack.

Chocolate Fruit and Nut Cookies

These simple, chunky gingerbread biscuits make a delicious gift, especially when presented in a decorative gift box. The combination of walnuts, almonds and cherries is very effective, but you can use any other mixture of glacé fruits and nuts.

Makes 20

INGREDIENTS

50g/2oz/4 tbsp caster sugar
75ml/3fl oz/⅓ cup water
225g/8oz plain chocolate, chopped
40g/1½oz/¾ cup walnut halves
75g/3oz/⅓ cup glacé cherries, chopped into small wedges
115g/4oz/1 cup whole blanched almonds
For the Lebkuchen
115g/4oz/½ cup unsalted butter
115g/4oz/⅔ cup light muscovado sugar
1 egg, beaten
115g/4oz/⅓ cup black treacle
400g/14oz/3½ cups self-raising flour
5ml/1 tsp ground ginger
2.5ml/½ tsp ground cloves
1.5ml/¼ tsp chilli powder

❦

Cook's Tip Carefully stack the biscuits in a pretty box or tin, lined with tissue paper, or tie in cellophane bundles.

1 To make the Lebkuchen, cream together the butter and sugar until pale and fluffy. Beat in the egg and black treacle. Sift the flour, ginger, cloves and chilli powder into the bowl. Using a wooden spoon, gradually mix the ingredients together to make a stiff paste. Turn on to a lightly floured work surface and knead lightly until smooth. Wrap and chill for 30 minutes.

2 Preheat the oven to 180°C/350°F/ Gas 4. Grease two baking sheets. Shape the dough into a roll, 20cm/8in long. Chill for 30 minutes. Cut into 20 slices and space them on the baking sheets. Bake for 10 minutes. Leave on the baking sheets for 5 minutes and then transfer to a wire rack and leave to cool.

3 Put the sugar and water in a small, heavy-based saucepan. Heat gently until the sugar dissolves. Bring to the boil and boil for 1 minute, until slightly syrupy. Leave for 3 minutes, to cool slightly, and then stir in the chocolate until it has melted and made a smooth sauce.

4 Place the wire rack of biscuits over a large tray or board. Spoon a little of the chocolate mixture over the biscuits, spreading it to the edges with the back of the spoon.

5 Gently press a walnut half into the centre of each biscuit. Arrange pieces of glacé cherry and almonds alternately around the nuts. Leave to set in a cool place.

Chocolate Almond Torronne

Serve this Italian speciality in thin slices.

Makes 20

INGREDIENTS

115g/4oz plain chocolate, chopped
50g/2oz/4 tbsp unsalted butter
1 egg white
115g/4oz/¹/₂ cup caster sugar
50g/2oz/¹/₂ cup ground almonds
75g/3oz/³/₄ cup chopped toasted almonds
75ml/5 tbsp chopped candied peel
For the coating
175g/6oz white chocolate, chopped
25g/1oz/2 tbsp unsalted butter
115g/4oz/1 cup flaked almonds, toasted

1 Melt the chocolate with the butter in a heatproof bowl over a saucepan of hot water, stirring until the mixture is smooth.

2 In a clean, grease-free bowl, whisk the egg white with the sugar until stiff. Gradually beat in the melted chocolate, then stir in the ground almonds, chopped toasted almonds and peel.

3 Tip the mixture on to a large sheet of non-stick baking paper and shape into a thick roll.

4 As the mixture cools, use the paper to press the roll firmly into a triangular shape. Twist the paper over the triangular roll and chill until completely set.

5 To make the coating, melt the white chocolate with the butter in a heatproof bowl over a saucepan of hot water. Unwrap the chocolate roll and spread the white chocolate quickly over the surface. Press the almonds in a thin even coating over the chocolate, working quickly before the chocolate sets.

6 Chill again until firm, then cut the torronne into fairly thin slices to serve.

Cook's Tip The mixture can be shaped into a simple round roll instead of the triangular shape if you prefer.

Chocolate Hazelnut Galettes

There's stacks of sophistication in these triple-tiered chocolate rounds sandwiched with a light fromage frais filling.

Makes 4

INGREDIENTS

175g/6oz plain chocolate, chopped
45ml/3 tbsp single cream
30ml/2 tbsp flaked hazelnuts
115g/4oz white chocolate, chopped
175g/6oz/³/₄ cup fromage frais
15ml/1 tbsp dry sherry
60ml/4 tbsp finely chopped hazelnuts, toasted
physalis (Cape gooseberries), dipped in white chocolate, to decorate

1 Melt the plain chocolate in a heatproof bowl over a saucepan of hot water, then remove from the heat and stir in the cream.

2 Draw 12 7.5cm/3in circles on sheets of non-stick baking paper. Turn the paper over and spread the plain chocolate over each marked circle, covering in a thin, even layer. Scatter flaked hazelnuts over four of the circles, then leave until set.

3 Melt the white chocolate in a heatproof bowl over a saucepan of hot water, then stir in the fromage frais and dry sherry. Fold in the chopped, toasted hazelnuts. Leave to cool until the mixture holds its shape.

Cook's Tip The chocolate could be spread over heart shapes instead, for a special Valentine's Day dessert.

4 Remove the plain chocolate rounds carefully from the paper and sandwich them together in stacks of 3, spooning the white chocolate hazelnut cream between each layer and using the hazelnut-covered rounds on top. Chill before serving.

5 To serve, place the galettes on individual plates and decorate with chocolate-dipped physalis.

Savoury
Treats

The earliest cookies were savoury, made with just flour, water and perhaps some salt, but as the practice of cookie-making became established the savoury version lost ground to sweet cookies. Now, there is a trend towards more savoury tastes with more wine being drunk, and quaffed more casually rather than consumed only as an accompaniment to special meals, and savoury cookies are making a comeback. This time, though, the recipes are far more varied and appetising. Variety is introduced by using different flours, and including ingredients such as oats, polenta and nuts for texture. Savoury cookie doughs are flavoured with cheese, herbs and spices, or topped with sesame or other seeds for extra crunch and savour.

Try sandwiching savoury cookies together in pairs with soft cheese, simply seasoned or flavoured with a complementary ingredient, such as chives with cheese biscuits. Triple-deckers can be created in the same way. Avoid filling cookies too far in advance, though, in case they soften.

Any type of savoury cookie is versatile — it can be served with drinks, soups and cheese, or taken in packed lunches and picnics.

Festive Nibbles

Shape these spicy cheese snacks in any way you wish –
stars, crescent moons, triangles, squares, hearts,
fingers or rounds. Serve them with drinks from
ice-cold cocktails to hot and spicy mulls.

Makes 60

INGREDIENTS

115g/4oz/1 cup plain flour, plus
extra for dusting
5ml/1 tsp mustard powder
pinch of salt
115g/4oz/¹/₂ cup butter
75g/3oz/³/₄ cup Cheddar cheese,
grated
pinch of cayenne pepper
30ml/2 tbsp water
1 egg, beaten
poppy seeds, sunflower seeds or
sesame seeds, to decorate

1 Preheat the oven to 200°C/400°F/
Gas 6. Grease two baking sheets.
Sift the flour, mustard powder and
salt into a bowl and rub in the butter
until the mixture resembles fine
breadcrumbs.

2 Stir in the cheese and cayenne
pepper and sprinkle on the water.
Add half the beaten egg, mix to a
firm dough and knead lightly until
smooth.

3 Roll out the dough on a lightly
floured surface and cut out a
variety of shapes. Re-roll the trimmings
and cut more shapes.

4 Place on the prepared baking
sheets and brush with the
remaining egg. Sprinkle on the seeds.
Bake for 8–10 minutes until golden.

Cheese Straws

Makes 50 straws and 8 rings

INGREDIENTS

115g/4oz/1 cup plain flour, plus
extra for dusting
5ml/1 tsp mustard powder
pinch of salt
115g/4oz/¹/₂ cup butter
75g/3oz/³/₄ cup Cheddar cheese,
grated
pinch of cayenne pepper
30ml/2 tbsp water
1 egg, beaten
poppy seeds, sunflower seeds or
sesame seeds, to decorate

1 Make the cheese pastry in the
same way as Festive Nibbles. Cut
the cheese pastry into fingers about
10cm/4in long and 5mm/¹/₄in wide.

2 Roll out the trimmings, cut
rounds using two pastry cutters
of different sizes, a 6cm/2¹/₂in one to
cut out the circle and a 5cm/2in
diameter one to stamp out the centre.
Cook as above.

3 To serve, push six or eight straws
through each ring.

Savoury Cheese Whirls

This make a tasty tea-time treat for children.

Makes 16

INGREDIENTS

*250g/9oz frozen puff pastry,
defrosted
2.5ml/¹/₂ tsp vegetable extract
1 egg, beaten
50g/2oz/¹/₂ cup grated red Leicester,
or Cheddar
cheese
carrot and cucumber sticks, to
serve*

1 Preheat the oven to 220°C/425°F/ Gas 7. Grease a large baking sheet. Roll out the pastry on a floured surface to a large rectangle, about 35 x 25cm/14 x 10in.

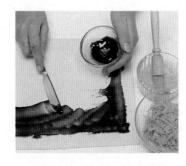

2 Spread the pastry with vegetable extract, leaving a 1cm/¹/₂in border. Brush the edges of the pastry with egg and sprinkle over the cheese to cover the vegetable extract.

3 Roll the pastry up quite tightly like a Swiss roll, starting from a longer edge. Brush the outside of the pastry with beaten egg.

4 Cut the pastry roll into thick slices and place on the prepared baking sheet.

5 Bake for 12–15 minutes, until the pastry is well risen and golden. Arrange on a serving plate and serve warm or cold with carrot and cucumber sticks.

Cook's Tip If the shapes become a little squashed when sliced, re-form into rounds by opening out the layers with the end of a knife.

Variation Omit the vegetable extract and use peanut butter, if preferred.

Cream Cheese Spirals

Makes 32

INGREDIENTS

225g/8oz/1 cup butter
225g/8oz/1 cup cream cheese
10ml/2 tsp granulated sugar
225g/8oz/2 cups plain flour
1 egg white beaten with 15ml/
1 tbsp water, for glazing
granulated sugar for sprinkling
For the filling
115g/4oz/1 cup walnuts or
pecans, finely chopped
75g/3oz/¹/₂ cup light brown sugar
5ml/1 tsp ground cinnamon

1 With an electric mixer, cream the butter, cream cheese, and sugar until soft. Sift over the flour and mix to form a dough. Gather into a ball and divide into halves. Flatten each piece, wrap in greaseproof paper and chill for at least 30 minutes.

2 To make the filling, mix together the chopped walnuts or pecans, brown sugar and cinnamon.

3 Preheat the oven to 190°C/375°F/ Gas 5. Grease two baking sheets.

4 Roll out each half of dough thinly into a circle about 28cm/11in in diameter. Trim the edges with a knife, using a dinner plate as a guide.

5 Brush the surface with the egg white glaze and sprinkle the dough evenly with half the filling.

6 Cut the dough into quarters and each quarter into four sections, to form 16 triangles.

7 Starting from the base of the triangles, roll up to form spirals.

8 Place on the prepared baking sheets and brush with the remaining glaze. Sprinkle with granulated sugar. Bake for 15– 20 minutes until golden. Transfer to a wire rack.

Bacon Twists

Making bread is always fun, so try this savoury version and add that extra twist to breakfast. Serve with soft cheese with herbs.

Makes 12

INGREDIENTS

450g/1lb/4 cups strong white flour
1 sachet easy-blend yeast
pinch of salt
400ml/14fl oz/1²/₃ cups hand-hot water
12 streaky bacon rashers
1 egg, beaten

Cook's Tip The same basic dough mix can be used to make rolls or a loaf of bread. Tap the base of the loaf – if it sounds hollow, it's cooked.

1 Mix the flour, yeast and salt in a bowl and stir them together. Add a little of the water and mix with a knife. Add the remaining water and use your hands to pull the mixture together, to make a sticky dough.

2 Turn the dough on to a lightly floured surface and knead for 5 minutes, until the dough is smooth and stretchy.

3 Divide the dough into 12 even-size pieces and roll each one into a sausage shape. Lightly oil a baking sheet.

4 Place each bacon rasher on a chopping board and run the back of the knife down its length, to stretch it slightly. Wind a rasher of bacon round each dough 'sausage'.

5 Brush the 'sausages' with beaten egg and arrange them on the prepared baking sheet. Leave in a warm place for 30 minutes, until doubled in size. Preheat the oven to 200°C/400°F/Gas 6. Bake the 'sausages' for 20–25 minutes, until cooked and browned.

Variations Make some meat-free versions of these twists for vegetarians by twisting the dough by hand and sprinkling with poppy or sesame seeds before baking.

Wisconsin Cheddar and Chive Biscuits

These soft biscuits are delicious warm, split and spread with butter;

serve with soup or as part of a main dish.

Makes 20

INGREDIENTS

200g/7oz/1³/₄ cups plain flour
10ml/2 tsp baking powder
2.5ml/¹/₂ tsp bicarbonate of soda
pinch of salt
1.5ml/¹/₄ tsp black pepper
65g/2¹/₂oz/5 tbsp unsalted butter,
chopped
50g/2oz/¹/₂ cup grated mature
Cheddar cheese
30ml/2 tbsp chopped fresh chives
175ml/6fl oz/³/₄ cup buttermilk

Variation For Cheddar and Bacon
Biscuits, substitute 45ml/3 tbsp
crumbled cooked bacon for the chives.

1 Preheat the oven to 200°C/400°F/
Gas 6. Grease a baking sheet.

2 Sift the flour, baking powder,
bicarbonate of soda, salt and
pepper into a large bowl. Rub the
butter into the dry ingredients until
the mixture resembles coarse
breadcrumbs. Add the cheese and
chives and stir to mix.

3 Make a well in the centre of the
mixture. Add the buttermilk and
stir vigorously until the batter comes
away from the sides of the bowl.

4 Drop in 30ml/2 tbsp mounds
spaced 5–7.5cm/2–3in apart on
the prepared baking sheet. Bake for
12–15 minutes, until golden brown.

Corn Oysters

Serve hot by themselves or as an accompaniment to meat or chicken dishes.

Makes about 8

INGREDIENTS

150g/5oz/1 cup grated fresh
sweetcorn kernels
1 egg, separated
30ml/2 tbsp plain flour
pinch of salt
1.5ml/¹/₄ tsp black pepper
25–50g/1–2oz/2–4 tbsp butter or
margarine
30–50ml/1–2fl oz/2–4 tbsp
vegetable oil

1 Combine the corn, egg yolk and
flour in a bowl. Mix well. Add
the salt and pepper.

2 In a separate bowl, beat the egg
white until it forms stiff peaks.
Fold it carefully into the corn
mixture.

3 Heat 30ml/2 tbsp butter or
margarine with 30ml/2 tbsp oil in
a frying pan. When the fats are very
hot and almost smoking, drop
tablespoonfuls of the corn mixture
into the pan. Fry until crisp and
brown on the undersides.

4 Turn the 'oysters' over and cook
for 1–2 minutes on the other side.
Drain on paper towels and keep hot.
Continue frying the 'oysters', adding
more fat as necessary.

Cook's Tip Thawed frozen or canned
sweetcorn kernels can also be used.
Drain them well and chop.

Cornmeal Biscuits

Serve these cookies hot, spread with butter.

Makes 12

INGREDIENTS

175g/6oz/1¼ cups plain flour
12.5ml/2½ tsp baking powder
pinch of salt
50g/2oz/½ cup cornmeal, plus extra for sprinkling
175g/6oz/⅓ cup lard or butter, chopped
175ml/6fl oz/¾ cup milk

1 Preheat the oven to 230°C/450°F/ Gas 8. Sprinkle an ungreased baking sheet lightly with cornmeal.

2 Sift the flour, baking powder and salt into a bowl. Stir in the cornmeal. Rub the lard or butter into the dry ingredients until the mixture resembles coarse breadcrumbs.

3 Make a well in the centre and pour in the milk. Stir in quickly with a wooden spoon until the dough begins to pull away from the sides.

4 Turn the dough on to a lightly floured surface and knead lightly 8–10 times only. Roll out to a thickness of 1cm/½in. Cut into rounds with a floured 5cm/2in biscuit cutter.

5 Arrange on the prepared baking sheet, about 2.5cm/1in apart. Sprinkle with cornmeal. Bake for 10–12 minutes, until golden brown.

Thyme and Mustard Biscuits

These aromatic biscuits are delicious served with herby cheese as a light savoury last course.

Makes 40

❧

INGREDIENTS

*175g/6oz/1¹/₂ cups wholemeal
plain flour
50g/2oz/²/₃ cup medium oatmeal
25g/1oz/2 tbsp caster sugar
10ml/2 tsp baking powder
30ml/2 tbsp fresh thyme leaves
50g/2oz/4 tbsp butter, chopped
25g/1oz/2 tbsp white vegetable
fat, chopped
45ml/3 tbsp milk
10ml/2 tsp Dijon mustard
30ml/2 tbsp sesame seeds
salt and black pepper*

❧

1 Preheat the oven to 200°C/400°F/
Gas 6. Grease two baking sheets.
Put the flour, oatmeal, sugar, baking
powder, thyme leaves and seasoning
into a bowl and mix. Add the fats to
the bowl, then rub in.

2 Mix the milk and mustard
together and stir into the flour
mixture until you have a soft dough.

3 Knead lightly on a floured surface
then roll out to a thickness of
5mm/¹/₄in. Stamp out 5cm/2in rounds
with a floured fluted biscuit cutter
and arrange, spaced slightly apart, on
the prepared baking sheets.

4 Re-roll the trimmings and
continue stamping out biscuits
until all the dough is used. Prick the
biscuits with a fork and sprinkle with
sesame seeds. Cook for 10–12
minutes, until lightly browned.

5 Cool on the sheets then pack into
a small airtight container. Store in
a cool place for up to 5 days.

Salted Peanut Cookies

The combinaton of salt and sweet flavours is delicious.

Makes 70

INGREDIENTS

*350g/12oz/3 cups plain flour
2.5ml/¹/₂ tsp bicarbonate of soda
115g/4oz/¹/₂ cup butter
115g/4oz/¹/₂ cup margarine
250g/9oz/1¹/₂ cups light brown
sugar
2 eggs
10ml/2 tsp vanilla essence
225g/8oz/2 cups salted peanuts*

1 Preheat the oven to 190°C/375°F/ Gas 5. Lightly grease two baking sheets. Grease the bottom of a glass and dip in sugar.

2 Sift together the flour and bicarbonate of soda. Set aside.

3 With an electric mixer, cream the butter, margarine and sugar until light and fluffy. Beat in the eggs and vanilla essence. Fold in the flour mixture.

Variation To make Cashew Cookies, substitute an equal amount of salted cashews for the peanuts, and add as above. The flavour is subtle and interesting.

4 Stir the peanuts into the butter mixture until evenly combined.

5 Drop teaspoonfuls 5cm/2in apart on the prepared sheets. Flatten with the prepared glass.

6 Bake for about 10 minutes, until lightly coloured. With a metal spatula, transfer to a wire rack to cool completely.

Cheddar Pennies

Serve these tasty snacks with pre-dinner drinks.

Makes 20

INGREDIENTS

*50g/2oz/4 tbsp butter
115g/4oz/1 cup Cheddar cheese,
grated
40g/1¹/₂oz/¹/₃ cup plain flour
pinch of salt
pinch of chilli powder*

1 With an electric mixer, cream the butter until soft.

2 Stir in the cheese, flour, salt and chilli. Gather to form a dough.

3 Transfer to a lightly floured surface. Shape into a cylinder about 3cm/1¹/₄in in diameter. Wrap in greaseproof paper and chill for 1–2 hours.

4 Preheat the oven to 180°C/350°F/ Gas 4. Grease 1–2 baking sheets.

5 Cut the dough into 5mm/¹/₄in thick slices and place on the prepared baking sheets. Bake for about 15 minutes, until golden. Transfer to a wire rack to cool.

Blue Cheese and Chive Crisps

Makes 48

INGREDIENTS

225g/8oz/2 cups blue cheese, crumbled
115g/4oz/¹/₂ cup unsalted butter
1 egg
1 egg yolk
30ml/2 tsp chopped fresh chives
black pepper
225g/8oz/2 cups plain flour, sifted

Cook's Tip The cheese crisps will keep up to 10 days in an airtight container.

1 The day before serving, beat together the cheese and butter until well blended. Add the egg, egg yolk, chives and a little pepper and beat until just blended.

2 Add the flour in three batches, folding in well between each addition.

3 Divide the dough in half and shape each half into a log about 5cm/2in in diameter. Wrap in greaseproof paper and chill overnight. Preheat the oven to 190°C/375°F/Gas 5. Lightly grease two baking sheets.

4 Cut the dough logs across into slices about 3mm/¹/₈in thick. Place on the prepared baking sheets. Bake for about 10 minutes, until just golden around the edges. Transfer to a wire rack to cool.

Cheese Muffins

Makes 9

INGREDIENTS

50g/2oz/4 tbsp butter
175g/6oz/1½ cups plain flour
10ml/2 tsp baking powder
30ml/2 tbsp caster sugar
pinch of salt
5ml/1 tsp paprika
2 eggs
120ml/4fl oz/½ cup milk
5ml/1 tsp dried thyme
50g/2oz mature Cheddar cheese,
cut into 1cm/½in dice

1 Preheat the oven to 190°C/375°F/ Gas 5. Grease nine muffin tins, or use paper liners. Melt the butter in a small saucepan.

2 In a mixing bowl, sift together the flour, baking powder, sugar, salt and paprika.

3 In another bowl, combine the eggs, milk, melted butter and thyme and whisk to blend.

4 Add the milk mixture to the dry ingredients and stir until just moistened; do not mix until smooth.

5 Place a heaped spoonful of batter into the prepared tins. Drop a few pieces of cheese over each, then top with another spoonful of batter.

6 Bake for about 25 minutes, until puffed and golden. Leave to stand for 5 minutes before unmoulding on to a wire rack. These muffins are best served warm or at room temperature.

Bacon Cornmeal Muffins

Serve these muffins fresh from the oven for a special breakfast.

Makes 14

❧

INGREDIENTS

8 bacon rashers
50g/2oz/4 tbsp butter
50g/2oz/4 tbsp margarine
115g/4oz/1 cup plain flour
15ml/1 tbsp baking powder
5ml/1 tsp caster sugar
pinch of salt
175g/6oz/1½ cups cornmeal
250ml/8fl oz/1 cup milk
2 eggs

❧

1 Preheat the oven to 200°C/400°F/ Gas 6. Grease 14 muffin tins, or use paper liners.

2 Fry the bacon until crisp. Drain on paper towels, then chop into small pieces. Set aside. Melt the butter and margarine in a saucepan over a low heat and set aside.

3 Sift the flour, baking powder, sugar and salt into a large mixing bowl. Stir in the cornmeal, then make a well in the centre. In another saucepan, heat the milk to lukewarm. In a small bowl, lightly whisk the eggs, then add to the milk. Stir in the melted fats.

4 Pour the milk mixture into the centre of the well and stir until smooth and well blended.

5 Fold in the bacon. Spoon the batter into the prepared tins, filling them halfway. Bake for about 20 minutes, until risen and lightly coloured.

Savoury Parmesan Puffs

Makes 6

❧

INGREDIENTS

115g/4oz/½ cup freshly grated
Parmesan cheese
115g/4oz/1 cup plain flour
pinch of salt
15ml/1 tbsp butter or margarine
2 eggs
250ml/8fl oz/1 cup milk

❧

1 Preheat the oven to 230°C/450°F/ Gas 8. Grease six individual baking tins. Sprinkle each tin with 15ml/1 tbsp of the grated Parmesan. Alternatively, you can use ramekins, in which case, heat them on a baking sheet in the oven then grease and sprinkle with Parmesan just before filling. Sift the flour and salt into a small bowl. Set aside. Melt the butter or margarine in a small saucepan.

2 In a mixing bowl, beat together the eggs, milk and melted butter or margarine. Add the flour mixture and stir until smoothly blended.

3 Divide the batter evenly among the containers, filling each one about half full. Bake for 15 minutes, then sprinkle the tops of the puffs with the remaining grated Parmesan cheese. Reduce the heat to 180°C/350°F/Gas 4 and continue baking for 20–25 minutes, until the puffs are firm and golden brown.

4 Remove the puffs from the oven. To unmould, run a thin knife around the inside of each container to loosen them. Gently ease out, then transfer to a wire rack to cool.

Herb Popovers

Makes 12

INGREDIENTS

25g/1oz/2 tbsp butter
3 eggs
250ml/8fl oz/1 cup milk
175g/6oz/¾ cup plain flour
pinch of salt
1 small sprig each mixed fresh
herbs, such as chives, tarragon,
dill and parsley

1 Preheat the oven to 220°C/425°F/ Gas 7. Grease 12 small ramekins or popover tins. Melt the butter in a small saucepan over a low heat.

2 With an electric mixer, beat the eggs until blended. Beat in the milk and melted butter.

3 Sift together the flour and salt, then beat into the egg mixture to combine thoroughly.

4 Strip the herb leaves from the stems and chop finely. Stir 30ml/ 2 tbsp into the batter.

5 Pour the batter into the prepared dishes or tins so they are half full.

6 Bake for 25–30 minutes, until golden. Do not open the oven door during baking time or the popovers may fall. For drier popovers, pierce each one with a knife after 30 minutes baking time and bake for 5 minutes more. Serve hot.

Cheese Popovers

Makes 12

INGREDIENTS

25ml/1½ tbsp butter
3 eggs
250ml/8fl oz/1 cup milk
75g/3oz/¾ cup plain flour
pinch of salt
1.5ml/¼ tsp paprika
75g/3oz/6 tbsp freshly grated
Parmesan cheese

1 Preheat the oven to 220°C/425°F/ Gas 7. Grease 12 small ramekins or popover tins. Melt the butter in a small saucepan over a low heat.

2 With an electric mixer, beat the eggs until blended. Beat in the milk and melted butter.

3 Sift together the flour, salt, and paprika, then beat into the egg mixture. Add the cheese and stir.

4 Fill the prepared dishes or tins so they are half full. Bake for 25– 30 minutes, until golden. Do not open the oven door during baking or the popovers will fall. For drier popovers, pierce each one with a knife after 30 minutes baking time and bake for 5 minutes more. Serve hot.

Tiny Cheese Puffs

These bite-sized portions of choux pastry are the ideal accompaniment
to a glass of wine before dinner.

Makes 45

INGREDIENTS

115g/4oz/1 cup plain flour
pinch of salt
5ml/1 tsp dry mustard powder
pinch of cayenne pepper
250ml/8fl oz/1 cup water
115g/4oz/½ cup butter, chopped
4 eggs
75g/3oz Gruyère cheese, finely
diced
15ml/1 tbsp finely chopped chives

Cook's Tip The puffs can be prepared ahead and are suitable for freezing. Reheat in a hot oven for 5 minutes, until crisp, before serving.

1 Preheat the oven to 200°C/400°F/ Gas 6. Lightly grease two large baking sheets. Sift together the flour, salt, dry mustard and cayenne pepper.

2 In a medium-size saucepan, bring the water and butter to the boil over a medium-high heat. Remove from the heat and add the flour mixture all at once, beating with a wooden spoon until the dough forms a ball. Return to the heat and beat constantly for 1–2 minutes to dry out. Remove from the heat and cool for 3–5 minutes.

3 Beat three of the eggs in to the dough, one at a time, beating well after each addition. Beat the fourth egg in a small bowl and add a teaspoon at a time, beating until the dough is smooth and shiny and falls slowly when dropped from a spoon. (You may not need all of the fourth egg; reserve any remaining egg for glazing.) Stir in the diced cheese and chives.

4 Using two teaspoons, drop small mounds of dough 5cm/2in apart on to the prepared baking sheets. Beat the reserved egg with 15ml/ 1 tbsp water and brush the tops with the glaze.

5 Bake for 8 minutes, then reduce the oven temperature to 180°C/350°F/Gas 4 and bake for 7– 8 minutes more, until puffed and golden. Transfer to a wire rack to cool. Serve warm.

Variation For Ham and Cheese Puffs, add 50g/2oz/¼ cup finely diced ham with the cheese. For Cheesy Herb Puffs, stir in 30ml/2 tbsp chopped fresh herbs or spring onions with the cheese.

Cheese Scones

These delicious scones make a good tea-time treat. They are best served fresh and still slightly warm.

Makes 12

INGREDIENTS

225g/8oz/2 cups plain flour
12.5ml/2½ tsp baking powder
2.5ml/½ tsp dry mustard powder
2.5ml/½ tsp salt
50g/2oz/4 tbsp cold butter, chopped
75g/3oz/¾ cup Cheddar cheese, grated
150ml/¼ pint/⅔ cup milk
1 egg, beaten

1 Preheat the oven to 230°C/450°F/ Gas 8. Sift the flour, baking powder, mustard powder and salt into a mixing bowl. Add the butter and rub into the flour mixture until the mixture resembles breadcrumbs.

2 Stir in 50g/2oz/½ cup of the cheese into the butter and flour mixture.

3 Make a well in the centre and gently stir in the milk and egg until smooth. Turn the dough on to a lightly floured surface.

4 Roll out the dough and cut into triangles or squares. Brush lightly with milk and sprinkle with the remaining cheese. Leave to rest for 15 minutes, then bake for 15 minutes, until well risen.

Oatcakes

These are very simple to make and are an excellent addition to a cheese board.

Makes 24

INGREDIENTS

225g/8oz/2 cups medium oatmeal, plus extra for sprinkling
75g/3oz/¾ cup plain flour
1.5ml/¼ tsp bicarbonate of soda
5ml/1 tsp salt
25g/1oz/2 tbsp lard
25g/1oz/2 tbsp butter

1 Preheat the oven to 220°C/425°F/ Gas 7. Place the oatmeal, flour, bicarbonate of soda and salt in a large bowl. Melt the two fats together in a small saucepan over a low heat.

2 Add the melted fat and enough boiling water to make a dough. Turn on to a surface sprinkled with a little oatmeal. Roll out thinly and cut into 24 circles. Bake on ungreased baking sheets for 15 minutes.

Ham and Tomato Scones

These make an ideal accompaniment for soup. Choose a strongly flavoured ham and chop it fairly finely, so that a little goes a long way.

Makes 12

❧

INGREDIENTS

225g/8oz/2 cups self-raising flour
5ml/1 tsp dry mustard
5ml/1 tsp paprika, plus extra for sprinkling
pinch of salt
25g/1oz/2 tbsp margarine, chopped
15ml/1 tbsp snipped fresh basil
50g/2oz/¹⁄₃ cup drained sun-dried tomatoes in oil, chopped
50g/2oz Black Forest ham, chopped
90–120ml/3–4fl oz/¹⁄₄–¹⁄₂ cup skimmed milk, plus extra for brushing.

❧

1 Preheat the oven to 200°C/400°F/ Gas 6. Flour a large baking sheet. Sift the flour, mustard, paprika and salt into a bowl. Using your fingers, rub in the margarine until the mixture resembles breadcrumbs.

2 Stir the basil, sun-dried tomatoes and ham into the bowl. Pour in enough milk to make a soft dough.

3 Turn the dough on to a lightly floured surface, knead lightly and roll out to a 20 x 15cm/8 x 6in rectangle. Cut into 5cm/2in squares and arrange on the baking sheet.

4 Brush the tops with milk, sprinkle with paprika and bake for 12–15 minutes. Transfer to a rack to cool.

Feta Cheese and Chive Scones

Feta cheese makes an excellent substitute for butter in these tangy savoury scones.

Makes 9

INGREDIENTS

*115g/4oz/1 cup self-raising white
flour
150g/5oz/1 cup self-raising
wholemeal flour
pinch of salt
75g/3oz feta cheese
15ml/1 tbsp snipped fresh chives
150ml/¼ pint/⅔ cup skimmed
milk, plus extra for glazing
1.5ml/¼ tsp cayenne pepper*

1 Preheat the oven to 200°C/400°F/
Gas 6. Sift the flours and salt into
a mixing bowl, adding any bran left
over from the flour in the sieve.

2 Crumble the feta cheese and rub
into the dry ingredients. Stir in
the chives, then add the milk and mix
to a soft dough.

3 Turn on to a floured surface and
lightly knead until smooth. Roll
out to 2cm/¾in thick and stamp out
nine scones with a floured 6cm/2½in
cookie cutter.

4 Transfer to a non-stick baking
sheet. Brush with skimmed milk,
then sprinkle over the cayenne
pepper. Bake for 15 minutes, until
golden brown. Serve warm or cold.

Wholemeal Herb Triangles

Stuffed with cooked chicken and salad, these make a good lunchtime snack, and are also an ideal accompaniment to a bowl of steaming soup.

Makes 8

❦

INGREDIENTS

225g/8oz/2 cups wholemeal plain
flour
115g/4oz/1 cup strong plain flour
pinch of salt
2.5ml/¹/₂ tsp bicarbonate of soda
5ml/1 tsp cream of tartar
2.5ml/¹/₂ tsp chilli powder
50g/2oz/¹/₄ cup margarine,
chopped
60ml/4 tbsp chopped mixed fresh
herbs
250ml/8fl oz/1 cup skimmed milk
15ml/1 tbsp sesame seeds

❦

1 Preheat the oven to 220°C/425°F/ Gas 7. Lightly flour a baking sheet. Put the wholemeal flour in a mixing bowl. Sift in the salt, bicarbonate of soda, cream of tartar and chilli powder, then rub in the margarine.

2 Add the herbs and milk and mix quickly to a soft dough. Turn on to a lightly floured surface. Knead only very briefly or the dough will become tough.

3 Roll the dough out to a 23cm/9in round and place on the prepared baking sheet. Brush lightly with water and sprinkle the top evenly with the sesame seeds.

4 Carefully cut the dough round into eight wedges, separate them slightly and bake for 15–20 minutes. Transfer to a wire rack to cool. Serve warm or cold.

Variation To make Sun-dried Tomato Triangles, replace the fresh mixed herbs with 30ml/2 tbsp drained chopped sun-dried tomatoes in oil and add 15ml/1 tbsp each mild paprika, chopped fresh parsley and chopped fresh marjoram.

Dill and Potato Cakes

Makes 10

❧

INGREDIENTS

225g/8oz/2 cups self-raising flour
40g/1¹/₂oz/3 tbsp butter
pinch of salt
15ml/1 tbsp finely chopped fresh
dill
175g/6oz/scant 1 cup mashed
potato, freshly made
30–45ml/2–3 tbsp milk

❧

1 Preheat the oven to 230°C/450°F/ Gas 8. Sift the flour into a bowl, and add the butter, salt and dill. Mix in the potato and enough milk to make a soft dough.

2 Roll out the dough until fairly thin. Cut into neat rounds with a floured 7.5cm/3in cutter. Place the cakes on a greased baking sheet, and bake for 20–25 minutes.

Chive and Potato Scones

These little scones should be fairly thin, soft and crisp on the outside. Serve them for breakfast.

Makes 20

INGREDIENTS

450g/1lb potatoes
115g/4oz/1 cup plain flour
30ml/2 tbsp olive oil
30ml/2 tbsp snipped chives
salt and black pepper

Cook's Tip Cook the scones over a constant low heat so that the outsides do not burn before the insides are cooked through.

1 Cook the potatoes in a saucepan of boiling salted water for 20 minutes, until tender, then drain thoroughly. Return the potatoes to the clean pan and mash them. Preheat a griddle or heavy frying pan.

2 Add the flour, olive oil, chives and a little salt and pepper to the mashed potato. Mix to a soft dough.

3 Roll out the dough on a well-floured surface to a thickness of 5mm/¼in and stamp out rounds with a floured 5cm/2in plain pastry cutter. Lightly grease the griddle or frying pan.

4 Cook the scones for about 10 minutes, turning once.

Curry Crackers

These spicy, crisp little biscuits are ideal for serving with drinks.

Makes 12

❧

INGREDIENTS

50g/2oz/¹/₂ cup plain flour
pinch of salt
5ml/1 tsp curry powder
1.5ml/¹/₄ tsp chilli powder
15ml/1 tbsp chopped fresh
coriander
30ml/2 tbsp water

❧

1 Preheat the oven to 180°C/350°F/ Gas 4. Sift the flour and salt into a mixing bowl, then add the curry powder and chilli powder. Make a well in the centre and add the chopped fresh coriander and water. Gradually incorporate the flour and mix to a firm dough.

2 Turn the dough on to a lightly floured surface, knead until smooth, then leave to rest for 5 minutes.

3 Cut the dough into 12 even-size pieces and knead into small balls. Roll each ball out very thinly to a 10cm/4in round, sprinkling more flour over the dough if necessary to prevent it from sticking to the rolling pin.

4 Arrange the rounds on two ungreased baking sheets, then bake for 15 minutes, turning over once during cooking. Transfer to a wire rack to cool.

147

Cocktail Shapes

Tiny savoury biscuits are always a welcome treat. Try using different flavours and shapes.

Makes 80

🌿

INGREDIENTS

350g/12oz/3 cups plain flour
pinch of salt
2.5ml/¹/₂ tsp black pepper
5ml/1 tsp whole grain mustard
175g/6oz/³/₄ cup butter, chopped
115g/4oz Cheddar cheese
1 egg, beaten
5ml/1 tsp chopped nuts
10ml/2 tsp dill seeds
10ml/2 tsp curry paste
10ml/2 tsp chilli sauce

🌿

1 Preheat the oven to 200°C/400°F/ Gas 6. Line several baking sheets with non-stick baking paper. Sift the flour into a mixing bowl and add the salt, pepper and mustard.

2 Rub the butter into the flour mixture until it resembles fine breadcrumbs. Grate the cheese then with a fork stir it into the butter and flour mixture. Add the egg, and mix together to form a soft dough.

3 Knead lightly on a floured surface and cut into four equal pieces.

4 Knead chopped nuts into one piece, dill seeds into another piece and curry paste and chilli sauce into each of the remaining pieces. Wrap each piece of flavoured dough in clear film and chill for at least 1 hour. Remove from the clear film and roll out one piece at a time.

5 Using a floured heart-shaped cutter, stamp out about 20 shapes from the curry-flavoured dough and use a club-shaped cutter to cut out the chilli-flavoured dough. Arrange the shapes well spaced apart on the prepared baking sheets and bake in the oven for 6–8 minutes, until slightly puffed and pale gold in colour. Cool on wire racks.

6 Repeat with the remaining flavoured dough using spade- and diamond-shaped cutters. Knead any trimmings together, re-roll and stamp out and bake as above.

Spiced Cocktail Biscuits

These savoury biscuits are ideal for serving with pre-dinner drinks.

Each of the spice seeds contributes to the flavour.

Makes 20–30

INGREDIENTS

150g/5oz/1¼ cups plain flour
10ml/2 tsp curry powder
115g/4oz/½ cup butter, chopped
75g/3oz/¾ cup grated Cheddar
cheese,
10ml/2 tsp poppy seeds
5ml/1 tsp black onion seeds
1 egg yolk
cumin seeds, to garnish

Variation Use caraway or sesame seeds instead of the poppy seeds if you wish.

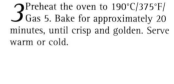

1 Grease two baking sheets. Sift the flour and curry powder into a large bowl. Rub in the butter until the mixture resembles breadcrumbs, then stir in the cheese, poppy seeds and black onion seeds. Stir in the egg yolk and mix to a firm dough. Wrap the dough in clear film and chill for 30 minutes.

2 Roll out the dough on a floured surface to a thickness of about 3mm/⅛in. Cut into rounds with a floured cookie cutter. Arrange on the prepared baking sheets and sprinkle with the cumin seeds. Chill for 15 minutes.

3 Preheat the oven to 190°C/375°F/ Gas 5. Bake for approximately 20 minutes, until crisp and golden. Serve warm or cold.

Brownies
and Bars

A brownie should be a moist, chewy bar, crisp on the outside but as if underdone inside. There are many recipes for brownies, varying in richness.

Bars are the quickest and easiest cookies to shape evenly. The cookie mixture is simply poured or pressed into the tin, baked, then cut to the required size with a large, sharp knife while still warm from the oven.

Some bar cookies are just a single layer, while others are double- or even triple-layered. The layers are sometimes added before baking, sometimes part of the way through the cooking, depending on the recipe.

Try to use the size of tin stated in a recipe. If you use one that is smaller, the layer of mixture will be deeper so the outside of the bars will become overcooked and too brown and crisp or hard before the inside is ready, whereas if too large a tin is used the mixture will be spread too thinly, and not only will it cook too quickly and dry out, but the ratio of centre to outside crust will be adversely affected. If you only have a larger tin, the size can be reduced by making a wide strip formed from a triple thickness of foil to fit across the tin at the right place. Fold up along a long edge to make a lap that the weight of the mixture will hold down, keeping the foil divider in place.

Bar cookies can be stored for a day or so in their baking tin. Cover the tin as tightly as you can with foil, or slide it into a plastic bag, gently press out as much air as possible and seal tightly.

White Chocolate Brownies

Makes 16

❧

INGREDIENTS

150g/5oz/1¼ cups plain flour
2.5ml/½ tsp baking powder
pinch of salt
175g/6oz fine quality white
chocolate, chopped
90g/3½oz/½ cup caster sugar
115g/4oz/½ cup unsalted butter,
chopped
2 eggs, lightly beaten
5ml/1 tsp vanilla essence
175g/6oz plain chocolate,
chopped, or plain chocolate chips
For the topping
200g/7oz milk chocolate, chopped
215g/7½oz/2 cups unsalted
macadamia nuts, chopped

❧

1 Preheat the oven to 180°C/350°F/ Gas 4. Grease a 23cm/9in springform tin. Sift together the flour, baking powder and salt. Set aside.

2 In a medium saucepan over medium heat, melt the white chocolate, sugar and butter, stirring until smooth.

3 Cool slightly, then beat in the eggs and vanilla essence. Stir in the flour until well blended. Stir in the chopped chocolate or chocolate chips. Spread evenly in the prepared tin, smoothing the top.

4 Bake for 20–25 minutes until a skewer inserted 5cm/2in from the side of the tin comes out clean. Remove from the oven. Sprinkle chopped milk chocolate evenly over the surface (avoid touching the side of tin) and return to oven for 1 minute.

5 Remove from the oven and, using the back of a spoon, spread the softened chocolate evenly over the top. Sprinkle with the macadamia nuts and gently press into the chocolate. Cool on a wire rack for 30 minutes, then chill until set. Run a sharp knife around the side of the tin to loosen; unclip the tin side and carefully remove. Cut into thin wedges.

Marbled Brownies

Makes 24

INGREDIENTS

225g/8oz plain chocolate, chopped
75g/3oz/⅓ cup butter, chopped
4 eggs
350g/12oz/1½ cups caster sugar
115g/4oz/1 cup plain flour
pinch of salt
5ml/1 tsp baking powder
10ml/2 tsp vanilla essence
115g/4oz/1 cup walnuts, chopped
For the plain batter
50g/2oz/4 tbsp butter
175g/6oz/⅔ cup cream cheese
115g/4oz/½ cup caster sugar
2 eggs
30ml/2 tbsp plain flour
5ml/1 tsp vanilla essence

1 Preheat the oven to 180°C/350°F/ Gas 4. Line a 33 x 23 cm/ 13 x 9in tin with greaseproof paper and grease the paper.

2 Melt the chocolate and butter in a saucepan over a very low heat.

3 Meanwhile, beat the eggs until light and fluffy. Gradually add the sugar and continue beating until blended. Sift over the flour, salt and baking powder and fold in.

4 Stir in the cooled chocolate mixture, and the vanilla essence and walnuts. Set aside 475ml/16fl oz/ 2 cups of the chocolate batter.

5 To make the plain batter, cream the butter and cream cheese with an electric mixer.

6 Add the sugar and continue beating until blended. Beat in the eggs, flour and vanilla essence.

7 Spread the unmeasured chocolate batter into the tin. Pour over the cream cheese mixture. Drop spoonfuls of the reserved chocolate batter on top.

8 With a metal spatula, swirl the mixtures to marble. Do not blend completely. Bake for 35–40 minutes, until just set. Unmould when cool and cut into squares for serving.

Fudgy Glazed Chocolate Slices

Makes 8–10

INGREDIENTS

*300g/11oz plain chocolate,
chopped*
*115g/4oz/¹/₂ cup unsalted butter,
chopped*
*90g/3¹/₂oz/generous ¹/₂ cup light
brown sugar*
50g/2oz/¹/₄ cup granulated sugar
2 eggs
15ml/1 tbsp vanilla essence
65g/2¹/₂oz/¹/₂ cup plain flour
*115g/4oz/1 cup pecans or
walnuts, toasted and chopped*
*150g/5oz fine quality white
chocolate, chopped*
For the Fudgy Chocolate Glaze
*175g/6oz plain chocolate,
chopped*
*50g/2oz/4 tbsp unsalted butter,
chopped*
30ml/2 tbsp golden syrup
10ml/2 tsp vanilla essence
5ml/1 tsp instant coffee powder
*pecan halves, to decorate
(optional)*

1 Preheat the oven to 180°C/350°F/
Gas 4. Invert a 20cm/8in square
baking tin and mould a piece of foil
over the bottom. Turn the tin over
and line with moulded foil. Lightly
grease the foil.

2 In a medium saucepan over a low
heat, melt the plain chocolate and
butter, stirring until smooth.

3 Stir in the sugars and continue
stirring for 2 minutes, until the
sugar has dissolved. Beat in the eggs
and vanilla essence. Stir in the flour,
nuts and white chocolate. Pour the
batter into the prepared tin.

4 Bake for 20–25 minutes, until a
skewer inserted 5cm/2in from the
centre comes out clean. Remove the
tin to a wire rack to cool for
30 minutes. Using the foil, lift from
the tin and cool on the wire rack for
2 hours.

5 To make the glaze, melt the
chocolate, butter, syrup, vanilla
essence and coffee powder in a
medium saucepan over a medium
heat, stirring frequently, until
smooth. Remove from the heat. Chill
for 1 hour, until thickened and
spreadable.

6 Invert the cake on to the wire
rack, remove the foil from the
bottom. Turn top side up. Using a
metal palette knife, spread a thick
layer of fudgy glaze over the top of
the cake just to the edges. Chill for
1 hour, until set. Cut into squares or
fingers. If you wish, top each with a
pecan half.

Chocolate Brownies

Traditional American brownies are usually rich in fat. This no-butter version still tastes dark and gooey, but is best eaten on the day it is made.

Makes 20

INGREDIENTS

120ml/4fl oz/½ cup sunflower oil
150g/5oz plain chocolate, chopped
2 eggs
115g/4oz/1 cup self-raising flour
115g/4oz/½ cup caster sugar
5ml/1 tsp vanilla essence
75g/3oz/¾ cup halved pecans

1 Preheat the oven to 200°C/400°F/ Gas 6. Use a little of the oil to grease a 23cm/9in square shallow cake tin and line with lightly oiled greaseproof paper.

Cook's Tip Ingredients can be melted easily in the microwave. To soften chocolate, butter, sugar or syrup, microwave on full power for a few minutes, until soft.

2 Melt the chocolate with the remaining oil in a heatproof bowl over a saucepan of water, stirring until smooth.

3 Beat the eggs lightly and add them to the chocolate, stirring vigorously. Beat in the flour, sugar and vanilla essence and pour the mixture into the prepared tin. Arrange the pecans over the top.

4 Bake for 10–15 minutes. If you like chewy brownies, take them out of the oven now. If you want a more cake-like finish, leave for another 5 minutes. Cut into squares and leave to cool before removing from the tin.

Nut and Chocolate Chip Brownies

These brownies are moist, dark and deeply satisfying.

Makes 16

INGREDIENTS

*150g/5oz plain chocolate,
chopped
120ml/4fl oz/¹/₂ cup sunflower oil
215g/7¹/₂oz/1¹/₄ cups light
muscovado sugar
2 eggs
5ml/1 tsp vanilla essence
65g/2¹/₂oz/²/₃ cup self-raising flour
60ml/4 tbsp cocoa powder
75g/3oz/³/₄ cup chopped walnuts
or pecans
60ml/4 tbsp milk chocolate chips*

Cook's Tip These brownies will freeze
for 3 months in an airtight container.

1 Preheat the oven to 180°C/350°F/
Gas 4. Lightly grease a shallow
19cm/7¹/₂in square cake tin. Melt the
plain chocolate in a heatproof bowl
over a saucepan of hot water.

2 With an electric whisk, beat the
oil, sugar, eggs and vanilla
essence together in a large bowl.

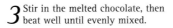

3 Stir in the melted chocolate, then
beat well until evenly mixed.

4 Sift the flour and cocoa powder
into the bowl and fold in
thoroughly. Stir in the chopped nuts
and chocolate chips, tip into the
prepared tin and spread evenly to the
edges. Bake for 30–35 minutes, until
the top is firm and crusty. Cool in the
tin before cutting into squares.

Banana Ginger Parkin

Parkin keeps well and actually improves with keeping. Store it in a covered container for up to 2 months.

Makes 26

INGREDIENTS

200g/7oz/1¾ cups plain flour
10ml/2 tsp bicarbonate of soda
10ml/2 tsp ground ginger
150g/5oz/1¾ cups medium oatmeal
60ml/4 tbsp dark muscovado sugar
75g/3oz/⅓ cup sunflower margarine, chopped
150g/5oz/⅔ cup golden syrup
1 egg, beaten
3 ripe bananas, mashed
75g/3oz/¾ cup icing sugar
stem ginger, to decorate

Cook's Tip These are nutritious, energy-giving squares that are a really good choice for packed lunches as they don't break up too easily.

1 Preheat the oven to 160°C/325°F/ Gas 3. Grease and line an 18 x 28cm/7 x 11in cake tin.

2 Sift together the flour, bicarbonate of soda and ginger, then stir in the oatmeal. Melt the sugar, margarine and syrup in a saucepan over a low heat, then stir into the flour mixture. Beat in the egg and mashed bananas.

3 Spoon into the prepared tin and bake for about 1 hour, until firm to the touch. Leave to cool in the tin, then turn out and cut into squares.

4 Sift the icing sugar into a bowl and stir in just enough water to make a smooth, runny icing. Drizzle the icing over each square and top with a piece of stem ginger.

Parkin Squares

The flavour of these squares will improve if they are stored in an airtight container for several days or a week before serving.

Makes 16–20

INGREDIENTS

300ml/¹/₂ pint/1¹/₄ cups milk
225g/8oz/³/₄ cup golden syrup
225g/8oz/³/₄ cup black treacle
115g/4oz/¹/₂ cup butter or
margarine, chopped
50g/2oz/¹/₃ cup dark brown sugar
450g/1lb/4 cups plain flour
2.5ml/¹/₂ tsp bicarbonate of soda
6.25ml/1¹/₄ tsp ground ginger
350g/12oz/4 cups medium
oatmeal
1 egg, beaten
icing sugar for dusting

1 Preheat the oven to 180°C/350°F/ Gas 4. Grease and line the base of a 20cm/8in square cake tin. Gently heat together the milk, syrup, treacle, butter or margarine and sugar, stirring until smooth; do not boil.

2 Stir together the flour, bicarbonate of soda, ginger and oatmeal. Make a well in the centre, pour in the egg, then slowly pour in the warmed mixture, stirring to make a smooth batter.

3 Pour the batter into the tin and bake for about 45 minutes, until firm to the touch. Cool slightly in the tin, then cool completely on a wire rack. Cut into squares and dust with icing sugar.

Chocolate Pecan Squares

Makes 16

INGREDIENTS

2 eggs
10ml/2 tsp vanilla essence
pinch of salt
175g/6oz/1½ cups pecans,
coarsely chopped
50g/2oz/½ cup plain flour
50g/2oz/4 tbsp granulated sugar
175g/6oz/½ cup treacle
75g/3oz/3 x 1oz plain chocolate,
finely chopped
45g/1½oz/3 tbsp butter
16 pecan halves for decorating

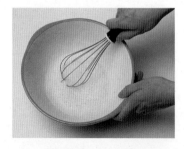 

1 Preheat the oven to 160°C/325°F/ Gas 3. Line the bottom and sides of a 20cm/8in square baking tin with paper and grease lightly.

2 Whisk together the eggs, vanilla essence and salt. In another bowl, mix together the pecans and flour. Set both bowls aside.

3 In a saucepan, bring the sugar and treacle to a boil.

4 Remove from the heat and stir in the chocolate and butter and blend thoroughly with a wooden spoon.

5 Mix in the beaten eggs, then fold in the pecan mixture. Pour the batter into the prepared tin and bake for about 35 minutes, until set.

6 Cool in the tin for 10 minutes before unmoulding. Cut into 5cm/2in squares and press pecan halves into the tops while warm. Cool completely on a wire rack.

Raisin Brownies

Makes 16

INGREDIENTS

115g/4oz/½ cup butter or
margarine, chopped
50g/2oz/½ cup cocoa powder
2 eggs
225g/8oz/1 cup caster sugar
5ml/1 tsp vanilla essence
40g/1½oz/⅓ cup plain flour
75g/3oz/¾ cup walnuts, chopped
65g/2½oz/½ cup raisins

1 Preheat the oven to 180°C/350°F/ Gas 4. Line a 20cm/8in square baking tin with greaseproof paper and grease the paper.

2 Melt the butter or margarine in a small saucepan over a low heat. Remove from the heat and stir in the cocoa powder.

3 With an electric mixer, beat together the eggs, sugar, and vanilla essence until light. Add the cocoa mixture and stir to blend.

4 Sift the flour over the cocoa mixture and gently fold in. Add the walnuts and raisins and scrape the batter into the prepared tin. Bake for 30 minutes. Do not overbake.

5 Leave in the tin to cool before cutting into 5cm/2in squares and removing. The brownies should be soft and moist. Dust with icing sugar before serving.

Chocolate Butterscotch Bars

Makes 24

INGREDIENTS

225g/8oz/2 cups plain flour
2.5ml/¹/₂ tsp baking powder
115g/4oz/¹/₂ cup unsalted butter,
chopped
50g/2oz/¹/₃ cup light muscovado
sugar
150g/5oz plain chocolate, melted
30ml/2 tbsp ground almonds
For the topping
175g/6oz/³/₄ cup unsalted butter
115g/4oz/¹/₂ cup caster sugar
30ml/2 tbsp golden syrup
175ml/6fl oz/³/₄ cup condensed
milk
150g/5oz/1¹/₄ cups whole toasted
hazelnuts
225g/8oz plain chocolate,
chopped

1 Preheat the oven to 160°C/325°F/ Gas 3. Grease a shallow 30 x 20cm/12 x 8in cake tin. Sift the flour and baking powder into a large bowl. Rub in the butter then stir in the sugar. Work in the melted chocolate and ground almonds.

2 Press the mixture into the prepared cake tin, prick the surface with a fork and bake for 25–30 minutes, until firm. Leave to cool.

3 To make the topping, mix the butter, sugar, golden syrup and condensed milk in a saucepan. Heat gently until the butter and sugar have melted. Simmer, stirring occasionally, until golden, then stir in the hazelnuts.

4 Pour over the cooked base and spread out evenly. Leave to set.

5 Melt the chocolate in a bowl over a saucepan of hot water. Spread over the butterscotch layer; leave to set before cutting into bars.

Soured Cream Streusel Bars

A deliciously different tea-time treat.

Makes 12–14

❧

INGREDIENTS

115g/4oz/¹/₂ cup butter
150g/5oz/²/₃ cup granulated sugar
3 eggs, at room temperature
175g/6oz/1¹/₂ cups plain flour
5ml/1 tsp bicarbonate of soda
5ml/1 tsp baking powder
250ml/8fl oz/1 cup soured cream
For the topping
175g/6oz/1 firmly packed cup
dark brown sugar
10ml/2 tsp ground cinnamon
115g/4oz/1 cup walnuts, finely
chopped
50g/2oz/4 tbsp butter, chopped

❧

1 Preheat the oven to 180°C/350°F/ Gas 4. Line the bottom of a 23cm/9in square cake tin with greaseproof paper and grease the paper.

4 Add the eggs, one at a time, beating well after each addition.

5 In another bowl, sift the flour, bicarbonate of soda and baking powder together three times.

2 To make the topping, place the brown sugar, cinnamon and walnuts in a bowl. Mix with your fingertips, then add the butter and continue working until the mixture resembles coarse crumbs.

3 Cream the butter with an electric mixer until soft. Add the sugar and continue beating until the mixture is light and fluffy.

6 Fold the dry ingredients into the butter mixture in three batches, alternating with the soured cream. Fold until blended after each addition.

7 Pour half of the batter into the prepared tin and sprinkle over half of the topping.

8 Pour the remaining batter on top and sprinkle over the remaining topping.

9 Bake for 60–70 minutes, until browned. Leave to stand for 5 minutes, then unmould and transfer to a wire rack to cool.

White Chocolate Macadamia Slices

Keep these luxury slices for someone special who will really appreciate
their superb rich flavour and crunchy texture.

Makes 16

INGREDIENTS

150g/5oz/1¼ cups macadamia
nuts, blanched almonds or
hazelnuts
400g/14oz white chocolate,
chopped
50g/2oz/⅓ cup ready-to-eat dried
apricots
75g/3oz/⅓ cup unsalted butter
5ml/1 tsp vanilla essence
3 eggs
150g/5oz/scant 1 cup light
muscovado sugar
115g/4oz/1 cup self-raising flour

1 Preheat the oven to 190°C/375°F/
Gas 5. Lightly grease two 20cm/
8in sandwich cake tins and line the
base of each with greaseproof paper
or non-stick baking paper.

2 Roughly chop the nuts and half
the white chocolate, making sure
that the pieces are more or less the
same size, then cut up the apricots to
similar-size pieces.

3 In the top of a double boiler or in
a heatproof bowl over a saucepan
of hot water, melt the remaining
white chocolate over a gentle heat
with the butter, stirring occasionally
until smooth. Remove the bowl from
the heat.

4 Stir in the vanilla essence. Whisk
the eggs and sugar in a mixing
bowl until thick and pale, then whisk
in the melted chocolate mixture.

5 Sift the flour over the mixture
and fold it in evenly. Stir in the
nuts, white chocolate and apricots.

6 Spoon the mixture into the
prepared tins and smooth the top
level with a spatula and bake for
30–35 minutes.

Cook's Tip You might find it easier
to use sharp kitchen scissors rather
than a knife to snip the apricots into
small pieces.

Toffee Bars

Makes 32

INGREDIENTS

350g/12oz/2 cups light brown
sugar
450g/1lb/2 cups butter or
margarine
2 egg yolks
7.5ml/1½ tsp vanilla essence
450g/1lb/4 cups plain or
wholemeal flour
pinch of salt
225g/8oz milk chocolate, chopped
115g/4oz/1 cup walnuts, chopped

1 Preheat the oven to 180°C/350°F/
Gas 4. Grease a 33 x 23 x 5cm/
13 x 9 x 2in cake tin. Beat together
the sugar and butter or margarine
until light and fluffy. Beat in the egg
yolks and vanilla essence. Stir in the
flour and salt.

2 Spread the dough in the prepared
cake tin. Bake for 25–30 minutes,
until lightly browned. The texture
will be soft.

3 Remove from the oven and
immediately place the chocolate
pieces on the hot cookie base. Leave
to stand until the chocolate softens,
then spread it evenly with a spatula.
Sprinkle with the nuts. While still
warm, cut into about 5 x 4cm/2 x
1½in bars.

Variation Use chopped pecan nuts
instead of walnuts if you prefer, or
try a mixture of both.

Chocolate Walnut Bars

Makes 24

❦

INGREDIENTS

50g/2oz/¹/₂ cup walnuts
75g/3oz/¹/₃ cup granulated sugar
75g/3oz/³/₄ cup plain flour, sifted
75g/3oz/6 tbsp cold unsalted
butter, chopped
For the topping
25g/1oz/2 tbsp unsalted butter
75g/3oz/¹/₃ cup water
40g/1¹/₂oz/¹/₃ cup cocoa powder
115g/4oz/¹/₂ cup granulated sugar
5ml/1 tsp vanilla essence
pinch of salt
2 eggs
icing sugar for dusting

❦

1 Preheat the oven to 180°C/350°F/
Gas 4. Grease the sides and
bottom of a 20cm/8in square cake tin.

2 Grind the walnuts with a few
tablespoons of the sugar in a
food processor, blender or nut
grinder.

3 In a bowl, combine the ground
walnuts, the remaining sugar, and
the flour. Rub in the butter until the
mixture resembles coarse crumbs.
Alternatively, put all the ingredients
in a food processor and process until
the mixture resembles coarse crumbs.

4 Pat the walnut mixture into the
bottom of the prepared tin in an
even layer. Bake for 25 minutes.

5 Meanwhile, to make the topping,
melt the butter with the water in
a small saucepan over a low heat.
Whisk in the cocoa and sugar.

6 Remove the pan from the heat,
stir in the vanilla essence and
salt and leave to cool for 5 minutes.

7 Whisk in the eggs until blended.
Pour the topping evenly over the
crust when it is cooked.

8 Return to the oven and bake for
about 20 minutes until set. Set
the tin on a wire rack to cool. Cut
into 7 x 2.5cm/2¹/₂ x 1in bars and
dust with icing sugar. Store in the
refrigerator.

Pecan Squares

Makes 36

❦

INGREDIENTS

225g/8oz/2 cups plain flour
pinch of salt
115g/4oz/¹/₂ cup granulated sugar
225g/8oz/1 cup cold butter or
margarine, chopped
1 egg
finely grated rind of 1 lemon
For the topping
175g/6oz/³/₄ cup butter
75g/3oz/¹/₄ cup honey
50g/2oz/¹/₄ cup granulated sugar
115g/4oz/¹/₂ firmly packed cup
dark brown sugar
75ml/5 tbsp whipping cream
450g/1lb/4 cups pecan halves

❦

1 Preheat the oven to 190°C/375°F/
Gas 5. Lightly grease a 37 x 27 x
2.5cm/15¹/₂ x 10¹/₂ x 1in Swiss roll tin.

2 Sift the flour and salt into a
mixing bowl. Stir in the sugar.
Cut and rub in the butter or
margarine until the mixture resembles
coarse crumbs. Add the egg and
lemon rind and blend with a fork
until the mixture just holds together.

3 Spoon the mixture into the
prepared tin. With floured
fingertips, press into an even layer.
Prick the pastry all over with a fork
and chill for 10 minutes.

4 Bake the pastry crust for
15 minutes. Remove the tin from
the oven, but keep the oven on while
making the topping.

5 To make the topping, melt the
butter, honey and both sugars.
Bring to the boil. Boil, without
stirring, for 2 minutes. Off the heat,
stir in the cream and pecans. Pour
over the crust, return to the oven and
bake for 25 minutes. Leave to cool.

6 When cool, run a knife around
the edge. Invert on to a baking
sheet, place another sheet on top and
invert again. Dip a sharp knife into
very hot water and cut into squares
for serving.

Hazelnut Squares

Makes 9

INGREDIENTS

50g/2oz plain chocolate, chopped
65g/2¹/₂oz/¹/₃ cup butter or
margarine
225g/8oz/1 cup caster sugar
50g/2oz/¹/₂ cup plain flour
2.5ml/¹/₂ tsp baking powder
2 eggs, beaten
2.5ml/¹/₂ tsp vanilla essence
115g/4oz/1 cup skinned
hazelnuts, roughly chopped

1 Preheat the oven to 180°C/350°F/ Gas 4. Grease a 20cm/8in square cake tin.

2 In a heatproof bowl set over a saucepan of hot water, melt the chocolate and butter or margarine, stirring until smooth.

3 Add the sugar, flour, baking powder, eggs, vanilla essence and half of the hazelnuts to the mixture and stir with a wooden spoon.

4 Pour the mixture into the prepared cake tin. Bake for 10 minutes, then sprinkle the remaining hazelnuts over the top. Return to the oven and continue baking for about 25 minutes, until firm to the touch.

5 Leave to cool in the tin, set on a wire rack, for 10 minutes, then transfer to the rack and leave to cool completely. Cut into squares for serving.

Almond-topped Squares

Makes 18

INGREDIENTS

75g/3oz/6 tbsp butter
50g/2oz/¹/₄ cup granulated sugar
1 egg yolk
grated rind and juice of ¹/₂ lemon
2.5ml/¹/₂ tsp vanilla essence
30ml/2 tbsp whipping cream
115g/4oz/1 cup plain flour
For the topping
225g/8oz/1 cup granulated sugar
75g/3oz/³/₄ cup sliced almonds
4 egg whites
2.5ml/¹/₂ tsp ground ginger
2.5ml/¹/₂ tsp ground cinnamon

1 Preheat the oven to 190°C/375°F/ Gas 5. Line a 33 x 23cm/13 x 9in Swiss roll tin with greaseproof paper and grease the paper.

2 With an electric mixer, cream the butter and sugar until light and fluffy. Beat in the egg yolk, lemon rind and juice, the vanilla essence and cream.

3 Gradually stir in the flour. Gather into a ball of dough. With lightly floured fingers, press the dough into the prepared tin. Bake for 15 minutes. Remove from the oven but leave the oven on.

4 To make the topping, combine all the ingredients in a heavy saucepan. Cook, stirring until the mixture comes to the boil. Boil for 1 minute. Pour over the dough, spreading evenly.

5 Return to the oven and bake for about 45 minutes. Remove and score into bars or squares.

Lemon Squares

Makes 12

❧

INGREDIENTS

225g/8oz/2 cups plain flour
50g/2oz/¹/₂ cup icing sugar
pinch of salt
175g/6oz/³/₄ cup butter or
margarine
5ml/1 tsp cold water
For the lemon layer
4 eggs
450g/1lb/2 cups caster sugar
25g/1oz/2 tbsp plain flour
2.5ml/¹/₂ tsp baking powder
5ml/1 tsp grated lemon rind
50ml/2fl oz/¹/₄ cup fresh lemon
juice
icing sugar for sprinkling

❧

1 Preheat the oven to 180°C/350°F/
Gas 4. Sift the flour, icing sugar
and salt into a mixing bowl.

2 Rub the butter or margarine into
the flour until the mixture
resembles coarse breadcrumbs. Add
the water and toss lightly with a fork
until the mixture forms a ball.

3 Press the mixture evenly into an
ungreased 33 x 23cm/13 x 9in
baking dish. Bake for 15–20 minutes,
until light golden brown. Remove from
the oven and leave to cool slightly.

4 Meanwhile, to make the lemon
layer, beat together the eggs,
caster sugar, flour, baking powder
and lemon rind and juice.

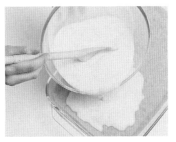

5 Pour the lemon mixture over the
baked dish. Return to the oven
and bake for 25 minutes. Leave to
cool in the baking dish, placed on a
wire rack.

6 Before serving, sprinkle the top
with icing sugar. Cut into squares
with a sharp knife.

Apricot and Almond Fingers

These apricot and almond fingers will stay moist for several days.

Makes 18

INGREDIENTS

225g/8oz/2 cups self-raising flour
115g/4oz/²⁄₃ cup light muscovado
sugar
50g/2oz/¹⁄₃ cup semolina
175g/6oz/1 cup ready-to-use
dried apricots, chopped
2 eggs
30ml/2 tbsp malt extract
30ml/2 tbsp clear honey
60ml/4 tbsp skimmed milk
60ml/4 tbsp sunflower oil
few drops of almond essence
30ml/2 tbsp flaked almonds

1 Preheat the oven to 160°C/325°F/
Gas 3. Lightly grease and line a
28 x 18cm/11 x 7in shallow cake tin.
Sift the flour into a bowl and add the
muscovado sugar, semolina, dried
apricots and eggs. Add the malt
extract, clear honey, milk, sunflower
oil and almond essence. Mix well
until smooth.

2 Turn the mixture into the
prepared cake tin, spread to the
edges and sprinkle with the flaked
almonds.

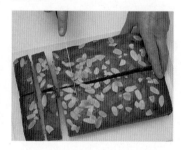

3 Bake for 30–35 minutes, until the
centre of the cake springs back
when lightly pressed. Transfer to a
wire rack to cool. Remove the paper,
place the cake on a board and cut it
into 18 slices with a sharp knife.

Apricot Bars

Makes 12

INGREDIENTS

*75g/3oz/¹/₂ cup firmly packed light
brown sugar
75g/3oz/³/₄ cup flour
75g/3oz/¹/₃ cup cold unsalted
butter, chopped
For the topping
175g/6oz/1 cup dried apricots
250ml/8fl oz/1 cup water
grated rind of 1 lemon
75g/3oz/¹/₃ cup granulated sugar
10ml/2 tsp cornflour
50g/2oz/¹/₂ cup walnuts, chopped*

1 Preheat the oven to 180°C/350°F/
Gas 4. Grease a 20cm/8in square
cake tin.

2 In a bowl, combine the sugar and
flour. Rub in the butter until the
mixture resembles coarse crumbs.

3 Press into the prepared cake tin.
Bake for 15 minutes. Remove
from the oven but leave the oven on.

4 To make the topping, combine the
apricots and water in a saucepan
and simmer for about 10 minutes,
until soft. Strain the liquid and
reserve. Chop the apricots.

5 Return the apricots to the
saucepan and add the lemon rind,
granulated sugar, cornflour, and
60ml/4 tbsp of the soaking liquid.
Cook for 1 minute.

6 Cool slightly before spreading the
topping over the base. Sprinkle
over the walnuts and continue baking
for 20 minutes more. Leave to cool in
the tin before cutting into bars.

Blueberry Streusel Slices

Makes 30

❦

INGREDIENTS

225g/8oz shortcrust pastry
50g/2oz/¹/₂ cup plain flour
1.5ml/¹/₄ tsp baking powder
40g/1¹/₂oz/3 tbsp butter or
margarine
25g/1oz/2 tbsp fresh white
breadcrumbs
50g/2oz/¹/₃ cup soft light brown
sugar
pinch of salt
50g/2oz/4 tbsp flaked or chopped
almonds
60ml/4 tbsp blackberry or bramble
jelly
115g/4oz/scant 1 cup blueberries,
fresh or frozen

❦

1 Preheat the oven to 180°C/350°F/
Gas 4. Roll out the pastry on a
lightly floured surface to fit an 18 x
28cm/7 x 11in Swiss roll tin. Grease
the Swiss roll tin.

2 Rub together the flour, baking
powder, butter or margarine,
breadcrumbs, sugar and salt until
really crumbly, then mix in the
almonds.

3 Place the rolled pastry in the
prepared tin. Spread the pastry
with the jelly, sprinkle with the
blueberries, then cover evenly with the
streusel topping, pressing down
lightly. Bake for 30–40 minutes,
lowering the temperature after 20
minutes to 160°C/325°F/Gas 3.

4 Remove from the oven. Cut into
slices while still hot, then transfer
to a wire rack to cool.

Sticky Date and Apple Squares

*If possible, allow this
mixture to mature for 1–2
days before cutting.*

Makes 16

❦

INGREDIENTS

115g/4oz/¹/₂ cup margarine
50g/2oz/4 tbsp soft dark brown
sugar
50g/2oz/4 tbsp golden syrup
115g/4oz/²/₃ cup chopped dates
115g/4oz/1¹/₃ cup rolled oats
115g/4oz/1 cup wholemeal self-
raising flour
2 eating apples, peeled, cored and
grated
5–10ml/1–2 tsp lemon juice
walnut halves

❦

1 Preheat the oven to 190°C/375°F/
Gas 5. Line an 18–20cm/7–8in
square or rectangle loose-based cake
tin. In a large saucepan, gently heat
the margarine, sugar and syrup
together until the margarine has
melted completely.

2 Add the dates and cook until they
have softened. Gradually work in
the oats, flour, apples and lemon juice
until well mixed.

3 Spoon into the prepared tin and
spread out evenly. Top with the
walnut halves. Bake for 30 minutes,
then reduce the temperature to
160°C/325°F/ Gas 3 and bake for
10–12 minutes more, until firm to the
touch and golden.

4 Cut into squares or bars while still
warm if you are going to eat it
straight away, or wrap in foil when
nearly cold and keep for 1–2 days
before eating.

Spiced Fig Bars

Makes 24

❧

INGREDIENTS

350g/12oz/2 cups dried figs
3 eggs
175g/6oz/³/₄ cup granulated sugar
75g/3oz/³/₄ cup plain flour
5ml/1 tsp baking powder
2.5ml/¹/₂ tsp ground cinnamon
1.5ml/¹/₄ tsp ground cloves
1.5ml/¹/₄ tsp grated nutmeg
pinch of salt
75g/3oz/³/₄ cup walnuts, finely chopped
30ml/2 tbsp brandy or cognac
icing sugar for dusting

❧

1 Preheat the oven to 160°C/325°F/ Gas 3. Line a 30 x 20 x 4cm/12 x 8 x 1¹/₂in cake tin with greaseproof paper and grease the paper.

2 With a sharp knife, chop the figs roughly. Set aside.

3 In a bowl, whisk the eggs and sugar until well blended. In another bowl, sift together the dry ingredients, then fold into the egg mixture in several batches.

4 Stir the figs, walnuts and brandy or cognac into the bowl until evenly combined.

5 Scrape the mixture into the prepared cake tin and bake for 35–40 minutes until the top is firm and brown. It should still be soft underneath. Leave to cool in the tin for 5 minutes, then unmould and transfer to a sheet of greaseproof paper lightly sprinkled with icing sugar. Cut into bars.

Creamy Lemon Bars

A delicious and luxurious treat, ideal for accompanying a cup of coffee.

Makes 36

❧

INGREDIENTS

50g/2oz/¹/₂ cup icing sugar
175g/6oz/1¹/₂ cups plain flour
pinch of salt
175g/6oz/³/₄ cup butter, chopped
For the topping
4 eggs
350g/12oz/1¹/₂ cups granulated sugar
grated rind of 1 lemon
120ml/4fl oz/¹/₂ cup fresh lemon juice
175g/6oz/³/₄ cup whipping cream
icing sugar for dusting

❧

1 Preheat the oven to 160°C/325°F/ Gas 3. Grease a 33 x 23cm/13 x 9in cake tin. Sift the sugar, flour and salt into a bowl. Rub in the butter until the mixture resembles coarse crumbs.

2 Press the mixture into the bottom of the prepared cake tin. Bake for about 20 minutes until golden brown.

3 Meanwhile, to make the topping, whisk together the eggs and sugar until blended. Add the lemon rind and juice and mix well.

4 Lightly whip the cream and fold into the egg mixture. Pour over the warm crust, return to the oven, and bake for about 40 minutes, until set. Cool completely before cutting into bars. Dust with icing sugar.

Chocolate Raspberry Macaroon Bars

Any seedless preserve, such as strawberry or apricot, can be substituted for raspberry.

Makes 16–18 bars

INGREDIENTS

115g/4oz/¹/₂ cup unsalted butter
50g/2oz/¹/₂ cup icing sugar
25g/1oz/¹/₄ cup cocoa powder
pinch of salt
5ml/1 tsp almond essence
150g/5oz/1¹/₄ cups plain flour
For the topping
150g/5oz/scant ¹/₂ cup seedless
raspberry preserve
15ml/1 tbsp raspberry-flavour
liqueur
175g/6oz/1 cup mini chocolate
chips
175g/6oz/1¹/₂ cups finely ground
almonds
4 egg whites
pinch of salt
200g/7oz/1 firmly packed cup
caster sugar
2.5ml/¹/₂ tsp almond essence
50g/2oz/¹/₂ cup flaked almonds

1 Preheat the oven to 160°C/325°F/ Gas 3. Invert a 23 x 33cm/9 x 13in cake tin. Mould a sheet of foil over the tin and smooth the foil evenly around the corners. Lift off the foil and turn the tin right side up; line with the moulded foil. Lightly grease the foil.

2 In a medium bowl, with an electric mixer, beat together the butter, sugar, cocoa and salt until well blended. Add in the almond essence and the flour and mix until the mixture forms a crumbly dough.

3 Turn the dough into the prepared tin and pat firmly over the bottom to make an even layer. Prick the dough with a fork.

4 Bake for 20 minutes, until just set. Remove from the oven and increase the temperature to 190°C/ 375°F/Gas 5.

5 To make the topping, in a small bowl, combine the raspberry preserve and raspberry-flavour liqueur. Spread the topping evenly over the chocolate crust, then sprinkle evenly with the chocolate chips.

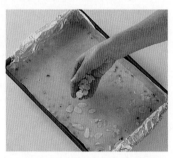

6 In a food processor fitted with a metal blade, process the almonds, egg whites, salt, sugar and almond essence until well blended and foamy. Gently pour over the jam layer, spreading evenly to the edges of the tin. Sprinkle with flaked almonds.

7 Bake for 20–25 minutes more, until the top is golden and puffed. Transfer to a wire rack to cool in the tin for 20 minutes, until firm.

8 Using the edges of the foil, carefully remove the cake from the tin and cool completely. Peel off the foil and, using a sharp knife, cut into bars.

Lemon Cheese Bars

Makes 24

INGREDIENTS

115g/4oz/1 cup plain flour
50g/2oz/¹/₂ cup chopped walnuts
75g/3oz/¹/₂ cup soft light brown
sugar
75g/3oz/¹/₃ cup unsalted butter
grated rind and juice of 1 small
lemon
225g/8oz/1 cup full-fat cream
cheese
50g/2oz/¹/₄ cup granulated sugar
15ml/1 tbsp milk
2.5ml/¹/₂ tsp vanilla essence
1 large egg

1 Preheat the oven to 180°C/350°F/ Gas 4. Grease a 23cm/9in square cake tin.

2 Beat together the flour, walnuts, brown sugar and butter. Divide the mixture in half. Press one half of the mixture into the prepared cake tin. Bake for 12–15 minutes, until lightly browned. Remove from the oven.

3 Beat together the lemon rind and juice, the cheese and sugar, then beat in the milk, vanilla essence and egg. Spoon over the partly cooked pastry and crumble the remaining mixture evenly over the top. Bake for a further 25 minutes, until the top is golden. Transfer to a wire rack to cool, then chill. Cut into bars.

Citrus Spice Bars

Makes 50

INGREDIENTS

115g/4oz/³/₄ cup candied orange
peel, chopped
50g/2oz/¹/₃ cup seedless raisins
75ml/5 tbsp rum
50g/2oz/3 tbsp clear honey
50g/2oz/3 tbsp black treacle
1 egg
115g/4oz/1 cup ground almonds
175g/6oz/1¹/₂ cups wholemeal
flour
2.5ml/¹/₂ tsp baking powder
large pinch bicarbonate of soda
5ml/1 tsp ground cinnamon
2.5ml/¹/₂ tsp ground ginger
115g/4oz/1 cup unblanched
almonds, chopped
50g/2oz/¹/₂ cup sifted icing sugar
45ml/about 3 tbsp orange juice

1 Preheat the oven to 200°C/400°F/ Gas 6. Lightly grease a 33 x 23cm/ 13 x 9in cake tin. Place the orange peel, raisins and rum in a bowl, cover and set aside for 1 hour.

2 Pour the honey and black treacle into a saucepan and bring to the boil. Set aside to cool, then beat in the egg. Mix together the ground almonds, flour, baking powder, bicarbonate of soda and spices and stir into the mixture. Stir in the chopped almonds and the rum mixture and form into a dough.

3 Press the dough into the prepared cake tin. Bake for about 20 minutes. Transfer to a wire rack to cool. Sift the icing sugar into a bowl and stir in just enough orange juice to make a spreading consistency. Set aside for 1 hour.

4 Spread the icing over the cake. Decorate if you wish and cut into generous bars.

Chocolate and Coconut Slices

Very simple to make, these slices are deliciously moist and sweet.

Makes 24

INGREDIENTS

115g/4oz/¹/₂ cup butter or margarine, chopped
175g/6oz digestive biscuits, crushed
50g/2oz/4 tbsp caster sugar
pinch of salt
75g/3oz/1 cup desiccated coconut
250g/9oz/1¹/₂ cups plain chocolate chips
250ml/8fl oz/1 cup sweetened condensed milk
115g/4oz/1 cup chopped walnuts

1 Preheat the oven to 180°C/350°F/ Gas 4. Melt the butter or margarine in a small saucepan over a low heat.

2 In a bowl, combine the crushed biscuits, sugar, salt and melted butter or margarine. Press the mixture evenly over the bottom of an ungreased 33 x 23cm/13 x 9in baking dish.

3 Sprinkle the coconut over the cookie base, then scatter over the chocolate chips. Pour the condensed milk evenly over the chocolate. Sprinkle the walnuts on top.

4 Bake for 30 minutes. Transfer to a wire rack and leave to cool, preferably overnight. When cooled, cut into slices.

Hermits

Makes 30

INGREDIENTS

*75g/3oz/¾ cup plain flour
7.5ml/1½ tsp baking powder
5ml/1 tsp ground cinnamon
2.5ml/½ tsp grated nutmeg
1.5ml/¼ tsp ground cloves
1.5ml/¼ tsp ground allspice
250g/9oz/1½ cups raisins
115g/4oz/½ cup butter or
margarine
115g/4oz/½ cup caster sugar
2 eggs
175g/6oz/½ cup black treacle
50g/2oz/½ cup walnuts, chopped*

1 Preheat the oven to 180°C/350°F/ Gas 4. Line the bottom and sides of a 33 x 23cm/13 x 9in tin with greaseproof paper and grease.

2 Sift together the flour, baking powder and spices into a bowl.

3 Place the raisins in another bowl and toss with a few tablespoons of the flour mixture.

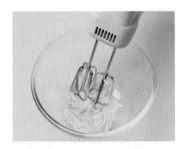

4 With an electric mixer, cream together the butter or margarine and sugar, until light and fluffy. Beat in the eggs, one at a time, then the black treacle. Stir in the flour mixture, raisins and walnuts.

5 Spread evenly in the prepared cake tin. Bake for 15–18 minutes, until just set. Leave to cool in the tin before cutting into squares or fingers.

Butterscotch Meringue Bars

Makes 12

INGREDIENTS

*50g/2oz/4 tbsp butter
175g/6oz/1 firmly packed cup
dark brown sugar
1 egg
2.5ml/½ tsp vanilla essence
50g/2oz/½ cup plain flour
pinch of salt
1.5ml/¼ tsp grated nutmeg
For the topping
1 egg white
pinch of salt
15ml/1 tbsp golden syrup
115g/4oz/½ cup granulated sugar
50g/2oz/½ cup walnuts, finely
chopped*

1 Combine the butter and brown sugar in a saucepan and cook until bubbling. Set aside to cool.

2 Preheat the oven to 180°C/350°F/ Gas 4. Line a 20cm/8in square cake tin with greaseproof paper and grease the paper.

3 Beat the egg and vanilla essence into the cooled sugar mixture. Sift over the flour, salt and nutmeg and fold in. Spread over the bottom of the prepared cake tin.

4 To make the topping, beat the egg white with the salt until it holds soft peaks. Beat in the golden syrup, then the sugar and continue beating until the mixture holds stiff peaks.

5 Fold in the nuts and spread on top of the mixture in the tin. Bake for 30 minutes. Cut into bars when cool.

Muffins
and Scones

Muffins are very easy to make and delicious to eat: to mix the batter, simply use a few swift strokes to stir the liquid ingredients, taking no more than 10–20 seconds. This will leave some lumps. Ignore them. If the batter is mixed for too long, the dough will be toughened and the muffins will be coarse-textured and full of tunnels. Rather than being mixed to a smooth, pouring consistency, the mixture should come off the spoon in coarse dollops.

Muffins are best eaten when freshly made and still warm, certainly on the day of baking. To re-warm muffins, wrap them loosely in foil and heat for approximately 5 minutes in an oven preheated to 230°C/450°F/Gas 8.

The well-risen, oven-baked scones that are now thought to be an essential part of a British afternoon tea, eaten while warm, split, spread with butter and served with cream (preferably clotted) and jam, did not exist before the introduction of raising agents and reliable ovens in Victorian times. The fore-runners of these modern scones were drop scones and griddle cakes, cooked on the stove top.

The secrets of perfect, light, tender scones are not making the dough too wet, handling it quickly and very lightly, and rolling it out with even pressure to the correct thickness – at least 2cm/³/₄in, and lastly, preheating the oven to quite a high temperature, usually about 220°C/425°F/Gas 7.

Oatmeal Buttermilk Muffins

Makes 12

INGREDIENTS

*115g/4oz/1 cup rolled oats
250ml/8fl oz/1 cup buttermilk
115g/4oz/¹/₂ cup butter
75g/3oz/¹/₂ cup dark brown sugar
1 egg
115g/4oz/1 cup plain flour
5ml/1 tsp baking powder
2.5ml/¹/₂ tsp bicarbonate of soda
pinch of salt
25g/1oz/¹/₄ cup raisins*

Cook's Tip If buttermilk is not available, add 5ml/1 tsp lemon juice or vinegar to 250ml/8fl oz/1 cup of milk. Let the mixture stand a few minutes to curdle before adding it to the oats.

1 In a bowl, combine the oats and buttermilk and leave to soak for 1 hour.

2 Grease 12 muffin tins, or use paper liners. Preheat the oven to 200°C/400°F/ Gas 6.

3 With an electric mixer, cream the butter and sugar until light and fluffy. Beat in the egg.

4 Sift together the flour, baking powder, bicarbonate of soda and salt. Stir into the butter mixture, alternating with the oat mixture. Fold in the raisins.

5 Fill the muffin tins two-thirds full. Bake for 20–25 minutes. Transfer to a wire rack to cool.

Pumpkin Muffins

Makes 14

INGREDIENTS

*115g/4oz/¹/₂ cup butter or margarine
175g/6oz/³/₄ cup firmly packed brown sugar
115g/4oz/¹/₃ cup black treacle
1 egg, beaten
225g/8oz/1 cup cooked or canned pumpkin
200g/7oz/1³/₄ cups plain flour
pinch of salt
5ml/1 tsp bicarbonate of soda
7.5ml/1¹/₂ tsp ground cinnamon
5ml/1 tsp grated nutmeg
50g/2oz/¹/₄ cup currants or raisins*

1 Preheat the oven to 200°C/400°F/ Gas 6. Grease 14 muffin tins, or use paper liners.

2 With an electric mixer, cream the butter or margarine until soft. Add the sugar and black treacle and beat until light and fluffy.

3 Add the egg and pumpkin and stir until well blended.

4 Sift over the flour, salt, bicarbonate of soda, cinnamon and nutmeg. Fold in until just blended, do not overmix.

5 Fold the currants or raisins into the pumpkin mixture until just evenly combined.

6 Spoon the batter into the prepared muffin tins, filling them two-thirds full.

7 Bake for 12–15 minutes, until the tops spring back when touched lightly. Serve warm or cold.

Banana Muffins

Makes 12

INGREDIENTS

225g/8oz/2 cups plain flour
5ml/1 tsp baking powder
5ml/1 tsp bicarbonate of soda
pinch of salt
2.5ml/¹/₂ tsp ground cinnamon
1.5ml/¹/₄ tsp grated nutmeg
3 large ripe bananas
1 egg
50g/2oz/¹/₃ cup dark brown sugar
50ml/2fl oz/¹/₄ cup vegetable oil
40g/1¹/₂oz/¹/₄ cup raisins

1 Preheat the oven to 190°C/375°F/ Gas 5.

2 Grease 12 muffin tins, or use paper liners.

3 Sift together the flour, baking powder, bicarbonate of soda, salt, cinnamon and nutmeg. Set aside.

4 With an electric mixer, mash the peeled bananas at moderate speed.

5 Beat the egg, sugar and oil into the mashed bananas.

6 Add the dry ingredients and beat in gradually, on low speed. Mix until just blended. With a wooden spoon, stir in the raisins. Fill the muffin tins two-thirds full.

7 Bake for 20–25 minutes, until the tops spring back when touched lightly. Transfer to a wire rack to cool.

Maple Pecan Muffins

Makes 20

❧

INGREDIENTS

150g/5oz/1¼ cups pecans
300g/11oz/2½ cups plain flour
5ml/1 tsp baking powder
5ml/1 tsp bicarbonate of soda
pinch of salt
1.5ml/¼ tsp ground cinnamon
115g/4oz/½ cup granulated sugar
50g/2oz/⅓ firmly packed cup light
brown sugar
45ml/3 tbsp maple syrup
150g/5oz/⅔ cup butter
3 eggs
300ml/½ pint/1¼ cups buttermilk
60 pecan halves to decorate

❧

Variation For Pecan Spice Muffins, substitute an equal quantity of black treacle for the maple syrup. Increase the cinnamon to 2.5ml/½ tsp, and add 5ml/1 tsp ground ginger and 2.5ml/½ tsp grated nutmeg, sifted with the flour and other dry ingredients.

1 Preheat the oven to 180°C/350°F/Gas 4. Grease 20 muffin tins, or use paper liners.

2 Spread the pecans on a baking sheet and toast in the oven for 5 minutes. Leave to cool, then chop coarsely and set aside.

3 In a bowl, sift together the flour, baking powder, bicarbonate of soda, salt and cinnamon. Set aside.

4 In a large mixing bowl, combine the granulated sugar, light brown sugar, maple syrup and butter. Beat with an electric mixer until light and fluffy.

5 Add the eggs, one at a time, beating to incorporate thoroughly after each addition.

6 Pour half of the buttermilk and half of the dry ingredients into the butter mixture, then stir until blended. Repeat with the remaining buttermilk and dry ingredients.

7 Fold the chopped pecans into the batter. Fill the muffin tins two-thirds full. Top with the pecan halves.

8 Bake for 20–25 minutes, until puffed up and golden. Leave to stand for 5 minutes before transferring to a wire rack to cool.

Raspberry Muffins

Low-fat buttermilk gives these muffins a light and spongy texture.

They are delicious to eat at any time of day.

Makes 10–12

INGREDIENTS

300g/11oz/2½ cups plain flour
15ml/1 tbsp baking powder
115g/4oz/½ cup caster sugar
1 egg
250ml/8fl oz/1 cup buttermilk
60ml/4 tbsp sunflower oil
150g/5oz/1 cup raspberries

Variation Cranberry Muffins: a tea or breakfast treat that is not too sweet.

350g/12oz/3 cups plain flour
15ml/1 tsp baking powder
pinch of salt
115g/4oz/½ cup caster sugar
2 eggs
150ml/¼ pint/⅔ cup milk
50ml/2fl oz/4 tbsp corn oil
finely grated rind of 1 orange
150g/5oz/1 cup cranberries

1 Preheat the oven to 190°C/375°F/ Gas 5. Line 12 deep muffin tins with paper cases. Mix the flour, baking powder, salt and caster sugar together. Lightly beat the eggs with the milk and oil.

2 Add the liquids to the dry ingredients and blend to make a smooth batter. Divide the mixture between the muffin cases and bake for 25 minutes, until risen and golden. Leave to cool in the tins for a few minutes, and serve warm or cold.

1 Preheat the oven to 200°C/400°F/ Gas 6. Arrange 12 paper cases in deep muffin tins. Sift the flour and baking powder into a mixing bowl, stir in the sugar, then make a well in the centre.

2 Mix the egg, buttermilk and sunflower oil together in a bowl, pour into the flour mixture and mix quickly until just combined.

3 Add the raspberries and lightly fold in with a metal spoon. Spoon the mixture into the paper cases.

4 Bake for 20–25 minutes, until golden brown and firm in the centre. Transfer to a wire rack and serve warm or cold.

Double Chocolate Chip Muffins

These marvellous muffins are packed with chunky plain and white chocolate chips.

Makes 16

INGREDIENTS

400g/14oz/3¹/₂ cups plain flour
15ml/1 tbsp baking powder
30ml/2 tbsp cocoa powder
115g/4oz/¹/₂ cup dark muscovado sugar
2 eggs
150ml/¹/₄ pint/²/₃ cup soured cream
150ml/¹/₄ pint/²/₃ cup milk
60ml/4 tbsp sunflower oil
175g/6oz white chocolate
175g/6oz plain chocolate
cocoa powder for dusting

Cook's Tip If soured cream is not available, sour 150ml/¹/₄ pint/²/₃ cup single cream by stirring in 5ml/1 tsp lemon juice and letting the mixture stand until thickened.

1 Preheat the oven to 190°C/375°F/ Gas 5. Place 16 paper muffin cases in muffin tins or deep patty tins. Sift the flour, baking powder and cocoa into a bowl and stir in the sugar. Make a well in the centre.

2 In a separate bowl, beat the eggs with the soured cream, milk and oil, then stir into the well in the dry ingredients. Beat well, gradually incorporating the flour mixture to make a thick and creamy batter.

Variation Make sure you use good quality chocolate with a high cocoa content, Vary the proportions of plain and white chocolate, or add in milk chocolate if you prefer.

3 Finely chop the chocolate and stir into the batter mixture.

4 Spoon the mixture into the muffin cases, filling them almost to the top. Bake for 25–30 minutes, until well risen and firm to the touch. Transfer to a wire rack to cool, then dust with cocoa powder.

Chocolate Walnut Muffins

Walnuts and chocolate are a delicious combination.

Makes 12

INGREDIENTS

175g/6oz/³/₄ cup unsalted butter, chopped
150g/5oz plain chocolate, chopped
225g/8oz/1 cup granulated sugar
50g/2oz/¹/₄ firmly packed cup dark brown sugar
4 eggs
5ml/1 tsp vanilla essence
1.5ml/¹/₄ tsp almond essence
75g/3oz/³/₄ cup plain flour
115g/4oz/1 cup walnuts, chopped

1 Preheat the oven to 180°C/350°F/ Gas 4. Grease muffin tins, or use paper liners.

2 Melt the butter with the chocolate in the top of a double boiler or a heatproof bowl over a saucepan of hot water. Transfer to a large mixing bowl.

3 Stir both the sugars into the chocolate mixture. Mix in the eggs, one at a time, then add the vanilla and almond essences.

4 Sift over the flour and fold in until evenly combined.

5 Stir the walnuts evenly into the chocolate mixture.

6 Fill the muffin tins almost to the top and bake for 30–35 minutes. Leave to stand for 5 minutes before transferring to a wire rack.

Chocolate Chip Muffins

Use the best quality chocolate chips you can find.

Makes 10

INGREDIENTS

115g/4oz/¹/₂ cup butter or margarine
75g/3oz/¹/₃ cup granulated sugar
30ml/2 tbsp dark brown sugar
2 eggs
175g/6oz/1¹/₂ cups plain flour
5ml/1 tsp baking powder
120ml/4fl oz/¹/₂ cup milk
175g/6oz/1 cup plain chocolate chips

1 Preheat the oven to 190°C/375°F/ Gas 5. Grease 10 muffin tins, or use paper liners.

2 With an electric mixer, cream the butter or margarine until soft. Add both sugars and beat until light and fluffy. Beat in the eggs, one at a time.

3 Sift the flour and baking powder, twice. Fold into the butter mixture, alternating with the milk.

4 Divide half of the mixture between the muffin tins. Sprinkle several chocolate chips on top, then cover with a spoonful of batter.

5 Bake for about 25 minutes, until lightly coloured. Leave to stand for 5 minutes before transferring to a wire rack to cool.

Banana and Nut Buns

Use walnut pieces instead of pecans if you prefer.

Makes 8

INGREDIENTS

150g/5oz/1¼ cup plain flour
7.5ml/1½ tsp baking powder
50g/2oz/¼ cup butter or
margarine
175g/6oz/¾ cup caster sugar
1 egg
1 tsp vanilla essence
3 medium bananas, mashed
50g/2oz/½ cup chopped pecans
75ml/3 fl oz/⅓ cup milk

1 Preheat the oven to 190°C/375°F/
Gas 5. Grease eight patty tins.

2 Sift the flour and baking powder
into a small bowl. Set aside.

3 With an electric mixer, cream
together the butter or margarine
and the sugar. Add the egg and
vanilla essence and beat until fluffy.
Mix in the bananas.

4 Add the pecans. With the mixer
on low speed, beat in the flour
mixture alternately with the milk.
Spoon the mixture into the prepared
tins. Bake for 20–25 minutes, until a
skewer or cake tester inserted in the
centre of a bun comes out clean.

5 Leave to cool in the patty tins for
10 minutes. Unmould on to the
wire rack. Cool for 10 minutes longer
before serving.

Fruit and Cinnamon Buns

Makes 8

INGREDIENTS

115g/4oz/1 cup plain flour
15ml/1 tbsp baking powder
pinch of salt
65g/2½oz/scant ½ cup light
brown sugar
1 egg
175ml/6fl oz/¾ cup milk
45ml/3 tbsp vegetable oil
10ml/2 tsp ground cinnamon
150g/5oz/1 cup fresh or thawed
frozen blueberries, or
blackcurrants

1 Preheat the oven to 190°C/375°F/
Gas 5. Grease eight patty tins.

2 With an electric mixer, beat
together the first eight ingredients
until smooth.

3 Fold the blueberries or
blackcurrants into the other
ingredients until just evenly combined.

4 Spoon the mixture into the patty
tins, filling them two-thirds full.
Bake for about 25 minutes, until a
skewer or cake tester inserted in the
centre of a bun comes out clean.

5 Leave to cool in the patty tins,
on a wire rack, for 10 minutes,
then transfer the buns to the wire
rack and leave to cool completely.

Carrot Muffins

Makes 12

INGREDIENTS

175g/6oz/³⁄₄ cup margarine
75g/3oz/¹⁄₂ cup dark brown sugar
1 egg
15ml/1 tbsp water
275g/10oz/2 cups grated carrots
150g/5oz/1¹⁄₄ cups plain flour
5ml/1 tsp baking powder
2.5ml/¹⁄₂ tsp bicarbonate of soda
5ml/1 tsp ground cinnamon
1.5ml/¹⁄₄ tsp grated nutmeg
pinch of salt

1 Preheat the oven to 180°C/350°F/ Gas 4. Grease 12 muffin tins, or use paper liners.

2 With an electric mixer, cream the margarine and sugar until light and fluffy. Beat in the egg and water.

3 Stir the grated carrots into the creamed mixture until evenly combined. Sift over the flour, baking powder, bicarbonate of soda, cinnamon, nutmeg and salt. Stir to blend evenly.

4 Spoon the batter into the prepared muffin tins, filling them almost to the top.

5 Bake for about 35 minutes, until the tops spring back when touched lightly. Leave to stand for 10 minutes before transferring to a wire rack to cool.

Dried Cherry Muffins

If you can't find dried cherries, use the same amount of dried cranberries.

Makes 16

INGREDIENTS

250ml/8fl oz/1 cup plain yogurt
225g/8oz/1 cup dried cherries
115g/4oz/¹⁄₂ cup butter
175g/6oz/³⁄₄ cup caster sugar
2 eggs
5ml/1 tsp vanilla essence
200g/7oz/1³⁄₄ cups plain flour
10ml/2 tsp baking powder
5ml/1 tsp bicarbonate of soda
pinch of salt

1 In a mixing bowl, combine the yogurt and cherries. Cover and leave to stand for 30 minutes.

2 Preheat the oven to 180°C/350°F/ Gas 4. Grease 16 muffin tins, or use paper liners.

3 With an electric mixer, cream together the butter and sugar until light and fluffy.

4 Add the eggs, one at a time, beating well after each addition. Add the vanilla essence and the cherry mixture and stir to blend. Set aside.

5 In another bowl, sift together the flour, baking powder, bicarbonate of soda and salt. Fold into the cherry mixture in three batches; do not overmix.

6 Fill the prepared muffin tins two-thirds full. Bake for about 20 minutes until the tops spring back when touched lightly. Transfer to a wire rack to cool.

Blueberry Muffins

Makes 12

INGREDIENTS

175g/6oz/1¼ cups plain flour
75g/3oz/⅓ cup caster sugar
10ml/2 tsp baking powder
pinch of salt
2 eggs
50g/2oz/4 tbsp butter, melted
175ml/6fl oz/¾ cup milk
5ml/1 tsp vanilla essence
5ml/1 tsp grated lemon rind
150g/5oz/1 cup fresh blueberries

1 Preheat the oven to 200°C/400°F/ Gas 6. Grease 12 muffin tins, or use paper liners.

2 Sift the flour, sugar, baking powder and salt into a bowl. Whisk the eggs until blended. Stir in the melted butter, milk, vanilla essence and lemon rind.

3 Make a well in the dry ingredients and pour in the egg mixture. With a large metal spoon, stir until the flour is just moistened, not until smooth.

4 Rinse the blueberries and dry well, then gently fold into the batter with a metal spoon, making sure they are distributed evenly.

5 Spoon the batter into the tins, leaving room for the muffins to rise. Bake for 20–25 minutes. Leave to cool for 5 minutes before transferring to a wire rack to cool.

Date and Apple Muffins

These muffins are delicious and very filling.

Makes 12

INGREDIENTS

*150g/5oz/1¼ cups self-raising
wholemeal flour
150g/5oz/1¼ cups self-raising
white flour
5ml/1 tsp ground cinnamon
5ml/1 tsp baking powder
25g/1oz/2 tbsp margarine
75g/3oz/½ cup light muscovado
sugar
1 eating apple
250ml/8fl oz/1 cup apple juice
30ml/2 tbsp pear and apple
spread
1 egg, lightly beaten
75g/3oz/½ cup chopped dates
15ml/1 tbsp chopped pecans*

1 Preheat the oven to 200°C/400°F/ Gas 6. Arrange 12 paper cases in a deep muffin tin. Put the wholemeal flour in a mixing bowl. Sift in the white flour with the cinnamon and baking powder. Rub in the margarine until the mixture resembles breadcrumbs, then stir in the muscovado sugar.

2 Quarter and core the apple, chop the flesh finely and set aside. Stir a little of the apple juice with the pear and apple spread until smooth. Mix in the remaining juice, then add to the rubbed-in mixture with the beaten egg.

3 Add the chopped apple to the bowl with the dates. Mix quickly until just combined. Divide the mixture among the muffin cases.

4 Sprinkle with the chopped pecans. Bake the muffins for 20–25 minutes, until golden brown and firm in the middle. Transfer to a wire rack and serve while still warm.

Blackberry Muffins

Other berries, such as elderberries or blueberries, can be substituted for the blackberries.

Makes 12

INGREDIENTS

275g/10oz/2½ cups plain white
flour
50g/2oz/generous ¼ cup light
brown sugar
20ml/4 tsp baking powder
pinch of salt
65g/2½oz/generous ½ cup
chopped blanched almonds
90g/3½oz/generous ½ cup fresh
blackberries
2 eggs
200ml/7fl oz/⅞ cup milk
65g/2½oz/4 tbsp butter, melted
15ml/1 tbsp sloe gin
15ml/1 tbsp rosewater

1 Mix the flour, sugar, baking powder and salt in a bowl and stir in the almonds and blackberries, mixing them well to coat with the flour mixture.

2 Preheat the oven to 200°C/ 400°F/Gas 6. Grease 12 muffin tins, or use paper liners.

3 In another bowl, mix the eggs with the milk, then gradually add the butter, sloe gin and rosewater. Make a well in the centre of the bowl of dry ingredients and add the egg and milk mixture. Stir well. Spoon the mixture into the muffin tins or cases. Bake for 20–25 minutes, until browned. Transfer to a wire rack to cool.

Chocolate Blueberry Muffins

Blueberries are one of the few fruits that combine deliciously with chocolate.

Makes 12

INGREDIENTS

115g/4oz/1/2 cup butter
75g/3oz plain chocolate, chopped
200g/7oz/generous 1 cup
granulated sugar
1 egg, lightly beaten
250ml/8fl oz/1 cup buttermilk
10ml/2 tsp vanilla essence
275g/10oz/2 1/2 cups plain flour
5ml/1 tsp bicarbonate of soda
175g/6oz/generous 1 cup fresh or
frozen blueberries, thawed
25g/1oz plain chocolate, melted,
to decorate

1 Preheat the oven to 190°C/375°F/ Gas 5. Grease 12 deep patty tins, or use paper liners. In a medium saucepan over a medium heat, melt the butter and chocolate until smooth, stirring frequently. Remove from the heat and leave to cool slightly.

2 Stir in the sugar, egg, buttermilk and vanilla essence. Gently fold in the flour and bicarbonate of soda until just blended. (Do not overblend; although the mixture may be lumpy with some unblended flour.) Fold in the berries.

3 Spoon the batter into the prepared bun tins, filling to the top. Bake for 25–30 minutes, until a skewer or cake tester inserted in the centre comes out with just a few crumbs attached. Remove the muffins in their paper liners to a wire rack immediately (if left in the tin they will go soggy). To decorate, drizzle with the melted chocolate and serve warm or cool.

Prune Muffins

Buy the ready-to-eat prunes if you can, as these are already soaked and pitted.

Makes 12

INGREDIENTS

1 egg
250ml/8fl oz/1 cup milk
50ml/2fl oz/¹⁄₄ cup vegetable oil
50g/2oz/¹⁄₄ cup granulated sugar
30ml/2 tbsp dark brown sugar
225g/8oz/2 cups plain flour
10ml/2 tsp baking powder
pinch of salt
1.5ml/¹⁄₄ tsp grated nutmeg
150g/5oz/³⁄₄ cup cooked pitted
prunes, chopped

1 Preheat the oven to 200°C/400°F/ Gas 6. Grease 12 muffin tins or use paper liners.

2 Break the egg into a mixing bowl and beat with a fork. Beat in the milk and oil.

3 Stir the sugars into the egg mixture. Set aside. Sift the flour, baking powder, salt and nutmeg into a mixing bowl. Make a well in the centre, pour in the egg mixture and stir. The batter should be slightly lumpy.

4 Gently fold the prunes into the batter until just evenly distributed. Fill the prepared muffin tins two-thirds full.

5 Bake for about 20 minutes, until golden brown. Leave to stand for 10 minutes before transferring to a wire rack. Serve warm or at room temperature.

Yogurt Honey Muffins

Makes 12

INGREDIENTS

50g/2oz/4 tbsp butter
75g/3oz/5 tbsp clear honey
250ml/8fl oz/1 cup plain yogurt
1 egg
grated rind of 1 lemon
50ml/2fl oz/¹⁄₄ cup lemon juice
115g/4oz/1 cup plain flour
115g/4oz/1 cup wholemeal flour
7.5ml/1¹⁄₂ tsp bicarbonate of soda
pinch of grated nutmeg

Variation For Walnut Yogurt Honey Muffins, add 50g/2oz/¹⁄₂ cup chopped walnuts, folded in with the flour. This makes a more substantial muffin.

1 Preheat the oven to 190°C/375°F/ Gas 5. Grease 12 muffin tins, or use paper liners.

2 In a saucepan, melt the butter and honey. Remove from the heat and set aside to cool slightly.

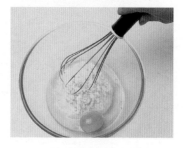

3 In a bowl, whisk together the yogurt, egg, lemon rind and juice. Add the butter and honey mixture. Set aside.

4 In another bowl, sift together the dry ingredients. Fold the dry ingredients into the yogurt mixture just to blend.

5 Fill the prepared muffin tins two-thirds full. Bake for 20–25 minutes until the tops spring back when touched lightly. Leave to cool in the pan for 5 minutes before transferring to a wire rack. Serve warm or at room temperature.

Raisin Bran Muffins

Makes 15

INGREDIENTS

*50g/2oz/4 tbsp butter or
margarine
75g/3oz/²/₃ cup plain flour
50g/2oz/¹/₂ cup wholemeal flour
7.5ml/1¹/₂ tsp bicarbonate of soda
pinch of salt
5ml/1 tsp ground cinnamon
25g/1oz/¹/₂ cup bran
75g/3oz/¹/₂ cup raisins
50g/2oz/¹/₃ cup dark brown sugar
50g/2oz/¹/₄ cup granulated sugar
1 egg
250ml/8fl oz/1 cup buttermilk
juice of ¹/₂ lemon*

1 Preheat the oven to 200°C/400°F/ Gas 6. Grease 15 muffin tins, or use paper liners.

2 Place the butter or margarine in a saucepan and melt over a low heat. Set aside. In a mixing bowl, sift together the plain flour, wholemeal flour, bicarbonate of soda, salt and cinnamon.

3 Add the bran, raisins, and sugars and stir until blended. In another bowl, mix together the egg, buttermilk, lemon juice and melted butter or margarine.

4 Add the buttermilk mixture to the dry ingredients and stir lightly and quickly until just moistened; do not mix until smooth.

5 Spoon the batter into the prepared muffin tins, filling them almost to the top. Bake for 15– 20 minutes, until golden. Serve warm or at room temperature.

Raspberry Crumble Muffins

Makes 12

❧

INGREDIENTS

175g/6oz/1½ cups plain flour
10ml/2 tsp baking powder
pinch of salt
5ml/1 tsp ground cinnamon
50g/2oz/¼ cup granulated sugar
50g/2oz/¼ firmly packed cup light
brown sugar
115g/4oz/½ cup butter, melted
1 egg
120ml/4fl oz/½ cup milk
225g/8oz/1¼ cups fresh
raspberries
grated rind of 1 lemon
For the crumble topping
50g/2oz/¼ cup pecans, finely
chopped
50g/2oz/¼ firmly packed cup dark
brown sugar
45ml/3 tbsp plain flour
5ml/1 tsp ground cinnamon
40g/1½oz/3 tbsp butter, melted

❧

1 Preheat the oven to 180°C/350°F/ Gas 4. Grease 12 muffin tins, or use paper liners. Sift the flour, baking powder, salt and cinnamon into a bowl. Add the sugars, and stir to blend.

2 Make a well in the centre of the mixture. Place the butter, egg and milk in the well and mix until just combined. Stir in the raspberries and lemon rind. Spoon the batter into the prepared muffin tins, filling them almost to the top.

3 To make the crumble topping, mix the pecans, dark brown sugar, flour and cinnamon in a bowl. Stir in the melted butter.

4 Spoon some of the crumble over each muffin. Bake for about 25 minutes. Transfer to a wire rack to cool slightly. Serve warm.

Nutty Muffins with Walnut Liqueur

Walnut liqueur gives a lift to these deep American muffins.

Makes 12–14

INGREDIENTS

225g/8oz/2 cups plain flour
20ml/4 tsp baking powder
2.5ml/¹/₂ tsp mixed spice
pinch of salt
115g/4oz/²/₃ cup soft light brown
sugar
75g/3oz/³/₄ cup chopped walnuts
50g/2oz/4 tbsp butter, melted
2 eggs
175ml/6fl oz/³/₄ cup milk
30ml/2 tbsp walnut liqueur
For the topping
30ml/2 tbsp soft dark brown
sugar
25g/1oz/¹/₄ cup chopped walnuts

1 Preheat the oven to 200°C/400°F/ Gas 6. Grease 12–14 muffin tins or deep bun tins, or use paper muffin cases supported in muffin tins. Sift the flour, baking powder, mixed spice and salt into a mixing bowl, then stir in the sugar and chopped walnuts.

2 In a jug, combine the melted butter, eggs, milk and liqueur.

3 Pour the butter mixture into the dry mixture and stir for just long enough to combine the ingredients. The batter should be lumpy.

4 Fill the muffin or bun tins two-thirds full, then top with a sprinkling of sugar and walnuts. Bake for 15 minutes until the muffins are golden brown. Leave in the tins for a few minutes, then transfer to a wire rack to cool.

Apple and Cinnamon Muffins

These spicy muffins are quick and easy to make and are perfect for serving for breakfast or tea.

Makes 6

INGREDIENTS

1 egg, beaten
40g/1½oz/3 tbsp caster sugar
120ml/4fl oz/½ cup milk
50g/2 oz/¼ cup butter, melted
150g/5oz/1¼ cups plain flour
7.5ml/1½ tsp baking powder
pinch of salt
2.5ml/½ tsp ground cinnamon
2 small eating apples, peeled, cored and finely chopped
For the topping
12 brown sugar cubes, roughly crushed
5ml/1 tsp ground cinnamon

Cook's Tip Do not overmix the muffin mixture – it should be lumpy.

1 Preheat the oven to 200°C/400°F/ Gas 6. Line six large muffin tins with paper cases. Mix the egg, sugar, milk and melted butter in a large bowl. Sift in the flour, baking powder, salt and cinnamon. Add the chopped apple and mix roughly.

2 Spoon the mixture into the prepared muffin cases. To make the topping, mix the crushed sugar cubes with the cinnamon. Sprinkle over the uncooked muffins.

3 Bake for 30–35 minutes, until well risen and golden. Transfer to a wire rack to cool.

Pineapple and Cinnamon Drop Scones

Making the batter with pineapple juice instead of milk cuts down on fat and adds to the taste.

Makes 24

INGREDIENTS

115g/4oz/1 cup self-raising wholemeal flour
115g/4oz/1 cup self-raising white flour
5ml/1 tsp ground cinnamon
15ml/1 tbsp caster sugar
1 egg
300ml/¹⁄₂ pint/1¹⁄₄ cups pineapple juice
75g/3oz/¹⁄₂ cup semi-dried pineapple, chopped

Cook's Tip Drop scones do not keep well and are best eaten freshly cooked.

1 Preheat a griddle, heavy-based frying pan or an electric frying pan. Put the wholemeal flour in a mixing bowl. Sift in the white flour, add the cinnamon and sugar and make a well in the centre. Add the egg with half of the pineapple juice.

2 Gradually incorporate the flour to make a smooth batter. Beat in the remaining juice with the chopped pineapple.

3 Lightly grease the griddle or pan. Drop tablespoons of the batter on to the surface, leaving them until they bubble and the bubbles begin to burst.

4 Turn the drop scones with a palette knife and cook until the underside is golden brown. Continue to cook in successive batches.

Chocolate Chip Banana Drop Scones

These delicious moist scones are topped with cream and toasted almonds.

Makes 16

〰

INGREDIENTS

2 ripe bananas
200ml/7fl oz/⅞ cup milk
2 eggs
150g/5oz/1¼ cups self-raising
flour
25g/1oz/¼ cup ground almonds
15ml/1 tbsp caster sugar
pinch of salt
25g/1oz/1½ tbsp plain chocolate
chips
butter for frying
For the topping
150ml/¼ pint/⅔ cup double
cream
15ml/1 tbsp icing sugar
50g/2oz/½ cup toasted flaked
almonds, to decorate

〰

Cook's Tip For banana and blueberry pancakes, replace the chocolate with 115g/4oz/1 cup fresh blueberries. Hot drop scones are also delicious when accompanied by ice cream.

1 In a bowl, mash the bananas with a fork, combine with half of the milk and beat in the eggs. Sieve in the flour, ground almonds, sugar and salt. Make a well in the centre and pour in the remaining milk. Add the chocolate chips and stir to produce a thick batter.

2 Heat a knob of butter in a non-stick frying pan. Spoon the pancake mixture into heaps, allowing room for them to spread. When the mixture starts to bubble, turn the pancakes over and cook briefly on the other side.

3 Lightly whip the cream with the icing sugar to sweeten it slightly. Spoon the cream on to the pancakes and decorate with flaked almonds.

Teatime Scones

Makes 16

❧

INGREDIENTS

225g/8oz/2 cups plain flour
pinch of salt
2.5ml/¹/₂ tsp bicarbonate of soda
5ml/1 tsp cream of tartar
25g/1oz/2 tbsp butter
about 150ml/¹/₄ pint/²/₃ cup milk
or buttermilk

❧

Variation These traditional favourites can be varied by adding 15–30ml/ 1–2 tbsp of chocolate drops or 5–10/1–2 tsp ground cinnamon.

1 Preheat the oven to 220°C/425°F/ Gas 7. Flour a baking sheet. Sift the flour, salt, bicarbonate of soda and cream of tartar into a bowl.

2 Rub in the fat until the mixture resembles fine breadcrumbs. Gradually stir in just enough milk to make a light, spongy dough.

3 Turn the dough on to a lightly-floured surface and knead until smooth. Roll to 2.5cm/1in thick. Cut into rounds with a floured 5cm/2in cutter (or a 4cm/1¹/₂in cutter for cocktail savouries).

4 Place the scones on the prepared baking sheet and brush the tops with milk. Bake for 7–10 minutes, until the scones are well risen and golden brown.

Lavender Scones

Serve these scented scones
warm, with plum jam and
clotted cream.

Makes 12

❧

INGREDIENTS

225g/8oz/2 cups flour
15ml/1 tbsp baking powder
50g/2oz/4 tbsp butter
40g/1¹/₂oz/¹/₄ cup caster sugar
10ml/2 tsp fresh lavender florets
or 5ml/1 tsp dried culinary
lavender, roughly chopped
about 175ml/6fl oz/³/₄ cup milk

❧

1 Preheat the oven to 220°C/425°F/ Gas 7. Grease a baking sheet. Sift together the flour and baking powder. Rub the butter into the dry ingredients until the mixture resembles breadcrumbs.

2 Stir in the sugar and lavender florets, reserving a pinch of lavender to sprinkle on the top of the scones before baking them.

3 Add enough milk to make a soft, sticky dough. Bind the mixture together and then turn the dough on to a well-floured work surface.

4 Shape the dough into a circle, and roll out to 2.5cm/1in depth. Using a floured cutter, stamp out 12 scones.

5 Place on the prepared baking sheet. Brush the tops with a little milk and sprinkle with the reserved lavender.

6 Bake for 10–12 minutes, until golden.

Sunflower Sultana Scones

Makes 10–12

INGREDIENTS

225g/8oz/2 cups self-raising flour
5ml/1 tsp baking powder
25g/1oz/2 tbsp margarine
30ml/2 tbsp golden caster sugar
50g/2oz/¹⁄₃ cup sultanas
30ml/2 tbsp sunflower seeds
150g/5oz/²⁄₃ cup natural yogurt
about 30–45ml/2–3 tbsp milk

1 Preheat the oven to 230°C/450°F/ Gas 8. Lightly oil a baking sheet. Sift the flour and baking powder into a bowl and rub in the margarine. Stir in the sugar, sultanas and half of the sunflower seeds, then mix in the natural yogurt.

2 Add just enough milk to the mixture to make a soft dough.

3 Roll out on a lightly floured surface to about 2cm/³⁄₄ in thick. Cut into 6cm/2¹⁄₂ in rounds with a floured biscuit cutter and lift on to the baking sheet.

4 Brush the tops of the scones with milk and sprinkle with the reserved sunflower seeds.

5 Bake for 10–12 minutes, until well risen and golden brown. Transfer to a wire rack. Serve while still warm, with jam, butter or low-fat spread.

Wholemeal Scones

Wholemeal scones are both delicious and healthy.

Makes 16

INGREDIENTS

175g/6oz/³/₄ cup cold butter
225g/8oz/2 cups wholemeal flour
115g/4oz/1 cup plain flour
30ml/2 tbsp caster sugar
pinch of salt
12.5ml/2¹/₂ tsp baking soda
2 eggs
175ml/6fl oz/³/₄ cup buttermilk
40g/1¹/₂oz/¹/₄ cup raisins

1 Preheat the oven to 200°C/400°F/ Gas 6. Grease and flour a large baking sheet.

2 Cut the butter into small pieces. Combine the dry ingredients in a bowl. Add the butter and rub in until the mixture resembles coarse crumbs. Set aside.

3 In another bowl, whisk together the eggs and buttermilk. Set aside 30ml/2 tbsp for glazing.

4 Stir the remaining egg mixture into the dry ingredients until it just holds together. Stir in the raisins.

5 Roll out the dough about 2cm/³/₄in thick. Stamp out circles with a floured cookie cutter. Place on the prepared baking sheet and brush with the glaze.

6 Bake for 12–15 minutes until golden. Allow to cool slightly before serving. Split in half with a fork while still warm and spread with butter and jam, if wished.

Orange Raisin Scones

Makes 16

INGREDIENTS

225g/8oz/2 cups plain flour
25ml/1¹/₂ tbsp baking powder
75g/3oz/¹/₃ cup caster sugar
pinch of salt
65g/2¹/₂oz/5 tbsp butter, chopped
grated rind of 1 large orange
50g/2oz/¹/₃ cup raisins
115ml/4oz/¹/₂ cup buttermilk
milk for glazing

1 Preheat the oven to 220°C/425°F/ Gas 7. Grease and flour a large baking sheet.

2 Combine the dry ingredients in a large bowl. Add the butter and rub in until the mixture resembles coarse crumbs.

3 Add the orange rind and raisins. Gradually stir in the buttermilk to form a soft dough.

4 Roll out the dough on a floured surface to about 2cm/³/₄in thick. Stamp out circles with a floured cookie cutter.

5 Place on the prepared baking sheet and brush the tops with milk. Bake for 12–15 minutes until golden. Serve hot or warm, with butter or whipped cream, and jam.

Cook's Tip For light, delicate scones, handle the dough as little as possible. If you wish, split the scones when cool and toast them under a preheated grill. Butter them while they are still hot.

Cookies
for Kids

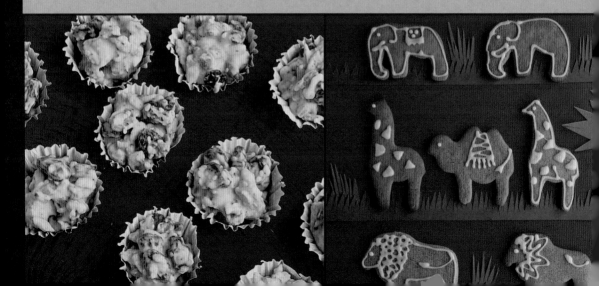

This chapter includes recipes that are suitable for children to eat, like Gingerbread Teddies, and recipes that children can make themselves. Quite a number of cookie recipes do not even need to be baked, such as Date Crunch, Fruit and Nut Clusters and Marshmallow Crispie Cakes.

Kids – before you embark on a cookie-making session, there are a few guidelines that will help you towards ending up with a batch to be proud of. Start by washing and drying your hands. If your hair is long, tie it back. Wear an apron both to protect your clothes from the food, and to protect the food from your clothes. Make sure the kitchen surfaces are clean and tidy before you begin.

Next, read through the recipe from start to finish very carefully so you can make sure you have all the ingredients and equipment you will need, and so you have a clear idea of what you are going to be doing and in what order. Now you can get out all the equipment you'll need, and assemble and carefully weigh all the ingredients.

Follow the recipe exactly and take your time. Avoid any distractions or interruptions, such as friends or brothers or sisters coming in, or the radio playing, in case you make a mistake or forget where you are in the recipe. If you are in any doubt about anything at all, at any time, or feel you need a hand, don't hesitate to ask a grown-up.

Chewy Fruit Muesli Slice

An easy recipe which needs just weighing out, mixing and baking.

Makes 8

INGREDIENTS

*75g/3oz/¹/₂ cup ready-to-eat dried
apricots, chopped
1 eating apple, cored and grated
150g/5oz/1¹/₄ cups Swiss-style
muesli
150ml/¹/₄ pint/²/₃ cup apple juice
15g/¹/₂oz/1 tbsp soft sunflower
margarine*

1 Preheat the oven to 190°C/375°F/ Gas 5. Place all the ingredients in a large bowl and mix well.

2 Press the mixture into a 20cm/8in non-stick sandwich tin and bake for 35–40 minutes, until lightly browned and firm.

3 Mark the muesli slice into eight wedges and leave to cool in the tin.

Oat and Apricot Clusters

*Here is a variation on an old favourite which children can easily make themselves,
so have plenty of the dried fruits and nuts ready for them to add.*

Makes 12

INGREDIENTS

*50g/2oz/4 tbsp butter or
margarine
50g/2oz/3 tbsp clear honey
50g/2oz/¹/₂ cup medium oatmeal
50g/2oz/¹/₃ cup chopped ready-to-
eat dried apricots
15ml/1 tbsp dried banana chips
15ml/1 tbsp dried shreds of
coconut
50–75g/2–3oz/2–3 cups
cornflakes or Rice Crispies*

1 Place the butter or margarine and honey in a small saucepan and warm over a low heat, stirring.

2 Add the oatmeal, apricots, banana chips, coconut and cornflakes or Rice Crispies and mix well.

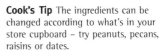

3 Spoon the mixture into 12 paper cake cases, piling it up roughly. Transfer to a baking sheet, or a tray, and chill until set and firm.

Cook's Tip The ingredients can be changed according to what's in your store cupboard – try peanuts, pecans, raisins or dates.

Fruit and Nut Clusters

This is a fun no-cook recipe which children will like.

Makes 24

INGREDIENTS

225g/8oz white chocolate
50g/2oz/¹⁄₃ cup sunflower seeds
50g/2oz/¹⁄₂ cup almond slivers
50g/2oz/¹⁄₃ cup sesame seeds
50g/2oz/¹⁄₃ cup seedless raisins
5ml/1 tsp ground cinnamon

1 Break the white chocolate into small pieces. Put the chocolate into a heatproof bowl over a saucepan of hot water on a low heat. Do not allow the water to touch the base of the bowl, or the chocolate may become too hot.

2 Alternatively, put the chocolate in a microwave-proof container and heat it on Medium for 3 minutes. Stir the melted chocolate until it is smooth and glossy.

3 Mix the remaining ingredients together, pour on the chocolate and stir well.

4 Using a teaspoon, spoon the mixture into paper cases and leave to set.

Marshmallow Crispie Cakes

Makes 45

❦

INGREDIENTS

250g/9oz bag of toffees
50g/2oz/4 tbsp butter
45ml/3 tbsp milk
115g/4oz/1 cup marshmallows
175g/6oz/6 cups Rice Crispies

❦

1 Lightly brush a 20 x 33cm/8 x 13in roasting tin with a little oil. Put the toffees, butter and milk in a saucepan and heat gently, stirring until the toffees have melted.

2 Add the marshmallows and cereal and stir until well mixed and the marshmallows have melted.

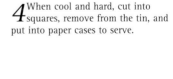

3 Spoon the mixture into the prepared roasting tin, level the surface and leave to set.

4 When cool and hard, cut into squares, remove from the tin, and put into paper cases to serve.

Date Crunch

Makes 24

INGREDIENTS

225g/8oz packet sweetmeal biscuits
75g/3oz/¹/₃ cup butter
30ml/2 tbsp golden syrup
75g/3oz/¹/₂ cup stoned dates, finely chopped
75g/3oz sultanas
150g/5oz milk or plain chocolate, chopped

Cook's Tip For an alternative topping, drizzle 75g/3oz melted white and 75g/3oz melted dark chocolate over.

1 Line an 18cm/7in square shallow cake tin with foil. Put the biscuits in a plastic bag and crush roughly with a rolling pin.

2 Gently heat the butter and syrup in a small saucepan until the butter has melted.

3 Stir in the crushed biscuits, the dates and sultanas and mix well. Spoon into the prepared tin, press flat with the back of a spoon and chill for 1 hour.

4 Melt the chocolate in a heatproof bowl, over a saucepan of hot water, stirring until smooth. Spoon over the cookie mixture, spreading evenly with a palette knife. Chill until set. Lift the foil out of the cake tin and peel away. Cut the crunch into 24 pieces and arrange on a plate.

Peanut Cookies

Packing up a picnic? Got a birthday party coming up?
Make sure some of these nutty cookies are on the menu.

Makes 25

❦

INGREDIENTS

225g/8oz/1 cup butter
30ml/2 tbsp smooth peanut butter
115g/4oz/1 cup icing sugar
50g/2oz/¹/₂ cup cornflour
225g/8oz/2 cups plain flour
115g/4oz/1 cup unsalted peanuts

❦

1 Put the butter and peanut butter in a bowl and beat together. Add the icing sugar, cornflour and plain flour and mix together to make a soft dough.

2 Preheat the oven to 180°C/350°F/ Gas 4. Lightly oil two baking sheets. Roll the mixture into 25 small balls, using your hands and place on the baking sheets. Leave plenty of room for the cookies to spread.

3 Press the tops of the balls of dough flat, using either the back of a fork or your fingertips.

4 Press a few of the peanuts into each of the cookies. Bake for 15–20 minutes, until lightly browned. Leave to cool for a few minutes before lifting them carefully on to a wire rack with a palette knife.

Cook's Tip Make really monster cookies by rolling bigger balls of dough. Remember to leave plenty of room on the baking sheets for them to spread, though.

Chocolate Crackle-tops

Older children will enjoy making these distinctive cookies.

Makes 38

INGREDIENTS

*200g/7oz plain chocolate,
chopped
90g/3¹/₂oz/scant ¹/₂ cup unsalted
butter
115g/4oz/¹/₂ cup caster sugar
3 eggs
5ml/1 tsp vanilla essence
215g/7¹/₂oz/scant 2 cups plain
flour
25g/1oz/¹/₄ cup unsweetened cocoa
2.5ml/¹/₂ tsp baking powder
pinch of salt
175g/6oz/1¹/₂ cups icing sugar for
coating*

1 In a medium saucepan over a low heat, melt the chocolate and butter together until smooth, stirring frequently.

2 Remove from the heat. Stir in the sugar, and continue stirring for 2–3 minutes, until the sugar dissolves. Add the eggs one at a time, beating well after each addition; stir in the vanilla.

3 Into a bowl, sift together the flour, cocoa, baking powder and salt. Gradually stir into the chocolate mixture in batches, until just blended.

4 Cover the dough and refrigerate for at least 1 hour, until the dough is cold and holds its shape.

5 Preheat the oven to 160°C/325°F/ Gas 3. Grease two or more large baking sheets. Place the icing sugar in a small, deep bowl. Using a small ice-cream scoop or round teaspoon, scoop cold dough into small balls and, between the palms of your hands, roll into 4cm/1¹/₂in balls.

6 Drop each ball into the icing sugar and roll until heavily coated. Remove with a slotted spoon and tap against the side of the bowl to remove excess sugar. Place on the prepared baking sheets 4cm/1¹/₂in apart.

7 Bake the cookies for 10– 15 minutes, until the tops feel slightly firm when touched. Remove the baking sheet to a wire rack for 2–3 minutes. With a metal palette knife, remove the cookies to a wire rack to cool completely.

Chocolate Dominoes

A recipe for children to eat rather than make. Ideal for birthday parties.

Makes 16

INGREDIENTS

175g/6oz/³/₄ cup soft margarine
175g/6oz/³/₄ cup caster sugar
150g/5oz/1¹/₄ cups self-raising flour
25g/1oz/¹/₄ cup cocoa powder, sifted
3 eggs
For the topping
175g/6oz/³/₄ cup butter
25g/1oz/¹/₄ cup cocoa powder
300g/11oz/2¹/₂ cups icing sugar
a few liquorice strips and
115g/4oz packet M & M's, for decoration

Variation To make Traffic Light Cakes, omit the cocoa and add an extra 25g/1oz/3 tbsp plain flour. Omit cocoa from the icing and add an extra 25g/1oz/4 tbsp icing sugar and 2.5ml/¹/₂ tsp vanilla essence. Spread over the cakes and decorate with red, yellow and green glacé cherries to look like traffic lights.

1 Preheat the oven to 180°C/350°F/ Gas 4. Lightly brush an 18 x 28cm/7 x 11in baking tin with a little oil and line the base of the tin with greaseproof paper.

2 Put all the cake ingredients in a bowl and beat until smooth.

3 Spoon into the prepared cake tin and level the surface with a palette knife.

4 Bake for 30 minutes, until the cake springs back when pressed with the fingertips.

5 Cool in the tin for 5 minutes, then loosen the edges with a knife and transfer to a wire rack. Peel off the paper and leave the cake to cool. Turn the cake on to a chopping board and cut into 16 bars.

6 To make the topping, place the butter in a bowl, sift in the cocoa and icing sugar and beat until smooth. Spread the topping evenly over the cakes with a palette knife.

7 Add a strip of liquorice to each cake, decorate with M & M's for domino dots and arrange the cakes on a serving plate.

Lemony Peanut Pairs

For those who don't like peanut butter, use buttercream or chocolate-and-nut spread instead.

Makes 8–10

INGREDIENTS

*40g/1¹/₂oz/¹/₄ cup soft light brown
sugar
50g/2oz/¹/₄ cup soft margarine
5ml/1 tsp grated lemon rind
75g/3oz/³/₄ cup wholemeal flour
50g/2oz/¹/₄ cup chopped
crystallized pineapple
25g/1oz/2 tbsp smooth peanut
butter
sifted icing sugar for dusting*

1 Preheat the oven to 190°C/375°F/
Gas 3. Grease a baking sheet.
Cream the sugar, margarine and
lemon rind together. Work in the
flour and knead until smooth.

2 Roll out thinly and cut into
rounds, then place on the baking
sheet. Press on pieces of pineapple
and bake for 15–20 minutes. Cool.
Sandwich together with peanut
butter, dust with icing sugar.

Ginger Cookies

*If your children enjoy cooking with you, mixing and rolling the dough, or cutting out
different shapes, this is the ideal recipe to let them practise on.*

Makes 16

INGREDIENTS

*115g/4oz/²/₃ cup soft brown sugar
115g/4oz/¹/₂ cup soft margarine
pinch of salt
few drops of vanilla essence
175g/6oz/1¹/₄ cups wholemeal
plain flour
15g/¹/₂oz/1 tbsp cocoa, sifted
10ml/2 tsp ground ginger
a little milk
glacé icing and glacé cherries, to
decorate*

1 Preheat the oven to 190°C/375°F/
Gas 5. Grease a baking sheet.
Cream together the sugar, margarine,
salt and vanilla essence until very
soft and light.

2 Work in the flour, cocoa and
ginger, adding a little milk, if
necessary, to bind the mixture. Knead
lightly on a floured surface until
smooth.

3 Roll out the dough to about
5mm/¹/₄in thick. Stamp out shapes
using floured biscuit cutters and place
on the prepared baking sheet.

4 Bake the cookies for 10–15
minutes. Leave to cool on the
baking sheets until firm, then transfer
to a wire rack to cool completely.
Decorate with glacé icing and pieces
of glacé cherries.

Gingerbread Jungle

Snappy biscuits in animal shapes, which can be decorated in your own style.

Makes 14

INGREDIENTS

175g/6oz/1¹/₂ cups self-raising
flour
2.5ml/¹/₂ tsp bicarbonate of soda
2.5ml/¹/₂ tsp ground cinnamon
10ml/2 tsp caster sugar
50g/2oz/¹/₄ cup butter
45ml/3 tbsp golden syrup
50g/2oz/¹/₂ cup icing sugar
5–10ml/1–2 tsp water

Cook's Tip Any cutters can be used with the same mixture. Obviously, the smaller the cutters, the more biscuits you will make.

1 Preheat the oven to 190°C/375°F/ Gas 5. Lightly oil two baking sheets.

2 Put the flour, bicarbonate of soda, cinnamon and caster sugar in a bowl and mix together. Melt the butter and syrup in a saucepan. Pour over the dry ingredients.

3 Mix together well and then use your hands to pull the mixture together to make a dough.

4 Turn on to a lightly floured surface and roll out to about 5mm/¹/₄in thick.

5 Use floured animal cutters to cut shapes from the dough and arrange on the prepared baking sheets, leaving enough room between them to rise.

6 Press the trimmings back into a ball, roll it out and cut more shapes. Continue until all the dough is used. Bake for 8–12 minutes, until lightly browned.

7 Leave to cool slightly, before transferring to a wire rack with a palette knife. Sift the icing sugar into a small bowl and add enough water to make a fairly soft icing.

8 Spoon the icing into a piping bag fitted with a small, plain nozzle and pipe decorations on the cookies.

Sweet Necklaces

These are too fiddly for young children to make but ideal as novelty Christmas presents.

Arrange in a pretty, tissue-lined box or tin for presentation.

Makes 12

❦

INGREDIENTS

1 quantity Lebkuchen mixture
200g/7oz royal icing
pink food colouring
selection of small sweets
6m/6 yards fine pink, blue or
white ribbon

❦

1 Preheat the oven to 180°C/350°F/ Gas 4. Grease two large baking sheets. Roll out slightly more than half of the Lebkuchen mixture on a lightly floured surface to a thickness of 5mm/¼in.

2 Cut out stars using a floured 2.5cm/1in star cutter. Transfer to a baking sheet, spacing them evenly. Taking care not to distort the shape of the stars, make a large hole in the centre of each, using a metal or wooden skewer.

3 Gather the trimmings together with the remaining dough. Roll the dough under the palms of your hands, to make a thick sausage about 2.5cm/1in in diameter. Cut in 1cm/½in slices. Using the skewer, make a hole in the centre of each. Put on the second baking sheet.

4 Bake for about 8 minutes, until slightly risen and just beginning to colour. Remove from the oven and, while still warm, re-make the skewer holes as the gingerbread will have spread slightly during baking. Leave to cool on a wire rack.

5 Put half the royal icing in a paper piping bag and snip off a tip. Use to pipe outlines around the stars. Colour the remaining icing with the pink colouring. Spoon into a paper piping bag fitted with a star nozzle.

6 Cut the sweets into smaller pieces and use to decorate the biscuits. Leave to harden.

7 Cut the ribbon into 50cm/20in lengths. Thread a selection of the biscuits on to each ribbon.

Choc-tipped Cookies

Get those cold hands wrapped round a steaming hot drink,

and tuck into choc-tipped cookies.

Makes 22

🌿

INGREDIENTS

115g/4oz/¹/₂ cup margarine
45ml/3 tbsp icing sugar, sifted
150g/5oz/1¹/₄ cups plain flour
few drops vanilla essence
75g/3oz plain chocolate, chopped

🌿

1 Preheat the oven to 180°C/350°F/ Gas 4. Lightly grease two baking sheets. Put the margarine and icing sugar in a bowl and cream them together until very soft. Mix in the flour and vanilla essence.

2 Spoon the mixture into a large piping bag fitted with a large star nozzle and pipe 10–13cm/4–5in lines on the prepared baking sheets. Cook for 15–20 minutes, until pale golden brown. Leave to cool slightly before lifting on to a wire rack. Leave the biscuits to cool completely.

3 Put the chocolate in a small heatproof bowl. Stand in a saucepan of hot, but not boiling, water and leave to melt. Dip both ends of each biscuit into the chocolate, put back on the rack and leave to set. Serve with hot chocolate topped with whipped cream.

Cook's Tip Make round biscuits if you prefer, and dip half of each biscuit in the melted chocolate.

Five-spice Fingers

Light, crumbly biscuits with an unusual Chinese five-spice flavouring.

Makes 28

🌿

INGREDIENTS

115g/4oz/¹/₂ cup margarine
50g/2oz/¹/₂ cup icing sugar
115g/4oz/1 cup plain flour
10ml/2 tsp five-spice powder
grated rind and juice of ¹/₂ orange

🌿

1 Preheat the oven to 180°C/
350°F/Gas 4. Lightly grease
two baking sheets. Put the margarine
and half the icing sugar in a bowl
and beat with a wooden spoon, until
the mixture is smooth and creamy.

2 Add the flour and five-spice
powder and beat again. Spoon
the mixture into a large piping bag
fitted with a large star nozzle.

3 Pipe short lines of mixture, about
7.5cm/3in long, on the prepared
baking sheets. Leave enough room for
them to spread.

4 Bake for 15 minutes, until lightly
browned. Leave to cool slightly,
before transferring to a wire rack
with a palette knife.

5 Sift the remaining icing sugar
into a small bowl and stir in the
orange rind. Add enough juice to
make a thin icing. Brush over the
biscuits while they are still warm.

Cook's Tip These biscuits are delicious
served with ice cream or creamy
desserts.

Gingerbread Teddies

These endearing teddies, dressed in striped pyjamas, would make a perfect gift for friends of any age. If you can't get a large cutter, make smaller teddies or use a traditional gingerbread-man cutter. You might need some help from an adult for the decorating.

Makes 6

❦

INGREDIENTS

75g/3oz white chocolate, chopped
175g/6oz ready-to-roll white sugar paste
blue food colouring
25g/1oz plain or milk chocolate
For the gingerbread
175g/6oz/1½ cups plain flour
1.5ml/¼ tsp bicarbonate of soda
pinch of salt
5ml/1 tsp ground ginger
5ml/1 tsp ground cinnamon
65g/2½oz/⅓ cup unsalted butter, chopped
75g/3oz/⅓ cup caster sugar
30ml/2 tbsp maple or golden syrup
1 egg yolk, beaten

❦

1 To make the gingerbread, sift together the flour, bicarbonate of soda, salt and spices into a large bowl. Rub the butter into the flour until the mixture resembles fine breadcrumbs.

2 Stir in the sugar, syrup and egg yolk and mix to a firm dough. Knead lightly. Wrap and chill for 30 minutes.

3 Preheat the oven to 180°C/350°F/ Gas 4. Grease two large baking sheets. Roll out the gingerbread dough on a floured surface and cut out teddies, using a floured 13cm/5in cookie cutter.

4 Transfer to the prepared baking sheets and bake for 10–15 minutes, until just beginning to colour around the edges. Leave on the baking sheets for 3 minutes and then transfer to a wire rack.

5 Melt half of the white chocolate. Put in a paper piping bag and snip off the tip. Make a neat template for the teddies' clothes: draw an outline of the cutter on to paper, finishing at the neck, halfway down the arms and around the legs.

6 Thinly roll the sugar paste on a surface dusted with icing sugar. Use the template to cut out the clothes, and secure them to the biscuits with the melted chocolate.

7 Use the sugar paste trimmings to add ears, eyes and snouts. Dilute the blue colouring with a little water and use it to paint the striped pyjamas.

8 Melt the remaining white chocolate and the plain or milk chocolate in separate bowls over saucepans of hot water. Put in separate paper piping bags and snip off the tips. Use the white chocolate to pipe a decorative outline around the pyjamas and use the plain or milk chocolate to pipe the faces.

Cookie
Treats
and Gifts

Everyone has times when they feel the need to indulge themselves. If your fancy is for something rich and sweet, or if you want to give someone a treat, delve into the next few pages and you will find just the ticket.

A delicious gift that is home-made is always received with delight, and cookies, because they have a special place in nearly everyone's heart, are doubly acceptable, even if they are simple. Of course, if the cookies require a little extra skill, such as Honey and Nut Clusters, they will be received with even more pleasure. With home-made cookies, it is so easy to hit upon an ideal gift every time, whether it is just a small token or something very special.

The slightly more complicated cookies are also particularly therapeutic to make and provide a rewarding job for a quiet morning or afternoon, or a rainy day when you want to bring a little sunshine into your life. However, none of the recipes in this chapter is beyond the bounds of a reasonably competent home cook.

Chocolate Nut Clusters

These are an ideal way to end a dinner party, or a gift for a special friend.

Makes 30

INGREDIENTS

550ml/18fl oz/2¼ cups double cream
25g/1oz/2 tbsp unsalted butter, chopped
350ml/12fl oz/1½ cups golden syrup
200g/7oz/scant 1 cup granulated sugar
90g/3½oz/½ packed cup light brown sugar
pinch of salt
15ml/1 tbsp vanilla essence
425g/15oz/3¾ cups hazelnuts, pecans, walnuts, brazil nuts or unsalted peanuts, or a combination
400g/14oz plain chocolate, chopped
25g/1oz/2 tbsp white vegetable fat

1 Lightly oil two baking sheets. In a heavy-based saucepan over a medium heat, cook the first six ingredients until the sugars dissolve and the butter melts. Bring to the boil and cook, stirring frequently, for about 1 hour, until the caramel reaches 119°C/238°F (soft ball stage) on a sugar thermometer.

2 Place the bottom of the saucepan in a pan of cold water to stop cooking, or transfer the caramel to a smaller saucepan. Cool slightly, then stir in the vanilla essence.

3 Stir the nuts into the caramel until well-coated. Using an oiled tablespoon, drop spoonfuls of the nut mixture on to the prepared sheets, about 2.5cm/1in apart. If the mixture hardens, return to the heat to soften.

4 Refrigerate the clusters for 30 minutes, until firm and cold, or leave in a cool place until hardened.

Cook's Tip If you do not possess a sugar thermometer, you can test cooked sugar for 'soft ball stage' by spooning a small amount into a bowl of cold water: when taken out it should form a soft ball when rolled between finger and thumb.

5 Using a metal palette knife, transfer the clusters to a wire rack placed over a baking sheet to catch drips.

6 In a medium saucepan, over a low heat, melt the chocolate and white vegetable fat, stirring until smooth. Cool slightly.

7 Spoon chocolate over each cluster, being sure to cover completely. Alternatively, using a fork, dip each cluster into chocolate and lift out, tapping on the edge of the saucepan to shake off excess.

8 Place on the wire rack over the baking sheet. Allow to set for 2 hours, until hardened.

Louisiana Pralines

This version of pralines resembles puddles of nut fudge and is deliciously indulgent.

Makes 30

INGREDIENTS

225g/8oz/2 cups pecan halves
450g/1lb/2 well-packed cups soft
light brown sugar
200g/7oz/scant 1 cup granulated
sugar
300ml/¹/₂ pint/1¹/₄ cups double
cream
175ml/6fl oz/³/₄ cup milk
5ml/1 tsp vanilla essence

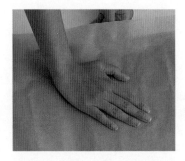

1 Roughly chop half of the pecans and set all the nuts aside. Line 2–3 baking sheets with non-stick baking paper.

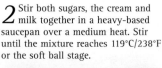

2 Stir both sugars, the cream and milk together in a heavy-based saucepan over a medium heat. Stir until the mixture reaches 119°C/238°F or the soft ball stage.

3 Remove from the heat immediately and beat with an electric beater or balloon whisk until the mixture loses its sheen and becomes creamy in texture and grainy looking. This could take 15 minutes by hand or about 5 minutes with an electric beater.

4 Stir in the vanilla essence and nuts. Drop tablespoons of the mixture on to the prepared baking sheets, allowing it to spread of its own accord. Leave to cool and set at room temperature. Store between layers of greaseproof paper in an airtight container.

Chocolate-coated Nut Brittle

Equal amounts of pecans and almonds set in crisp caramel, then coated

in dark chocolate, make a sensational gift.

Makes 20–24

INGREDIENTS

115g/4oz/1 cup mixed pecans and whole almonds
115g/4oz/½ cup caster sugar
60ml/4 tbsp water
200g/7oz plain chocolate, chopped

Cook's Tip These look best in rough chunks, so don't worry if the pieces break unevenly, or if there are gaps in the chocolate coating.

1 Lightly grease a baking sheet. Mix the nuts, sugar and water in a heavy-based saucepan. Place the pan over a low heat, stirring without boiling until the sugar has dissolved.

2 Bring to the boil, then lower the heat to medium and cook until the mixture turns a rich golden brown and registers 148°C/300°F on a sugar thermometer.

3 To test without a thermometer, drop a small amount of the mixture into a cup of iced water. The mixture should become brittle enough to snap with your fingers.

4 Quickly remove the pan from the heat and tip the mixture on to the prepared baking sheet, spreading it evenly. Leave until completely cold and hard.

5 Break the nut brittle into bite-size pieces. Melt the chocolate in a heatproof bowl over a saucepan of hot water and dip the pieces to half-coat them. Leave on a sheet of non-stick baking paper to set.

Chocolate Fudge Triangles

This fudge can be stored in an airtight container in the fridge for up to 2 weeks.

Makes 48

❦

INGREDIENTS

*600g/1lb 5oz fine quality white
chocolate, chopped
400ml/14fl oz can sweetened
condensed milk
15ml/1 tbsp vanilla essence
7.5ml/1½ tsp lemon juice
pinch of salt
215g/7½oz/scant 2 cups hazelnuts
or pecans, chopped (optional)
175g/6oz plain chocolate,
chopped
40g/1½oz/3 tbsp unsalted butter,
chopped
50g/2oz plain chocolate, melted,
to decorate*

❦

1 Line a 20cm/8in square baking tin with foil. In a saucepan over a low heat, melt the chocolate and condensed milk, stirring frequently. Remove from the heat and stir in the vanilla essence, lemon juice, salt, and nuts, if using. Spread half of the mixture in the tin. Chill for 15 minutes.

2 In a saucepan over a low heat, melt the plain chocolate and butter, stirring until smooth. Remove from the heat, cool slightly, then pour over the chilled white layer and chill for 15 minutes.

3 Gently re-heat the remaining white chocolate mixture and pour over the set plain chocolate layer. Smooth the top, then chill for 2–4 hours, until set.

4 Using the foil to lift it, remove the fudge from the tin and turn on to a cutting board. Remove the foil and, using a sharp knife, cut into 24 squares. Cut each square into two triangles. To decorate, drizzle with melted chocolate.

Honey and Nut Clusters

These are popular in Italy. To serve, cut in squares or fingers and keep in the refrigerator. They are delightfully sticky!

Makes 48

❦

INGREDIENTS

115g/4oz/²/₃ cup blanched almonds
115g/4oz/1 cup shelled hazelnuts
whites of 2 eggs
115g/4oz/¹/₃ cup clear honey
115g/4oz/¹/₂ cup caster sugar

❦

1 Preheat the oven to the lowest temperature. Line a 20cm/8in square tin with baking paper.

2 Spread the almonds and hazelnuts on separate baking sheets and toast in the oven for about 30 minutes. Tip on to a cloth and rub off the skins. Roughly chop both types of nut.

3 Whisk the egg whites until they are stiff, and stir in the chopped nuts.

4 Put the honey and sugar into a small, heavy-based saucepan and bring to the boil. Stir in the nut mixture and cook over a medium heat for 10 minutes.

5 Turn the mixture into the prepared tin and level the top. Cover with another piece of non-stick paper, put weights (such as food cans) on top and chill for at least 2 days.

6 To present as a tree decoration, wrap slices in non-stick baking paper and then in gift-wrap or cotton fabric, or in foil.

Peppermint and Coconut Chocolate Sticks

Desiccated coconut gives these chocolate mint sticks a unique flavour and texture.

Makes 80

INGREDIENTS

115g/4oz/¹/₂ cup granulated sugar
150ml/¹/₄ pint/²/₃ cup water
2.5ml/¹/₂ tsp peppermint essence
*200g/7oz plain dark chocolate,
chopped*
*60ml/4 tbsp toasted desiccated
coconut*

1 Lightly oil a large baking sheet. Place the sugar and water in a small, heavy-based saucepan and heat gently, stirring occasionally, until the sugar has dissolved completely.

2 Bring to the boil and boil rapidly without stirring until the syrup registers 138°C/280°F on a sugar thermometer. Remove the pan from the heat and add the peppermint essence, then pour on to the prepared baking sheet and leave until set and completely cold.

3 Break up the peppermint mixture into a bowl and use the end of a rolling pin to crush it into pieces.

4 Melt the chocolate in a heatproof bowl over a saucepan of hot water. Remove from the heat and stir in the mint pieces and desiccated coconut.

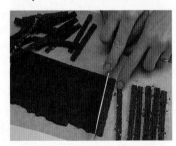

5 Place a 30 x 25cm/12 x 10in sheet of non-stick baking paper on a flat surface. Spread the mixture over the paper, leaving a narrow border all around. Leave to set. When firm, use a sharp knife to cut into thin sticks.

Chocolate Peppermint Crisps

If you do not have a sugar thermometer, test cooked sugar for "hard ball stage"

by spooning a few drops into a bowl of cold water; it should form

a hard ball when rolled between fingers.

Makes 30

❦

INGREDIENTS

50g/2oz/¼ cup granulated sugar
50ml/2fl oz/¼ cup water
5ml/1 tsp peppermint essence
225g/8oz plain chocolate,
chopped

❦

1 Lightly brush a large baking sheet with unflavoured oil. In a saucepan over a medium heat, heat the sugar and water, swirling the pan gently until the sugar dissolves. Boil rapidly to 138°C/280°F on a sugar thermometer. Remove the pan from the heat and add the peppermint essence; swirl to mix. Pour on to the prepared baking sheet and leave to set and cool completely.

2 When cold, break into pieces. Place in a food processor fitted with a metal blade and process to fine crumbs form; do not over-process.

3 Line two baking sheets with non-stick baking paper. Place the chocolate in a small heatproof bowl over a small saucepan of hot water. Place over a very low heat until the chocolate has melted, stirring frequently until smooth. Remove from the heat and stir in the peppermint mixture.

4 Using a teaspoon, drop small mounds on to the prepared sheets. Using the back of the spoon, spread to 4cm/1½in rounds. Cool, then refrigerate for about 1 hour, until set. Peel off the paper and store in airtight containers with non-stick baking paper between the layers.

Striped Biscuits

These biscuits may be made in different flavours and colours and look wonderful tied in bundles or packed into boxes. Eat them with ice cream or light desserts.

Makes 25

INGREDIENTS

25g/1oz white chocolate, melted
red and green food colouring dusts
2 egg whites
90g/3¹/₂oz/¹/₃ cup caster sugar
50g/2oz/¹/₂ cup plain flour
50g/2oz/4 tbsp unsalted butter, melted

1 Preheat the oven to 190°C/375°F/ Gas 5. Line two baking sheets with non-stick baking paper. Divide the melted chocolate in half and add a little food colouring dust to each half to colour the chocolate red and green. Using two greaseproof paper piping bags, fill with each colour chocolate and fold down the tops. Snip off the points.

2 Place the egg whites in a bowl and whisk until stiff. Add the sugar gradually, whisking well after each addition, to make a thick meringue. Add the flour and melted butter and whisk until smooth.

3 Drop four separate teaspoonfuls of the mixture on to the prepared baking sheets and spread into thin rounds. Pipe lines or zigzags of green and red chocolate over each round.

4 Bake one sheet at a time for 3–4 minutes, until pale golden in colour. Loosen the rounds with a palette knife and return to the oven for a few seconds to soften. Have two or three lightly oiled wooden spoon handles at hand.

5 Taking one round biscuit out of the oven at a time, roll it around a spoon handle and leave for a few seconds to set. Repeat to shape the remaining biscuits. Put the second sheet of biscuits in to bake.

6 When the biscuits are set, slip them off the spoon handles on to a wire rack. Repeat with the remaining mixture and the red and green chocolate until all the mixture has been used, baking only one sheet of biscuits at a time. If the biscuits are too hard to shape, simply return them to the oven for a few seconds to soften.

7 When the biscuits are cold, tie them together with coloured ribbon and pack into boxes, tins or glass jars.

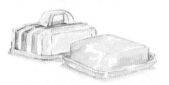

Almond Fingers

A very simple Middle Eastern sweetmeat which is especially popular in Arab countries.

Makes 40–50

INGREDIENTS

200g/7oz/1³/₄ cups ground almonds
50g/2oz/¹/₂ cup ground pistachios
50g/2oz/¹/₄ cup granulated sugar
15ml/1 tbsp rosewater
2.5ml/¹/₂ tsp ground cinnamon
12 sheets of filo pastry
115g/4oz/¹/₂ cup butter, melted
icing sugar for dusting

1 Preheat the oven to 160°C/325°F/ Gas 3. Butter a baking sheet. Mix together the almonds, pistachios, sugar, rosewater and cinnamon.

2 Cut each sheet of filo pastry into four rectangles. Work with one at a time, and cover the remaining rectangles with a damp dish towel.

3 Brush one rectangle with melted butter, place a teaspoon of the nut filling in the centre.

4 Fold the sides and roll into a cigar shape. Continue until all the filling has been used.

5 Place the 'cigars' on the baking sheet and bake for 30 minutes. Transfer to a wire rack to cool, then dust with icing sugar.

Basbousa

These delicious Middle Eastern coconut sweetmeats can be served either hot as a dessert or cold with tea.

Makes 12

INGREDIENTS

115g/4oz/¹/₂ cup unsalted butter
175g/6oz/³/₄ cup caster sugar
50g/2oz/¹/₂ cup plain flour
150g/5oz/1¹/₄ cups semolina
75g/3oz/1¹/₂ cups grated coconut
175ml/6fl oz/³/₄ cup milk
5ml/1 tsp baking powder
5ml/1 tsp vanilla essence
almonds, to decorate
For the syrup
115g/4oz/¹/₂ cup caster sugar
150ml/¹/₄ pint/²/₃ cup water
15ml/1 tbsp lemon juice

1 To make the syrup, place the sugar, water and lemon juice in a saucepan, bring to the boil, simmer for 6–8 minutes then cool before chilling.

2 Preheat the oven to 180°C/350°F/ Gas 4. Melt the butter in a saucepan. Add the remaining ingredients and mix thoroughly.

3 Pour the cake mixture into a shallow baking tin, flatten the top and bake for 30–35 minutes.

4 Remove the Basbousa from the oven and cut into diamond-shaped lozenges. Pour the cold syrup evenly over the top and decorate with an almond placed in each centre.

Semolina and Nut Halva

*Semolina is a popular ingredient in many desserts and pastries in the
Eastern Mediterranean. Here it provides a spongy base for
soaking up a deliciously fragrant spicy syrup.*

Makes 20–24

INGREDIENTS

*115g/4oz/¹/₂ cup unsalted butter
115g/4oz/¹/₂ cup caster sugar
finely grated rind of 1 orange
30ml/2 tbsp orange juice
3 eggs
175g/6oz/1 cup semolina
10ml/2 tsp baking powder
115g/4oz/1 cup ground hazelnuts
50g/2oz/¹/₂ cup unblanched
hazelnuts, toasted and chopped
50g/2oz/¹/₂ cup blanched almonds,
toasted and chopped
shredded rind of 1 orange
For the syrup
350g/12oz/1¹/₂ cups caster sugar
550ml/18fl oz/2¹/₄ cups water
2 cinnamon sticks, halved
juice of 1 lemon
60ml/4 tbsp orange flower water*

1 Preheat the oven to 220°C/425°F/
Gas 7. Grease and line the base of
a deep 23cm/9in square heavy-based
cake tin.

2 Lightly cream the butter in a
bowl. Add the sugar, orange rind
and juice, the eggs, semolina, baking
powder and hazelnuts and beat the
ingredients together until smooth.

3 Turn into the prepared tin and
level the surface. Bake for 20–
25 minutes, until just firm and
golden. Leave to cool in the tin.

4 To make the syrup, put the sugar
in a heavy-based saucepan with
the water and cinnamon sticks. Heat
gently, until the sugar has dissolved.

5 Bring to the boil and boil hard
for 5 minutes. Measure half the
syrup in a jug and add the lemon
juice and orange flower water to it.
Pour over the halva. Reserve the
remainder of the syrup in the pan.

6 Leave the halva in the tin until
the syrup is absorbed, then turn
it out on to a plate and cut
diagonally into diamond-shaped
portions. Scatter with the nuts.

7 Boil the remaining syrup until
slightly thickened then pour it
over the halva. Scatter the shredded
orange rind over the cake and serve
with lightly whipped cream.

Jewelled Elephants

These stunningly robed elephants make a lovely gift for animal-lovers, or an edible decoration for a special occasion. If you make holes in them before baking, you could use them as original Christmas tree decorations.

Makes 10

INGREDIENTS

1 quantity Lebkuchen mixture
1 quantity Icing Glaze
red food colouring
225g/8oz ready-to-roll sugar
paste
small candy-covered
chocolates or chews
gold dragees

1 Preheat the oven to 180°C/350°F/ Gas 4. Grease two large baking sheets. Make a paper template for the elephant. Roll out the Lebkuchen mixture. Use the template and a sharp knife to cut out elephant shapes. Space them, slightly apart, on the baking sheet for 3 minutes and then transfer to a wire rack to cool.

2 Put a little Icing Glaze in a paper piping bag fitted with a fine nozzle. Alternatively, cut off the tip of the bag.

3 Knead some red food colouring into half of the sugar paste. Roll a little red sugar paste under your fingers into ropes. Secure them around the feet and tips of the trunk, using icing from the bag. Shape more red sugar paste into flat oval shapes, about 2cm/¾in long, and stick them to the elephants' heads. Shape smaller ovals and secure them at the top of the trunks.

4 Roll out the white sugar paste. Cut out circles, using a 6cm/2½in biscuit cutter. Secure to the elephants' backs with royal icing so that the edge of the sugar paste is about 2.5cm/1in above the top of the legs. Trim off the excess paste around the top of the white sugar paste shapes.

5 Pipe 1cm/½in tassels around the edges. Pipe dots of white icing at the tops of the trunks, around the necks and at the tops of the tails and also use it to draw small eyes. Halve the small sweets and press the halves into the sugar paste, above the tassels. Decorate the headdress, sweets and white sugar paste with gold dragees, securing them with dots of icing. Leave for several hours, to harden.

Index

Index

NOTES

NOTES

NOTES

NOTES

NOTES

NOTES

THE GREAT BIG
BAKING BOOK

THE GREAT BIG
BAKING BOOK

CAROLE CLEMENTS

LORENZ BOOKS

This edition is published by Lorenz Books, an imprint of Anness Publishing Ltd,
Blaby Road, Wigston, Leicestershire LE18 4SE

Email: info@anness.com

Web: www.lorenzbooks.com; www.annesspublishing.com

If you like the images in this book and would like to investigate using them for publishing, promotions or
advertising, please visit our website www.practicalpictures.com for more information.

Publisher: Joanna Lorenz
Project editor: Carole Clements
Designer: Sheila Volpe
Photography, styling: Amanda Heywood
Food styling: Elizabeth Wolf-Cohen, Carla Capalbo
Steps: Cara Hobday, Teresa Goldfinch, Nicola Fowler

ETHICAL TRADING POLICY
Because of our ongoing ecological investment programme, you, as our customer, can have the pleasure and
reassurance of knowing that a tree is being cultivated on your behalf to naturally replace the materials used
to make the book you are holding. For further information about this scheme,
go to www.annesspublishing.com/trees

A CIP catalogue record for this book is available from the British Library.

Previously published as *Baking*

NOTES
Bracketed terms are intended for American readers.
For all recipes, quantities are given in both metric and imperial measures and,
where appropriate, in standard cups and spoons.
Follow one set of measures, but not a mixture, because they are not interchangeable.
Standard spoon and cup measures are level. 1 tsp = 5ml, 1 tbsp = 15ml, 1 cup = 250ml/8fl oz.
Australian standard tablespoons are 20ml.
Australian readers should use 3 tsp in place of 1 tbsp for measuring small quantities.
American pints are 16fl oz/2 cups.
American readers should use 20fl oz/2.5 cups in place of 1 pint when measuring liquids.
Electric oven temperatures in this book are for conventional ovens.
When using a fan oven, the temperature will probably need to be reduced by about 10–20°C/20–40°F.
Since ovens vary, you should check with your manufacturer's instruction book for guidance.
Medium (US large) eggs are used unless otherwise stated.

PUBLISHER'S NOTE

CONTENTS

INTRODUCTION

Nothing equals the satisfaction of home baking. No commercial cake mix or shop-bought biscuit can match one that is made from the best fresh ingredients with all the added enjoyment that baking at home provides – the enticing aromas that fill the house and stimulate appetites, the delicious straight-from-the-oven flavour, as well as the pride of having created such wonderful goodies yourself.

This book is filled with familiar favourites as well as many other lesser known recipes. Explore the wealth of biscuits, cookies, buns, tea breads, yeast breads, pies, tarts, and cakes within these pages. Even if you are a novice baker, the easy-to-follow and clear step-by-step photographs will help you achieve good results. For the more experienced home baker, this book will provide some new recipes to add to your repertoire.

Baking is an exact science and needs to be approached in an ordered way. First read through the recipe from beginning to end. Set out all the required ingredients before you begin. Medium eggs are assumed unless specified otherwise, and they should be at room temperature for best results. Sift the flour after you have measured it, and incorporate other dry ingredients as specified in the individual recipes. If you sift the flour from a fair height, it will have more chance to aerate and lighten.

When a recipe calls for folding one ingredient into another, it should be done in a way that incorporates as much air as possible into the mixture. Use either a large metal spoon or a long rubber or plastic scraper. Gently plunge the spoon or scraper deep into the centre of the mixture and, scooping up a large amount of the mixture, fold it over. Turn the bowl slightly so each scoop folds over another part of the mixture.

No two ovens are alike. Buy a reliable oven thermometer and test the temperature of your oven. When possible bake in the centre of the oven where the heat is more likely to be constant. If using a fan-assisted oven, follow the manufacturer's guidelines for baking. Good quality baking tins can improve your results, as they conduct heat more efficiently.

Practice, patience and enthusiasm are the keys to confident and successful baking. The recipes that follow will inspire you to start sifting flour, breaking eggs and stirring up all sorts of delectable homemade treats – all guaranteed to bring great satisfaction to both the baker and those lucky enough to enjoy the results.

BISCUITS, COOKIES & BARS

KEEP THE BISCUIT TIN FILLED WITH THIS WONDERFUL ARRAY OF BISCUITS, COOKIES AND BARS – SOME SOFT AND CHEWY, SOME CRUNCHY AND NUTTY, SOME RICH AND SINFUL, AND SOME PLAIN AND WHOLESOME. ALL ARE IRRESISTIBLE.

Farmhouse Cookies

Makes 18

115g/4oz/¹/₂ cup butter or margarine,
  at room temperature

90g/3¹/₂ oz/generous 1 cup light
  brown sugar

65g/2¹/₂ oz/¹/₄ cup crunchy peanut butter

1 egg

50g/2oz/¹/₂ cup plain (all-purpose) flour

2.5ml/¹/₂ tsp baking powder

2.5ml/¹/₂ tsp ground cinnamon

pinch of salt

175g/6oz/1¹/₂ cups muesli (granola)

50g/2oz/¹/₃ cup raisins

50g/2oz/¹/₂ cup chopped walnuts

1 Preheat the oven to 180°C/350°F/
Gas 4. Grease a baking sheet.

2 With an electric mixer, cream the
butter or margarine and sugar until
light and fluffy. Beat in the peanut
butter. Beat in the egg.

3 ▲ Sift the flour, baking powder,
cinnamon and salt over the peanut
butter mixture and stir to blend. Stir
in the muesli, raisins and walnuts.
Taste the mixture to see if it needs
more sugar, as muesli varies.

4 ▲ Drop rounded tablespoonfuls of
the mixture on to the prepared baking
sheet about 2.5cm/1in apart. Press
gently with the back of a spoon to
spread each mound into a circle.

5 Bake until lightly coloured, about
15 minutes. With a metal spatula,
transfer to a rack to cool. Store in
an airtight container.

Crunchy Oatmeal Cookies

Makes 14

175g/6oz/³/₄ cup butter or margarine,
  at room temperature

175g/6oz/scant 1 cup caster
  (superfine) sugar

1 egg yolk

175g/6oz/1¹/₂ cups plain (all-purpose) flour

5ml/1 tsp bicarbonate of soda
  (baking soda)

2.5ml/¹/₂ tsp salt

50g/2oz/¹/₂ cup rolled oats

50g/2oz/¹/₂ cup small crunchy
  nugget cereal

~ VARIATION ~

For Nutty Oatmeal Cookies,
substitute an equal quantity of
chopped walnuts or pecan nuts for
the cereal, and prepare as described.

1 ▲ With an electric mixer, cream
the butter or margarine and sugar
together until light and fluffy. Mix in
the egg yolk.

2 Sift over the flour, bicarbonate of
soda and salt, then stir into the butter
mixture. Add the oats and cereal
and stir to blend. Chill for at least
20 minutes. Meanwhile, preheat the
oven to 190°C/375°F/Gas 5. Grease a
baking sheet.

3 ▼ Roll the mixture into balls.
Place them on the sheet and flatten
with the bottom of a floured glass.

4 Bake until golden, 10–12 minutes.
With a metal spatula, transfer to a
rack to cool completely. Store in an
airtight container.

Farmhouse Cookies (top), Crunchy Oatmeal Cookies

Oaty Coconut Cookies

Makes 48

175g/6oz/1¾ cups quick-cooking oats

75g/3oz/1 cup desiccated (dry unsweetened) coconut

225g/8oz/1 cup butter or margarine, at room temperature

115g/4oz/generous ½ cup caster (superfine) sugar, plus 30ml/2 tbsp

50g/2oz/¼ cup soft dark brown sugar

2 eggs

60ml/4 tbsp milk

7.5ml/1½ tsp vanilla extract

115g/4oz/1 cup plain (all-purpose) flour

2.5ml/½ tsp bicarbonate of soda (baking soda)

2.5ml/½ tsp salt

5ml/1 tsp ground cinnamon

1 Preheat the oven to 200°C/400°F/ Gas 6. Lightly grease two baking sheets.

2 ▲ Spread the oats and coconut on an ungreased baking sheet. Bake until golden brown, 8–10 minutes, stirring occasionally.

3 With an electric mixer, cream the butter or margarine and both sugars until light and fluffy. Beat in the eggs, one at a time, then the milk and vanilla. Sift over the dry ingredients and fold in. Stir in the oats and coconut.

4 ▼ Drop spoonfuls of the mixture 2.5–5cm/1–2in apart on the prepared sheets and flatten with the bottom of a greased glass dipped in sugar. Bake until golden, 8–10 minutes. Transfer to a rack to cool.

Crunchy Jumbles

Makes 36

115g/4oz/½ cup butter or margarine, at room temperature

225g/8oz/generous 1 cup caster (superfine) sugar

1 egg

5ml/1 tsp vanilla extract

150g/5oz/¾ cup plain (all-purpose) flour

2.5ml/½ tsp bicarbonate of soda (baking soda)

pinch of salt

50g/2oz crisped rice cereal

175g/6oz chocolate chips

~ VARIATION ~

For even crunchier biscuits, add 50g/2oz/⅓ cup walnuts, coarsely chopped, with the cereal and chocolate chips.

1 Preheat the oven to 180°C/350°F/ Gas 4. Lightly grease two baking sheets.

2 ▲ With an electric mixer, cream the butter or margarine and sugar until light and fluffy. Beat in the egg and vanilla. Sift over the flour, bicarbonate of soda and salt and fold in carefully.

3 ▼ Add the cereal and chocolate chips. Stir to mix thoroughly.

4 Drop spoonfuls of the mixture 2.5–5cm/1–2in apart on the sheets. Bake until golden, 10–12 minutes. Transfer to a rack to cool.

Oaty Coconut Cookies (top), Crunchy Jumbles

Ginger Cookies

MAKES 36

225g/8oz/generous 1 cup caster (superfine) sugar

90g/3¹/₂oz/generous 1 cup soft light brown sugar

115g/4oz/¹/₂ cup butter, at room temperature

115g/4oz/¹/₂ cup margarine, at room temperature

1 egg

90ml/6 tbsp black treacle (molasses)

250g/9oz/2¹/₄ cups plain (all-purpose) flour

10ml/2 tsp ground ginger

2.5ml/¹/₂ tsp freshly grated nutmeg

5ml/1 tsp ground cinnamon

10ml/2 tsp bicarbonate of soda (baking soda)

2.5ml/¹/₂ tsp salt

1 Preheat the oven to 170°C/325°F/ Gas 3. Line two or three baking sheets with baking parchment; grease lightly.

2 ▲ With an electric mixer, cream half the caster sugar, the brown sugar, butter and margarine until light and fluffy. Add the egg and continue beating to blend well. Add the treacle.

3 ▲ Sift the flour, spices and bicarbonate of soda three times, then stir into the butter mixture. Refrigerate for 30 minutes.

4 ▲ Place the remaining sugar in a shallow dish. Roll tablespoonfuls of the biscuit mixture into balls, then roll the balls in the sugar to coat.

5 Place the balls 5cm/2in apart on the prepared sheets and flatten slightly. Bake until golden around the edges but soft in the middle, 12–15 minutes. Leave to stand for 5 minutes before transferring to a rack to cool.

~ VARIATION ~

To make Gingerbread Men, increase the amount of flour by 25g/1oz/ ¹/₄ cup. Roll out the mixture and cut out shapes with a special cutter. Decorate with icing, if you like.

Orange Cookies

MAKES 30

115g/4oz/¹/₂ cup butter, at room temperature

200g/7oz/1 cup caster (superfine) sugar

2 egg yolks

15ml/1 tbsp fresh orange juice

grated rind of 1 large orange

200g/7oz/scant 2 cups plain (all-purpose) flour

10g/¹/₄oz/1 tbsp cornflour (cornstarch)

2.5ml/¹/₂ tsp salt

5ml/1 tsp baking powder

1 ▲ With an electric mixer, cream the butter and sugar until light and fluffy. Add the yolks, orange juice and rind, and continue beating to blend. Set aside.

2 In another bowl, sift together the flour, cornflour, salt and baking powder. Add to the butter mixture and stir until it forms a dough.

4 Preheat the oven to 190°C/375°F/ Gas 5. Grease two baking sheets.

6 ▼ Press down with a fork to flatten. Bake until golden brown, 8–10 minutes. With a metal spatula transfer to a rack to cool.

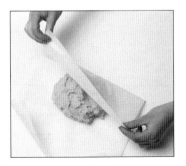

3 ▲ Wrap the dough in baking parchment and chill for 2 hours.

5 ▲ Roll spoonfuls of the dough into balls and place 2.5–5cm/1–2in apart on the prepared sheets.

Cinnamon-coated Cookies

MAKES 30

115g/4oz/¹/₂ cup butter, at
  room temperature

350g/12oz/1³/₄ cups caster
  (superfine) sugar

5ml/1 tsp vanilla extract

2 eggs

50ml/2fl oz/¹/₄ cup milk

400g/14oz/3¹/₂ cups plain (all-purpose) flour

5ml/1 tsp bicarbonate of soda
  (baking soda)

50g/2oz/¹/₂ cup finely chopped walnuts

FOR THE COATING

65g/2¹/₂oz/5 tbsp sugar

30ml/2 tbsp ground cinnamon

1 Preheat the oven to 190°C/375°F/
Gas 5. Grease two baking sheets.

2 With an electric mixer, cream the
butter until light. Add the sugar and
vanilla and continue mixing until
fluffy. Beat in the eggs, then the milk.

3 ▲ Sift the flour and bicarbonate of
soda over the butter mixture and stir
to blend. Stir in the nuts. Refrigerate
for 15 minutes.

4 ▲ For the coating, mix the sugar
and cinnamon. Roll tablespoonfuls of
the mixture into walnut-size balls.
Roll the balls in the sugar mixture.
You may need to work in batches.

5 Place 5cm/2in apart on the
prepared sheets and flatten slightly.
Bake until golden, about 10 minutes.
Transfer to a rack to cool.

Chewy Chocolate Cookies

MAKES 18

4 egg whites

275g/10oz/scant 2¹/₂ cups icing
  (confectioners') sugar

115g/4oz/1 cup unsweetened cocoa powder

30ml/2 tbsp plain (all-purpose) flour

5ml/1 tsp instant coffee

15ml/1 tbsp water

115g/4oz/¹/₂ cup finely chopped walnuts

1 Preheat the oven to 180°C/350°F/
Gas 4. Line two baking sheets with
baking parchment and grease the paper.

~ VARIATION ~

If wished, add 75g/3oz chocolate
chips to the mixture with the nuts.

2 With an electric mixer, beat the
egg whites until frothy.

3 ▼ Sift the sugar, cocoa, flour and
coffee into the whites. Add the water
and continue beating on low speed to
blend, then on high for a few minutes
until the mixture thickens. With a
rubber spatula, fold in the walnuts.

4 ▲ Place generous spoonfuls of the
mixture 2.5cm/1in apart on the
prepared sheets. Bake until firm and
cracked on top but soft on the inside,
12–15 minutes. With a metal spatula,
transfer to a rack to cool.

Cinnamon-coated Cookies (top), Chewy Chocolate Cookies

Chocolate Pretzels

MAKES 28

150g/5oz/1¼ cups plain
(all-purpose) flour

pinch of salt

25g/³/₄oz/1 tbsp unsweetened cocoa powder

115g/4oz/½ cup butter, at
room temperature

130g/4½oz/scant ¾ cup caster
(superfine) sugar

1 egg

1 egg white, lightly beaten, for glazing

sugar crystals, for sprinkling

1 Sift together the flour, salt and cocoa powder. Set aside. Grease two baking sheets.

2 ▲ With an electric mixer, cream the butter until light. Add the sugar and continue beating until light and fluffy. Beat in the egg. Add the dry ingredients and stir to blend. Gather the dough into a ball, wrap in clear film (plastic wrap), and chill for 1 hour or freeze for 30 minutes.

3 ▲ Roll the dough into 28 small balls. Chill the balls until needed. Preheat the oven to 190°C/375°F/ Gas 5.

4 ▲ Roll each ball into a rope about 25cm/10in long. With each rope, form a loop with the two ends facing you. Twist the ends and fold back on to the circle, pressing in to make a pretzel shape. Place on the sheets.

5 ▲ Brush the pretzels with the egg white. Sprinkle sugar crystals over the tops and bake until firm, 10–12 minutes. Transfer to a rack to cool.

Cream Cheese Spirals

MAKES 32

225g/8oz/1 cup butter, at
  room temperature

225g/8oz/1 cup cream cheese

10ml/2 tsp caster (superfine) sugar

225g/8oz/2 cups plain (all-purpose) flour

1 egg white beaten with 15ml/1 tbsp
  water, for glazing

caster sugar, for sprinkling

FOR THE FILLING

115g/4oz/1 cup finely chopped walnuts

115g/4oz/¹/2 cup soft light brown sugar

5ml/1 tsp ground cinnamon

1 With an electric mixer, cream the butter, cream cheese and sugar until soft. Sift over the flour and mix until combined. Gather into a ball and divide in half. Flatten each half, wrap in baking parchment and chill for at least 30 minutes.

2 Meanwhile, make the filling. Mix together the chopped walnuts, the brown sugar and the cinnamon, and set aside.

3 Preheat the oven to 190°C/375°F/Gas 5. Grease two baking sheets.

4 ▲ Working with one half of the mixture at a time, roll out thinly into a circle about 28cm/11in in diameter. Trim the edges with a knife, using a dinner plate as a guide.

5 ▼ Brush the surface with the egg white glaze and then sprinkle evenly with half the filling.

6 Cut the circle into quarters, and each quarter into four sections, to form 16 triangles.

7 ▲ Starting from the base of the triangles, roll up to form spirals.

8 Place on the sheets and brush with the remaining glaze. Sprinkle with caster sugar. Bake until golden, 15–20 minutes. Cool on a rack.

Vanilla Crescents

MAKES 36

175g/6oz/1 cup unblanched almonds

115g/4oz/1 cup plain (all-purpose) flour

pinch of salt

225g/8oz/1 cup unsalted (sweet) butter

115g/4oz/generous 1/2 cup granulated sugar

5ml/1 tsp vanilla extract

icing (confectioners') sugar, for dusting

1 Grind the almonds with a few tablespoons of the flour in a food processor, blender or nut grinder.

2 Sift the remaining flour with the salt into a bowl. Set aside.

3 With an electric mixer, cream together the butter and sugar until light and fluffy.

4 ▼ Add the almonds, vanilla essence and the flour mixture. Stir to mix well. Gather the dough into a ball, wrap in baking parchment, and chill for at least 30 minutes.

5 Preheat the oven to 160°C/325°F/ Gas 3. Lightly grease two baking sheets.

6 ▲ Break off walnut-size pieces of dough and roll into small cylinders about 1cm/1/2in in diameter. Bend into small crescents and place on the prepared baking sheets.

7 Bake for about 20 minutes until dry but not brown. Transfer to a wire rack to cool only slightly. Set the rack over a baking sheet and dust with an even layer of icing sugar. Leave to cool completely.

Walnut Crescents

MAKES 9

115g/4oz/2/3 cup walnuts

225g/8oz/1 cup unsalted (sweet) butter

115g/4oz/generous 1/2 cup granulated sugar

2.5ml/1/2 tsp vanilla extract

225g/8oz/2 cups plain (all-purpose) flour

1.5ml/1/4 tsp salt

icing (confectioners') sugar, for dusting

1 Preheat the oven to 180°C/350°F/ Gas 4.

2 Grind the walnuts in a food processor, blender or nut grinder until they are almost a paste. Transfer to a bowl.

3 Add the butter to the walnuts and mix with a wooden spoon until blended. Add the granulated sugar and vanilla, and stir to blend.

4 ▼ Sift the flour and salt into the walnut mixture. Work into a dough.

5 Shape the dough into small cylinders about 4cm/11/2in long. Bend into crescents and place evenly spaced on an ungreased baking sheet.

6 ▲ Bake until lightly browned, about 15 minutes. Transfer to a rack to cool only slightly. Set the rack over a baking sheet and dust lightly with icing sugar.

Vanilla Crescents (top), Walnut Crescents

Pecan Puffs

MAKES 24

115g/4oz/¹/₂ cup unsalted (sweet) butter

25g/1oz/2 tbsp granulated sugar

pinch of salt

5ml/1 tsp vanilla extract

115g/4oz/²/₃ cup pecan nuts

115g/4oz/1 cup plain (all-purpose)
  flour, sifted

icing (confectioners') sugar, for dusting

1 Preheat the oven to 150°C/300°F/
Gas 2. Grease two baking sheets.

2 ▲ Cream the butter and sugar
until light and fluffy. Stir in the salt
and vanilla extract.

3 Grind the nuts in a food processor,
blender or nut grinder. Stir several
times to prevent them becoming oily.
If necessary, grind in batches.

4 ▲ Push the ground nuts through a
sieve (strainer) set over a bowl to aerate
them. Pieces too large to go through
the sieve can be ground again.

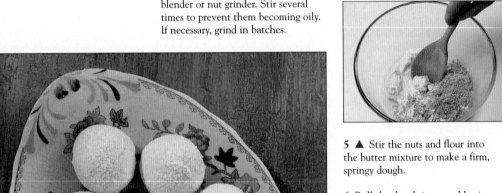

5 ▲ Stir the nuts and flour into
the butter mixture to make a firm,
springy dough.

6 Roll the dough into marble-size
balls between the palms of your
hands. Place on the prepared baking
sheets and bake for 30 minutes.

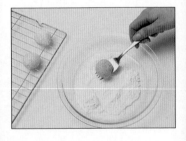

7 ▲ While the puffs are still hot,
roll them in icing sugar. Leave to cool
completely, then roll once more in
icing sugar.

Pecan Tassies

MAKES 24

115g/4oz/1/2 cup cream cheese
115g/4oz/1/2 cup butter
115g/4oz/1 cup plain (all-purpose) flour
FOR THE FILLING
2 eggs
115g/4oz/1/2 cup soft dark brown sugar
5ml/1 tsp vanilla extract
pinch of salt
25g/1oz/2 tbsp butter, melted
115g/4oz/2/3 cup pecan nuts

1 Place a baking sheet in the oven and preheat to 180°C/350°F/Gas 4. Grease 24 mini-muffin tins.

2 Chop the cream cheese and butter into cubes. Put them in a mixing bowl. Sift over half the flour and mix. Add the remaining flour and continue mixing to form a dough.

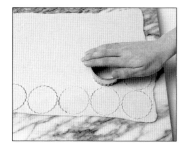

3 ▲ Roll out the dough thinly. With a floured, fluted pastry cutter, stamp out 24 6cm/2½in rounds. Line the tins with the rounds and chill.

~ VARIATION ~

To make Jam Tassies, fill the cream cheese pastry shells with raspberry or blackberry jam, or other fruit jams. Bake as described.

4 To make the filling, lightly whisk the eggs in a bowl. Gradually whisk in the brown sugar, and add the vanilla extract, salt and butter. Set aside until required.

5 ▼ Reserve 24 undamaged pecan halves and chop the rest coarsely with a sharp knife.

6 ▲ Place a spoonful of chopped nuts in each muffin tin and cover with the filling. Set a pecan half on the top of each.

7 Bake on the hot baking sheet for about 20 minutes, until puffed and set. Transfer to a wire rack to cool. Serve at room temperature.

Lady Fingers

MAKES 18

90g/3¹/₂oz/³/₄ cup plain (all-purpose) flour

pinch of salt

4 eggs, separated

115g/4oz/generous ¹/₂ cup granulated sugar

2.5ml/¹/₂ tsp vanilla extract

icing (confectioners') sugar, for sprinkling

1 Preheat the oven to 150°C/300°F/
Gas 2. Grease two baking sheets, then
coat lightly with flour, and shake off
the excess.

2 Sift the flour and salt together
twice in a bowl.

~ COOK'S TIP ~

To make the biscuits all the
same length, mark parallel lines
10cm/4in apart on the
greased baking sheets.

3 With an electric mixer beat the
egg yolks with half the sugar until
thick enough to leave a ribbon trail
when the beaters are lifted.

4 ▲ In another bowl, beat the egg
whites until stiff. Beat in the
remaining sugar until glossy.

5 Sift the flour over the yolks and
spoon a large dollop of egg whites
over the flour. Carefully fold in with
a large metal spoon, adding the
vanilla extract. Gently fold in the
remaining whites.

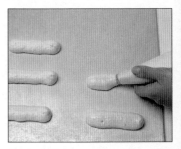

6 ▲ Spoon the mixture into a piping
(pastry) bag fitted with a large plain
nozzle. Pipe 10cm/4in long lines on
the prepared baking sheets about
2.5cm/1in apart. Sift over a layer of
icing sugar. Turn the sheet upside
down to dislodge any excess sugar.

7 Bake for about 20 minutes until
crusty on the outside but soft in the
centre. Cool slightly on the baking
sheets before transferring to a wire
rack to cool completely.

Walnut Cookies

MAKES 60

115g/4oz/¹/₂ cup butter or margarine

175g/6oz/scant 1 cup caster
(superfine) sugar

115g/4oz/1 cup plain (all-purpose) flour

10ml/2 tsp vanilla extract

115g/4oz/²/₃ cup walnuts, finely chopped

~ VARIATION ~

To make Almond Cookies,
use an equal amount of finely
chopped unblanched almonds
instead of walnuts. Replace
half the vanilla with 2.5ml/
¹/₂ tsp almond essence.

1 Preheat the oven to 150°C/300°F/
Gas 2. Grease two baking sheets.

2 ▲ With an electric mixer, cream
the butter or margarine until soft. Add
50g/2oz/¹/₄ cup of the sugar and continue
beating until light and fluffy. Stir in
the flour, vanilla extract and walnuts.

3 Drop teaspoonfuls of the batter
2.5–5cm/1–2in apart on the prepared
baking sheets and flatten slightly.
Bake for about 25 minutes.

4 ▼ Transfer to a wire rack set over
a baking sheet and sprinkle with the
remaining sugar.

Lady Fingers (top), Walnut Cookies

Italian Almond Biscotti

MAKES 48

200g/7oz/generous 1 cup whole unblanched almonds

215g/7¹/₂oz/scant 2 cups plain (all-purpose) flour

90g/3¹/₂oz/¹/₂ cup caster (superfine) sugar

pinch of salt

pinch of saffron threads

2.5ml/¹/₂ tsp bicarbonate of soda (baking soda)

2 eggs

1 egg white, lightly beaten

~ COOK'S TIP ~

Dunk biscotti in sweet white wine, such as an Italian Vin Santo or a French Muscat de Beaumes-de-Venise.

1 Preheat the oven to 190°C/375°F/ Gas 5. Grease and flour two baking sheets.

2 ▲ Spread the almonds in a baking tray and bake until lightly browned, about 15 minutes. When cool, grind 50g/2oz/¹/₃ cup of the almonds in a food processor, blender, or coffee grinder until pulverized. Coarsely chop the remaining almonds into two or three pieces each. Set aside.

3 ▲ Combine the flour, sugar, salt, saffron, bicarbonate of soda and ground almonds in a bowl and mix to blend. Make a well in the centre and add the eggs. Stir to form a rough dough. Transfer to a floured surface and knead until well blended. Knead in the chopped almonds.

4 ▲ Divide the dough into three equal parts. Roll into logs about 2.5cm/1in in diameter. Place on one of the prepared sheets, brush with the egg white and bake for 20 minutes. Remove from the oven.

5 ▲ With a very sharp knife, cut into each log at an angle making 1cm/ ¹/₂in slices. Return the slices on the baking sheets to a 140°C/275°F/Gas 1 oven and bake for 25 minutes more. Transfer to a rack to cool.

Christmas Cookies

MAKES 30

175g/6oz/³/₄ cup unsalted (sweet) butter, at room temperature

275g/10oz/scant 1¹/₂ cups caster (superfine) sugar

1 egg

1 egg yolk

5ml/1 tsp vanilla extract

grated rind of 1 lemon

1.5ml/¹/₄ tsp salt

275g/10oz/2¹/₂ cups plain (all-purpose) flour

FOR DECORATING (OPTIONAL)

coloured icing and small decorations

1 Preheat oven to 350°F/180°C/Gas 4.

2 ▲ With an electric mixer, cream the butter until soft. Add the sugar gradually and continue beating until light and fluffy.

3 ▲ Using a wooden spoon, slowly mix in the whole egg and the egg yolk. Add the vanilla, lemon rind and salt. Stir to mix well.

4 Add the flour and stir until blended. Gather the mixture into a ball, wrap in baking parchment, and chill for at least 30 minutes.

5 ▼ On a floured surface, roll out the mixture to 3mm/¹/₈in thick.

6 ▲ Stamp out shapes or rounds with biscuit (cookie) cutters.

7 Bake until lightly coloured, about 8 minutes. Transfer to a rack and leave to cool completely before icing and decorating, if wished.

Toasted Oat Meringues

MAKES 12

50g/2oz/¹/₂ cup rolled oats
2 egg whites
pinch of salt
7.5ml/1¹/₂ tsp cornflour (cornstarch)
175g/6oz/scant 1 cup caster (superfine) sugar

1 Preheat the oven to 140°C/275°F/ Gas 1. Spread the oats on a baking sheet and toast in the oven until golden, about 10 minutes. Lower the heat to 120°C/250°F/Gas ¹/₂. Grease and flour a baking sheet.

~ **VARIATION** ~

Add 2.5ml/¹/₂ tsp ground cinnamon with the oats, and fold in gently.

2 ▼ With an electric mixer, beat the egg whites and salt until they start to form soft peaks.

3 Sift over the cornflour and continue beating until the whites hold stiff peaks. Add half the sugar and whisk until glossy.

4 ▲ Add the remaining sugar and fold in, then fold in the oats.

5 Gently spoon the mixture on to the prepared sheet and bake for 2 hours.

6 When done, turn off the oven. Lift the meringues from the sheet, turn over, and set in another place on the sheet to prevent sticking. Leave in the oven as they cool down.

Meringues

MAKES 24

4 egg whites
pinch of salt
275g/10oz/scant 1¹/₂ cups caster (superfine) sugar
2.5ml/¹/₂ tsp vanilla or almond extract (optional)
250ml/8fl oz/1 cup whipped cream (optional)

1 Preheat the oven to 110°C/225°F/ Gas ¹/₄. Grease and flour two large baking sheets.

2 With an electric mixer, beat the egg whites and salt in a very clean metal bowl on low speed. When they start to form soft peaks, add half the sugar and continue beating until the mixture holds stiff peaks.

3 ▲ With a large metal spoon, fold in the remaining sugar and vanilla or almond extract, if using.

4 ▼ Pipe the meringue mixture or spoon it on to the prepared sheet.

5 Bake for 2 hours. Turn off the oven. Loosen the meringues, invert, and set in another place on the sheets to prevent sticking. Leave in the oven as they cool. Serve sandwiched with whipped cream, if you wish.

Toasted Oat Meringues (top), Meringues

Chocolate Macaroons

MAKES 24

50g/2oz plain (semisweet) chocolate
175g/6oz/1 cup blanched almonds
225g/8oz/generous 1 cup caster (superfine) sugar
3 egg whites
2.5ml/¹/₂ tsp vanilla extract
1.5ml/¹/₄ tsp almond extract
icing (confectioners') sugar, for dusting

1 Preheat the oven to 300°F/150°C/ Gas 2. Line two baking sheets with baking parchment and grease the paper.

2 ▼ Melt the chocolate in the top of a double boiler, or in a heatproof bowl set over a pan of hot water.

3 ▲ Grind the almonds finely in a food processor, blender or grinder. Transfer to a mixing bowl.

4 ▲ In a mixing bowl, whisk the egg whites until they form soft peaks. Fold in the sugar, vanilla and almond extracts, ground almonds and cooled melted chocolate Chill for 15 minutes.

5 ▲ Use a teaspoon and your hands to shape the mixture into walnut-size balls. Place on the sheets and flatten slightly. Brush each ball with a little water and sift over a thin layer of icing sugar. Bake until just firm, 20–25 minutes. With a metal spatula, transfer to a rack to cool.

> **~ VARIATION ~**
>
> For Chocolate Pine Nut Macaroons, spread 75g/3oz/³/₄ cup pine nuts in a shallow dish. Press the chocolate macaroon balls into the nuts to cover one side and bake as described, nut-side up.

Coconut Macaroons

MAKES 24

40g/1¹/₂oz/¹/₃ cup plain (all-purpose) flour
pinch of salt
225g/8oz/scant 3 cups desiccated (dry unsweetened) coconut
175ml/6fl oz/³/₄ cup sweetened condensed milk
5ml/1 tsp vanilla extract

1 Preheat the oven to 180°C/350°F/ Gas 4. Grease two baking sheets.

2 Sift the flour and salt into a bowl. Stir in the coconut.

3 ▲ Pour in the milk. Add the vanilla and stir from the centre to make a very thick mixture.

4 Drop heaped tablespoonfuls of mixture 2.5cm/1in apart on the sheets. Bake until golden brown, about 20 minutes. Cool on a rack.

Chocolate Macaroons (top), Coconut Macaroons

Almond Tuiles

MAKES 40

50g/2oz/¹/₃ cup blanched almonds

115g/4oz/generous ¹/₂ cup caster (superfine) sugar

50g/2oz/¹/₄ cup unsalted (sweet) butter

2 egg whites

40g/1¹/₂oz/¹/₃ cup plain (all-purpose) flour

2.5ml/¹/₂ tsp vanilla extract

115g/4oz/1 cup flaked (sliced) almonds

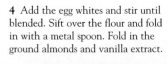

1 Grind the blanched almonds with 30ml/2 tbsp of the sugar in a food processor, blender or nut grinder. If necessary, grind in batches.

2 Preheat the oven to 220°C/425°F/ Gas 7. Grease two baking sheets.

3 ▲ Put the butter in a large bowl and mix in the remaining sugar, using a metal spoon. With an electric mixer, cream them together until light and fluffy.

4 Add the egg whites and stir until blended. Sift over the flour and fold in with a metal spoon. Fold in the ground almonds and vanilla extract.

5 ▲ Working in small batches, drop tablespoonfuls of the mixture 7.5cm/3in apart on one of the prepared sheets. With the back of a spoon, spread out into thin, almost transparent circles about 6cm/2¹/₂in in diameter. Sprinkle each circle with some of the flaked almonds.

6 Bake until the outer edges have browned slightly, about 4 minutes.

7 ▲ Remove from the oven. With a metal spatula, quickly drape the biscuits over a rolling pin to form a curved shape. Transfer to a rack when firm. If the biscuits harden too quickly to shape, reheat them briefly. Repeat the baking and shaping process until the mixture is used up. Store in an airtight container.

Florentines

MAKES 36

40g/1½oz/3 tbsp butter
120ml/4fl oz/½ cup whipping cream
130g/4½oz/scant ¾ cup caster (superfine) sugar
130g/4½oz/generous 1 cup flaked (sliced) almonds
50g/2oz/⅓ cup orange or mixed (candied) peel, finely chopped
40g/1½oz/¼ cup glacé (candied) cherries, chopped
65g/2½oz/9 tbsp plain (all-purpose) flour, sifted
225g/8oz plain (semisweet) chocolate
5ml/1 tsp vegetable oil

1 ▲ Preheat the oven to 180°C/ 350°F/Gas 4. Grease two baking sheets. Melt the butter, cream and sugar together and slowly bring to the boil. Take off the heat and stir in the almonds, orange or mixed peel, cherries and flour until blended.

2 Drop teaspoonfuls of the batter 2.5–5cm/1–2in apart on the prepared sheets and flatten with a fork.

3 Bake for about 10 minutes until brown at the edges. Remove from the oven and correct the shape whilst they are hot by quickly pushing in any uneven edges with a knife or a round biscuit (cookie) cutter. If necessary, return to the oven for a few moments to soften. While still hot, use a metal spatula to transfer the florentines to a clean, flat surface.

4 Melt the chocolate in the top of a double boiler or in a heatproof bowl set over a pan of hot water. Add the oil and stir to blend.

5 ▲ With a palette knife (metal spatula), spread the smooth underside of the cooled florentines with a thin coating of the melted chocolate.

6 ▼ When the chocolate is about to set, draw a serrated knife across the surface with a slight sawing motion to make wavy lines. Store in an airtight container in a cool place.

Nut Lace Wafers

MAKES 18

65g/2¹/₂oz/¹/₂ cup whole blanched almonds

50g/2oz/¹/₄ cup butter

40g/1¹/₂oz/¹/₃ cup plain (all-purpose) flour

90g/3¹/₂oz/¹/₂ cup caster (superfine) sugar

30ml/2 tbsp double (heavy) cream

2.5ml/¹/₂ tsp vanilla extract

1 Preheat the oven to 190°C/375°F/ Gas 5. Grease one or two baking sheets.

2 With a sharp knife, chop the almonds as finely as possible. Alternatively, use a food processor, blender, or coffee grinder to chop the nuts very finely.

3 ▼ Melt the butter in a pan over low heat. Remove from the heat and stir in the remaining ingredients and the almonds.

4 Drop teaspoonfuls 6cm/2¹/₂in apart on the prepared sheets. Bake until golden, about 5 minutes. Cool on the baking sheets briefly, just until the wafers are stiff enough to remove.

5 ▲ With a palette knife (metal spatula), transfer to a rack to cool completely.

~ VARIATION ~

Add 50g/2oz finely chopped orange peel to the mixture.

Oatmeal Lace Rounds

MAKES 36

165g/5¹/₂oz/11 tbsp butter or margarine

130g/4¹/₂oz/1¹/₄ cups quick-cooking rolled oats

175g/6oz/scant 1 cup soft dark brown sugar

150g/5oz/³/₄ cup caster (superfine) sugar

40g/1¹/₂oz/¹/₃ cup plain (all-purpose) flour

1.5ml/¹/₄ tsp salt

1 egg, lightly beaten

5ml/1 tsp vanilla extract

65g/2¹/₂oz/¹/₂ cup pecan nuts or walnuts, finely chopped

1 Preheat the oven to 180°C/350°F/ Gas 4. Grease two baking sheets.

2 Melt the butter in a pan over low heat. Set aside.

3 In a mixing bowl, combine the oats, brown sugar, caster sugar, flour and salt.

4 ▲ Make a well in the centre and add the butter or margarine, egg and vanilla.

5 ▼ Mix until blended, then stir in the chopped nuts.

6 Drop rounded teaspoonfuls of the mixture about 5cm/2in apart on the prepared sheets. Bake until lightly browned on the edges and bubbling, 5–8 minutes. Leave to cool on the sheet for 2 minutes, then transfer to a rack to cool completely.

Nut Lace Wafers (top), Oatmeal Lace Rounds

Raspberry Sandwich Cookies

MAKES 32

175g/6oz/1 cup blanched almonds
175g/6oz/1½ cups plain (all-purpose) flour
175g/6oz/¾ cup butter, at room temperature
115g/4oz/generous ½ cup caster (superfine) sugar
grated rind of 1 lemon
5ml/1 tsp vanilla extract
1 egg white
pinch of salt
25g/1oz/¼ cup flaked (sliced) almonds
250ml/8fl oz/1 cup raspberry jam
15ml/1 tbsp fresh lemon juice

1 Place the blanched almonds and 20g/¾oz/3 tbsp of the flour in a food processor, blender or coffee grinder and process until finely ground. Set aside.

2 With an electric mixer, cream the butter and sugar together until light and fluffy. Stir in the lemon rind and vanilla. Add the ground almonds and remaining flour, and mix well until combined. Gather into a ball, wrap in baking parchment, and chill for at least 1 hour.

3 Preheat the oven to 160°C/325°F/ Gas 3. Line two baking sheets with baking parchment.

4 Divide the cookie mixture into four equal parts. Working with one section at a time, roll out to a thickness of 3mm/⅛in on a lightly floured surface. With a 6cm/2½in fluted pastry (cookie) cutter, stamp out circles. Gather the scraps, roll out and stamp out more circles. Repeat with the remaining sections.

5 ▲ Using a 2cm/¾in piping nozzle or pastry cutter, stamp out the centres from half the circles. Place the rings and circles 2.5cm/1in apart on the prepared sheets.

6 ▲ Whisk the egg white with the salt until just frothy. Chop the flaked almonds. Brush only the biscuit rings with the egg white, then sprinkle over the almonds. Bake until very lightly browned, 12–15 minutes. Let cool for a few minutes on the sheets before transferring to a rack.

7 ▲ In a pan, melt the jam with the lemon juice until it comes to a simmer. Brush the jam over the biscuit circles and sandwich together with the rings. Store in an airtight container with sheets of baking parchment between the layers.

Brandysnaps

MAKES 18

50g/2oz/¹/₄ cup butter, at room temperature

150g/5oz/³/₄ cup caster (superfine) sugar

15ml/1 tbsp golden (light corn) syrup

40g/1¹/₂oz/¹/₃ cup plain (all-purpose) flour

2.5ml/¹/₂ tsp ground ginger

FOR THE FILLING

250ml/8fl oz/1 cup whipping cream

30ml/2 tbsp brandy

1 With an electric mixer, cream together the butter and sugar until light and fluffy, then beat in the golden syrup. Sift over the flour and ginger and mix together.

2 ▲ Transfer the mixture to a work surface and knead until smooth. Cover and chill for 30 minutes.

3 Preheat the oven to 190°C/375°F/ Gas 5. Grease a baking sheet.

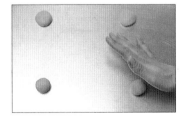

4 ▲ Working in batches of four, form the mixture into walnut-size balls. Place far apart on the sheet and flatten slightly. Bake until golden and bubbling, about 10 minutes.

5 ▼ Remove from the oven and let cool a few moments. Working quickly, slide a metal spatula under each one, turn over, and wrap around the handle of a wooden spoon (have four spoons ready). If they firm up too quickly, reheat for a few seconds to soften. When firm, slide the snaps off and place on a rack to cool.

6 ▲ When all the brandy snaps are cool, prepare the filling. Whip the cream and brandy until soft peaks form. Fill a piping (pastry) bag with the brandy cream. Pipe into each end of the brandy snaps just before serving.

Shortbread

MAKES 8

165g/5¹/₂oz/11 tbsp unsalted (sweet) butter, at room temperature

90g/3¹/₂oz/¹/₂ cup caster (superfine) sugar

185g/6¹/₂oz/1²/₃ cups plain (all-purpose) flour

50g/2oz/¹/₂ cup rice flour

1.5ml/¹/₄ tsp baking powder

pinch of salt

1 Preheat the oven to 170°C/325°F/Gas 3. Grease a shallow 20cm/8in cake tin (pan), preferably with a removable base.

2 With an electric mixer, cream the butter and sugar together until light and fluffy. Sift over the flours, baking powder and salt, and mix well.

3 ▲ Press the dough neatly into the prepared tin, smoothing the surface with the back of a spoon.

4 Prick all over with a fork, then score into eight equal wedges.

5 ▲ Bake until golden, 40–45 minutes. Leave in the tin until cool enough to handle, then turn out and recut the wedges while still hot. Store in an airtight container.

Flapjacks

MAKES 8

50g/2oz/¹/₄ cup butter

15ml/1 tbsp golden (light corn) syrup

75g/3oz/¹/₃ cup soft dark brown sugar

90g/3¹/₂oz/1 cup quick-cooking rolled oats

pinch of salt

1 ▲ Preheat the oven to 180°C/350°F/Gas 4. Line a 20cm/8in cake tin with baking parchment and grease.

2 ▼ Place the butter, golden syrup and sugar in a pan over a low heat. Cook, stirring, until melted and combined.

~ VARIATION ~

If you like, add 5ml/1 tsp ground ginger to the melted butter.

3 ▲ Remove from the heat and add the oats and salt. Stir to blend.

4 Spoon into the prepared tin and smooth the surface. Place in the centre of the oven and bake until golden brown, 20–25 minutes. Leave in the tin until cool enough to handle, then turn out and cut into wedges while still hot.

Shortbread (top), Flapjacks

Chocolate Delights

MAKES 50

25g/1oz plain (semisweet) chocolate

25g/1oz dark (bittersweet)
  cooking chocolate

225g/8oz/2 cups plain (all-purpose) flour

2.5ml/½ tsp salt

225g/8oz/1cup unsalted (sweet) butter,
  at room temperature

225g/8oz/generous 1 cup caster
  (superfine) sugar

2 eggs

5ml/1 tsp vanilla extract

115g/4oz/1 cup finely chopped walnuts

1 Melt the chocolates in the top of a
double boiler, or in a heatproof bowl
set over a pan of gently simmering
water. Set aside.

2 ▼ In a small bowl, sift together the
flour and salt. Set aside.

3 With an electric mixer, cream the
butter until soft. Add the sugar and
continue beating until the mixture is
light and fluffy.

4 Mix the eggs and vanilla, then
gradually stir into the butter mixture.

5 ▲ Stir in the chocolate, then the
flour. Stir in the nuts.

6 ▲ Divide the mixture into four
equal parts, and roll each into 5cm/
2in diameter logs. Wrap tightly in foil
and refrigerate or freeze until firm.

7 Preheat the oven to 190°C/375°F/
Gas 5. Grease two baking sheets.

8 With a sharp knife, cut the logs
into 5mm/¼in slices. Place the rounds
on the prepared sheets and bake until
lightly coloured, about 10 minutes.
Transfer to a rack to cool.

~ VARIATION ~

For two-tone biscuits, melt only
half the chocolate. Combine all
the ingredients, except the
chocolate, as above. Divide the
mixture in half. Add the chocolate
to one half. Roll out the plain
mixture on to a flat sheet. Roll out
the chocolate mixture, place on
top of the plain one and roll up.
Wrap, slice and bake as described.

Cinnamon Treats

MAKES 50

250g/9oz/2¼ cups plain (all-purpose) flour

2.5ml/½ tsp salt

10ml/2 tsp ground cinnamon

225g/8oz/1 cup unsalted (sweet) butter, at room temperature

225g/8oz/generous 1 cup caster (superfine) sugar

2 eggs

5ml/1 tsp vanilla extract

1 In a bowl, sift together the flour, salt and cinnamon. Set aside.

2 ▲ With an electric mixer, cream the butter until soft. Add the sugar and continue beating until the mixture is light and fluffy.

3 Beat the eggs and vanilla, then gradually stir into the butter mixture.

4 ▲ Stir in the dry ingredients.

5 ▲ Divide the mixture into four equal parts, then roll each into 5cm/2in diameter logs. Wrap tightly in foil and chill or freeze until firm.

6 Preheat the oven to 190°C/375°F/ Gas 5. Grease two baking sheets.

7 ▼ With a sharp knife, cut the logs into 5mm/¼in slices. Place the rounds on the prepared sheets and bake until lightly coloured, about 10 minutes. With a metal spatula, transfer to a rack to cool.

Peanut Butter Cookies

MAKES 24

150g/5oz/1¼ cups plain (all-purpose) flour

2.5ml/½ tsp bicarbonate of soda (baking soda)

2.5ml/½ tsp salt

115g/4oz/½ cup butter, at room temperature

165g/5½oz/¾ cup soft light brown sugar

1 egg

5ml/1 tsp vanilla extract

265g/9½oz/1¼ cups crunchy peanut butter

1 Sift together the flour, bicarbonate of soda and salt, and set aside.

2 With an electric mixer, cream the butter and sugar together until light and fluffy.

3 In another bowl, mix together the egg and vanilla, then gradually beat into the butter mixture.

4 ▲ Stir in the peanut butter and blend thoroughly. Stir in the dry ingredients. Chill for at least 30 minutes, or until firm.

5 Preheat the oven to 180°C/350°F/ Gas 4. Grease two baking sheets.

6 Spoon out rounded teaspoonfuls of the dough and roll into balls.

7 ▲ Place the balls on the prepared sheets and press flat with a fork into circles about 6cm/2½in in diameter, making a criss-cross pattern. Bake until lightly coloured, 12–15 minutes. Transfer to a rack to cool.

> ~ VARIATION ~
>
> Add 75g/3oz/½ cup peanuts, coarsely chopped, with the peanut butter.

Chocolate Chip Cookies

MAKES 24

115g/4oz/½ cup butter or margarine, at room temperature

50g/2oz/¼ cup caster (superfine) sugar

90g/3½oz/scant ½ cup soft dark brown sugar

1 egg

2.5ml/½ tsp vanilla extract

175g/6oz/1½ cups plain (all-purpose) flour

2.5ml/½ tsp bicarbonate of soda (baking soda)

pinch of salt

175g/6oz chocolate chips

50g/2oz/⅓ cup walnuts, chopped

1 Preheat the oven to 180°C/350°F/ Gas 4. Grease two large baking sheets.

2 ▼ With an electric mixer, cream the butter or margarine and two sugars together until light and fluffy.

3 In another bowl, mix the egg and vanilla, then gradually beat into the butter mixture. Sift over the flour, bicarbonate of soda and salt, and stir.

4 ▲ Add the chocolate chips and walnuts, and mix to combine well.

5 Place heaped teaspoonfuls of the dough 5cm/2in apart on the prepared sheets. Bake until lightly coloured, 10–15 minutes. Transfer to a rack to cool.

Peanut Butter Cookies (top), Chocolate Chip Cookies

Salted Peanut Cookies

MAKES 70

350g/12oz/3 cups plain (all-purpose) flour

2.5ml/¹/₂ tsp bicarbonate of soda (baking soda)

115g/4oz/¹/₂ cup butter

115g/4oz/¹/₂ cup margarine

250g/9oz/generous 1 cup soft light brown sugar

2 eggs

10ml/2 tsp vanilla extract

225g/8oz/1¹/₃ cups salted peanuts

1 Preheat the oven to 190°C/375°F/ Gas 5. Lightly grease two baking sheets. Grease the bottom of a glass and dip in sugar.

2 Sift together the flour and bicarbonate of soda. Set aside.

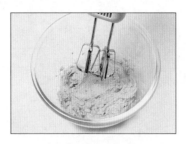

3 ▲ Cream the butter, margarine and sugar. Beat in the eggs and vanilla extract. Fold in the flour mixture.

4 ▲ Stir the peanuts into the butter mixture until evenly combined.

5 ▲ Drop teaspoonfuls 5cm/2in apart on the prepared sheets. Flatten with the prepared glass.

6 Bake for about 10 minutes, until lightly coloured. With a metal spatula, transfer to a wire rack to cool.

~ **VARIATION** ~

To make Cashew Cookies, substitute an equal amount of salted cashew nuts for the peanuts, and add as above.

Cheddar Pennies

MAKES 20

50g/2oz/¹/₄ cup butter

115g/4oz/1¹/₃ cups Cheddar cheese, grated

40g/1¹/₂oz/¹/₃ cup plain (all-purpose) flour

pinch of salt

pinch of chilli powder

1 Put the butter in a large bowl and cut into 2.5cm/1in cubes. With an electric mixer, cream the butter until soft and fluffy.

2 ▲ Stir in the cheese, flour, salt and chilli. Gather to form a dough.

3 Transfer to a lightly floured surface. Shape into a cylinder about 3cm/ 1¹/₄in in diameter. Wrap in baking parchment and chill for 1–2 hours.

4 Preheat the oven to 180°C/350°F/ Gas 4. Grease one or two baking sheets.

5 ▲ Cut the dough into 5mm/¹/₄in thick slices and place on the prepared baking sheets. Bake for about 15 minutes, until golden. Transfer to a wire rack to cool.

Salted Peanut Cookies (top), Cheddar Pennies

Chocolate Chip Brownies

MAKES 24

115g/4oz plain (semisweet) chocolate

115g/4oz/½ cup butter

3 eggs

200g/7oz/1 cup caster (superfine) sugar

2.5ml/½ tsp vanilla extract

pinch of salt

150g/5oz/1¼ cups plain (all-purpose) flour

175g/6oz chocolate chips

1 ▼ Preheat the oven to 180°C/350°F/ Gas 4. Line a 33 × 23cm/13 × 9in tin (pan) with baking parchment and grease.

2 ▲ Melt the chocolate and butter in the top of a double boiler, or in a heatproof bowl set over a pan of gently simmering water.

3 ▲ Beat together the eggs, sugar, vanilla and salt. Stir in the chocolate mixture. Sift over the flour and fold in. Add the chocolate chips.

4 ▲ Pour the mixture into the prepared tin and spread evenly. Bake until just set, about 30 minutes. Do not overbake; the brownies should be slightly moist inside. Cool in the pan.

5 To turn out, run a knife all around the edge and invert on to a baking sheet. Remove the paper. Place another sheet on top and invert again so the brownies are right-side up. Cut into squares for serving.

Marbled Brownies

MAKES 24

225g/8oz plain (semisweet) chocolate

75g/3oz/6 tbsp butter

4 eggs

300g/11oz/generous 1¹/₂ cups caster (superfine) sugar

150g/5oz/1¹/₄ cups plain (all-purpose) flour

2.5ml/¹/₂ tsp salt

5ml/1 tsp baking powder

10ml/2 tsp vanilla extract

115g/4oz/²/₃ cups walnuts, chopped

FOR THE PLAIN MIXTURE

50g/2oz/¹/₄ cup butter, at room temperature

175g/6oz/³/₄ cup cream cheese

90g/3¹/₂oz/¹/₂ cup caster (superfine) sugar

2 eggs

25g/1oz/¹/₄ cup plain (all-purpose) flour

5ml/1 tsp vanilla extract

1 Preheat the oven to 180°C/350°F/ Gas 4. Line a 33 × 23cm/13 × 9in tin (pan) with baking parchment and grease.

2 Melt the chocolate and butter over very low heat, stirring constantly. Set aside to cool.

3 Meanwhile, beat the eggs until light and fluffy. Gradually add the sugar and continue beating until blended. Sift over the flour, salt and baking powder, and fold to combine.

4 ▲ Stir in the cooled chocolate mixture. Add the vanilla and walnuts. Measure and set aside 475ml/16fl oz/ 2 cups of the chocolate mixture.

5 ▲ For the plain mixture, cream the butter and cream cheese with an electric mixer.

6 Add the sugar and continue beating until blended. Beat in the eggs, flour and vanilla.

7 Spread the unmeasured chocolate mixture in the tin. Pour over the plain mixture. Drop spoonfuls of the reserved chocolate mixture on top.

8 ▲ With a palette knife (metal spatula), swirl the mixtures to marble. Do not blend completely. Bake until just set, 35–40 minutes. Turn out when cool and cut into squares for serving.

Nutty Chocolate Squares

MAKES 16

2 eggs

10ml/2 tsp vanilla extract

pinch of salt

175g/6oz/1 cup pecan nuts,
  coarsely chopped

50g/2oz/¹/₂ cup plain (all-purpose) flour

50g/2oz/¹/₄ cup caster (superfine) sugar

120ml/4fl oz/¹/₂ cup golden
  (light corn) syrup

75g/3oz plain (semisweet) chocolate,
  finely chopped

45ml/3 tbsp butter

16 pecan halves, for decorating

1 Preheat the oven to 160°C/325°F/
Gas 3. Line the base and sides of a
20cm/8in square baking tin (pan) with
baking parchment and grease lightly.

2 ▼ Whisk together the eggs, vanilla
and salt. In another bowl, mix
together the pecan nuts and flour.
Set both aside.

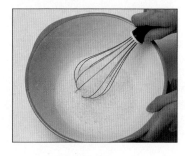

3 In a pan, bring the sugar and
golden syrup to the boil. Remove
from the heat and stir in the
chocolate and butter and blend
thoroughly with a wooden spoon.

4 ▲ Mix in the beaten eggs, then
fold in the pecan mixture.

5 Pour the mixture into the prepared
tin and bake until set, about
35 minutes. Cool in the tin for
10 minutes before turning out. Cut
into 5cm/2in squares and press pecan
halves into the tops while warm. Cool
completely on a rack.

Raisin Brownies

MAKES 16

115g/4oz/¹/₂ cup butter or margarine

50g/2oz/¹/₂ cup unsweetened cocoa
  powder

2 eggs

225g/8oz/generous 1 cup caster
  (superfine) sugar

5ml/1 tsp vanilla extract

40g/1¹/₂oz/¹/₃ cup plain (all-purpose) flour

75g/3oz/³/₄ cup chopped walnuts

75g/3oz/²/₃ cup raisins

1 Preheat the oven to 180°C/350°F/
Gas 4. Line the base and sides of a
20cm/8in square baking tin (pan)
with baking parchment and grease
the paper.

2 ▼ Gently melt the butter or
margarine in a small pan. Remove
from the heat and stir in the
cocoa powder.

3 With an electric mixer, beat the
eggs, sugar and vanilla together until
light. Add the cocoa mixture and stir
to blend.

4 ▲ Sift the flour over the cocoa
mixture and gently fold in. Add the
walnuts and raisins, and scrape the
mixture into the prepared tin.

5 Bake in the centre of the oven for
30 minutes. Do not overbake. Leave
in the tin to cool before cutting into
5cm/2in squares and removing. The
brownies should be soft and moist.

Nutty Chocolate Squares (top), Raisin Brownies

Chocolate Walnut Bars

MAKES 24

50g/2oz/¹/₃ cup walnuts

65g/2¹/₂oz/¹/₄ cup caster (superfine) sugar

115g/4oz/1 cup plain (all-purpose) flour, sifted

75g/3oz/6 tbsp cold unsalted (sweet) butter, cut into pieces

FOR THE TOPPING

25g/1oz/2 tbsp unsalted (sweet) butter

90ml/6 tbsp water

25g/1oz/¹/₄ cup unsweetened cocoa powder

90g/3¹/₂oz/¹/₂ cup caster sugar

5ml/1 tsp vanilla extract

pinch of salt

2 eggs

icing (confectioners') sugar, for dusting

1 Preheat the oven to 180°C/350°F/ Gas 4. Grease the base and sides of a 20cm/8in square baking tin (pan).

2 ▼ Grind the walnuts with a few tablespoons of the sugar in a food processor, blender or coffee grinder.

3 In a bowl, combine the ground walnuts, remaining sugar and flour. With your fingertips, rub in the butter until the mixture resembles coarse breadcrumbs. Alternatively, process all the ingredients in a food processor until the mixture resembles coarse breadcrumbs.

4 ▲ Pat the walnut mixture into the base of the prepared tin in an even layer. Bake for 25 minutes.

5 ▲ Meanwhile, for the topping, melt the butter with the water. Whisk in the cocoa and sugar. Remove from the heat, stir in the vanilla and salt and let cool for 5 minutes. Whisk in the eggs until blended.

6 ▲ Pour the topping over the crust when baked.

7 Return to the oven and bake until set, about 20 minutes. Set the tin on a rack to cool. Cut into 6 × 2.5cm/ 2¹/₂ × 1in bars and dust with icing sugar. Store in the refrigerator.

Pecan Squares

MAKES 36

225g/8oz/2 cups plain (all-purpose) flour

pinch of salt

115g/4oz/generous ½ cup granulated sugar

225g/8oz/1 cup cold butter or
   margarine, chopped

1 egg

finely grated rind of 1 lemon

FOR THE TOPPING

175g/6oz/¾ cup butter

75g/3oz/scant ⅓ cup honey

50g/2oz/¼ cup granulated sugar

115g/4oz/½ cup soft dark brown sugar

75ml/5 tbsp whipping cream

450g/1lb/2⅔ cups pecan halves

1 Preheat the oven to 190°C/375°F/
Gas 5. Lightly grease a 38 × 27 × 2.5cm/
15½ × 10½ × 1in Swiss roll tin (jelly
roll pan).

2 ▲ Sift the flour and salt into a
mixing bowl. Stir in the sugar. Cut
and rub in the butter or margarine
until the mixture resembles coarse
breadcrumbs. Add the egg and lemon
rind and blend with a fork until the
mixture just holds together.

3 ▼ Spoon the mixture into the
prepared tin. With floured fingertips,
press into an even layer. Prick the
pastry all over with a fork and chill
for 10 minutes.

4 Bake the pastry crust for 15 minutes.
Remove the tin from the oven, but
keep the oven on while making
the topping.

5 ▲ To make the topping, melt the
butter, honey and both sugars. Bring
to the boil. Boil, without stirring, for
2 minutes. Off the heat, stir in the
cream and pecan halves. Pour over
the crust, return to the oven and bake
for 25 minutes. Leave to cool.

6 When cool, run a knife around the
edge. Invert on to a baking sheet,
place another sheet on top and invert
again. Dip a sharp knife into very hot
water and cut into squares for serving.

Figgy Bars

Makes 48

350g/12oz/2 cups dried figs

3 eggs

175g/6oz/scant 1 cup caster (superfine) sugar

75g/3oz/²/₃ cup plain (all-purpose) flour

5ml/1 tsp baking powder

2.5ml/¹/₂ tsp ground cinnamon

1.5ml/¹/₄ tsp ground cloves

1.5ml/¹/₄ tsp freshly grated nutmeg

1.5ml/¹/₄ tsp salt

75g/3oz/³/₄ cup finely chopped walnuts

30ml/2 tbsp brandy or cognac

icing (confectioners') sugar, for dusting

1 Preheat the oven to 160°C/325°F/ Gas 3.

2 Line a 30 × 20 × 4cm/12 × 8 × 1¹/₂in tin (pan) with baking parchment and grease the paper.

3 ▲ With a sharp knife, chop the figs roughly. Set aside.

4 In a bowl, whisk the eggs and sugar until well blended. In another bowl, sift together the dry ingredients, then fold into the egg mixture in several batches.

5 ▼ Stir in the figs, walnuts and brandy or cognac.

6 Scrape the mixture into the prepared tin and bake until the top is firm and brown, 35–40 minutes. It should still be soft underneath.

7 Cool in the tin for 5 minutes, then turn out and transfer to a sheet of baking parchment lightly sprinkled with icing sugar. Cut into bars.

Lemon Bars

Makes 36

50g/2oz/¹/₂ cup icing (confectioners') sugar

175g/6oz/1¹/₂ cups plain (all-purpose) flour

2.5ml/¹/₂ tsp salt

175g/6oz/³/₄ cup butter, cut in small pieces

For the topping

4 eggs

350g/12oz/1³/₄ cups caster (superfine) sugar

grated rind of 1 lemon

120ml/4fl oz/¹/₂ cup fresh lemon juice

175ml/6fl oz/³/₄ cup whipping cream

icing (confectioners') sugar, for dusting

1 Preheat the oven to 160°C/325°F/ Gas 3.

2 Grease a 33 × 23cm/13 × 9in baking tin (pan).

3 Sift the sugar, flour and salt into a bowl. With a pastry blender, cut in the butter until the mixture resembles coarse breadcrumbs.

4 ▲ Press the mixture into the base of the prepared tin (pan). Bake until golden brown, about 20 minutes.

5 Meanwhile, for the topping, whisk the eggs and sugar together until blended. Add the lemon rind and juice, and mix well.

6 ▲ Lightly whip the cream and fold into the egg mixture. Pour over the still-warm base, return to the oven, and bake until set, about 40 minutes.

7 Cool completely before cutting into bars. Dust with icing sugar.

Figgy Bars (top), Lemon Bars

Apricot Specials

MAKES 12

90g/3¹/₂oz/generous ¹/₃ cup soft light
brown sugar

75g/3oz/²/₃ cup plain (all-purpose) flour

75g/3oz/6 tbsp cold unsalted (sweet)
butter, cut in pieces

FOR THE TOPPING

150g/5oz/generous ¹/₂ cup ready-to-eat
dried apricots

250ml/8fl oz/1 cup water

grated rind of 1 lemon

55g/2¹/₂oz/5 tbsp caster (superfine) sugar

10ml/2 tsp cornflour (cornstarch)

50g/2oz/¹/₂ cup chopped walnuts

1 Preheat the oven to 180°C/350°F/
Gas 4.

2 ▲ In a bowl, combine the brown
sugar and flour. With a pastry blender,
cut in the butter until the mixture
resembles coarse breadcrumbs.

3 ▲ Transfer to a 20cm/8in square
baking tin (pan) and press level. Bake
for 15 minutes. Remove from the
oven but leave the oven on.

4 Meanwhile, for the topping,
combine the apricots and water in
a pan and simmer until soft, about
10 minutes. Strain the liquid and
reserve. Chop the apricots.

5 ▲ Return the apricots to the
pan and add the lemon rind, caster
sugar, cornflour, and 60ml/4 tbsp
of the soaking liquid. Cook for
1 minute.

6 ▲ Cool slightly before spreading
the topping over the base. Sprinkle
over the walnuts and continue baking
for 20 minutes more. Leave to cool in
the tin before cutting into bars.

Almond-topped Squares

MAKES 18

75g/3oz/²/3 cup butter
50g/2oz/¹/4 cup granulated sugar
1 egg yolk
grated rind and juice of ¹/2 lemon
2.5ml/¹/2 tsp vanilla extract
30ml/2 tbsp whipping cream
115g/4oz/1 cup plain (all-purpose) flour
FOR THE TOPPING
225g/8oz/generous 1 cup granulated sugar
75g/3oz/³/4 cup flaked (sliced) almonds
4 egg whites
2.5ml/¹/2 tsp ground ginger
2.5ml/¹/2 tsp ground cinnamon

1 ▲ Preheat the oven to 190°C/375°F/Gas 5. Line a 33 × 23cm/13 × 9in Swiss roll tin (jelly roll pan) with baking parchment; grease the paper.

2 Cream the butter and sugar. Beat in the egg yolk, lemon rind and juice, vanilla extract and cream.

3 ▲ Gradually stir in the flour. Gather into a ball of dough.

4 With lightly floured fingers, press the dough into the prepared tin. Bake for 15 minutes. Remove from the oven but leave the oven on.

5 ▲ To make the topping, combine all the ingredients in a heavy pan. Cook, stirring until the mixture comes to the boil.

6 Continue boiling until just golden, about 1 minute. Pour over the dough, spreading evenly.

7 ▲ Return to the oven and bake for about 45 minutes. Remove and score into bars or squares. Cool completely before cutting into squares and serving.

Spiced Raisin Bars

MAKES 30

115g/4oz/1 cup plain (all-purpose) flour

7.5ml/1½ tsp baking powder

5ml/1 tsp ground cinnamon

2.5ml/½ tsp freshly grated nutmeg

1.5ml/¼ tsp ground cloves

1.5ml/¼ tsp ground allspice

200g/7oz/1½ cups raisins

115g/4oz/½ cup butter or margarine,
   at room temperature

90g/3½oz/½ cup sugar

2 eggs

165g/5½oz/scant ½ cup black treacle
   (molasses)

50g/2oz/⅓ cup walnuts, chopped

1 Preheat the oven to 180°C/350°F/
Gas 4. Line a 33 × 23cm/13 × 9in tin
(pan) with baking parchment; grease.

2 Sift together the flour, baking
powder and spices.

3 ▲ Place the raisins in another bowl
and toss with a few tablespoons of the
flour mixture.

4 ▲ With an electric mixer, cream
the butter or margarine and sugar
together until light and fluffy. Beat
in the eggs, one at a time, then the
molasses. Stir in the flour mixture,
raisins and walnuts.

5 Spread evenly in the tin. Bake until
just set, 15–18 minutes. Cool in the
tin before cutting into bars.

Toffee Meringue Bars

MAKES 12

50g/2oz/¼ cup butter

215g/7½oz/scant 1 cup soft dark
   brown sugar

1 egg

2.5ml/½ tsp vanilla extract

65g/2½oz/9 tbsp plain (all-purpose) flour

2.5ml/½ tsp salt

1.5ml/¼ tsp freshly grated nutmeg

FOR THE TOPPING

1 egg white

pinch of salt

15ml/l tbsp golden (light corn) syrup

90g/3½oz/½ cup caster (superfine) sugar

50g/2oz/⅓ cup walnuts, finely chopped

1 ▲ Combine the butter and brown
sugar in a pan and heat until
bubbling. Set aside to cool.

2 Preheat the oven to 180°C/350°F/
Gas 4. Line the base and sides of a
20cm/8in square cake tin (pan) with
baking parchment and grease.

3 Beat the egg and vanilla into the
cooled sugar mixture. Sift over the
flour, salt and nutmeg, and fold in.
Spread in the base of the tin.

4 ▲ For the topping, beat the egg white
with the salt until it holds soft peaks.
Beat in the golden syrup, then the
sugar and continue beating until
the mixture holds stiff peaks. Fold
in the nuts and spread on top. Bake
for 30 minutes. Cut into bars when cool.

Spiced Raisin Bars (top), Toffee Meringue Bars

BUNS & TEA BREADS

EASY TO MAKE AND SATISFYING TO
EAT, THESE BUNS AND TEA BREADS
WILL FILL THE HOUSE WITH
MOUTHWATERING SCENTS AND LURE
YOUR FAMILY AND FRIENDS TO
LINGER OVER BREAKFAST, COFFEE
OR TEA – AND THEY ARE GREAT FOR
SNACKS OR LUNCH.

Blueberry Muffins

MAKES 12

185g/6¹/₂oz/1²/₃ cups plain
(all-purpose) flour

65g/2¹/₂oz/5 tbsp caster (superfine) sugar

10ml/2 tsp baking powder

1.5ml/¹/₄ tsp salt

2 eggs

50g/2oz/¹/₄ cup butter, melted

175ml/6fl oz/³/₄ cup milk

5ml/1 tsp vanilla extract

5ml/1 tsp grated lemon rind

175g/6oz/1¹/₂ cups fresh blueberries

1 Preheat the oven to 200°C/400°F/
Gas 6.

2 ▼ Grease a 12-cup muffin tray.

3 ▲ Sift the flour, sugar, baking
powder and salt into a bowl.

4 In another bowl, whisk the eggs
until blended. Add the melted butter,
milk, vanilla and lemon rind, and stir
to combine.

5 Make a well in the dry ingredients
and pour in the egg mixture. With a
large metal spoon, stir just until the
flour is moistened, not until smooth.

6 ▲ Fold in the blueberries.

7 ▲ Spoon the batter into the tray,
leaving room for the muffins to rise.

8 Bake until the tops spring back
when touched lightly, 20–25 minutes.
Leave to cool in the tray for 5 minutes
before turning out.

Apple and Cranberry Muffins

MAKES 12

50g/2oz/¹/₄ cup butter or margarine
1 egg
90g/3¹/₂oz/¹/₂ cup caster (superfine) sugar
grated rind of 1 large orange
120ml/4fl oz/¹/₂ cup freshly squeezed orange juice
150g/5oz/1¹/₄ cups plain (all-purpose) flour
5ml/1 tsp baking powder
2.5ml/¹/₂ tsp bicarbonate of soda (baking soda)
5ml/1 tsp ground cinnamon
2.5ml/¹/₂ tsp freshly grated nutmeg
2.5ml/¹/₂ tsp ground allspice
1.5ml/¹/₄ tsp ground ginger
1.5ml/¹/₄ tsp salt
1–2 eating apples
150g/6oz/1¹/₂ cups cranberries
50g/2oz/¹/₃ cup walnuts, chopped
icing (confectioners') sugar, for dusting (optional)

1 Preheat the oven to 180°C/350°F/Gas 4. Grease a 12-cup muffin tray or use paper cases.

2 Melt the butter or margarine over gentle heat. Set aside to cool.

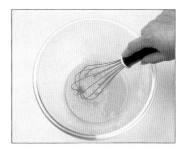

3 ▲ Place the egg in a mixing bowl and whisk lightly. Add the melted butter or margarine and whisk to combine.

4 Add the sugar, orange rind and juice. Whisk to blend, then set aside.

5 In a large bowl, sift together the flour, baking powder, bicarbonate of soda, cinnamon, nutmeg, allspice, ginger and salt. Set aside.

6 ▲ Quarter, core and peel the apples. With a sharp knife, chop coarsely.

7 Make a well in the dry ingredients and pour in the egg mixture. With a spoon, stir until just blended.

8 ▲ Add the apples, cranberries and walnuts, and stir to blend.

9 Fill the cups three-quarters full and bake until the tops spring back when touched lightly, 25–30 minutes. Transfer to a rack to cool. Dust with icing sugar, if you like.

Chocolate Chip Muffins

MAKES 10

115g/4oz/¹/₂ cup butter or margarine,
    at room temperature

65g/2¹/₂oz/5 tbsp caster (superfine) sugar

25g/1oz/2 tbsp soft dark brown sugar

2 eggs, at room temperature

215g/7¹/₂oz/scant 2 cups plain
    (all-purpose) flour

5ml/1 tsp baking powder

120ml/4fl oz/¹/₂ cup milk

175g/6oz/ plain chocolate chips

1 Preheat the oven to 190°C/375°F/
Gas 5. Grease 10 muffin cups or use
paper cases.

2 ▼ With an electric mixer, cream
the butter or margarine until soft. Add
both sugars and beat until light and
fluffy. Beat in the eggs, one at a time.

3 Sift together the flour and baking
powder, twice. Fold into the butter
mixture, alternating with the milk.

4 ▲ Divide half the mixture between
the muffin cups. Sprinkle several
chocolate chips on top, then cover
with a spoonful of the batter. To
ensure even baking, half-fill any
empty cups with water.

5 Bake until lightly coloured, about
25 minutes. Leave to stand for
5 minutes before turning out.

Chocolate Walnut Muffins

MAKES 12

175g/6oz/³/₄ cup unsalted (sweet) butter

150g/5oz plain (semisweet) chocolate

200g/7oz/1 cup caster (superfine) sugar

50g/2oz/¹/₄ cup soft dark brown sugar

4 eggs

5ml/1 tsp vanilla extract

1.5ml/¹/₄ tsp almond extract

90g/3¹/₂oz/³/₄ cup plain (all-purpose) flour

15ml/1 tbsp unsweetened cocoa powder

115g/4oz/²/₃ cup walnuts, chopped

1 Preheat the oven to 180°C/350°F/
Gas 4. Grease a 12-cup muffin tray or
use paper cases.

2 ▼ Melt the butter with the
chocolate in the top of a double boiler
or in a heatproof bowl set over a pan
of hot water. Transfer to a large
mixing bowl.

3 Stir both the sugars into the
chocolate mixture. Mix in the eggs,
one at a time, then add the vanilla
and almond extracts.

4 Sift over the flour and cocoa.

5 ▲ Fold in and stir in the walnuts.

6 Fill the prepared cups almost to the
top and bake until a skewer inserted in
the centre barely comes out clean,
30–35 minutes. Leave to stand for
5 minutes before turning out on to a
rack to cool completely.

Chocolate Chip Muffins (top), Chocolate Walnut Muffins

Raisin Bran Buns

MAKES 15

50g/2oz/¼ cup butter or margarine

40g/1½oz/⅓ cup plain (all-purpose) flour

50g/2oz/½ cup wholemeal (whole-wheat) flour

7.5ml/1½ tsp bicarbonate of soda (baking soda)

pinch of salt

5ml/1 tsp ground cinnamon

25g/1oz/¼ cup bran

75g/3oz/generous ½ cup raisins

65g/2½oz/5 tbsp soft dark brown sugar

50g/2oz/¼ cup caster (superfine) sugar

1 egg

250ml/8fl oz/1 cup buttermilk

juice of ½ lemon

1 Preheat the oven to 200°C/400°F/Gas 6. Grease 15 bun-tray cups.

2 ▲ Place the butter or margarine in a pan and melt over gentle heat. Set aside.

3 In a mixing bowl, sift together the flours, bicarbonate of soda, salt and cinnamon.

4 ▲ Add the bran, raisins and sugars and stir until blended.

5 In another bowl, mix together the egg, buttermilk, lemon juice and melted butter.

6 ▲ Add the buttermilk mixture to the dry ingredients and stir lightly and quickly until just moistened; do not mix until smooth.

7 ▲ Spoon the mixture into the prepared bun tray, filling the cups almost to the top. Half-fill any empty cups with water.

8 Bake until golden, 15–20 minutes. Serve warm or at room temperature.

Raspberry Crumble Buns

MAKES 12

175g/6oz/1¹/₂ cups plain (all-purpose) flour
50g/2oz/¹/₄ cup caster (superfine) sugar
50g/2oz/¹/₄ cup soft light brown sugar
10ml/2 tsp baking powder
pinch of salt
5ml/1 tsp ground cinnamon
115g/4oz/¹/₂ cup butter, melted
1 egg
120ml/4fl oz/¹/₂ cup milk
150g/5oz/scant 1 cup fresh raspberries
grated rind of 1 lemon
FOR THE CRUMBLE TOPPING
25g/1oz/¹/₄ cup finely chopped pecan nuts or walnuts
50g/2oz/¹/₄ cup soft dark brown sugar
20g/³/₄oz/3 tbsp plain (all-purpose) flour
5ml/1 tsp ground cinnamon
40g/1¹/₂oz/3 tbsp butter, melted

1 Preheat the oven to 180°C/350°F/ Gas 4. Lightly grease a 12-cup bun tray or use paper cases.

2 Sift the flour into a bowl. Add the sugars, baking powder, salt and cinnamon, and stir to blend.

3 ▲ Make a well in the centre. Place the butter, egg and milk in the well and mix until just combined. Stir in the raspberries and lemon rind. Spoon the mixture into the prepared bun tray, filling the cups almost to the top.

4 ▼ For the crumble topping, mix the nuts, dark brown sugar, flour and cinnamon in a bowl. Add the melted butter and stir to blend.

5 ▲ Spoon some of the crumble over each bun. Bake until browned, about 25 minutes. Transfer to a rack to cool slightly. Serve warm.

Carrot Buns

MAKES 12

175g/6oz/³/4 cup margarine,
   at room temperature

90g/3¹/2oz/generous ¹/3 cup soft dark
   brown sugar

1 egg, at room temperature

15ml/1 tbsp water

225g/8oz/1 cup carrots, grated

150g/5oz/1¹/4 cups plain (all-purpose) flour

5ml/1 tsp baking powder

2.5ml/¹/2 tsp bicarbonate of soda
   (baking soda)

5ml/1 tsp ground cinnamon

1.5ml/¹/4 tsp freshly grated nutmeg

2.5ml/¹/2 tsp salt

1 Preheat the oven to 180°C/350°F/
Gas 4. Grease a 12-cup bun tray or
use paper cases.

2 With an electric mixer, cream the
margarine and sugar until light and
fluffy. Beat in the egg and water.

3 ▲ Stir in the carrots.

4 Sift over the flour, baking powder,
bicarbonate of soda, cinnamon,
nutmeg and salt. Stir to blend.

5 ▼ Spoon the mixture into the
prepared bun tray, filling the cups
almost to the top. Bake until the tops
spring back when touched lightly,
about 35 minutes. Leave to stand for
10 minutes before transferring to a rack.

Dried Cherry Buns

MAKES 16

250ml/8fl oz/1 cup natural (plain) yogurt

175g/6oz/³/4 cup dried cherries

115g/4oz/¹/2 cup butter, at
   room temperature

175g/6oz/scant 1 cup caster
   (superfine) sugar

2 eggs, at room temperature

5ml/1 tsp vanilla essence (extract)

200g/7oz/1³/4 cups plain (all-purpose) flour

10ml/2 tsp baking powder

5ml/1 tsp bicarbonate of soda (baking soda)

pinch of salt

1 In a mixing bowl, combine the
yogurt and cherries. Cover and leave
to stand for 30 minutes.

2 Preheat the oven to 180°C/350°F/
Gas 4. Grease 16 bun-tray cups or use
paper cases.

3 With an electric mixer, cream the
butter and sugar together until light
and fluffy.

4 ▼ Add the eggs, one at a time,
beating well after each addition. Add
the vanilla and the cherry mixture and
stir to blend. Set aside.

5 ▲ In another bowl, sift together
the flour, baking powder, bicarbonate
of soda and salt. Fold into the cherry
mixture in three batches.

6 Fill the prepared cups two-thirds
full. For even baking, half-fill any
empty cups with water. Bake until
the tops spring back when touched
lightly, about 20 minutes. Transfer
to a rack to cool.

Carrot Buns (top), Dried Cherry Buns

Oat and Raisin Muffins

MAKES 12

75g/3oz/scant 1 cup rolled oats
250ml/8fl oz/1 cup buttermilk
115g/4oz/¹/₂ cup butter, at room temperature
90g/3¹/₂oz/generous ¹/₃ cup soft dark brown sugar
1 egg, at room temperature
115g/4oz/1 cup plain (all-purpose) flour
5ml/1 tsp baking powder
2.5ml/¹/₂ tsp bicarbonate of soda (baking soda)
1.5ml/¹/₄ tsp salt
25g/1oz/2 tbsp raisins

~ COOK'S TIP ~

If buttermilk is not available, add 5ml/1 tsp lemon juice or vinegar to milk. Let the mixture stand for a few minutes to curdle.

1 ▲ In a bowl, combine the oats and buttermilk, and leave to soak for 1 hour.

2 ▲ Lightly grease a 12-cup muffin tray or use paper cases.

3 ▲ Preheat the oven to 200°C/ 400°F/Gas 6. With an electric mixer, cream the butter and sugar until light and fluffy. Beat in the egg.

4 In another bowl, sift the flour, baking powder, bicarbonate of soda and salt. Stir into the butter mixture, alternating with the oat mixture. Fold in the raisins. Do not overmix.

5 Fill the prepared cups two-thirds full. Bake until a skewer inserted in the centre comes out clean, 20–25 minutes. Transfer to a rack to cool.

Pumpkin Muffins

MAKES 14

115g/4oz/¹/₂ cup butter or margarine, at room temperature
150g/5oz/²/₃ cup soft dark brown sugar
60ml/4 tbsp black treacle (molasses)
1 egg, at room temperature, beaten
225g/8oz cooked or canned pumpkin
225g/8oz/2 cups plain (all-purpose) flour
1.5ml/¹/₄ tsp salt
5ml/1 tsp bicarbonate of soda (baking soda)
7.5ml/1¹/₂ tsp ground cinnamon
5ml/1 tsp freshly grated nutmeg
25g/1oz/2 tbsp currants or raisins

1 Preheat the oven to 200°C/400°F/ Gas 6. Grease 14 muffin cups or use paper cases.

2 With an electric mixer, cream the butter or margarine until soft. Add the sugar and molasses and beat until light and fluffy.

3 ▲ Add the egg and pumpkin and stir until well blended.

4 Sift over the flour, salt, bicarbonate of soda, cinnamon and nutmeg. Fold just enough to blend; do not overmix.

5 ▼ Fold in the currants or raisins.

6 Spoon the mixture into the prepared muffin cups, filling them three-quarters full.

7 Bake until the tops spring back when touched lightly, 12–15 minutes. Serve warm or cold.

Prune Muffins

MAKES 12

1 egg

250ml/8fl oz/1 cup milk

120ml/4fl oz/¹/₂ cup vegetable oil

50g/2oz/¹/₄ cup caster (superfine) sugar

25g/1oz/2 tbsp soft dark brown sugar

275g/10oz/2¹/₂ cups plain (all-purpose) flour

10ml/2 tsp baking powder

2.5ml/¹/₂ tsp salt

1.5ml/¹/₄ tsp grated nutmeg

115g/4oz/¹/₂ cup cooked pitted
    prunes, chopped

1 Preheat the oven to 200°C/400°F/
Gas 6. Grease a 12-cup muffin tray.

2 Break the egg into a mixing bowl
and beat with a fork. Beat in the
milk and oil.

3 ▼ Stir in the sugars. Set aside.

4 Sift the flour, baking powder, salt
and nutmeg into a mixing bowl. Make
a well in the centre, pour in the egg
mixture and stir until moistened. Do
not overmix; the batter should be
slightly lumpy.

5 ▲ Fold in the prunes.

6 Fill the prepared cups two-thirds
full. Bake until golden brown, about
20 minutes. Leave to stand for
10 minutes before turning out. Serve
warm or at room temperature.

Yogurt and Honey Muffins

MAKES 12

50g/2oz/¹/₄ cup butter

75ml/5 tbsp clear honey

250ml/8fl oz/1 cup natural (plain) yogurt

1 large egg, at room temperature

grated rind of 1 lemon

50ml/2fl oz/¹/₄ cup lemon juice

150g/5oz/1¹/₄ cups plain (all-purpose) flour

175g/6oz/1²/₃ cups wholemeal
    (whole-wheat) flour

7.5ml/1¹/₂ tsp bicarbonate of soda
    (baking soda)

pinch of freshly grated nutmeg

~ VARIATION ~

For Walnut Yogurt Honey Muffins,
add 50g/2oz/¹/₂ cup chopped walnuts,
folded in with the flour. This
makes a more substantial muffin.

---

1 Preheat the oven to 190°C/375°F/
Gas 5. Grease a 12-cup muffin tray or
use paper cases.

2 In a pan, melt the butter and
honey. Remove from the heat and set
aside to cool slightly.

3 ▲ In a bowl, whisk together the
yogurt, egg, lemon rind and juice.
Add the butter and honey mixture.
Set aside.

4 ▲ In another bowl, sift together
the dry ingredients.

5 Fold the dry ingredients into the
yogurt mixture to blend.

6 Fill the prepared cups two-thirds
full. Bake until the tops spring back
when touched lightly, 20–25 minutes.
Cool in the tray for 5 minutes before
turning out. Serve warm or at room
temperature.

Prune Muffins (top), Yogurt and Honey Muffins

Banana Muffins

MAKES 10

250g/9oz/2¼ cups plain (all-purpose) flour

5ml/1 tsp baking powder

5ml/1 tsp bicarbonate of soda
   (baking soda)

1.5ml/¼ tsp salt

2.5ml/½ tsp ground cinnamon

1.5ml/¼ tsp freshly grated nutmeg

3 large ripe bananas

1 egg

65g/2½oz/scant ⅓ cup soft dark
   brown sugar

50ml/2fl oz/¼ cup vegetable oil

25g/1oz/2 tbsp raisins

1 ▼ Preheat the oven to 190°C/
375°F/Gas 5. Lightly grease or line
ten deep muffin cups with paper cases.

2 Sift together the flour, baking
powder, bicarbonate of soda, salt,
cinnamon and nutmeg. Set aside.

3 ▲ With an electric mixer, beat
the peeled bananas at moderate speed
until mashed.

4 ▲ Beat in the egg, sugar and oil.

5 Add the dry ingredients and beat in
gradually, on low speed. Mix just until
blended. With a wooden spoon, stir in
the raisins.

6 Fill the prepared cups two-thirds
full. For even baking, half-fill any
empty cups with water.

7 ▲ Bake until the tops spring back
when touched lightly, 20–25 minutes.
Transfer to a rack to cool.

Maple Pecan Muffins

MAKES 20

175g/6oz/1 cup pecan nuts
350g/12oz/3 cups plain (all-purpose) flour
5ml/1 tsp baking powder
5ml/1 tsp bicarbonate of soda (baking soda)
1.5ml/¼ tsp salt
1.5ml/¼ tsp ground cinnamon
90g/3½oz/½ cup caster (superfine) sugar
65g/2½oz/scant ⅓ cup soft light brown sugar
45ml/3 tbsp maple syrup
150g/5oz/10 tbsp butter, at room temperature
3 eggs, at room temperature
300ml/½ pint/1¼ cups buttermilk
60 pecan halves, for decorating

1 Preheat the oven to 180°C/350°F/ Gas 4. Lightly grease 20 deep muffin cups or use paper cases.

2 ▲ Spread the pecan nuts on a baking sheet and toast in the oven for 5 minutes. When cool, chop coarsely and set aside.

3 In a bowl, sift together the flour, baking powder, bicarbonate of soda, salt and cinnamon. Set aside.

4 ▲ In a large mixing bowl, combine the caster sugar, light brown sugar, maple syrup and butter. Beat with an electric mixer until light and fluffy.

5 Add the eggs, one at a time, beating to incorporate thoroughly after each addition.

6 ▲ Pour half the buttermilk and half the dry ingredients into the butter mixture, then stir until blended. Repeat with the remaining buttermilk and dry ingredients.

7 Fold in the chopped pecan nuts. Fill the prepared cups two-thirds full. Top with the pecan halves. For even baking, half-fill any empty cups with water.

8 Bake until puffed up and golden, 20–25 minutes. Leave to stand for 5 minutes before turning out.

~ VARIATION ~

For Pecan Spice Muffins, substitute an equal quantity of golden (light corn) syrup for the maple syrup. Increase the cinnamon to 2.5ml/½ tsp, and add 5ml/1 tsp ground ginger and 2.5ml/½ tsp freshly grated nutmeg, sifted with the dry ingredients.

Cheese Muffins

MAKES 9

50g/2oz/¹/₄ cup butter

200g/7oz/1³/₄ cups plain (all-purpose) flour

10ml/2 tsp baking powder

30ml/2 tbsp sugar

1.5ml/¹/₄ tsp salt

5ml/1 tsp paprika

2 eggs

120ml/4fl oz/¹/₂ cup milk

5ml/1 tsp dried thyme

50g/2oz/¹/₂ cup mature Cheddar cheese, cut into 1cm/¹/₂in dice

1 Preheat the oven to 190°C/375°F/ Gas 5. Thickly grease nine deep muffin cups or use paper cases.

2 Melt the butter and set aside.

3 ▼ In a mixing bowl, sift together the flour, baking powder, sugar, salt and paprika.

4 ▲ In another bowl, combine the eggs, milk, melted butter and thyme, and whisk to blend.

5 Add the milk mixture to the dry ingredients and stir until just moistened; do not mix until smooth.

6 ▲ Place a heaped spoonful of batter into the prepared cups. Drop a few pieces of cheese over each, then top with another spoonful of batter. For even baking, half-fill any empty muffin cups with water.

7 ▲ Bake until puffed and golden, about 25 minutes. Leave to stand for 5 minutes before turning out on to a rack. Serve warm or at room temperature.

Bacon and Cornmeal Muffins

MAKES 14

8 bacon rashers (strips)
50g/2oz/¼ cup butter
50g/2oz/¼ cup margarine
115g/4oz/1 cup plain (all-purpose) flour
15ml/1 tbsp baking powder
5ml/1 tsp sugar
1.5ml/¼ tsp salt
225g/8oz/2 cups cornmeal
120ml/4fl oz/½ cup milk
2 eggs

1 Preheat the oven to 200°C/400°F/ Gas 6. Lightly grease 14 deep muffin cups or use paper cases.

2 ▲ Fry the bacon until crisp. Drain on kitchen paper, then chop into small pieces. Set aside.

3 Gently melt the butter and margarine, and set aside.

4 ▲ Sift the flour, baking powder, sugar, and salt into a large mixing bowl. Stir in the cornmeal, then make a well in the centre.

5 In a pan, heat the milk to lukewarm. In a small bowl, lightly whisk the eggs, then add to the milk. Stir in the melted fats.

6 ▼ Pour the milk mixture into the centre of the well and stir until smooth and well blended.

7 ▲ Stir the bacon into the mixture, then spoon the mixture into the prepared cups, filling them half-full. Bake until risen and lightly coloured, about 20 minutes. Serve hot or warm.

Corn Bread

MAKES 1 LOAF

115g/4oz/1 cup plain (all-purpose) flour

65g/2¹/₂oz/5 tbsp caster (superfine) sugar

5ml/1 tsp salt

15ml/1 tbsp baking powder

175g/6oz/1¹/₂ cups cornmeal or polenta

350ml/12fl oz/1¹/₂ cups milk

2 eggs

75g/3oz/6 tbsp butter, melted

115g/4oz/¹/₂ cup margarine, melted

1 Preheat the oven to 200°C/400°F/ Gas 6. Line a 23 × 13cm/9 × 5in loaf tin (pan) with baking parchment and grease.

2 Sift the flour, sugar, salt and baking powder into a mixing bowl.

3 ▼ Add the cornmeal and stir to blend. Make a well in the centre.

4 ▲ Whisk together the milk, eggs, butter and margarine. Pour the mixture into the well. Stir until just blended; do not overmix.

5 Pour into the tin and bake until a skewer inserted into the centre comes out clean, about 45 minutes. Serve hot or at room temperature.

Spicy Corn Bread

MAKES 9 SQUARES

3–4 whole canned chilli peppers, drained

2 eggs

450ml/³/₄ pint/scant 2 cups buttermilk

50g/2oz/¹/₄ cup butter, melted

50g/2oz/¹/₂ cup plain (all-purpose) flour

5ml/1 tsp bicarbonate of soda (baking soda)

10ml/2 tsp salt

175g/6oz/1¹/₂ cups cornmeal, or polenta

350g/12oz/2 cups canned corn, drained, or frozen corn, thawed

1 Preheat the oven to 200°C/400°F/ Gas 6. Line the bottom and sides of a 23cm/9in square cake tin (pan) with baking parchment and grease lightly.

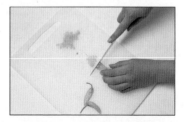

2 ▲ With a sharp knife, finely chop the chillies and set aside.

3 ▲ In a large bowl, whisk the eggs until frothy, then whisk in the buttermilk. Add the melted butter.

4 In another large bowl, sift together the flour, bicarbonate of soda and salt. Fold into the buttermilk mixture in three batches, then fold in the cornmeal in three batches.

5 ▲ Fold in the chillies and corn.

6 Pour the mixture into the prepared tin and bake until a skewer inserted in the middle comes out clean, 25–30 minutes. Leave to stand for 2–3 minutes before turning out. Cut into squares and serve warm.

Corn Bread (top), Spicy Corn Bread

Fruity Tea Bread

MAKES 1 LOAF

225g/8oz/2 cups plain (all-purpose) flour

115g/4oz/generous ¹/₂ cup caster (superfine) sugar

15ml/1 tbsp baking powder

2.5ml/¹/₂ tsp salt

grated rind of 1 large orange

170ml/5¹/₂fl oz/scant ³/₄ cup fresh orange juice

2 eggs, lightly beaten

75g/3oz/6 tbsp butter or margarine, melted

115g/4oz/1 cup fresh cranberries, or bilberries

50g/2oz/¹/₂ cup chopped walnuts

1 Preheat the oven to 180°C/350°F/ Gas 4. Line a 23 × 13cm/9 × 5in loaf tin (pan) with baking parchment and grease.

2 Sift the flour, sugar, baking powder and salt into a mixing bowl.

3 ▼ Stir in the orange rind.

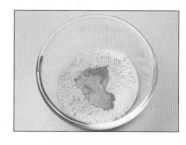

4 ▲ Make a well in the centre and add the orange juice, eggs and melted butter or margarine. Stir from the centre until the ingredients are blended; do not overmix.

5 ▲ Add the berries and walnuts, and stir until blended.

6 Transfer the mixture to the prepared tin and bake until a skewer inserted into the centre comes out clean, 45–50 minutes.

7 ▲ Leave to cool in the tin for 10 minutes before transferring to a rack to cool completely. Serve thinly sliced, toasted or plain, with butter or cream cheese and jam.

Date and Pecan Loaf

MAKES 1 LOAF

175g/6oz/1 cup pitted dates, chopped
175ml/6fl oz/³/4 cup boiling water
50g/2oz/¹/4 cup unsalted (sweet) butter, at room temperature
50g/2oz/¹/4 cup soft dark brown sugar
50g/2oz/¹/4 cup caster (superfine) sugar
1 egg, at room temperature
30ml/2 tbsp brandy
165g/5¹/2oz/1¹/4 cups plain (all-purpose) flour
10ml/2 tsp baking powder
2.5ml/¹/2 tsp salt
4ml/³/4 tsp freshly grated nutmeg
75g/3oz/³/4 cup coarsely chopped pecan nuts or walnuts

1 ▲ Place the dates in a bowl and pour over the boiling water. Set aside to cool.

2 Preheat the oven to 180°C/350°F/ Gas 4. Line a 23 × 13cm/9 × 5in loaf tin (pan) with baking parchment and grease.

4 Sift the flour, baking powder, salt and nutmeg together, three times.

5 ▼ Fold the dry ingredients into the sugar mixture in three batches, alternating with the dates and water.

6 ▲ Fold in the nuts.

7 Pour the mixture into the prepared tin and bake until a skewer inserted into the centre comes out clean, 45–50 minutes. Leave to cool in the tin for 10 minutes before transferring to a rack to cool completely.

3 ▲ With an electric mixer, cream the butter and sugars until light and fluffy. Beat in the egg and brandy, then set aside.

Orange and Honey Tea Bread

Makes 1 loaf

375g/13oz/3¼ cups plain (all-purpose) flour

12.5ml/2½ tsp baking powder

2.5ml/½ tsp bicarbonate of soda (baking soda)

2.5ml/½ tsp salt

25g/1oz/2 tbsp margarine

250ml/8fl oz/1 cup clear honey

1 egg, at room temperature, lightly beaten

25ml/1½ tbsp grated orange rind

175ml/6fl oz/¾ cup freshly squeezed orange juice

115g/4oz/1 cup walnuts, chopped

1 Preheat the oven to 160°C/325°F/ Gas 3.

2 Sift together the flour, baking powder, bicarbonate of soda and salt.

3 Line the bottom and sides of a 23 × 13cm/9 × 5in loaf tin (pan) with baking parchment and grease.

4 ▲ With an electric mixer, cream the margarine until soft. Stir in the honey until blended, then stir in the egg. Add the orange rind and stir to combine thoroughly.

5 ▲ Fold the flour mixture into the honey and egg mixture in three batches, alternating with the orange juice. Stir in the walnuts.

6 Pour into the tin and bake until a skewer inserted into the centre comes out clean, 60–70 minutes. Leave to stand for 10 minutes before turning out on to a rack to cool.

Apple Loaf

Makes 1 loaf

1 egg

250ml/8fl oz/1 cup bottled or homemade apple sauce

50g/2oz/¼ cup butter or margarine, melted

115g/4oz/½ cup soft dark brown sugar

50g/2oz/¼ cup caster (superfine) sugar

275g/10oz/2½ cups plain (all-purpose) flour

10ml/2 tsp baking powder

2.5ml/½ tsp bicarbonate of soda (baking soda)

2.5ml/½ tsp salt

5ml/1 tsp ground cinnamon

2.5ml/½ tsp freshly grated nutmeg

65g/2½oz/½ cup currants or raisins

50g/2oz/⅓ cup pecan nuts or walnuts, chopped

1 Preheat the oven to 180°C/350°F/ Gas 4. Line a 23 × 13cm/9 × 5in loaf tin (pan) with baking parchment and grease.

2 ▲ Break the egg into a bowl and beat lightly. Stir in the apple sauce, butter or margarine and both sugars. Set aside.

3 In another bowl, sift together the flour, baking powder, bicarbonate of soda, salt, cinnamon and nutmeg. Fold the dry ingredients into the apple sauce mixture in three batches.

4 ▼ Stir in the currants or raisins, and nuts.

5 Pour into the prepared tin and bake until a skewer inserted into the centre comes out clean, about 1 hour. Leave to stand for 10 minutes. Turn out on to a rack and cool completely.

Orange and Honey Tea Bread (top), Apple Loaf

Lemon and Walnut Tea Bread

MAKES 1 LOAF

115g/4oz/¹/₂ cup butter or margarine, at room temperature

90g/3¹/₂oz/¹/₂ cup sugar

2 eggs, at room temperature, separated

grated rind of 2 lemons

30ml/2 tbsp lemon juice

225g/8oz/2 cups plain (all-purpose) flour

10ml/2 tsp baking powder

120ml/4fl oz/¹/₂ cup milk

50g/2oz/¹/₃ cup walnuts, chopped

pinch of salt

1 Preheat the oven to 180°C/350°F/ Gas 4. Line a 23 × 13cm/9 × 5in loaf tin (pan) with baking parchment and grease.

2 With an electric mixer, cream the butter or margarine with the sugar until light and fluffy.

3 ▲ Beat in the egg yolks.

4 Add the lemon rind and juice, and stir until blended. Set aside.

5 ▲ In another bowl, sift together the flour and baking powder, three times. Fold into the butter mixture in three batches, alternating with the milk. Fold in the walnuts. Set aside.

6 ▲ Beat the egg whites and salt until stiff peaks form. Fold a large dollop of the egg whites into the walnut mixture to lighten it. Fold in the remaining egg whites carefully until just blended.

7 ▲ Pour the batter into the prepared tin and bake until a skewer inserted into the centre of the loaf comes out clean, 45–50 minutes. Leave to stand for 5 minutes before turning out on to a rack to cool completely.

Apricot Nut Loaf

MAKES 1 LOAF

115g/4oz/¹/₂ cup ready-to-eat dried apricots
1 large orange
75g/3oz/²/₃ cup raisins
150g/5oz/³/₄ cup caster (superfine) sugar
85ml/3fl oz/generous ¹/₃ cup oil
2 eggs, lightly beaten
250g/9oz/2¹/₄ cups plain (all-purpose) flour
10ml/2 tsp baking powder
2.5ml/¹/₂ tsp salt
5ml/1 tsp bicarbonate of soda (baking soda)
50g/2oz/¹/₂ cup chopped walnuts

1 Preheat the oven to 180°C/350°F/ Gas 4. Line a 23 × 13cm/9 × 5in loaf tin (pan) with baking parchment and grease.

2 Place the apricots in a bowl, cover with lukewarm water and leave to stand for 30 minutes.

3 ▲ With a vegetable peeler, remove the orange rind, leaving the pith.

4 With a sharp knife, finely chop the orange rind strips.

5 Drain the apricots and chop coarsely. Place in a bowl with the orange rind and raisins. Set aside.

6 Squeeze the peeled orange. Measure the juice and add enough hot water to obtain 175ml/6fl oz/³/₄ cup liquid.

7 ▼ Pour the orange juice mixture over the apricot mixture. Stir in the sugar, oil and eggs. Set aside.

8 In another bowl, sift together the flour, baking powder, salt and bicarbonate of soda. Fold the flour mixture into the apricot mixture in three batches.

9 ▲ Stir in the walnuts.

10 Spoon the mixture into the prepared tin and bake until a skewer inserted into the centre comes out clean, 55–60 minutes. If the loaf browns too quickly, protect the top with a sheet of foil. Leave to cool in the tin for 10 minutes before transferring to a rack to cool completely.

Mango Tea Bread

MAKES 2 LOAVES

275g/10oz/2¹/₂ cups plain (all-purpose) flour
10ml/2 tsp bicarbonate of soda (baking soda)
10ml/2 tsp ground cinnamon
2.5ml/¹/₂ tsp salt
115g/4oz/¹/₂ cup margarine, at room temperature
3 eggs, at room temperature
300g/11oz/generous 1¹/₂ cups caster (superfine) sugar
120ml/4fl oz/¹/₂ cup vegetable oil
1 large ripe mango, peeled and chopped
90g/3¹/₂oz/generous 1 cup desiccated (dry unsweetened) coconut
65g/2¹/₂oz/¹/₂ cup raisins

1 Preheat the oven to 180°C/350°F/ Gas 4. Line the bottom and sides of two 23 × 13cm/9 × 5in loaf tins (pans) with baking parchment and grease.

2 Sift together the flour, bicarbonate of soda, cinnamon and salt. Set aside.

3 With an electric mixer, cream the margarine until soft.

4 ▼ Beat in the eggs and sugar until light and fluffy. Beat in the oil.

5 Fold the dry ingredients into the creamed ingredients in three batches.

6 Fold in the mango, two-thirds of the coconut and the raisins.

7 ▲ Spoon the batter into the pans.

8 Sprinkle over the remaining coconut. Bake until a skewer inserted into the centre comes out clean, 50–60 minutes. Leave to stand for 10 minutes before turning out on to a rack to cool completely.

Courgette Tea Bread

MAKES 1 LOAF

50g/2oz/¹/₄ cup butter
3 eggs
250ml/8fl oz/1 cup vegetable oil
300g/11oz/generous 1¹/₂ cups sugar
2 medium unpeeled courgettes (zucchini), grated
275g/10oz/2¹/₂ cups plain (all-purpose) flour
10ml/2 tsp bicarbonate of soda (baking soda)
5ml/1 tsp baking powder
5ml/1 tsp salt
5ml/1 tsp ground cinnamon
5ml/1 tsp freshly grated nutmeg
1.5ml/¹/₄ tsp ground cloves
115g/4oz/²/₃ cup walnuts, chopped

1 Preheat the oven to 180°C/350°F/ Gas 4.

2 Line the base and sides of a 23 × 13cm/9 × 5 in loaf tin (pan) with baking parchment and grease.

3 ▲ In a pan, melt the butter over low heat. Set aside.

4 With an electric mixer, beat the eggs and oil together until thick. Beat in the sugar. Stir in the melted butter and courgettes. Set aside.

5 ▲ In another bowl, sift all the dry ingredients together three times. Carefully fold into the courgette mixture. Fold in the walnuts.

6 Pour into the tin and bake until a skewer inserted into the centre comes out clean, 60–70 minutes. Leave to stand for 10 minutes before turning out on to a wire rack to cool completely.

Mango Tea Bread (top), Courgette Tea Bread

Wholemeal Banana Nut Loaf

MAKES 1 LOAF

115g/4oz/¹/2 cup butter, at room temperature

115g/4oz/generous ¹/2 cup caster (superfine) sugar

2 eggs, at room temperature

115g/4oz/1 cup plain (all-purpose) flour

5ml/1 tsp bicarbonate of soda (baking soda)

1.5ml/¹/4 tsp salt

5ml/1 tsp ground cinnamon

50g/2oz/¹/2 cup wholemeal (whole-wheat) flour

3 large ripe bananas

5ml/1 tsp vanilla extract

50g/2oz/¹/3 cup chopped walnuts

1 Preheat the oven to 180°C/350°F/ Gas 4. Line the base and sides of a 23 × 13cm/9 × 5in loaf tin (pan) with baking parchment and grease the paper.

2 With an electric mixer, cream the butter and sugar together until light and fluffy.

3 ▲ Add the eggs, one at a time, beating well after each addition.

4 Sift the plain flour, bicarbonate of soda, salt and cinnamon over the butter mixture and stir to blend.

5 ▲ Stir in the wholemeal flour.

6 ▲ With a fork, mash the bananas to a purée, then stir into the mixture. Stir in the vanilla and nuts.

7 ▲ Pour the mixture into the prepared tin and spread level.

8 Bake until a skewer inserted into the centre comes out clean, 50–60 minutes. Leave to stand for 10 minutes before transferring to a rack.

Dried Fruit Loaf

MAKES 1 LOAF

450g/1lb/2²/₃ cups mixed dried fruit, such as currants, raisins, chopped ready-to-eat dried apricots and dried cherries

300ml/¹/₂ pint/1¹/₄ cups cold strong tea

200g/7oz/scant 1 cup soft dark brown sugar

grated rind and juice of 1 small orange

grated rind and juice of 1 lemon

1 egg, lightly beaten

200g/7oz/1³/₄ cups plain (all-purpose) flour

15ml/1 tbsp baking powder

pinch of salt

1 ▲ In a bowl, mix the dried fruit with the tea and soak overnight.

2 Preheat the oven to 180°C/350°F/Gas 4. Line the base and sides of a 23 × 13cm/9 × 5in loaf tin (pan) with baking parchment and grease the paper.

3 ▲ Strain the fruit, reserving the liquid. In a bowl, combine the brown sugar, grated orange and lemon rind, and fruit.

4 ▼ Pour the orange and lemon juice into a measuring jug (cup); if the quantity is less than 250ml/8fl oz/1 cup, top up with the soaking liquid.

5 Stir the citrus juices and egg into the dried fruit mixture.

6 In another bowl, sift together the flour, baking powder and salt. Stir into the fruit mixture until blended.

7 Transfer to the prepared tin and bake until a skewer inserted into the centre comes out clean, about 1¹/₄ hours. Leave to stand for 10 minutes before turning out.

Bilberry Tea Bread

MAKES 8 PIECES

50g/2oz/¹/₄ cup butter or margarine,
  at room temperature

175g/6oz/scant 1 cup caster (superfine) sugar

1 egg, at room temperature

120ml/4fl oz/¹/₂ cup milk

225g/8oz/2 cups plain (all-purpose) flour

10ml/2 tsp baking powder

2.5ml/¹/₂ tsp salt

275g/10oz/2¹/₂ cups fresh bilberries,
  or blueberries

FOR THE TOPPING

115g/4oz/generous ¹/₂ cup sugar

40g/1¹/₂oz/¹/₃ cup plain (all-purpose) flour

2.5ml/¹/₂ tsp ground cinnamon

50g/2oz/¹/₄ cup butter, cut in pieces

1 Preheat the oven to 190°C/375°F/
Gas 5. Grease a 23cm/9in baking dish.

2 With an electric mixer, cream the butter or margarine with the sugar until light and fluffy. Add the egg, beat to combine, then mix in the milk until blended.

3 ▼ Sift over the flour, baking powder and salt, and stir just enough to blend the ingredients.

4 ▲ Add the berries and stir.

5 Transfer to the baking dish.

6 ▲ For the topping, place the sugar, flour, cinnamon and butter into a mixing bowl. Cut in with a pastry blender until the mixture resembles coarse breadcrumbs.

7 ▲ Sprinkle the topping over the mixture in the baking dish.

8 Bake until a skewer inserted into the centre comes out clean, about 45 minutes. Serve warm or cold.

Chocolate Chip Walnut Loaf

MAKES 1 LOAF

90g/3¹/₂oz/¹/₂ cup caster (superfine) sugar

90g/3¹/₂oz/³/₄ cup plain (all-purpose) flour

5ml/1 tsp baking powder

60ml/4 tbsp cornflour (cornstarch)

130g/4¹/₂oz/generous ¹/₂ cup butter, at room temperature

2 eggs, at room temperature

5ml/1 tsp vanilla extract

30ml/2 tbsp currants or raisins

25g/1oz/¹/₄ cup walnuts, finely chopped

grated rind of ¹/₂ lemon

45ml/3 tbsp plain (semisweet) chocolate chips

icing (confectioners') sugar, for dusting

1 Preheat the oven to 180°C/350°F/ Gas 4. Grease and line a 21 × 12cm/ 8¹/₂ × 4¹/₂in loaf tin (pan).

2 ▲ Sprinkle 25ml/1¹/₂ tbsp of the caster sugar into the pan and tilt to distribute the sugar in an even layer over the base and sides. Shake out any excess.

~ VARIATION ~

For the best results, the eggs should be at room temperature. If they are too cold when folded into the creamed butter mixture, they may separate. If this happens, add a spoonful of the flour to help stabilize the mixture.

3 ▼ Sift together the flour, baking powder and cornflour into a mixing bowl, three times. Set aside.

4 With an electric mixer, cream the butter until soft. Add the remaining sugar and continue beating until light and fluffy. Add the eggs, one at a time, beating to incorporate thoroughly after each addition.

5 Gently fold the dry ingredients into the butter mixture, in three batches; do not overmix.

6 ▲ Fold in the vanilla, currants or raisins, walnuts, lemon rind, and chocolate chips until just blended.

7 Pour the mixture into the prepared tin and bake until a skewer inserted into the centre comes out clean, 45–50 minutes. Leave to cool in the tin for 5 minutes before transferring to a rack to cool completely. Dust over an even layer of icing sugar before serving.

Glazed Banana Spice Loaf

MAKES 1 LOAF

1 large ripe banana

115g/4oz/½ cup butter, at room temperature

165g/5½oz/generous ¾ cup caster (superfine) sugar

2 eggs, at room temperature

215g/7½oz/scant 2 cups plain (all-purpose) flour

5ml/1 tsp salt

5ml/1 tsp bicarbonate of soda (baking soda)

2.5ml/½ tsp freshly grated nutmeg

1.5ml/¼ tsp ground allspice

1.5ml/¼ tsp ground cloves

175ml/6fl oz/¾ cup sour cream

5ml/1 tsp vanilla extract

FOR THE GLAZE

115g/4oz/1 cup icing (confectioners') sugar

15–30ml/1–2 tbsp lemon juice

1 Preheat the oven to 180°C/350°F/ Gas 4. Line a 21 × 11cm/8½ × 4½in loaf tin (pan) with baking parchment; grease.

2 ▼ With a fork, mash the banana in a bowl. Set aside.

3 With an electric mixer, cream the butter and sugar until light and fluffy. Add the eggs, one at a time, beating to blend well after each addition.

4 Sift together the flour, salt, bicarbonate of soda, nutmeg, allspice and cloves. Add to the butter mixture and stir to combine well.

5 ▲ Add the sour cream, banana, and vanilla and mix just enough to blend. Pour into the prepared tin.

6 ▲ Bake until the top springs back when touched lightly, 45–50 minutes. Leave to cool in the pan for 10 minutes. Turn out on to a wire rack to cool.

7 ▲ For the glaze, combine the icing sugar and lemon juice, then stir until smooth.

8 To glaze, place the cooled loaf on a rack set over a baking sheet. Pour the glaze over the top of the loaf and allow to set.

Sweet Sesame Loaf

MAKES 1 OR 2 LOAVES

75g/3oz/6 tbsp sesame seeds
275g/10oz/2½ cups plain (all-purpose) flour
5ml/1 tsp salt
12.5ml/2½ tsp baking powder
50g/2oz/¼ cup butter or margarine, at room temperature
130g/4½oz/scant ¾ cup sugar
2 eggs, at room temperature
grated rind of 1 lemon
350ml/12fl oz/1½ cups milk

1 Preheat the oven to 180°C/350°F/ Gas 4. Line a 23 × 13cm/9 × 5in loaf tin (pan) with baking parchment and grease.

2 ▲ Reserve 30ml/2 tbsp of the sesame seeds. Spread the remainder on a baking sheet and bake until lightly toasted, about 10 minutes.

3 Sift the flour, salt and baking powder into a bowl.

4 ▲ Stir in the toasted sesame seeds and set aside.

5 With an electric mixer, cream the butter or margarine and sugar together until light and fluffy. Beat in the eggs, then stir in the lemon rind and milk.

6 ▼ Pour the milk mixture over the dry ingredients and fold in with a large metal spoon until just blended.

7 ▲ Pour into the tin and sprinkle over the reserved sesame seeds.

8 Bake until a skewer inserted into the centre comes out clean, about 1 hour. Leave to cool in the tin for about 10 minutes. Turn out on to a wire rack to cool completely.

Wholemeal Scones

MAKES 16

175g/6oz/3/4 cup cold butter

350g/12oz/3 cups wholemeal (whole-wheat) flour

150g/5oz/1¼ cups plain (all-purpose) flour

30ml/2 tbsp caster (superfine) sugar

2.5ml/½ tsp salt

12.5ml/2½ tsp bicarbonate of soda (baking soda)

2 eggs

175ml/6fl oz/3/4 cup buttermilk

35g/1¼oz/2½ tbsp raisins

1 Preheat the oven to 200°C/400°F/ Gas 6. Grease and flour a large baking sheet.

2 ▲ Cut the butter into small pieces.

3 Combine the dry ingredients in a bowl. Add the butter and rub in with your fingertips until the mixture resembles coarse breadcrumbs. Set aside.

4 In another bowl, whisk together the eggs and buttermilk. Set aside 30ml/2 tbsp for glazing.

5 Stir the remaining egg mixture into the dry ingredients until it just holds together. Stir in the raisins.

6 Roll out the dough to about 2cm/ 3/4in thick. Stamp out circles with a biscuit (cookie) cutter. Place on the prepared sheet and brush with the glaze.

7 Bake until golden, 12–15 minutes. Allow to cool slightly before serving. Split in two with a fork while still warm and spread with butter and jam, if you like.

Orange and Raisin Scones

MAKES 16

275g/10oz/2½ cups plain (all-purpose) flour

7.5ml/1½ tsp baking powder

60g/2¼oz/4½ tbsp sugar

2.5ml/½ tsp salt

65g/2½oz/5 tbsp butter, diced

65g/2½oz/5 tbsp margarine, diced

grated rind of 1 large orange

50g/2oz/4 tbsp raisins

120ml/4fl oz/½ cup buttermilk

milk, for glazing

1 Preheat the oven to 220°C/425°F/ Gas 7. Grease and flour a large baking sheet.

2 Combine the dry ingredients in a large bowl. Add the butter and margarine and rub in with your fingertips until the mixture resembles coarse breadcrumbs.

3 ▲ Add the orange rind and raisins.

4 Gradually stir in the buttermilk to form a soft dough.

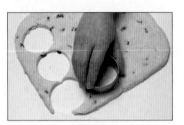

5 ▲ Roll out the dough to about 2cm/3/4in thick. Stamp out circles with a biscuit (cookie) cutter.

6 ▲ Place on the prepared sheet and brush the tops with milk.

7 Bake until golden, 12–15 minutes. Serve hot or warm, with butter, or whipped or clotted cream, and jam.

~ COOK'S TIP ~

For light, tender scones, handle the dough as little as possible. If you wish, split the scones when cool and toast them under a preheated grill (broiler). Butter them while still hot.

Wholemeal Scones (top), Orange and Raisin Scones

Buttermilk Scones

Makes 15

200g/7oz/1¾ cups plain (all-purpose) flour

5ml/1 tsp salt

5ml/1 tsp baking powder

2.5ml/½ tsp bicarbonate of soda (baking soda)

60ml/4 tbsp cold butter or margarine

175ml/6fl oz/¾ cup buttermilk

1 Preheat the oven to 220°C/425°F/ Gas 7. Grease and flour a baking sheet.

2 Sift the dry ingredients into a bowl. Rub in the butter or margarine with your fingertips until the mixture resembles breadcrumbs.

3 ▼ Gradually pour in the buttermilk, stirring with a fork to form a soft dough.

4 ▲ Roll out the dough to about 1cm/½in thick. Stamp out rounds with a 5cm/2in biscuit (cookie) cutter.

5 Place on the prepared baking sheet and bake until golden, 12–15 minutes. Serve warm or at room temperature.

Traditional Sweet Scones

Makes 8

175g/6oz/1½ cups plain (all-purpose) flour

30ml/2 tbsp sugar

15ml/1 tbsp baking powder

pinch of salt

75ml/5 tbsp cold butter, cut in pieces

120ml/4fl oz/½ cup milk

1 Preheat the oven to 220°C/425°F/ Gas 7. Grease and flour a baking sheet.

~ VARIATION ~

To make a delicious and speedy dessert, split the scones in half while still warm. Butter one half, top with lightly sugared fresh strawberries, raspberries or blueberries, and sandwich with the other half. Serve at once with dollops of whipped cream.

2 ▲ Sift the flour, sugar, baking powder, and salt into a bowl.

3 Cut in the butter with a pastry blender until the mixture resembles coarse crumbs.

4 Pour in the milk and stir with a fork to form a soft dough.

5 ▲ Roll out the dough to about 5mm/¼in thick. Stamp out rounds using a 6cm/2½in biscuit (cookie) cutter.

6 Place on the prepared sheet and bake until golden, about 12 minutes. Serve hot or warm, with butter and jam, to accompany tea or coffee.

Buttermilk Scones (top), Traditional Sweet Scones

Herb Popovers

MAKES 12

3 eggs

250ml/8fl oz/1 cup milk

25g/1oz/2 tbsp butter, melted

75g/3oz/²/3 cup plain (all-purpose) flour

pinch of salt

1 small sprig each mixed fresh herbs, such
as chives, tarragon, dill and parsley

1 Preheat the oven to 220°C/425°F/
Gas 7. Grease 12 small ramekins or
individual baking cups.

2 With an electric mixer, beat the
eggs until blended. Beat in the milk
and melted butter.

3 Sift together the flour and salt,
then beat into the egg mixture to
combine thoroughly.

4 ▼ Strip the herb leaves from the
stems and chop finely. Mix together
and measure out 30ml/2 tbsp. Stir the
herbs into the batter.

5 ▲ Fill the prepared cups half-full.

6 Bake until golden, 25–30 minutes.
Do not open the oven door during
baking time or the popovers may
collapse. For drier popovers, pierce
each one with a knife after the
30 minute baking time and bake
for 5 minutes more. Serve hot.

Cheese Popovers

MAKES 12

3 eggs

250ml/8fl oz/1 cup milk

25g/1oz/2 tbsp butter, melted

75g/3oz/²/3 cup plain (all-purpose) flour

1.5ml/¹/4 tsp salt

1.5ml/¹/4 tsp paprika

25g/1oz/¹/3 cup freshly grated
Parmesan cheese

~ VARIATION ~

For traditional Yorkshire Pudding,
omit the cheese and paprika, and
use 50–75g/2–3oz/4–6 tbsp of beef
dripping to replace the butter.
Put them into the oven in time to
serve warm as an accompaniment
for roast beef.

1 Preheat the oven to 220°C/425°F/
Gas 7.

2 ▲ Grease 12 small ramekins or
individual baking cups. With an
electric mixer, beat the eggs until
they are blended. Beat in the milk
and melted butter.

3 ▲ Sift together the flour, salt
and paprika, then beat into the egg
mixture. Add the cheese and stir.

4 Fill the prepared cups half-full and
bake until golden, 25–30 minutes. Do
not open the oven door or the popovers
may collapse. For drier popovers,
pierce each one with a knife after the
30 minute baking time and bake for
5 minutes more. Serve hot.

Herb Popovers (top), Cheese Popovers

YEAST BREADS

THOUGH THE PACE OF TODAY'S LIFE
LEAVES LITTLE TIME FOR BAKING,
BREADMAKING CAN BE VERY
THERAPEUTIC. THE PROCESS IS
SIMPLE YET INFINITELY VARIABLE,
AS THE LOAVES THAT FOLLOW
PROVE. ROLL UP YOUR SLEEVES AND
CREATE A TRADITION.

White Bread

MAKES 2 LOAVES

50ml/2fl oz/¹/₄ cup lukewarm water

15ml/1 tbsp active dried yeast

30ml/2 tbsp sugar

450ml/16fl oz/2 cups lukewarm milk

25g/1oz/2 tbsp butter or margarine,
   at room temperature

10ml/2 tsp salt

850–900g/1lb 14oz–2lb/7¹/₂–8 cups strong
   white bread flour

2 ▼ Pour the milk into a large bowl. Add the remaining sugar, the butter or margarine, and salt. Stir in the yeast mixture.

1 Combine the water, dried yeast and 15ml/1 tbsp of sugar in a measuring cup and leave to stand for 15 minutes until the mixture is frothy.

3 Stir in the flour, 150g/5oz/1¹/₄ cups at a time, until a stiff dough is obtained. Alternatively, use a food processor.

4 ▲ Transfer the dough to a floured surface. To knead, push the dough away from you with the palm of your hand, then fold it towards you. Repeat until the dough is smooth and elastic.

5 Place the dough in a large greased bowl, cover with a plastic bag, and leave to rise in a warm place until doubled in volume, 2–3 hours.

6 Grease two 23 × 13cm/9 × 5in tins (pans).

7 ▲ Knock back (punch down) the risen dough with your fist and divide in half. Form into a loaf shape and place in the tins, seam-side down. Cover and leave to rise in a warm place until almost doubled in volume, about 45 minutes. Preheat the oven to 190°C/375°F/Gas 5.

8 Bake until firm and brown, 45–50 minutes. Turn out and tap the bottom of a loaf: if it sounds hollow the loaf is done. If necessary, return to the oven and bake a few minutes more. Leave to cool on a rack.

Country Bread

MAKES 2 LOAVES

350g/12oz/3 cups wholemeal
(whole-wheat) flour

350g/12oz/3 cups plain (all-purpose) flour

150g/5oz/1¼ cups strong white bread flour

20ml/4 tsp salt

50g/2oz/¼ cup butter, at room temperature

475ml/16fl oz/2 cups lukewarm milk

FOR THE STARTER

15ml/1 tbsp active dry yeast

250ml/8fl oz/1 cup lukewarm water

150g/5oz/1¼ cups strong white bread flour

1.5ml/¼ tsp caster (superfine) sugar

1 ▲ For the starter, combine the yeast, water, flour and sugar in a bowl and stir with a fork. Cover and leave in a warm place for 2–3 hours, or leave overnight in a cool place.

2 Place the flours, salt and butter in a food processor and process until just blended, 1–2 minutes.

3 Stir together the milk and starter, then slowly pour into the processor, with the motor running, until the mixture forms a dough. If necessary, add more water. Alternatively, the dough can be mixed by hand. Transfer to a floured surface and knead until smooth and elastic.

4 Place in an ungreased bowl, cover with a plastic bag, and leave to rise in a warm place until doubled in volume, about 1½ hours.

5 Transfer to a floured surface and knead briefly. Return to the bowl and leave to rise until tripled in volume, about 1½ hours.

6 ▲ Divide the dough in half. Cut off one-third of the dough from each half and shape into balls. Shape the larger remaining portion of each half into balls. Grease a baking sheet.

7 ▲ For each loaf, top the large ball with the small ball, and press the centre with the handle of a wooden spoon to secure. Cover with a plastic bag, slash the top, and leave to rise.

8 Preheat the oven to 200°C/400°F/Gas 6. Dust the dough with flour and bake until the top is browned and the bottom sounds hollow when tapped, 45–50 minutes. Cool on a rack.

Braided Loaf

MAKES 1 LOAF

15ml/1 tbsp active dried yeast
5ml/1 tsp honey
250ml/8fl oz/1 cup lukewarm milk
50g/2oz/1/4 cup butter, melted
425g/15oz/3 1/2 cups strong white bread flour
5ml/1 tsp salt
1 egg, lightly beaten
1 egg yolk beaten with 5ml/1 tsp milk, for glazing

1 ▼ Combine the yeast, honey, milk and butter. Stir and leave for 15 minutes to dissolve.

2 In a large bowl, mix together the flour and salt. Make a well in the centre and add the yeast mixture and egg. With a wooden spoon, stir from the centre, incorporating flour with each turn, to obtain a rough dough.

3 Transfer to a floured surface and knead until smooth and elastic. Place in a clean bowl, cover and leave to rise in a warm place until doubled in volume, about 1 1/2 hours.

4 Grease a baking sheet. Knock back (punch down) the dough and divide into three equal pieces. Roll to shape each piece into a long, thin strip.

5 ▲ Begin braiding with the centre strip, tucking in the ends. Cover loosely and leave to rise in a warm place for 30 minutes.

6 ▲ Preheat the oven to 190°C/375°F/Gas 5. Place the bread in a cool place while the oven heats. Brush with the glaze and bake until golden, 40–45 minutes. Turn out on to a rack to cool.

Sesame Seed Bread

MAKES 1 LOAF

10ml/2 tsp active dried yeast
300ml/¹/₂ pint/1¹/₄ cups lukewarm water
200g/7oz/1³/₄ cups strong white bread flour
200g/7oz/1³/₄ cups strong wholemeal (whole-wheat) bread flour
10ml/2 tsp salt
65g/2¹/₂oz/5 tbsp toasted sesame seeds
milk, for glazing
25g/1oz/2 tbsp sesame seeds, for sprinkling

1 Combine the yeast and 75ml/5 tbsp of the water and leave to dissolve for 15 minutes. Mix the flours and salt in a large bowl. Make a well in the centre and pour in the yeast and water.

2 ▲ With a wooden spoon, stir from the centre, incorporating flour with each turn, to obtain a rough dough.

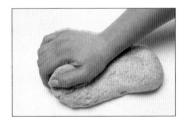

3 ▲ Transfer to a lightly floured surface. To knead, push the dough away from you with the palm of your hand, then fold it towards you and push away again. Repeat until smooth and elastic, then return to the bowl and cover with a plastic bag. Leave the dough in a warm place for about 1¹/₂–2 hours, until doubled in volume.

4 ▲ Grease a 23cm/9in cake tin (pan). Knock back (punch down) the dough and knead in the sesame seeds. Divide the dough into 16 balls and place in the tin. Cover with a plastic bag and leave in a warm place until risen above the rim of the tin.

5 ▼ Preheat the oven to 220°C/ 425°F/Gas 7. Brush the loaf with milk and sprinkle with the sesame seeds. Bake for 15 minutes. Lower the heat to 190°C/375°F/Gas 5 and bake until the bottom sounds hollow when tapped, about 30 minutes. Cool on a rack.

Wholemeal Bread

MAKES 1 LOAF

600g/1lb 5oz/5¼ cups strong wholemeal (whole-wheat) bread flour

10ml/2 tsp salt

20ml/4 tsp active dried yeast

425ml/15fl oz/generous 1⅔ cups lukewarm water

30ml/2 tbsp honey

45ml/3 tbsp oil

40g/1½oz wheatgerm

milk, for glazing

1 Combine the flour and salt in a bowl and place in the oven at its lowest setting until warmed, 8–10 minutes.

2 Meanwhile, combine the yeast with half of the water in a small bowl and leave to dissolve.

3 ▼ Make a well in the centre of the flour. Pour in the yeast mixture, the remaining water, honey, oil and wheatgerm. With a wooden spoon, stir from the centre until smooth.

4 Transfer the dough to a lightly floured surface and knead just enough to shape into a loaf.

5 ▲ Grease a 23 × 13cm/9 × 5in loaf tin (pan), place the dough in it and cover with a plastic bag. Leave in a warm place until the dough is about 2.5cm/1in higher than the tin rim, about 1 hour.

6 Preheat the oven to 200°C/400°F/ Gas 6. Bake until the bottom sounds hollow when tapped, 35–40 minutes. Cool.

Rye Bread

MAKES 1 LOAF

200g/7oz/1¾ cups rye flour

450ml/¾ pint/scant 2 cups boiling water

120ml/4fl oz/½ cup black treacle (molasses)

65g/2½oz/5 tbsp butter, cut in pieces

15ml/1 tbsp salt

30ml/2 tbsp caraway seeds

15ml/1 tbsp active dried yeast

120ml/4fl oz/½ cup lukewarm water

about 850g/1lb 14oz/7½ cups strong white bread flour

semolina or flour, for dusting

~ COOK'S TIP ~

To bring out the flavour of the caraway seeds, toast them lightly. Spread the seeds on a baking tray and place in a preheated 160°C/325°F/ Gas 3 oven for about 7 minutes.

1 ▲ Mix the rye flour, boiling water, treacle, butter, salt and caraway seeds in a large bowl. Leave to cool.

2 In another bowl, mix the yeast and lukewarm water and leave to dissolve. Stir into the rye flour mixture. Stir in just enough strong flour to obtain a stiff dough. If it becomes too stiff, stir with your hands.

3 Transfer to a floured surface and knead until the dough is no longer sticky and is smooth and shiny.

4 Place in a greased bowl, cover with a plastic bag, and leave in a warm place until doubled in volume. Knock back (punch down) the dough, cover, and leave to rise again for 30 minutes.

5 Preheat the oven to 180°C/350°F/ Gas 4. Dust a baking sheet with semolina.

6 ▼ Shape the dough into a ball. Place on the sheet and score several times across the top. Bake until the bottom sounds hollow when tapped, about 40 minutes. Cool on a rack.

Wholemeal Bread (top), Rye Bread

Buttermilk Graham Bread

MAKES 8

10ml/2 tsp active dried yeast

120ml/4fl oz/¹/₂ cup lukewarm water

225g/8oz/2 cups graham or strong
   wholemeal (whole-wheat)
   bread flour

350g/12oz/3 cups strong white
   bread flour

130g/4¹/₂oz/generous 1 cup cornmeal

10ml/2 tsp salt

30ml/2 tbsp sugar

60ml/4 tbsp butter, at room temperature

475ml/16fl oz/2 cups lukewarm buttermilk

1 beaten egg, for glazing

sesame seeds, for sprinkling

1 Combine the yeast and water, stir, and leave for 15 minutes to dissolve.

2 ▲ Mix together the two flours, cornmeal, salt and sugar in a large bowl. Make a well in the centre and pour in the yeast mixture, then add the butter and the buttermilk.

3 ▲ Stir from the centre, mixing in the flour until a rough dough is formed. If too stiff, use your hands.

4 ▲ Transfer to a floured surface and knead until smooth. Place in a clean bowl, cover, and leave in a warm place for 2–3 hours.

5 ▲ Grease two 20cm/8in square baking tins (pans). Knock back (punch down) the dough. Divide into eight pieces and roll them into balls. Place four in each tin. Cover and leave in a warm place for about 1 hour.

6 Preheat the oven to 190°C/375°F/Gas 5. Brush with the glaze, then sprinkle over the sesame seeds. Bake for about 50 minutes, or until the bottoms sound hollow when tapped. Cool on a wire rack.

Multi-grain Bread

MAKES 2 LOAVES

15ml/1 tbsp active dried yeast
50ml/2fl oz/¼ cup lukewarm water
65g/2½oz/⅔ cup rolled oats (not quick cook)
450ml/¾ pint/scant 2 cups milk
10ml/2 tsp salt
50ml/2fl oz/¼ cup oil
50g/2oz/¼ cup soft light brown sugar
30ml/2 tbsp honey
2 eggs, lightly beaten
25g/1oz wheatgerm
175g/6oz/1½ cups soya flour
350g/12oz/3 cups strong wholemeal (whole-wheat) bread flour
about 450g/1lb/4 cups strong white bread flour

1 Combine the yeast and water, stir, and leave for 15 minutes to dissolve.

2 ▲ Place the oats in a large bowl. Scald the milk, then pour over the rolled oats.

3 Stir in the salt, oil, sugar and honey. Leave until lukewarm.

~ VARIATION ~

Different flours may be used in this recipe, such as rye, barley, buckwheat or cornmeal. Try replacing the wheatgerm and the soya flour with one or two of these, using the same total amount.

4 ▲ Stir in the yeast mixture, eggs, wheatgerm, soya and wholemeal flours. Gradually stir in enough white flour to obtain a rough dough.

5 Transfer the dough to a floured surface and knead, adding flour if necessary, until smooth and elastic. Return to a clean bowl, cover and leave to rise in a warm place until doubled in volume, about 2½ hours.

6 Grease two 21 × 12cm/8½ × 4½in bread tins (pans). Knock back (punch down) the risen dough and knead briefly.

7 Divide the dough into quarters. Roll each quarter into a cylinder 4cm/1½in thick. Twist together 2 cylinders and put in a tin; repeat for the remaining pieces.

8 Cover and leave to rise until doubled in size, about 1 hour.

9 Preheat the oven to 190°C/375°F/Gas 5.

10 ▲ Bake for 45–50 minutes, until the bottoms sound hollow when tapped lightly. Cool on a rack.

Potato Bread

MAKES 2 LOAVES

20ml/4 tsp active dried yeast
250ml/8fl oz/1 cup lukewarm milk
225g/8oz potatoes, boiled (reserve 250ml/ 8fl oz/1 cup of potato cooking liquid)
30ml/2 tbsp oil
20ml/4 tsp salt
850–900g/1lb 14oz–2lb/7^1/$_2$–8 cups strong white bread flour

1 Combine the yeast and milk in a large bowl and leave to dissolve, about 15 minutes.

2 Meanwhile, mash the potatoes.

3 ▲ Add the potatoes, oil and salt to the yeast mixture and mix well. Stir in the reserved cooking water, then stir in the flour, in six separate batches, to form a stiff dough.

4 Transfer to a floured surface and knead until smooth and elastic. Return to the bowl, cover, and leave in a warm place until doubled in size, 1–1^1/$_2$ hours. Knock back (punch down), then leave to rise for another 40 minutes.

5 Grease two 23 × 13cm/9 × 5in loaf tins (pans). Roll the dough into 20 small balls. Place two rows of balls in each tin. Leave until the dough has risen above the rim of the tins.

6 Preheat the oven to 200°C/400°F/ Gas 6. Bake for 10 minutes, then lower the heat to 190°C/375°F/Gas 5. Bake until the bottoms sound hollow when tapped, 40 minutes. Cool on a rack.

Irish Soda Bread

MAKES 1 LOAF

275g/10oz/2^1/$_2$ cups plain (all-purpose) flour
150g/5oz/1^1/$_4$ cups wholemeal (whole-wheat) flour
5ml/1 tsp bicarbonate of soda (baking soda)
5ml/1 tsp salt
25g/1oz/2 tbsp butter or margarine, at room temperature
300ml/^{1}/$_2$ pint/1^1/$_4$ cups buttermilk
15ml/1 tbsp plain flour, for dusting

1 Preheat the oven to 200°C/400°F/ Gas 6. Grease a baking sheet.

2 Sift the flours, bicarbonate of soda and salt together into a bowl. Make a well in the centre and add the butter or margarine and buttermilk. Working outwards from the centre, stir with a fork until a soft dough is formed.

3 ▲ With floured hands, gather the dough into a ball.

4 ▲ Transfer to a floured surface and knead for 3 minutes. Shape the dough into a large round.

5 ▲ Place on the baking sheet. Cut a cross in the top with a sharp knife.

6 ▲ Dust with flour. Bake until brown, 40–50 minutes. Transfer to a rack to cool.

Potato Bread (top), Irish Soda Bread

Anadama Bread

MAKES 2 LOAVES

10ml/2 tsp active dried yeast
60ml/4 tbsp lukewarm water
50g/2oz/1/2 cup cornmeal
45ml/3 tbsp butter or margarine
60ml/4 tbsp black treacle (molasses)
175ml/6fl oz/3/4 cup boiling water
1 egg
350g/12oz/3 cups strong white bread flour
30ml/2 tbsp salt

1 Combine the yeast and lukewarm water, stir well, and leave for 15 minutes to dissolve.

2 ▼ Meanwhile, combine the cornmeal, butter or margarine, black treacle and boiling water in a large bowl. Add the yeast, egg, and half the flour. Stir together to blend.

3 ▲ Stir in the remaining flour and salt. When the dough becomes too stiff, stir with your hands until it comes away from the sides of the bowl. If it is too sticky, add more flour; if too stiff, add a little water.

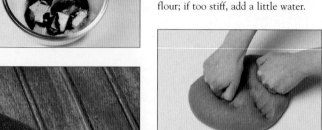

4 ▲ Transfer to a floured surface and knead until smooth and elastic. Place in a bowl, cover with a plastic bag, and leave in a warm place until doubled in size, 2–3 hours.

5 Grease two 18 × 7.5cm/7 × 3in bread tins (pans). Knock back (punch down) the dough. Shape into two loaves and place in the tins, seam-side down. Cover and leave in a warm place for 1–2 hours.

6 ▲ Preheat the oven to 190°C/375°F/Gas 5. Bake for 50 minutes. Remove and cool on a wire rack.

Oatmeal Bread

MAKES 2 LOAVES

450ml/³/₄ pint/scant 2 cups milk
25g/1oz/2 tbsp butter
50g/2oz/¹/₄ cup soft dark brown sugar
10ml/2 tsp salt
15ml/1 tbsp active dried yeast
50ml/2fl oz/¹/₄ cup lukewarm water
400g/14oz/4 cups rolled oats (not quick-cook)
700–850g/1¹/₂lb–1lb 14oz/6–7¹/₂ cups strong white bread flour

1 ▲ Scald the milk. Remove from the heat and stir in the butter, brown sugar and salt. Leave until lukewarm.

2 Combine the yeast and warm water in a large bowl and leave until the yeast is dissolved and the mixture is frothy. Stir in the milk mixture.

3 ▲ Add 270g/10oz/2¹/₄ cups of the oats and enough flour to obtain a soft dough.

4 Transfer to a floured surface and knead until smooth and elastic.

5 ▲ Place in a greased bowl, cover with a plastic bag, and leave until doubled in volume, 2–3 hours.

6 Grease a large baking sheet. Transfer the dough to a lightly floured surface and divide in half.

7 ▼ Shape into rounds. Place on the baking sheet, cover with a dish towel and leave to rise until doubled in volume, about 1 hour.

8 Preheat the oven to 200°C/400°F/ Gas 6. Score the tops and sprinkle with the remaining oats. Bake until the bottoms sound hollow when tapped, 45–50 minutes. Cool on racks.

Sourdough Bread

MAKES 1 LOAF

350g/12oz/3 cups strong white bread flour

15ml/1 tbsp salt

250ml/8fl oz/1 cup Sourdough Starter

120ml/4fl oz/¹/₂ cup lukewarm water

1 ▲ Combine the flour and salt in a large bowl. Make a well in the centre and add the starter and water. With a wooden spoon, stir from the centre, incorporating more flour with each turn, to obtain a rough dough.

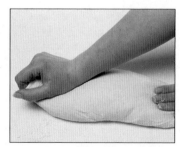

2 ▲ Transfer the dough to a floured surface. To knead, push the dough away from you with the palm of your hand, then fold it towards you, and push it away again. Repeat the process until the dough has become smooth and elastic.

3 Place in a clean bowl, cover, and leave to rise in a warm place until doubled in volume, for about 2 hours.

4 Lightly grease a 20 × 10cm/8 × 4in bread tin (pan).

5 ▼ Knock back (punch down) the dough with your fist. Knead briefly, then form into a loaf shape and place in the tin, seam-side down. Cover with a plastic bag, and leave to rise in a warm place, for about 1¹/₂ hours.

6 Preheat the oven to 220°C/425°F/Gas 7. Dust the top of the loaf with flour, then score lengthways. Bake for 15 minutes. Lower the heat to 190°C/375°F/Gas 5 and bake for about 30 minutes more, or until the bottom sounds hollow when tapped.

Sourdough Starter

MAKES 750ML/1¹/₄ PINTS

5ml/1 tsp active dried yeast

175ml/6fl oz/³/₄ cup lukewarm water

50g/2oz/¹/₂ cup strong white bread flour

~ COOK'S TIP ~

After using, feed the remaining starter with a handful of flour and enough water to restore it to a thick batter. The starter can be chilled for up to 1 week, but must be brought back to room temperature before using.

1 ▲ Combine the yeast and water, stir and leave for 15 minutes to dissolve.

2 ▼ Sprinkle over the flour, and whisk until it forms a batter. Cover and leave to rise in a warm place for at least 24 hours or preferably 2–4 days, before using.

Sourdough French Loaves

MAKES 2 LOAVES

10ml/2 tsp active dried yeast
350ml/12fl oz/1¹/₂ cups lukewarm water
250ml/8fl oz/1 cup Sourdough Starter
700g/1lb 8oz/6 cups strong white bread flour
15ml/1 tbsp salt
5ml/1 tsp sugar
cornmeal, for sprinkling
5ml/1 tsp cornflour (cornstarch)
120ml/4fl oz/¹/₂ cup water

1 In a large bowl, combine the yeast and lukewarm water, stir and leave for 15 minutes to dissolve.

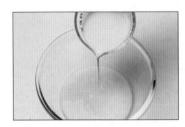

2 ▲ Pour in the Sourdough Starter. Add 450g/1lb/4 cups of the flour, the salt and the sugar. Stir until smooth. Cover the bowl with a plastic bag and leave the dough to rise in a warm place until doubled in volume, about 1¹/₂ hours.

3 Stir in just enough flour to obtain a rough dough. Transfer to a floured surface and knead until the dough is smooth and elastic. Divide in half, then shape each half into a 35cm/14in cylinder with rounded ends.

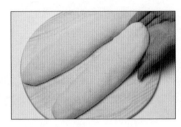

4 ▲ Place the loaves on a wooden board or tray sprinkled with cornmeal. Cover loosely with a dishtowel and leave to rise in a warm place until nearly doubled in volume.

5 Preheat the oven to 220°C/425°F/ Gas 7. Place a 38 × 30cm/15 × 12in baking sheet in the oven. Half-fill a shallow baking dish with hot water and put it on the bottom of the oven.

6 Mix the cornflour and water in a small pan. Bring to the boil.

7 ▲ With a sharp knife, make several diagonal slashes across the loaves. Slide on to the hot baking sheet and brush over the cornflour mixture. Bake until the tops are golden and the bottoms sound hollow when tapped, about 25 minutes. Cool on a wire rack.

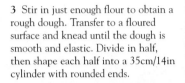

Sourdough Rye Bread

MAKES 2 LOAVES

10ml/2 tsp active dried yeast
120ml/4fl oz/¹/₂ cup lukewarm water
25g/1oz/2 tbsp butter, melted
15ml/1 tbsp salt
115g/4oz/1 cup strong wholemeal (whole-wheat) bread flour
400–450g/14–16oz/3¹/₂–4 cups strong white bread flour
1 egg mixed with 15ml/1 tbsp water, for glazing

FOR THE STARTER

15ml/1 tbsp active dried yeast
350ml/12fl oz/1¹/₂ cups lukewarm water
45ml/3 tbsp black treacle (molasses)
30ml/2 tbsp caraway seeds
250g/9oz/2¹/₄ cups rye flour

1 For the starter, combine the yeast and water, stir and leave for 15 minutes to dissolve.

2 ▲ Stir in the black treacle, caraway seeds and rye flour. Cover and leave in a warm place for 2–3 days.

3 In a large bowl, combine the yeast and water, stir and leave for 10 minutes. Stir in the melted butter, salt, wholemeal flour and 400g/14oz/ 3¹/₂ cups of the white flour.

4 ▲ Make a well in the centre and pour in the starter.

5 Stir to obtain a rough dough, then transfer to a floured surface and knead until smooth and elastic. Return to the bowl, cover and leave to rise in a warm place until doubled in volume, about 2 hours.

6 Grease a large baking sheet. Knock back (punch down) the dough and knead briefly. Cut the dough in half and form each half into log-shaped loaves.

7 ▼ Place the loaves on the baking sheet and score the tops with a sharp knife. Cover and leave to rise in a warm place until almost doubled, about 50 minutes.

8 Preheat the oven to 190°C/375°F/ Gas 5. Brush the loaves with the egg wash to glaze them, then bake until the bottoms sound hollow when tapped, about 50–55 minutes. If the tops brown too quickly, place a sheet of foil over the tops to protect them. Cool on a wire rack.

Wholemeal Rolls

MAKES 12

10ml/2 tsp active dried yeast

50ml/2fl oz/¹/₄ cup lukewarm water

5ml/1 tsp caster (superfine) sugar

175ml/6fl oz/³/₄ cup lukewarm buttermilk

1.5ml/¹/₄ tsp bicarbonate of soda
   (baking soda)

5ml/1 tsp salt

40g/1¹/₂oz/3 tbsp butter,
   at room temperature

200g/7oz/1³/₄ cups strong wholemeal
   (whole-wheat) bread flour

150g/5oz/1¹/₄ cups strong white
   bread flour

1 beaten egg, for glazing

1 In a large bowl, combine the yeast,
water and sugar. Stir, and leave for
15 minutes to dissolve.

2 ▲ Add the buttermilk, bicarbonate
of soda, salt and butter, and stir to
blend. Stir in the wholemeal flour.

3 Add just enough of the white flour
to obtain a rough dough.

4 Transfer to a floured surface and
knead until smooth and elastic.
Divide into three equal parts.
Roll each into a cylinder, then cut
into four.

5 ▼ Form the pieces into torpedo
shapes. Place on a greased baking
sheet, cover and leave in a warm
place until doubled in volume.

6 Preheat the oven to 200°C/400°F/
Gas 6. Brush the rolls with the glaze.
Bake until firm, 15–20 minutes. Cool
on a rack.

French Bread

MAKES 2 LOAVES

15ml/1 tbsp active dried yeast

450ml/³/₄ pint/scant 2 cups lukewarm water

15ml/1 tbsp salt

850g–1.2kg/1lb 14oz–2¹/₂lb/7¹/₂–10 cups
   strong white bread flour

semolina or flour, for sprinkling

1 Combine the yeast and water, stir,
and leave for 15 minutes to dissolve.
Stir in the salt.

2 Add the flour, 150g/5oz/1¹/₄ cups at
a time. Beat in with a wooden spoon,
adding just enough flour to obtain a
smooth dough. Alternatively, use an
electric mixer with a dough hook.

3 Transfer to a floured surface and
knead until smooth and elastic.

4 Shape into a ball, place in a greased
bowl and cover with a plastic bag.
Leave to rise in a warm place until
doubled in volume, 2–4 hours.

5 ▲ Transfer to a lightly floured
board and shape into two long loaves.
Place on a baking sheet sprinkled with
semolina or flour and leave to rise for
5 minutes.

6 ▲ Score the tops in several places
with a very sharp knife. Brush with
water and place in a cold oven. Set a
pan of boiling water on the bottom of
the oven and set the oven to 200°C/
400°F/Gas 6. Bake until crusty and
golden, about 40 minutes. Cool
on a rack.

Wholemeal Rolls (top), French Bread

Pleated Rolls

MAKES 48

15ml/1 tbsp active dried yeast
475ml/16fl oz/2 cups lukewarm milk
115g/4oz/¹/₂ cup margarine
75ml/5 tbsp sugar
10ml/2 tsp salt
2 eggs
975g–1.2kg/2lb 3oz–2¹/₂lb/8²/₃–10 cups strong white bread flour
50g/2oz/¹/₄ cup butter

1 Combine the yeast and 120ml/
4fl oz/¹/₂ cup milk in a large bowl. Stir
and leave for 15 minutes to dissolve.

2 Scald the remaining milk, cool
for 5 minutes, then beat in the
margarine, sugar, salt and eggs.
Leave to cool to lukewarm.

3 ▲ Pour the milk mixture into
the yeast mixture. Stir in half the
flour with a wooden spoon. Add the
remaining flour, 150g/5oz/1¹/₄ cups at a
time, until a rough dough is obtained.

4 Transfer the dough to a lightly
floured surface and knead until
smooth and elastic. Place in a clean
bowl, cover with a plastic bag and
leave to rise in a warm place until
doubled in volume, about 2 hours.

5 In a pan, melt the butter and set
aside. Grease two baking sheets.

6 Knock back (punch down) the dough
and divide into four equal pieces. Roll
each piece into a 30 × 20cm/12 × 8in
rectangle, about 5mm/¹/₄in thick.

7 ▲ Cut each rectangle into four
long strips. Cut each strip into three
10 × 5cm/4 × 2in rectangles.

8 ▲ Brush each rectangle with
melted butter, then fold the rectangles
in half, so that the top extends about
1cm/¹/₂in over the bottom.

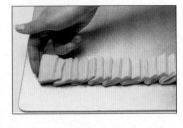

9 ▲ Place the rectangles slightly
overlapping on the baking sheet, with
the longer side facing up. Cover and
chill for 30 minutes. Preheat the oven
to 180°C/350°F/Gas 4. Bake until
golden, about 18–20 minutes. Allow
to cool slightly before slicing or
breaking the rolls.

Clover Leaf Rolls

MAKES 24

300ml/¹/₂ pint/1¹/₄ cups milk
30ml/2 tbsp caster (superfine) sugar
50g/2oz/¹/₄ cup butter, at room temperature
10ml/2 tsp active dried yeast
1 egg
10ml/2 tsp salt
500–575g/1lb 2oz–1lb 4oz/4¹/₂–5 cups strong white bread flour
melted butter, for glazing

1 ▲ Heat the milk until lukewarm; test the temperature with your knuckle. Pour into a large bowl and stir in the sugar, butter and yeast. Leave for 15 minutes to dissolve.

2 Stir the egg and salt into the yeast mixture. Gradually stir in 500g/1lb 2oz/4¹/₂ cups of the flour. Add just enough extra flour to obtain a rough dough.

3 ▲ Transfer to a floured surface and knead until smooth and elastic. Place in a greased bowl, cover and leave in a warm place until doubled in volume, about 1¹/₂ hours.

4 Grease two 12-cup bun trays.

5 ▼ Knock back (punch down) the dough. Cut into four equal pieces. Roll each piece into a rope 35cm/14in long. Cut each rope into 18 pieces, then roll each into a ball.

6 ▲ Place three balls, side by side, in each bun cup. Cover loosely and leave to rise in a warm place until doubled in volume, about 1¹/₂ hours.

7 Preheat the oven to 200°C/400°F/ Gas 6. Brush the rolls with glaze. Bake until lightly browned, about 20 minutes. Cool slightly before serving.

Poppyseed Knots

MAKES 12

300ml/¹/₂ pint/1¹/₄ cups lukewarm milk

50g/2oz/¹/₄ cup butter, at room temperature

5ml/1 tsp caster (superfine) sugar

10ml/2 tsp active dried yeast

1 egg yolk

10ml/2 tsp salt

500–575g/1lb 2oz–1lb 4oz/4¹/₂–5 cups
 strong white bread flour

1 egg beaten with 10ml/2 tsp of water,
 for glazing

poppyseeds, for sprinkling

1 In a large bowl, stir together the milk, butter, sugar and yeast. Leave for 15 minutes to dissolve.

2 Stir in the egg yolk, salt and 275g/10oz/2¹/₂ cups flour. Add half the remaining flour and stir to obtain a soft dough.

3 Transfer to a floured surface and knead, adding flour if necessary, until smooth and elastic. Place in a bowl, cover and leave in a warm place until doubled in volume, 1¹/₂–2 hours.

4 ▲ Grease a baking sheet. Knock back (punch down) the dough and cut into 12 pieces the size of golf balls.

5 ▲ Roll each piece to a rope, twist to form a knot and place 2.5cm/1in apart on the sheet. Cover and leave to rise until doubled in volume, 1–1¹/₂ hours.

6 Preheat the oven to 180°C/350°F/Gas 4.

7 ▲ Brush the knots with the egg glaze and sprinkle over the poppyseeds. Bake until the tops are lightly browned, 25–30 minutes. Cool slightly on a rack before serving.

Bread Sticks

MAKES 18–20

15ml/1 tbsp active dried yeast
300ml/¹/₂ pint/1¹/₄ cups lukewarm water
425g/15oz/3²/₃ cups strong white bread flour
10ml/2 tsp salt
5ml/1 tsp caster (superfine) sugar
30ml/2 tbsp olive oil
150g/5oz/10 tbsp sesame seeds
1 beaten egg, for glazing
coarse salt, for sprinkling

1 Combine the yeast and water, stir and leave for 15 minutes to dissolve.

2 ▲ Place the flour, salt, sugar and olive oil in a food processor. With the motor running, slowly pour in the yeast mixture, and process until the dough forms a ball. If sticky, add more flour; if dry, add more water.

3 Transfer to a floured surface and knead until smooth and elastic. Place in a bowl, cover and leave to rise in a warm place for 45 minutes.

4 ▲ Lightly toast the sesame seeds in a frying pan. Grease two baking sheets.

5 ▼ Roll small handfuls of dough into cylinders, about 30cm/12in long. Place on the baking sheets.

~ VARIATION ~

If you like, use other seeds, such as poppy or caraway, or, for plain bread sticks, omit the seeds and salt.

6 ▲ Brush with egg glaze, sprinkle with the sesame seeds, then sprinkle over some coarse salt. Leave to rise, uncovered, until almost doubled in volume, about 20 minutes.

7 Preheat the oven to 200°C/400°F/ Gas 6. Bake until golden, about 15 minutes. Turn off the heat but leave the bread sticks in the oven for 5 minutes more. Serve warm or cool.

Croissants

MAKES 18

15ml/1 tbsp active dried yeast
335ml/11fl oz/generous 1¼ cups lukewarm milk
10ml/2 tsp caster (superfine) sugar
7.5ml/1½ tsp salt
425–505g/15oz–1lb 2oz/3⅔–4½ cups strong white bread flour
225g/8oz/1 cup cold unsalted (sweet) butter
1 egg beaten with 10ml/2 tsp water, for glazing

1 Stir together the yeast and warm milk in a large bowl. Leave for 15 minutes to dissolve. Stir in the sugar, salt and 150g/5oz/1¼ cups of the flour.

2 Using a dough hook, on low speed, gradually add the remaining flour. Beat on high until the dough pulls away from the sides of the bowl. Cover and let rise in a warm place until doubled, about 1½ hours.

3 On a floured surface, knead the dough until smooth. Wrap it in baking parchment and chill for 15 minutes.

4 ▲ Divide the butter into two halves and place each between two sheets of baking parchment. With a rolling pin, flatten each to form a 15 × 10cm/6 × 4in rectangle. Set aside.

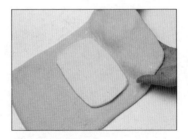

5 ▲ On a floured surface, roll out the dough to 30 × 20cm/12 × 8in. Place a butter rectangle in the centre. Fold the bottom third of dough over the butter and press gently to seal. Top with the other butter rectangle, then fold over the top dough third.

6 ▲ Turn the dough so that the short side is facing you, with the long folded edge on the left and the long open edge on the right, like a book.

7 Roll the dough gently into a 30 × 20cm/12 × 8in rectangle; do not press the butter out. Fold in thirds again and mark one corner with your fingertip to indicate the first turn. Wrap and chill for 30 minutes.

8 Repeat twice more: again position the dough like a book, roll, fold in thirds, mark, wrap, and chill. After the third fold, chill for at least 2 hours (or overnight).

9 Roll out the dough about 3mm/⅛in thick to a rectangle about 33cm/13in wide. Trim the sides to neaten.

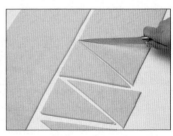

10 ▲ Cut the dough in half lengthways, then cut into triangles 15cm/6in high with a 10cm/4in base.

11 ▲ Gently go over the triangles lengthways with a rolling pin to stretch slightly. Roll up from base to point. Place point down on baking sheets and curve to form a crescent. Cover and leave to rise in a warm place until more than doubled in volume, 1–1½ hours. (Or, chill overnight and bake the next day.)

12 ▲ Preheat the oven to 240°C/475°F/Gas 9. Brush with the glaze. Bake for 2 minutes. Lower the heat to 190°C/375°F/Gas 5. Bake until golden, 10–12 more minutes. Serve warm.

Dill Bread

MAKES 2 LOAVES

20ml/4 tsp active dried yeast
475ml/16fl oz/2 cups lukewarm water
30ml/2 tbsp sugar
1.05kg/2lb 5¹/₂oz/9¹/₄ cups strong white bread flour
¹/₂ onion, chopped
60ml/4 tbsp oil
1 large bunch of dill, finely chopped
2 eggs, lightly beaten
165g/5¹/₂oz/¾ cup cottage cheese
20ml/4 tsp salt
milk, for glazing

1 Mix together the yeast, water and sugar in a large bowl and leave for 15 minutes to dissolve.

2 ▼ Stir in about half of the flour. Cover and leave to rise in a warm place for 45 minutes.

3 ▲ In a frying pan, cook the onion in 15ml/1 tbsp of the oil until soft. Set aside to cool, then stir into the yeast mixture. Stir the dill, eggs, cottage cheese, salt and remaining oil into the yeast. Gradually add the remaining flour until too stiff to stir.

4 ▲ Transfer to a floured surface and knead until smooth and elastic. Place in a bowl, cover and leave to rise until doubled in volume, 1–1¹/₂ hours.

5 ▲ Grease a large baking sheet. Cut the dough in half and shape into two rounds. Leave to rise in a warm place for 30 minutes.

6 Preheat the oven to 190°C/375°F/ Gas 5. Score the tops, brush with the milk and bake until browned, about 50 minutes. Cool on a rack.

Spiral Herb Bread

MAKES 2 LOAVES

30ml/2 tbsp active dried yeast
600ml/1 pint/2¹/₂ cups lukewarm water
425g/15oz/3²/₃ cups strong white bread flour
505g/1lb 2oz/4¹/₂ cups strong wholemeal (whole-wheat) bread flour
15ml/3 tsp salt
25g/1oz/2 tbsp butter
1 large bunch of parsley, finely chopped
1 bunch of spring onions (scallions), chopped
1 garlic clove, finely chopped
salt and ground black pepper
1 egg, lightly beaten
milk, for glazing

1 Combine the yeast and 50ml/2fl oz/ ¹/₄ cup of the water, stir and leave for 15 minutes to dissolve.

2 Combine the flours and salt in a large bowl. Make a well in the centre and pour in the yeast mixture and the remaining water. With a wooden spoon, stir from the centre, working outwards to obtain a rough dough.

3 Transfer the dough to a floured surface and knead until smooth and elastic. Return to the bowl, cover with a plastic bag, and leave until doubled in volume, about 2 hours.

4 ▲ Meanwhile, combine the butter, parsley, spring onions and garlic in a large frying pan. Cook over low heat, stirring, until softened. Season and set aside.

5 Grease two 23 × 13cm/9 × 5in tins (pans). When the dough has risen, cut in half and roll each half into a rectangle about 35 × 23cm/14 × 9in.

6 ▼ Brush both with the beaten egg. Divide the herb mixture between the two, spreading just up to the edges.

7 ▲ Roll up to enclose the filling and pinch the short ends to seal. Place in the tins, seam-side down. Cover, and leave in a warm place until the dough rises above the rim of the tins.

8 Preheat the oven to 190°C/375°F/ Gas 5. Brush with milk and bake until the bottoms sound hollow when tapped, about 55 minutes. Cool on a rack.

Pizza

MAKES 2

505g/1lb 2oz/4¹/₂ cups strong white bread flour

5ml/1 tsp salt

10ml/2 tsp active dried yeast

300ml/¹/₂ pint/1¹/₄ cups lukewarm water

50–120ml/2–4fl oz/¹/₄–¹/₂ cup extra-virgin olive oil

tomato sauce, grated cheese, olives and herbs, for topping

1 Combine the flour and salt in a large mixing bowl. Make a well in the centre and add the yeast, water and 30ml/2 tbsp of the olive oil. Leave for 15 minutes to dissolve the yeast.

2 With your hands, stir until the dough just holds together. Transfer to a floured surface and knead until smooth and elastic. Avoid adding too much flour while kneading.

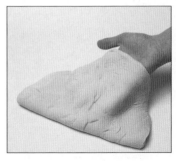

3 ▲ Brush the inside of a clean bowl with 15ml/1 tbsp of the oil. Place the dough in the bowl and roll around to coat with the oil. Cover with a plastic bag and leave to rise in a warm place until more than doubled in volume, about 45 minutes.

4 Divide the dough into two balls. Preheat the oven to 200°C/400°F/Gas 6.

5 ▲ Roll each ball into a 25cm/10in circle. Flip the circles over and on to your palm. Set each circle on the work surface and rotate, stretching the dough as you turn, until it is about 30cm/12in in diameter.

6 ▲ Brush two pizza pans with oil. Place the dough circles in the pans and neaten the edges. Brush with oil.

7 ▲ Cover with the toppings and bake until golden, 10–12 minutes.

Cheese Bread

MAKES 1 LOAF

15ml/1 tbsp active dried yeast
250ml/8fl oz/1 cup lukewarm milk
25g/1oz/2 tbsp butter
425g/15oz/3²/₃ cups strong white bread flour
10ml/2 tsp salt
90g/3¹/₂oz mature Cheddar cheese, grated

1 Combine the yeast and milk. Stir and leave for 15 minutes to dissolve.

2 Melt the butter, leave to cool, and add to the yeast mixture.

3 Mix the flour and salt together in a large bowl. Make a well in the centre and pour in the yeast mixture.

4 With a wooden spoon, stir from the centre, incorporating flour with each turn, to obtain a rough dough. If the dough seems too dry, add 30–45ml/2–3 tbsp water.

5 Transfer to a floured surface and knead until smooth and elastic. Return to the bowl, cover and leave to rise in a warm place until doubled in volume, 2–3 hours.

6 ▲ Grease a 23 × 13cm/9 × 5in loaf tin (pan). Knock back (punch down) the dough with your fist. Knead in the cheese, distributing it as evenly as possible.

7 ▼ Twist the dough, form into a loaf shape and place in the tin, tucking the ends under. Leave in a warm place until the dough rises above the rim of the tin.

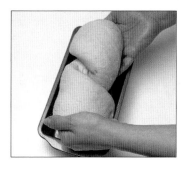

8 ▲ Preheat the oven to 200°C/400°F/Gas 6. Bake for 15 minutes, then lower to 190°C/375°F/Gas 5 and bake until the bottom sounds hollow when tapped, about 30 minutes more.

Italian Flat Bread with Sage

MAKES 1 LOAF

10ml/2 tsp active dried yeast
250ml/8fl oz/1 cup lukewarm water
350g/12oz/3 cups strong white bread flour
10ml/2 tsp salt
75ml/5 tbsp extra virgin olive oil
12 fresh sage leaves, chopped

1 Combine the yeast and water, stir and leave for 15 minutes until the yeast has completely dissolved.

2 Mix the flour and salt in a large bowl, and make a well in the centre.

3 Stir in the yeast mixture and 60ml/ 4 tbsp of the oil. Stir from the centre, incorporating flour with each turn, to obtain a rough dough.

4 ▲ Transfer the dough to a lightly floured surface and knead until it is smooth and elastic. Shape into a ball and place in a lightly oiled bowl. Cover and leave to rise in a warm place until doubled in volume, for about 2 hours.

5 Preheat the oven to 200°C/400°F/ Gas 6 and place a baking sheet in the centre of the oven.

6 Knock back (punch down) the dough. Knead in the sage leaves, then roll into a 30cm/12in round. Leave to rise slightly.

7 ▼ Dimple the surface all over with your finger. Drizzle the remaining oil on top. Slide a floured board under the bread, carry to the oven, and slide off on the hot baking sheet. Bake for about 35 minutes, or until golden brown. Cool on a rack.

Courgette Yeast Bread

MAKES 1 LOAF

450g/1lb courgettes (zucchini), grated
30ml/2 tbsp salt
10ml/2 tsp active dried yeast
300ml/1/2 pint/11/4 cups lukewarm water
400g/14oz/31/2 cups strong white bread flour
olive oil, for brushing

1 ▼ In a colander, alternate the layers of grated courgettes and salt. Leave for 30 minutes, then squeeze out the moisture with your hands.

2 Combine yeast with 50ml/2fl oz/1/4 cup warm water. Leave for 15 minutes.

3 ▲ Place the courgettes, yeast and flour in a bowl. Stir together and add just enough of the remaining water to obtain a rough dough.

4 Transfer to a floured surface and knead until smooth and elastic. Return the dough to the bowl, cover with a plastic bag, and leave to rise in a warm place until doubled in volume, for about 11/2 hours.

5 Knock back (punch down) the risen dough with your fist and knead into a tapered cylinder. Place on a greased baking sheet, cover and leave to rise in a warm place until doubled in volume.

6 ▼ Preheat the oven to 220°C/ 425°F/Gas 7. Brush the bread with olive oil and bake for 40–45 minutes, or until the loaf is a golden colour.

Italian Flat Bread with Sage (top), Courgette Yeast Bread

Olive Bread

MAKES 2 LOAVES

20ml/4 tsp active dried yeast

475ml/16fl oz/2 cups warm water

400g/14oz/3½ cups strong white
  bread flour

175g/6oz/1½ cups strong wholemeal
  (whole-wheat) bread flour

65g/2½oz/generous ½ cup cornmeal

10ml/2 tsp salt

30ml/2 tbsp olive oil

115g/4oz/1 cup mixed pitted green and
  black olives, cut in half

cornmeal, for sprinkling

1 Combine the yeast and water, stir
and leave for 5 minutes to dissolve.

2 Stir in 225g/8oz/2 cups of the white
flour, cover and leave in a warm place
for 1 hour.

3 In a large mixing bowl, combine
the remaining white flour, the
wholemeal flour, cornmeal and salt.
Make a well in the centre; pour in
the olive oil and yeast mixture.

4 ▼ With a wooden spoon, stir from
the centre, incorporating flour with
each turn. When the dough becomes
stiff, stir with your hands until a rough
dough is obtained.

5 Transfer to a floured surface and
knead until smooth and elastic.
Return to the bowl, cover and leave
to rise in a warm place until doubled
in volume, about 1½ hours.

6 ▲ Knock back (punch down) the
dough. Add the olives and knead.

7 Cut the dough in half and shape
each half into a round. Sprinkle a
baking sheet with cornmeal. Place
the rounds on the sheet, seam-side
down. Cover and leave to rise until
nearly doubled in volume.

8 Place a baking tin (pan) in the
bottom of the oven and half fill it
with hot water. Preheat the oven to
220°C/425°F/Gas 7.

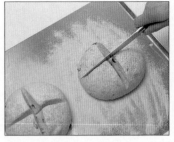

9 ▲ With a sharp knife, score
the tops of the loaves. Bake for
20 minutes. Lower the heat to
190°C/375°F/Gas 5 and bake for
25–30 minutes more, or until the
bottoms sound hollow when tapped.
Cool on a wire rack.

Pumpkin Spice Bread

MAKES 1 LOAF

30ml/2 tbsp active dried yeast
250ml/8fl oz/1 cup lukewarm water
10ml/2 tsp ground cinnamon
5ml/1 tsp ground ginger
5ml/1 tsp ground allspice
1.5ml/¼ tsp ground cloves
5ml/1 tsp salt
75g/3oz/6 tbsp dried skimmed milk
175g/6oz cooked or canned pumpkin
350g/12oz/1¾ cups sugar
115g/4oz/½ cup butter, melted
600g/1lb 6oz/5½ cups strong white bread flour
50g/2oz/⅓ cup pecan nuts, finely chopped

1 Using an electric mixer, combine the yeast and water, stir and leave for 15 minutes to dissolve. In another bowl, mix the spices together.

2 To the yeast, add the salt, milk, pumpkin, 115g/4oz/generous ½ cup of the sugar, 45ml/3 tbsp of the melted butter, 10ml/2 tsp of the spice mixture and 225g/8oz/2 cups of the flour.

3 ▲ With the dough hook, mix on low speed until blended. Gradually add the remaining flour and mix on medium speed until a rough dough is formed. Alternatively, mix by hand.

4 Transfer to a floured surface and knead until smooth. Place in a bowl, cover and leave to rise in a warm place until doubled, 1–1½ hours.

5 ▼ Knock back (punch down) and knead briefly. Divide the dough into thirds. Roll each third into an 45cm/18in rope. Cut each rope into 18 equal pieces, then roll into balls.

6 Grease a 25cm/10in tube tin. Stir the remaining sugar into the remaining spice mixture. Roll the balls in the remaining melted butter, then in the sugar and spice mixture.

7 ▲ Place 18 balls in the tin and sprinkle over half the nuts. Add the remaining balls, then sprinkle over the remaining nuts. Cover and leave to rise in a warm place until almost doubled, about 45 minutes.

8 Preheat the oven to 180°C/350°F/Gas 4. Bake for 55 minutes. Cool in the tin for 20 minutes, then turn out on a rack. Serve warm.

Walnut Bread

MAKES 1 LOAF

425g/15oz/3²/₃ cups strong wholemeal (whole-wheat) bread flour

150g/5oz/1¹/₄ cups strong white bread flour

12.5ml/2¹/₂ tsp salt

550ml/18fl oz/2¹/₂ cups lukewarm water

15ml/1 tbsp honey

15ml/1 tbsp active dried yeast

150g/5oz/1 cup walnut pieces, plus extra for decorating

1 beaten egg, for glazing

1 Combine the flours and salt in a large bowl. Make a well in the centre and add 250ml/8fl oz/1 cup of the water, the honey and the yeast.

2 Set aside until the yeast dissolves and the mixture is frothy.

3 Add the remaining water. With a wooden spoon, stir from the centre, incorporating flour with each turn, to obtain a smooth dough. Add more flour if the dough is too sticky and use your hands if the dough becomes too stiff to stir.

4 Transfer to a floured board and knead, adding flour if necessary, until the dough is smooth and elastic. Place in a greased bowl and roll the dough around in the bowl to coat thoroughly on all sides.

5 ▲ Cover with a plastic bag and leave in a warm place until doubled in volume, about 1¹/₂ hours.

6 ▲ Knock back (punch down) the dough and knead in the walnuts evenly.

7 Grease a baking sheet. Shape into a round loaf and place on the baking sheet. Press in walnut pieces to decorate the top. Cover and leave to rise in a warm place until doubled, 25–30 minutes.

8 Preheat the oven to 220°C/425°F/ Gas 7.

9 ▲ With a sharp knife, score the top. Brush with the glaze. Bake for 15 minutes. Lower the heat to 190°C/ 375°F/Gas 5 and bake until the bottom sounds hollow when tapped, about 40 minutes. Cool on a rack.

Pecan Rye Bread

MAKES 2 LOAVES

25ml/1¹/₂ tbsp active dried yeast
700ml/24fl oz/2³/₄ cups lukewarm water
670g/1¹/₂lb/6 cups strong white bread flour
505g/1lb 2oz/4¹/₂ cups rye flour
30ml/2 tbsp salt
15ml/1 tbsp honey
10ml/2 tsp caraway seeds, (optional)
115g/4oz/¹/₂ cup butter, at room temperature
225g/8oz/1¹/₃ cups pecan nuts, chopped

1 Combine the yeast and 120ml/ 4fl oz/¹/₂ cup of the water. Stir and leave for 15 minutes to dissolve.

2 In the bowl of an electric mixer, combine the flours, salt, honey, caraway seeds, if using, and butter. With the dough hook, mix on low speed until well blended.

3 Add the yeast mixture and the remaining water and mix on medium speed until the dough forms a ball.

4 ▲ Transfer to a floured surface and knead in the pecan nuts.

5 Return the dough to a bowl, cover with a plastic bag and leave in a warm place until doubled, about 2 hours.

6 Grease two 21 × 12cm/8¹/₂ × 4¹/₂in bread tins (pans).

7 ▲ Knock back (punch down) the risen dough.

8 Divide the dough in half and form into loaves. Place in the tins, seam-side down. Dust the tops with flour. Cover with plastic bags and leave to rise in a warm place until doubled in volume, about 1 hour.

9 Preheat the oven to 190°C/375°F/ Gas 5.

10 ▼ Bake until the bottoms sound hollow when tapped, 45–50 minutes. Cool on racks.

Sticky Buns

MAKES 18

170ml/5¹/₂fl oz/scant ³/₄ cup milk

15ml/1 tbsp active dried yeast

30ml/2 tbsp caster (superfine) sugar

425–450g/15oz–1lb/3¹/₂–4 cups strong
    white bread flour

5ml/1 tsp salt

115g/4oz/¹/₂ cup cold butter, cut into pieces

2 eggs, lightly beaten

grated rind of 1 lemon

FOR THE TOPPING AND FILLING

275g/10oz/1¹/₄ cups soft dark brown sugar

65g/2¹/₂oz/5 tbsp butter

120ml/4fl oz/¹/₂ cup water

75g/3oz/¹/₂ cup pecan nuts or walnuts,
    chopped

45ml/3 tbsp caster (superfine) sugar

10ml/2 tsp ground cinnamon

165g/5¹/₂oz/generous 1 cup raisins

1 Heat the milk to lukewarm. Add
the yeast and sugar, and leave until
frothy, about 15 minutes.

2 Combine the flour and salt in a
large mixing bowl. Add the butter and
rub in with your fingertips until the
mixture resembles coarse breadcrumbs.

3 ▲ Make a well in the centre and
add the yeast mixture, eggs and lemon
rind. With a wooden spoon, stir from
the centre, incorporating flour with
each turn. When it becomes too stiff,
stir by hand to obtain a rough dough.

4 Transfer to a floured surface
and knead until smooth and elastic.
Return to the bowl, cover with a
plastic bag and leave to rise in a warm
place until doubled in volume, about
2 hours.

5 Meanwhile, for the topping, make
the syrup. Combine the brown sugar,
butter and water in a heavy pan.
Bring to the boil and boil gently until
thick and syrupy, about 10 minutes.

6 ▲ Place 15ml/1 tbsp of the syrup
in the bottom of each of 18 4cm/1¹/₂in
muffin cups. Sprinkle in a thin layer
of chopped nuts, reserving the rest for
the filling.

7 Knock back (punch down) the
dough. Roll out to a 45 × 30cm/
18 × 12in rectangle.

8 ▲ For the filling, combine the
caster sugar, cinnamon, raisins and
reserved nuts. Sprinkle over the
dough in an even layer.

9 ▲ Roll up tightly, from the long
side, to form a cylinder.

10 ▲ Cut the cylinder into 2.5cm/
1in rounds. Place each in a prepared
muffin cup, cut-side up. Leave to rise
in a warm place until increased by
half, about 30 minutes.

11 Preheat the oven to 180°C/350°F/
Gas 4. Place foil under the tins (pans)
to catch any syrup that bubbles over.
Bake until golden, about 25 minutes.

12 Remove from the oven and invert
the tins on to a baking sheet. Leave
for 3–5 minutes, then remove the
buns from the tins. Transfer to a rack
to cool. Serve sticky-side up.

~ COOK'S TIP ~

To save time and energy, make
double the recipe and freeze half
for another occasion.

Raisin Bread

MAKES 2 LOAVES

15ml/1 tbsp active dried yeast
475ml/16fl oz/2 cups lukewarm milk
150g/5oz/1 cup raisins
65g/2¹/₂oz/generous ¹/₄ cup currants
15ml/1 tbsp sherry or brandy
2.5ml/¹/₂ tsp freshly grated nutmeg
grated rind of 1 large orange
65g/2¹/₂oz/5 tbsp sugar
15ml/1 tbsp salt
115g/4oz/¹/₂ cup butter, melted
700–850g/1¹/₂lb–1lb 14oz/6–7¹/₂ cups strong white bread flour
1 egg beaten with 15ml/1 tbsp cream, for glazing

1 Stir together the yeast and 125ml/ 4fl oz/¹/₂ cup of the milk and leave to stand for 15 minutes to dissolve.

2 ▲ Mix the raisins, currants, sherry or brandy, nutmeg and orange rind together and set aside.

3 In another bowl, mix the remaining milk, sugar, salt and half the butter. Add the yeast mixture. With a wooden spoon, stir in half the flour, 150g/5oz/1¹/₄ cups at a time, until blended. Add the remaining flour as needed for a stiff dough.

4 Transfer to a floured surface and knead until smooth and elastic. Place in a greased bowl, cover and leave to rise in a warm place until doubled in volume, about 2¹/₂ hours.

5 Knock back (punch down) the dough, return to the bowl, cover and leave in a warm place for 30 minutes.

6 Grease two 21 × 12cm/8¹/₂ × 4¹/₂in bread tins (pans). Divide the dough in half and roll each half into a 50 × 18cm/20 × 7in rectangle.

7 ▲ Brush the rectangles with the remaining melted butter. Sprinkle over the raisin mixture, then roll up tightly, tucking in the ends slightly as you roll. Place in the prepared tins, cover, and leave to rise until almost doubled in volume.

8 ▲ Preheat the oven to 200°C/ 400°F/Gas 6. Brush the loaves with the glaze. Bake for 20 minutes. Lower to 180°C/350°F/Gas 4 and bake until golden, 25–30 minutes. Cool on racks.

Prune Bread

MAKES 1 LOAF

225g/8oz/1 cup dried prunes

15ml/1 tbsp active dried yeast

75g/3oz/²/₃ cup strong wholemeal (whole-wheat) bread flour

375–425g/13–15oz/3¹/₄–3²/₃ cups strong white bread flour

2.5ml/¹/₂ tsp bicarbonate of soda (baking soda)

5ml/1 tsp salt

5ml/1 tsp pepper

25g/1oz/2 tbsp butter, at room temperature

175ml/6fl oz/³/₄ cup buttermilk

50g/2oz/¹/₃ cup walnuts, chopped

milk, for glazing

1 Simmer the prunes in water to cover until soft, or soak overnight. Drain, reserving 50ml/2fl oz/¹/₄ cup of the soaking liquid. Pit and chop the prunes.

2 Combine the yeast and the reserved prune liquid. Leave for 15 minutes.

3 In a large bowl, stir together the flours, bicarbonate of soda, salt and pepper. Make a well in the centre.

4 ▲ Add the chopped prunes, butter, and buttermilk. Pour in the yeast mixture. With a wooden spoon, stir from the centre, incorporating more flour with each turn, to obtain a rough dough.

5 Transfer to a floured surface and knead until smooth and elastic. Return to the bowl, cover with a plastic bag and leave to rise in a warm place until doubled in volume, about 1¹/₂ hours.

6 Grease a baking sheet.

7 ▲ Punch down the dough with your fist, then knead in the walnuts.

8 Shape the dough into a long, cylindrical loaf. Place on the baking sheet, cover loosely, and leave to rise in a warm place for 45 minutes.

9 Preheat the oven to 220°C/425°F/Gas 7.

10 ▼ With a sharp knife, score the top deeply. Brush with milk and bake for 15 minutes. Lower to 190°C/375°F/Gas 5 and bake until the bottom sounds hollow when tapped, 35 minutes. Cool.

Braided Prune Bread

MAKES 1 LOAF

15ml/1 tbsp active dried yeast
50ml/2fl oz/¹/₄ cup lukewarm water
50ml/2fl oz/¹/₄ cup lukewarm milk
50g/2oz/¹/₄ cup caster (superfine) sugar
2.5ml/¹/₂ tsp salt
1 egg
50g/2oz/¹/₄ cup butter, at room temperature
425–505g/15oz–1lb 2oz/3²/₃–4¹/₂ cups strong white bread flour
1 egg beaten with 10ml/2 tsp water, for glazing

FOR THE FILLING

200g/7oz/scant 1 cup cooked prunes, pitted
10ml/2 tsp grated lemon rind
5ml/1 tsp grated orange rind
1.5ml/¹/₄ tsp freshly grated nutmeg
40g/1¹/₂oz/3 tbsp butter, melted
50g/2oz/¹/₄ cup very finely chopped walnuts
25g/1oz/2 tbsp caster sugar

1 In a large bowl, combine the yeast and water, stir and leave for 15 minutes to dissolve.

2 Stir in the milk, sugar, salt, egg and butter. Gradually stir in 350g/12oz/3 cups of the flour to obtain a soft dough.

3 Transfer to a floured surface and knead in just enough flour to obtain a dough that is smooth and elastic. Put into a clean bowl, cover and leave to rise in a warm place until doubled in volume, about 1¹/₂ hours.

~ VARIATION ~

For Plaited Apricot Bread, replace the prunes with the same amount of dried apricots. It is not necessary to cook them, but, to soften, soak them in hot tea and discard the liquid before using.

4 ▲ Meanwhile, for the filling, combine the prunes, lemon and orange rinds, nutmeg, butter, walnuts and sugar, and stir together to blend. Set aside.

5 Grease a large baking sheet. Knock back (punch down) the dough and transfer to a lightly floured surface. Knead briefly, then roll out into a 38 × 25cm/15 × 10in rectangle. Carefully transfer to the baking sheet.

6 ▲ Spread the filling in the centre.

7 ▲ With a sharp knife, cut ten strips at an angle on either side of the filling, cutting just to the filling.

8 ▲ For a braided pattern, fold up one end neatly, then fold over the strips from alternating sides until all the strips are folded over. Tuck excess dough underneath at the ends.

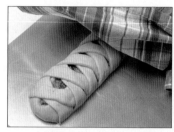

9 ▲ Cover loosely with a dish towel and leave to rise in a warm place until almost doubled in volume.

10 ▲ Preheat the oven to 190°C/375°F/Gas 5. Brush with the glaze. Bake until browned, about 30 minutes. Transfer to a rack to cool.

Kugelhopf

MAKES 1 LOAF

115g/4oz/²/₃ cup raisins
15ml/1 tbsp Kirsch or brandy
15ml/1 tbsp active dried yeast
120ml/4fl oz/¹/₂ cup lukewarm water
115g/4oz/¹/₂ cup unsalted (sweet) butter, at room temperature
90g/3¹/₂oz/¹/₂ cup sugar
3 eggs, at room temperature
grated rind of 1 lemon
5ml/1 tsp salt
2.5ml/¹/₂ tsp vanilla extract
425g/15oz/3²/₃ cups strong white bread flour
120ml/4fl oz/¹/₂ cup milk
25g/1oz/¹/₄ cup flaked (sliced) almonds
90g/3¹/₂oz/scant 1 cup whole blanched almonds, chopped
icing (confectioners') sugar, for dusting

1 ▼ In a bowl, combine the raisins and Kirsch or brandy. Set aside.

2 Combine the yeast and water, stir and leave for 15 minutes to dissolve.

3 With an electric mixer, cream the butter and sugar until thick and fluffy. Beat in the eggs, one at a time. Add the lemon rind, salt and vanilla. Stir in the yeast mixture.

4 ▲ Add the flour, alternating with the milk, until the mixture is well blended. Cover and leave to rise in a warm place until doubled in volume, about 2 hours.

5 ▲ Grease a 4¹/₂ pint Kugelhopf mould, then sprinkle the flaked almonds evenly over the bottom.

6 Work the raisins and whole almonds into the dough, then spoon into the mould. Cover with a plastic bag, and leave to rise in a warm place until the dough almost reaches the top of the mould, about 1 hour.

7 Preheat the oven to 180°C/350°F/ Gas 4.

8 Bake until golden brown, about 45 minutes. If the top browns too quickly, protect with a sheet of foil. Leave to cool in the mould for 15 minutes, then turn out on to a rack. Dust the top lightly with icing sugar before serving.

Panettone

MAKES 1 LOAF

150ml/¼ pint/⅔ cup lukewarm milk
15ml/1 tbsp active dried yeast
350–400g/12–14oz/3–3½ cups strong white bread flour
65g/2½oz/5 tbsp sugar
10ml/2 tsp salt
2 eggs
5 egg yolks
175g/6oz/¾ cup unsalted (sweet) butter, at room temperature
130g/4½oz/scant 1 cup raisins
grated rind of 1 lemon
75g/3oz/½ cup mixed peel

1 Combine the milk and yeast in a large warmed bowl and leave for 10 minutes to dissolve.

2 Stir in 115g/4oz/1 cup of the flour, cover loosely and leave in a warm place for 30 minutes.

3 Sift over the remaining flour and stir into the dough mixture. Make a well in the centre and add the sugar, salt, eggs and egg yolks.

4 ▲ Stir with a wooden spoon until stiff, then stir with your hands to obtain a very elastic and sticky dough. Add a little more flour if necessary, but keep the dough as soft as possible.

5 ▲ To incorporate the butter, smear it over the dough, then work it in with your hands. When the butter is evenly distributed, cover and leave to rise in a warm place until doubled in volume, 3–4 hours.

6 Grease a 2 litre/3½ pint/9 cup charlotte tin (pan) or a 1kg/2¼lb coffee tin and line the bottom with baking parchment. Grease the paper.

7 Knock back (punch down) the dough. Knead in the raisins, lemon rind and mixed peel.

8 ▲ Put the dough in the tin. Cover and leave to rise in a warm place until it is well above the top of the tin, about 2 hours.

9 Preheat the oven to 200°C/400°F/Gas 6. Bake for 15 minutes, cover the top with foil and lower the heat to 180°C/350°F/Gas 4. Bake for 30 minutes more. Cool in the tin for 5 minutes, then transfer to a rack.

Danish Wreath

SERVES 10–12

10g/¹/₄oz active dried yeast
175ml/6fl oz/³/₄ cup lukewarm milk
50g/2oz/¹/₄ cup caster (superfine) sugar
450g/1lb/4 cups strong white bread flour
2.5ml/¹/₂ tsp salt
2.5ml/¹/₂ tsp vanilla extract
1 egg, beaten
225g/8oz/1 cup blocks unsalted (sweet) butter
1 egg yolk beaten with 10ml/2 tsp water, for glazing
115g/4oz/1 cup icing (confectioners') sugar
15–30ml/1–2 tbsp water
chopped pecan nuts or walnuts, for sprinkling
FOR THE FILLING
200g/7oz/scant 1 cup soft dark brown sugar
5ml/1 tsp ground cinnamon
50g/2oz/¹/₃ cup pecan nuts or walnuts, toasted and chopped

1 Combine the yeast, milk and 2.5ml/ ¹/₂ tsp of the sugar. Stir and leave for 15 minutes to dissolve.

2 Combine the flour, sugar and salt. Make a well in the centre and add the yeast mixture, vanilla and egg. Stir until a rough dough is formed.

3 Transfer to a floured surface and knead until smooth and elastic. Wrap and chill for 15 minutes.

~ VARIATION ~

For a different filling, substitute 3 tart apples, peeled and grated, the grated rind of 1 lemon, 15ml/1 tbsp lemon juice, 2.5ml/¹/₂ tsp ground cinnamon, 45ml/3 tbsp sugar, 35g/1¹/₄oz/1¹/₄ tbsp currants, and 25g/1oz/2 tbsp chopped walnuts. Combine well and use as described.

4 ▲ Meanwhile, place the butter between two sheets of baking parchment. With a rolling pin, flatten to form two 15 × 10cm/6 × 4in rectangles. Set aside.

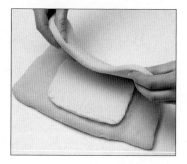

5 ▲ Roll out the dough to a 30 × 20cm/12 × 8in rectangle. Place one butter rectangle in the centre. Fold the bottom third of dough over the butter and seal the edge. Place the other butter rectangle on top and cover with the top third of the dough.

6 Turn the dough so the shorter side faces you. Roll into a 30 × 20cm/ 12 × 8in rectangle. Fold into thirds, and indent one edge with your finger to indicate the first turn. Wrap in clear film (plastic wrap) and chill for 30 minutes.

7 Repeat two more times; rolling, folding, marking and chilling between each turn. After the third fold chill for 1–2 hours, or longer.

8 Grease a large baking sheet. In a bowl, stir together all the filling ingredients until blended.

9 ▲ Roll out the dough to a 62 × 15cm/ 25 × 6in strip. Spread over the filling, leaving a 1cm/¹/₂in border.

10 Roll up the dough lengthways into a cylinder. Place on the baking sheet and form into a circle, pinching the edges together to seal. Cover with an inverted bowl and leave in a warm place to rise for 45 minutes.

11 ▲ Preheat the oven to 200°C/ 400°F/Gas 6. Slash the top every 5cm/2in, cutting about 1cm/¹/₂in deep. Brush with the egg glaze. Bake until golden, 35–40 minutes. Cool on a rack. To serve, mix the icing sugar and water, then drizzle over the wreath. Sprinkle with the pecan nuts or walnuts.

PIES &
TARTS

HERE IS EVERY SORT OF FILLING –
FROM ORCHARD FRUITS TO AUTUMN
NUTS, TANGY CITRUS TO LUSCIOUS
CHOCOLATE – FOR THE MOST
MEMORABLE PIES AND TARTS. SOME
ARE PLAIN AND SOME ARE FANCY,
BUT ALL ARE DELICIOUS.

Plum Pie

SERVES 8

900g/2lb red or purple plums

grated rind of 1 lemon

15ml/1 tbsp lemon juice

115–175g/4–6oz/^{3}/$_4$–scant 1 cup caster (superfine) sugar

45ml/3 tbsp quick-cooking tapioca

pinch of salt

2.5ml/^{1}/$_2$ tsp ground cinnamon

1.5ml/^{1}/$_4$ tsp freshly grated nutmeg

FOR THE PASTRY

275g/10oz/2^1/$_2$ cups plain (all-purpose) flour

5ml/1 tsp salt

75g/3oz/6 tbsp cold butter, cut in pieces

50g/2oz/^{1}/$_4$ cup cold white vegetable fat (shortening), cut in pieces

50–120ml/2–4fl oz/^{1}/$_4$–^{1}/$_2$ cup iced water

milk, for glazing

1 ▼ For the pastry, sift the flour and salt into a bowl. Add the butter and fat and cut in with a pastry blender until the mixture resembles coarse breadcrumbs.

2 Stir in just enough water to bind the pastry. Gather into two balls, one slightly larger than the other. Wrap and chill for 20 minutes.

3 Preheat a baking sheet in the centre of a 220°C/425°F/Gas 7 oven.

4 On a lightly floured surface, roll out the larger pastry ball to about 3mm/^{1}/$_8$in thick. Transfer to a 23cm/9in pie dish and trim the edge.

5 ▲ Halve the plums, discard the stones (pits), and cut into large pieces. Mix all the filling ingredients together (if the plums are tart, use extra sugar). Transfer to the pastry case (pie shell).

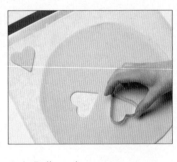

6 ▲ Roll out the remaining pastry and place on a baking tray lined with baking parchment. With a cutter, stamp out four hearts. Transfer the pastry lid to the pie using the paper.

7 Trim to leave a 2cm/^{3}/$_4$in overhang. Fold the top edge under the bottom and pinch to seal. Arrange the hearts on top. Brush with the milk. Bake for 15 minutes. Reduce the heat to 180°C/350°F/Gas 4 and bake for 30–35 minutes more. If the crust browns too quickly, protect with a sheet of foil.

Lattice Berry Pie

SERVES 8

450g/1lb/4 cups berries, such as bilberries, blueberries, blackcurrants etc
115g/4oz/generous ¹/₂ cup caster (superfine) sugar
45ml/3 tbsp cornflour (cornstarch)
30ml/2 tbsp lemon juice
25g/1oz/2 tbsp butter, diced
FOR THE PASTRY
275g/10oz/2¹/₂ cups plain (all-purpose) flour
4ml/³/₄ tsp salt
115g/4oz/¹/₂ cup cold butter, cut in pieces
40g/1¹/₂oz/3 tbsp cold white vegetable fat (shortening), cut in pieces
75–90ml/5–6 tbsp iced water
1 egg beaten with 15ml/1 tbsp water, for glazing

1 For the pastry, sift the flour and salt into a bowl. Add the butter and fat, and cut in with a pastry blender until the mixture resembles coarse breadcrumbs. With a fork, stir in just enough water to bind the pastry. Form into two balls, wrap in baking parchment, and chill for 20 minutes.

2 On a lightly floured surface, roll out one ball about 3mm/¹/₈in thick. Transfer to a 23cm/9in pie dish and trim to leave a 1cm/¹/₂in overhang. Brush the base with egg glaze.

3 ▲ Mix all the filling ingredients together, except the butter (reserve a few berries for decoration). Spoon into the pastry case and dot with the butter. Brush the egg glaze around the rim of the pastry case (pie shell).

4 Preheat a baking sheet in the centre of a 220°C/425°F/Gas 7 oven.

5 ▼ Roll out the remaining pastry on a baking tray lined with baking parchment. With a serrated pastry wheel, cut out 24 thin pastry strips. Roll out the scraps and cut out leaf shapes. Mark veins in the leaves with the point of a knife.

6 ▲ Weave the strips in a close lattice, then transfer to the pie using the paper. Press the edges to seal and trim. Arrange the pastry leaves around the rim. Brush with egg glaze.

7 Bake for 10 minutes. Reduce the heat to 180°C/350°F/Gas 4 and bake until the pastry is golden, 40–45 minutes more. Decorate with berries.

Raspberry Tart

SERVES 8

4 egg yolks

65g/2¹/₂oz/5 tbsp caster (superfine) sugar

45ml/3 tbsp plain (all-purpose) flour

300ml/¹/₂ pint/1¹/₄ cups milk

pinch of salt

2.5ml/¹/₂ tsp vanilla extract

450g/1lb/2²/₃ cups fresh raspberries

75ml/5 tbsp red currant jelly

15ml/1 tbsp fresh orange juice

FOR THE PASTRY

190g/6¹/₂oz/1²/₃ cups plain (all-purpose) flour

2.5ml/¹/₂ tsp baking powder

1.5ml/¹/₄ tsp salt

15ml/1 tbsp sugar

grated rind of ¹/₂ orange

75g/3oz/6 tbsp cold butter, cut in pieces

1 egg yolk

45–60ml/3–4 tbsp whipping cream

1 For the pastry, sift the flour, baking powder and salt into a bowl. Stir in the sugar and orange rind. Add the butter and cut in with a pastry blender until the mixture resembles coarse breadcrumbs. Stir in the egg yolk and just enough cream to bind the dough. Gather into a ball, wrap in baking parchment and chill.

2 For the custard filling, beat the egg yolks and sugar until thick and lemon-coloured. Gradually stir in the flour.

3 In a pan, bring the milk and salt just to the boil, then remove from the heat. Whisk into the egg yolk mixture, return to the pan and continue whisking over medium high heat until just bubbling. Cook for 3 minutes to thicken. Transfer immediately to a bowl. Add the vanilla and stir to blend.

4 ▲ Cover with baking parchment to prevent a skin from forming.

5 ▲ Preheat the oven to 200°C/ 400°F/Gas 6. On a floured surface, roll out the pastry 3mm/¹/₈in thick, transfer to a 25cm/10in pie dish and trim. Prick the base with a fork and line with crumpled baking parchment. Fill with baking beans and bake for 15 minutes. Remove the paper and beans. Continue baking until golden, 6–8 minutes more. Leave to cool.

6 ▲ Spread an even layer of the pastry cream filling in the pastry case (pie shell) and arrange the raspberries on top. Melt the jelly and orange juice in a pan and brush on top to glaze.

Rhubarb and Cherry Pie

SERVES 8

450g/1lb rhubarb, cut into
 2.5cm/1in pieces

450g/1lb canned pitted tart red or black
 cherries, drained

275g/10oz/1½ cups caster (superfine) sugar

25g/1oz quick-cooking tapioca

FOR THE PASTRY

275g/10oz/2½ cups plain (all-purpose) flour

5ml/1 tsp salt

75g/3oz/6 tbsp cold butter, cut in pieces

50g/2oz/⅓ cup cold white vegetable fat
 (shortening), cut in pieces

50–120ml/2–4fl oz/¼–½ cup iced water

milk, for glazing

1 ▲ For the pastry, sift the flour and salt into a bowl. Add the butter and fat to the dry ingredients and cut in with a pastry blender until the mixture resembles coarse breadcrumbs.

2 With a fork, stir in just enough water to bind the pastry. Gather into two balls, one slightly larger than the other. Wrap the pastry in baking parchment and chill for at least 20 minutes.

3 Preheat a baking sheet in the centre of a 200°C/400°F/Gas 6 oven.

4 On a lightly floured surface, roll out the larger pastry ball to a thickness of about 3mm/⅛in.

5 ▼ Roll the pastry around the rolling pin and transfer to a 23cm/9in pie dish. Trim the edge to leave a 1cm/½in overhang.

6 Chill the pastry case (pie shell) while making the filling.

7 In a mixing bowl, combine the rhubarb, cherries, sugar and tapioca, and spoon into the pie shell.

8 ▲ Roll out the remaining pastry and cut out leaf shapes.

9 Transfer the pastry lid to the pie and trim to leave a 2cm/¾in overhang. Fold the top edge under the bottom, and flute. Roll small balls from the scraps. Mark veins in the pastry leaves and place on top with the balls.

10 Glaze the top and bake until golden, 40–50 minutes.

Peach Leaf Pie

SERVES 8

1.2kg/2¹/₂lb ripe peaches

juice of 1 lemon

90g/3¹/₂oz/¹/₂ cup caster (superfine) sugar

45ml/3 tbsp cornflour (cornstarch)

1.5ml/¹/₄ tsp grated nutmeg

2.5ml/¹/₂ tsp ground cinnamon

25g/1oz/2 tbsp butter, diced

FOR THE CRUST

275g/10oz/2¹/₂ cups plain (all-purpose) flour

4ml/³/₄ tsp salt

115g/4oz/¹/₂ cup cold butter,
   cut into pieces

60g/2¹/₄oz/generous ¹/₃ cup cold white
   vegetable fat (shortening), cut
   into pieces

60–75ml/5–6 tbsp iced water

1 egg beaten with 15ml/1 tbsp water,
   for glazing

1 For the pastry, sift the flour and salt into a bowl. Add the butter and fat and rub in with your fingertips until the mixture resembles coarse breadcrumbs.

2 ▲ With a fork, stir in just enough water to bind the dough. Gather into two balls, one slightly larger than the other. Wrap in clear film (plastic wrap) and chill for 20 minutes.

3 Place a baking sheet in the oven and preheat to 220°C/425°F/Gas 7.

4 ▲ Drop a few peaches at a time into boiling water for 20 seconds, then transfer to a bowl of cold water. When cool, peel off the skins.

5 Slice the peaches and combine with the lemon juice, sugar, cornflour and spices. Set aside.

6 ▲ On a lightly floured surface, roll out the larger dough ball to about 3mm/¹/₈in thick. Transfer to a 23cm/9in pie tin (pan) and trim. Chill.

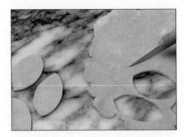

7 ▲ Roll out the remaining dough 5mm/¹/₄in thick. Cut out leaf shapes 7.5cm/3in long, using a template if needed. Mark veins with a knife. With the scraps, roll a few balls.

8 ▲ Brush the bottom of the pastry case (pie shell) with egg glaze. Add the peaches, piling them higher in the centre. Dot with the butter.

9 ▲ To assemble, start from the outside edge and cover the peaches with a ring of leaves. Place a second ring of leaves above, staggering the positions. Continue with rows of leaves until covered. Place the balls in the centre. Brush with glaze.

10 Bake for 10 minutes. Lower the heat to 180°C/350°F/Gas 4 and bake for 35–40 minutes more.

~ COOK'S TIP ~

Baking the pie on a preheated baking sheet helps to make the bottom crust crisp. The moisture from the filling keeps the bottom crust more humid than the top, but this baking method helps to compensate for the top crust being more exposed to the heat source.

Peach Tart with Almond Cream

<u>SERVES 8–10</u>

4 large ripe peaches

115g/4oz/²/₃ cup blanched almonds

30ml/2 tbsp plain (all-purpose) flour

90g/3¹/₂oz/7 tbsp unsalted (sweet) butter,
   at room temperature

115g/4oz/¹/₂ cup plus 30ml/2 tbsp caster
   (superfine) sugar

1 egg

1 egg yolk

2.5ml/¹/₂ tsp vanilla extract,
   or 10ml/2 tsp rum

<u>FOR THE PASTRY</u>

190g/6¹/₂oz/1²/₃ cups plain (all-purpose) flour

4ml/³/₄ tsp salt

90g/3¹/₂oz/7 tbsp cold unsalted (sweet)
   butter, cut in pieces

1 egg yolk

40–45ml/2¹/₂–3 tbsp iced water

1 ▲ For the pastry, sift the flour and
salt into a bowl.

2 Add the butter and cut in with
a pastry blender until the mixture
resembles coarse breadcrumbs. Stir
in the egg yolk and just enough water
to bind the pastry. Gather into a ball,
wrap in baking parchment and chill
for at least 20 minutes.

3 Preheat a baking sheet in the
centre of a 200°C/400°F/Gas 6 oven.

4 ▲ On a floured surface, roll out
the pastry to 3mm/¹/₈in thick. Transfer
to a 25cm/10in pie dish. Trim the
edge, prick the base and chill.

5 ▲ Score the bottoms of the
peaches. Drop the peaches, one at a
time, into boiling water. Boil for
20 seconds, then dip in cold water.
Peel off the skins using a sharp knife.

6 ▲ Grind the almonds finely with
the flour in a food processor, blender
or grinder. With an electric mixer, cream
the butter and 115g/4oz/generous ¹/₂
cup of the sugar until light and fluffy.
Gradually beat in the egg and yolk. Stir
in the almonds and vanilla or rum.
Spread in the pastry case(pie shell).

7 ▲ Halve the peaches and remove
the stones (pits). Cut crossways in
thin slices and arrange on top of the
almond cream like the spokes of a
wheel; keep the slices of each peach-
half together. Fan out by pressing
down gently at a slight angle.

8 ▲ Bake until the pastry begins to
brown, 10–15 minutes. Lower the
heat to 180°C/350°F/Gas 4 and
continue baking until the almond
cream sets, about 15 minutes more.
Ten minutes before the end of the
cooking time, sprinkle with the
remaining 30ml/2 tbsp of sugar.

~ VARIATION ~

For a Nectarine and Apricot Tart
with Almond Cream, replace the
peaches with nectarines, prepared
and arranged the same way. Peel
and chop three fresh apricots. Fill
the spaces between the fanned-out
nectarines with 15ml/1 tbsp of
chopped apricots. Bake as above.

Apple and Cranberry Lattice Pie

SERVES 8

grated rind of 1 orange

45ml/3 tbsp fresh orange juice

2 large, tart cooking apples

175g/6oz/1¹/₂ cups cranberries

65g/2¹/₂oz/¹/₂ cup raisins

25g/1oz/2 tbsp walnuts, chopped

215g/7¹/₂oz/generous 1 cup caster
(superfine) sugar

115g/4oz/¹/₂ cup soft dark brown sugar

30ml/2 tbsp plain (all-purpose) flour

FOR THE CRUST

275g/10oz/2¹/₂ cups plain flour

2.5ml/¹/₂ tsp salt

75g/3oz/6 tbsp cold butter, cut into pieces

75g/3oz/¹/₂ cup cold white vegetable fat
(shortening), cut into pieces

60–120ml/2–4fl oz/¹/₄–¹/₂ cup iced water

1 ▼ For the crust, sift the flour and salt into a bowl. Add the butter and fat and rub in with your fingertips until the mixture resembles coarse breadcrumbs. With a fork, stir in just enough water to bind the dough. Gather into two equal balls, wrap in clear film (plastic wrap), and chill for at least 20 minutes.

2 ▲ Put the orange rind and juice into a mixing bowl. Peel and core the apples and grate into the bowl. Stir in the cranberries, raisins, walnuts, all except 15g/¹/₂oz/1 tbsp of the caster sugar, the brown sugar and flour.

3 Place a baking sheet in the oven and preheat to 200°C/400°F/Gas 6.

4 On a lightly floured surface, roll out one ball of dough to about 3mm/¹/₈in thick. Transfer to a 23cm/9in pie plate and trim. Spoon the cranberry and apple mixture into the pastry case (pie shell).

5 ▲ Roll out the remaining dough to a circle about 28cm/11in in diameter. With a serrated pastry wheel, cut the dough into ten strips, 2cm/³/₄in wide. Place five strips horizontally across the top of the tart at 2.5cm/1in intervals. Weave in five vertical strips and trim. Sprinkle the top with the remaining sugar.

6 Bake the pie for 20 minutes. Reduce the heat to 180°C/350°F/Gas 4 and bake for about 15 minutes more, until the crust is golden and the filling is bubbling.

Open Apple Pie

SERVES 8

1.3kg/3lb sweet, tart firm eating or cooking apples
50g/2oz/¹/4 cup caster (superfine) sugar
10ml/2 tsp ground cinnamon
grated rind and juice of 1 lemon
25g/1oz/2 tbsp butter, diced
30–45ml/2–3 tbsp honey
FOR THE CRUST
275g/10oz/2¹/2 cups plain (all-purpose) flour
2.5ml/¹/2 tsp salt
115g/4oz/¹/2 cup cold butter, cut into pieces
60g/2¹/4oz/generous ¹/3 cup cold white vegetable fat (shortening), cut into pieces
75–90ml/5–6 tbsp iced water

1 For the crust, sift the flour and salt into a bowl. Add the butter and fat and rub in with your fingertips until the mixture resembles coarse breadcrumbs.

2 ▲ With a fork, stir in just enough water to bind the dough. Gather into a ball, wrap in clear film (plastic wrap), and chill for at least 20 minutes.

3 Place a baking sheet in the centre of the oven and preheat to 200°C/ 400°F/Gas 6.

4 ▼ Peel, core, and slice the apples. Combine the sugar and cinnamon in a bowl. Add the apples, lemon rind and juice, and stir.

5 On a lightly floured surface, roll out the dough to a circle about 30cm/12in in diameter. Transfer to a 23cm/9in diameter deep pie dish; leave the dough hanging over the edge. Fill with the apple slices.

6 ▲ Fold in the edges and crimp loosely for a decorative border. Dot the apples with diced butter.

7 Bake on the hot sheet until the pastry is golden and the apples are tender, about 45 minutes.

8 Melt the honey in a pan and brush over the apples to glaze. Serve warm or at room temperature.

Apple Pie

SERVES 8

900g/2lb tart cooking apples
30ml/2 tbsp plain (all-purpose) flour
115g/4oz/generous ¹/₂ cup caster (superfine) sugar
25ml/1¹/₂ tbsp fresh lemon juice
2.5ml/¹/₂ tsp ground cinnamon
2.5ml/¹/₂ tsp ground allspice
1.5ml/¹/₄ tsp ground ginger
1.5ml/¹/₄ tsp freshly grated nutmeg
1.5ml/¹/₄ tsp salt
50g/2oz/¹/₄ cup butter, diced

FOR THE PASTRY

275g/10oz/2¹/₂ cups plain (all-purpose) flour
5ml/1 tsp salt
75g/3oz/6 tbsp cold butter, cut in pieces
50g/2oz/¹/₃ cup cold white vegetable fat (shortening), cut in pieces
50–120ml/2–4fl oz/¹/₄–¹/₂ cup iced water

1 ▲ For the crust, sift the flour and salt into a bowl.

2 Add the butter and fat and cut in with a pastry blender or rub between your fingertips until the mixture resembles coarse breadcrumbs. With a fork, stir in just enough water to bind the pastry.

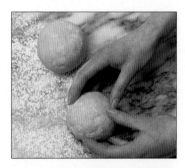

3 ▲ Form two balls, wrap in clear film (plastic wrap). Chill for 20 minutes.

4 ▲ On a lightly floured surface, roll out one ball 3mm/¹/₈in thick. Transfer to a 23cm/9in pie dish and trim the edge. Preheat a baking sheet in the centre of a 220°C/425°F/Gas 7 oven.

5 ▲ Peel, core and slice the apples into a bowl. Toss with the flour, sugar, lemon juice, spices and salt. Spoon into the pastry case (pie shell), dot with butter.

6 ▲ Roll out the remaining pastry. Place on top of the pie and trim to leave a 2cm/³/₄in overhang. Fold the overhang under the pastry base and press to seal. Crimp the edge.

7 ▲ Roll out the scraps and cut out leaf shapes and roll balls. Arrange on top of the pie. Cut steam vents.

8 Bake for 10 minutes. Reduce the heat to 180°C/350°F/Gas 4 and bake until golden, 40–45 minutes more. If the pie browns too quickly, protect with foil.

~ COOK'S TIP ~

Instead of using cooking apples, choose crisp eaters such as Granny Smith, which will not soften too much during cooking.

Pear and Apple Crumble Pie

SERVES 8

3 firm pears

4 cooking apples

175g/6oz/scant 1 cup caster (superfine) sugar

30ml/2 tbsp cornflour (cornstarch)

pinch of salt

grated rind of 1 lemon

30ml/2 tbsp fresh lemon juice

75g/3oz/²⁄₃ cup raisins

75g/3oz/²⁄₃ cup plain (all-purpose) flour

5ml/1 tsp ground cinnamon

75g/3oz/6 tbsp cold butter, cut in pieces

FOR THE PASTRY

150g/5oz/1¹⁄₄ cups plain flour

2.5ml/¹⁄₂ tsp salt

65g/2¹⁄₂oz/scant ¹⁄₂ cup cold white vegetable fat (shortening), cut in pieces

30ml/2 tbsp iced water

1 For the pastry, combine the flour and salt in a bowl. Add the fat and cut in with a pastry blender until the mixture resembles coarse breadcrumbs. Stir in just enough water to bind the pastry. Gather into a ball and transfer to a lightly floured surface. Roll out 3mm/¹⁄₈in thick.

2 ▲ Transfer to a shallow 23cm/9in pie dish and trim to leave a 1cm/¹⁄₂in overhang. Fold the overhang under for double thickness. Flute the edge. Chill.

3 Preheat a baking sheet in the centre of a 230°C/450°F/Gas 8 oven.

4 ▲ Peel and core the pears. Slice them into a bowl. Peel, core and slice the apples. Add to the pears. Stir in one-third of the sugar, the cornflour, salt and lemon rind. Add the lemon juice and raisins, and stir to blend.

5 For the crumble topping, combine the remaining sugar, flour, cinnamon, and butter in a bowl. Blend with your fingertips until the mixture resembles coarse breadcrumbs. Set aside.

6 ▲ Spoon the fruit filling into the pastry case (pie shell). Sprinkle the crumbs lightly and evenly over the top.

7 Bake for 10 minutes, then reduce the heat to 180°C/350°F/Gas 4. Cover the top of the pie loosely with a sheet of foil and continue baking until browned, 35–40 minutes more.

Chocolate Pear Tart

SERVES 8

115g/4oz plain (semisweet)
  chocolate, grated

3 large firm, ripe pears

1 egg

1 egg yolk

120ml/4fl oz/½ cup single (light) cream

2.5ml/½ tsp vanilla extract

45ml/3 tbsp caster (superfine) sugar

FOR THE PASTRY

150g/5oz/1¼ cups plain (all-purpose) flour

pinch of salt

30ml/2 tbsp sugar

115g/4oz/½ cup cold unsalted (sweet)
  butter, cut into pieces

1 egg yolk

15ml/1 tbsp fresh lemon juice

1 For the pastry, sift the flour and salt into a bowl. Add the sugar and butter. Cut in with a pastry blender until the mixture resembles coarse breadcrumbs. Stir in the egg yolk and lemon juice until the mixture forms a ball. Wrap in clear film (plastic wrap) and chill for at least 20 minutes.

2 Preheat a baking sheet in the centre of a 200°C/400°F/Gas 6 oven.

3 On a lightly floured surface, roll out the pastry 3mm/⅛in thick. Transfer to a 25cm/10in tart dish and trim.

4 ▲ Sprinkle the base of the pastry case (pie shell) with the grated chocolate.

5 ▲ Peel, halve and core the pears. Cut in thin slices crossways, then fan them out slightly.

6 Transfer the pear halves to the tart with the help of a metal spatula and arrange on top of the chocolate like the spokes of a wheel.

7 ▼ Whisk together the egg and egg yolk, cream and vanilla. Ladle over the pears, then sprinkle with sugar.

8 Bake for 10 minutes. Reduce the heat to 180°C/350°F/Gas 4 and cook until the custard is set and the pears begin to caramelize, about 20 minutes more. Serve warm.

Caramelized Upside-down Pear Pie

SERVES 8

5–6 firm, ripe pears
175g/6oz/scant 1 cup sugar
115g/4oz/¹/₂ cup unsalted (sweet) butter
whipped cream, for serving
FOR THE PASTRY
115g/4oz/1 cup plain (all-purpose) flour
1.5ml/¹/₄ tsp salt
130g/4¹/₂oz/generous ¹/₂ cup cold butter, cut into pieces
40g/1¹/₂oz/¹/₄ cup cold white vegetable fat (shortening), cut into pieces
60ml/4 tbsp iced water

1 ▲ For the pastry, combine the flour and salt in a bowl. Add the butter and vegetable fat and cut in with a pastry blender until the mixture resembles coarse crumbs. With a fork, stir in enough iced water to bind the dough. Gather into a ball, wrap in clear film (plastic wrap) and chill for at least 20 minutes. Preheat the oven to 200°C/400°F/Gas 6.

~ VARIATION ~

For Caramelized Upside-Down Apple Pie, replace the pears with 8–9 firm, tart apples. There may seem to be too many apples, but they shrink slightly as they cook.

2 ▲ Quarter, peel and core the pears. Place in a bowl and toss with a few tablespoons of the sugar.

3 ▲ In a 27cm/10¹/₂in ovenproof frying pan, melt the butter over moderately high heat. Add the remaining sugar. When it starts to colour, arrange the pears evenly around the edge and in the centre.

4 ▲ Continue cooking, uncovered, until caramelized, about 20 minutes.

5 ▲ Leave the fruit to cool. Roll out a circle of dough slightly larger than the diameter of the pan. Place the dough on top of the pears, tucking it around the edges. Transfer the pan to the oven and bake for 15 minutes, then reduce the heat to 180°C/350°F/ Gas 4. Bake until golden, about 15 minutes more.

6 ▲ Let the pie cool in the pan for about 3–4 minutes. Run a knife around the edge of the pan to loosen the pie, ensuring that the knife reaches down to the bottom of the pan. Invert a plate on top and, protecting your hands with oven gloves, hold plate and pan firmly, and turn them both over quickly.

7 Lift off the pan. If any pears stick to the pan, remove them gently with a metal spatula and replace them carefully on the pie. Serve warm, with the whipped cream passed round separately.

Lime Tart

SERVES 8

3 large egg yolks

1 × 400g/14oz can sweetened condensed milk

15ml/1 tbsp grated lime rind

120ml/4fl oz/¹/₂ cup fresh lime juice

green food colouring (optional)

120ml/4fl oz/¹/₂ cup whipping cream

FOR THE BASE

115g/4oz/2 cups digestive biscuits (graham crackers), crushed

65g/2¹/₂oz/5 tbsp butter or margarine, melted

1 Preheat the oven to 180°C/350°F/Gas 4.

2 ▲ For the base, place the crushed biscuits in a bowl and add the butter or margarine. Mix to combine.

~ VARIATION ~

Use lemons instead of limes, with yellow food colouring.

3 Press the mixture evenly over the base and sides of a 23cm/9in pie dish. Bake for 8 minutes. Leave to cool.

4 ▲ Beat the yolks until thick. Beat in the milk, lime rind and juice and colouring, if using. Pour into the pastry case (pie shell) and chill until set, about 4 hours. To serve, whip the cream. Pipe a lattice pattern on top.

Fruit Tartlets

MAKES 8

175ml/6fl oz/³/₄ cup redcurrant jelly

15ml/1 tbsp fresh lemon juice

175ml/6fl oz/³/₄ cup whipping cream

675g/1¹/₂lb fresh fruit, such as strawberries, raspberries, kiwi fruit, peaches, grapes or currants, peeled and sliced as necessary

FOR THE PASTRY

150g/5oz/10 tbsp cold butter, cut in pieces

65g/2¹/₂oz/generous ¹/₄ cup soft dark brown sugar

45ml/3 tbsp unsweetened cocoa powder

200g/7oz/1³/₄ cups plain (all-purpose) flour

1 egg white

1 For the pastry, combine the butter, brown sugar and cocoa over low heat. When the butter is melted, remove from the heat and sift over the flour. Stir, then add just enough egg white to bind the mixture. Gather into a ball, wrap in clear film (plastic wrap) and chill for 30 minutes.

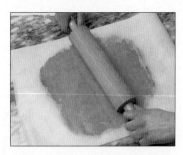

2 ▲ Grease eight 7.5cm/3in tartlet tins (muffin pans). Roll out pastry between 2 sheets of baking parchment. Cut eight 10cm/4in rounds with a fluted cutter.

3 Line the tartlet tins. Prick the base. Chill for 15 minutes. Preheat the oven to 180°C/350°F/Gas 4.

4 Bake until firm, 20–25 minutes. Cool, then remove from the tins.

5 ▲ Melt the jelly with the lemon juice. Brush a thin layer in the bottom of the tartlets. Whip the cream and spread a thin layer in the tartlet cases. Arrange the fruit on top. Brush with the glaze and serve.

Lime Tart (top), Fruit Tartlets

Chocolate Lemon Tart

SERVES 8–10

250g/9oz/1¼ cups caster (superfine) sugar

6 eggs

grated rind of 2 lemons

175ml/6fl oz/¾ cup lemon juice

175ml/6fl oz/¾ cup whipping cream

chocolate curls, for decorating

FOR THE CRUST

190g/6½oz/1⅔ cups plain
   (all-purpose) flour

30ml/2 tbsp unsweetened cocoa powder

25g/1oz/¼ cup icing (confectioners') sugar

2.5ml/½ tsp salt

115g/4oz/½ cup butter or margarine

15ml/1 tbsp water

1 ▲ Grease a 25cm/10in tart tin (pan).

2 For the crust, sift the flour, cocoa powder, icing sugar and salt into a bowl. Set aside.

3 ▲ Melt the butter and water over a low heat. Pour over the flour mixture and stir with a wooden spoon until the dough is smooth and the flour has absorbed all the liquid.

4 Press the dough evenly over the base and side of the prepared tart tin. Chill the pastry case (pie shell) while preparing the filling.

5 Preheat a baking sheet in a 190°C/375°F/Gas 5 oven.

6 ▲ Whisk the sugar and eggs until the sugar is dissolved. Add the lemon rind and juice, and mix well. Add the cream. Taste the mixture and add more lemon juice or sugar if needed. It should taste tart but also sweet.

7 Pour the filling into the tart shell and bake on the hot sheet until the filling is set, 20–25 minutes. Cool on a rack. When cool, decorate with the chocolate curls.

Lemon Almond Tart

SERVES 8

165g/5¹/₂oz/scant 1 cup whole
   blanched almonds

90g/3¹/₂oz/¹/₂ cup sugar

2 eggs

grated rind and juice of 1¹/₂ lemons

115g/4oz/¹/₂ cup butter, melted

strips of lemon rind, for decorating

FOR THE CRUST

190g/6¹/₂oz/1²/₃ cups plain (all-purpose) flour

15ml/1 tbsp caster (superfine) sugar

2.5ml/¹/₂ tsp salt

2.5ml/¹/₂ tsp baking powder

75g/3oz/6 tbsp cold unsalted (sweet)
   butter, cut into pieces

45–60ml/3–4 tbsp whipping cream

1 For the crust, sift the flour, sugar, salt and baking powder into a bowl. Add the butter and rub in with your fingertips until the mixture resembles coarse breadcrumbs.

2 ▲ With a fork, stir in just enough cream to bind the dough.

3 Gather into a ball and transfer to a lightly floured surface. Roll out the dough about 3mm/¹/₈in thick and carefully transfer to a 23cm/9in tart tin (pan). Trim and prick the base all over with a fork. Chill for at least 20 minutes.

4 Preheat a baking sheet in a 200°C/400°F/Gas 6 oven.

5 Line the tart shell with crumpled baking parchment and fill with dried beans. Bake for 12 minutes. Remove the paper and beans and continue baking until golden, 6–8 minutes more. Reduce the oven temperature to 180°C/350°F/Gas 4.

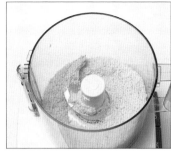

6 ▲ Grind the almonds finely with 15ml/1 tbsp of the sugar in a food processor, blender, or coffee grinder.

7 ▲ Set a mixing bowl over a pan of hot water. Add the eggs and the remaining sugar, and beat with an electric mixer until the mixture is thick enough to leave a ribbon trail when the beaters are lifted.

8 Stir in the lemon rind and juice, butter and ground almonds.

9 Pour into the pastry case (pie shell). Bake until the filling is golden and set, 35 minutes. Decorate with lemon rind.

Lemon Meringue Pie

SERVES 8

grated rind and juice of 1 large lemon

250ml/8fl oz/1 cup plus 15ml/1 tbsp
   cold water

115g/4oz/generous 1/2 cup plus 75g/3oz/
   6 tbsp caster (superfine) sugar

25g/1oz/2 tbsp butter

45ml/3 tbsp cornflour (cornstarch)

3 eggs, separated

pinch of salt

pinch of cream of tartar

FOR THE PASTRY

150g/5oz/11/4 cups plain (all-purpose) flour

2.5ml/1/2 tsp salt

65g/21/2oz/scant 1/2 cup cold white
   vegetable fat (shortening), cut in pieces

30ml/2 tbsp iced water

1 For the pastry, sift the flour and salt
into a bowl. Add the fat and cut in
with a pastry blender until the mixture
resembles coarse breadcrumbs. With a
fork, stir in just enough water to bind
the mixture. Gather into a ball.

2 ▲ On a lightly floured surface,
roll out the pastry about 3mm/1/8in
thick. Transfer to a 23cm/9in pie
dish and trim the edge to leave a
2cm/1/2in overhang.

3 ▲ Fold the overhang under and
crimp the edge. Chill the pastry case
(pie shell) for at least 20 minutes.

4 Preheat oven to 200°C/400°F/Gas 6.

5 ▲ Prick the case all over with
a fork. Line with crumpled baking
parchment and fill with baking beans.
Bake for 12 minutes. Remove the
paper and beans and continue baking
until golden, 6–8 minutes more.

6 In a pan, combine the lemon rind
and juice, 250ml/8fl oz/1 cup of the
water, 115g/4oz/generous 1/2 cup of the
sugar, and butter. Bring the mixture to
the boil.

7 Meanwhile, in a mixing bowl,
dissolve the cornflour in the
remaining water.

~ VARIATION ~

For Lime Meringue Pie, substitute
the grated rind and juice of two
medium-size limes for the lemon.

8 ▲ Add the egg yolks to the lemon
mixture and return to the boil,
whisking continuously until the
mixture thickens, about 5 minutes.

9 Cover the surface with baking
parchment and leave to cool.

10 ▲ For the meringue, using an
electric mixer beat the egg whites with
the salt and cream of tartar until they
hold stiff peaks. Add the remaining
sugar and beat until glossy.

11 ▲ Spoon the lemon mixture into
the pastry case and level. Spoon the
meringue on top, smoothing it up to
the pastry rim to seal. Bake until
golden, 12–15 minutes.

Orange Tart

SERVES 8

200g/7oz/1 cup sugar

250ml/8fl oz/1 cup fresh orange juice, strained

2 large navel oranges

165g/5½oz/scant 1 cup whole blanched almonds

50g/2oz/¼ cup butter

1 egg

15ml/1 tbsp plain (all-purpose) flour

45ml/3 tbsp apricot jam

FOR THE CRUST

215g/7½oz/scant 2 cups plain flour

2.5ml/½ tsp salt

50g/2oz/¼ cup cold butter, cut into pieces

40g/1½oz/3 tbsp cold margarine, cut into pieces

45–60ml/3–4 tbsp iced water

1 For the crust, sift the flour and salt into a bowl. Add the butter and margarine and rub in with your fingertips until the mixture resembles coarse breadcrumbs. Stir in just enough water to bind the dough. Gather into a ball, wrap in clear film (plastic wrap), and chill for at least 20 minutes.

2 On a lightly floured surface, roll out the dough 5mm/¼in thick and transfer to an 20cm/8in tart tin (pan). Trim off the overhang. Chill until needed.

3 In a pan, combine 165g/5½oz/ generous ¾ cup of the sugar and the orange juice and boil until thick and syrupy, about 10 minutes.

4 ▲ Cut the oranges into 5mm/¼in slices. Do not peel. Add to the syrup. Simmer gently for 10 minutes, or until glazed. Transfer to a rack to dry. When cool, cut in half. Reserve the syrup. Place a baking sheet in the oven and heat to 200°C/400°F/Gas 6.

5 Grind the almonds finely in a food processor, blender or coffee grinder. With an electric mixer, cream the butter and remaining sugar until light and fluffy. Beat in the egg and 30ml/ 2 tbsp of the orange syrup. Stir in the almonds and flour.

6 Melt the jam over a low heat, then brush over the pastry case (pie shell). Pour in the almond mixture. Bake until set, about 20 minutes. Leave to cool.

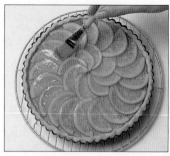

7 ▲ Arrange overlapping orange slices on top. Boil the remaining syrup until thick. Brush on top to glaze.

Pumpkin Pie

SERVES 8

450g/1lb cooked or canned pumpkin
250ml/8fl oz/1 cup whipping cream
2 eggs
115g/4oz/1/2 cup soft dark brown sugar
60ml/4 tbsp golden (light corn) syrup
7.5ml/1 1/2 tsp ground cinnamon
5ml/1 tsp ground ginger
1.5ml/1/4 tsp ground cloves
2.5ml/1/2 tsp salt
FOR THE PASTRY
175g/6oz/1 1/2 cups plain (all-purpose) flour
2.5ml/1/2 tsp salt
75g/3oz/6 tbsp cold butter, cut into pieces
40g/1 1/2oz/3 tbsp cold white vegetable fat (shortening), cut into pieces
45–60ml/3–4 tbsp iced water

1 For the pastry, sift the flour and salt into a bowl. Cut in the butter and fat until it resembles coarse crumbs. Bind with iced water. Wrap in clear film (plastic wrap) and chill for 20 minutes.

2 Roll out the dough and line a 23cm/9in pie tin (pan). Trim off the overhang. Roll out the trimmings and cut out leaf shapes. Wet the rim of the pastry case (pie shell) with a brush dipped in water.

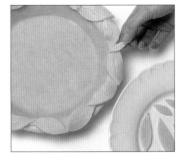

3 ▲ Place the dough leaves around the rim of the pastry case. Chill for about 20 minutes. Preheat the oven to 200°C/400°F/Gas 6.

4 ▲ Line the pastry case with baking parchment. Fill with baking beans and bake for 12 minutes. Remove paper and beans and bake until golden, 6–8 minutes more. Reduce the heat to 190°C/375°F/Gas 5.

5 ▼ Beat together the pumpkin, cream, eggs, sugar, golden syrup, spices and salt. Pour into the pastry case and bake until set, 40 minutes.

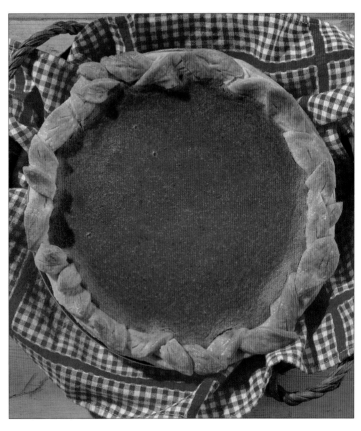

Maple Walnut Tart

SERVES 8

3 eggs

pinch of salt

50g/2oz/¼ cup caster (superfine) sugar

50g/2oz/¼ cup butter or margarine, melted

250ml/8fl oz/1 cup pure maple syrup

115g/4oz/1 cup chopped walnuts

whipped cream, for decorating

FOR THE PASTRY

65g/2½oz/9 tbsp plain (all-purpose) flour

65g/2½oz/9 tbsp wholemeal
    (whole-wheat) flour

pinch of salt

50g/2oz/¼ cup cold butter, cut in pieces

40g/1½oz/3 tbsp cold white vegetable fat
    (shortening), cut in pieces

1 egg yolk

30–45ml/2–3 tbsp iced water

1 ▼ For the pastry, mix the flours and salt in a bowl. Add the butter and fat and cut in with a pastry blender until the mixture resembles coarse breadcrumbs. With a fork, stir in the egg yolk and just enough water to bind the pastry. Form into a ball.

2 Wrap in baking parchment and chill for 20 minutes.

3 Preheat oven to 220°C/425°F/Gas 7.

4 On a lightly floured surface, roll out the pastry about 3mm/⅛in thick and transfer to a 23cm/9in pie dish. Trim the edge. To decorate, roll out the trimmings. With a small heart-shaped cutter, stamp out enough hearts to go around the rim of the pie. Brush the edge with water, then arrange the pastry hearts all around.

5 ▲ Prick the bottom with a fork. Line with crumpled baking parchment and fill with baking beans. Bake for 10 minutes. Remove the paper and beans and continue baking until golden brown, 3–6 minutes more.

6 In a bowl, whisk the eggs, salt and sugar together. Stir in the butter and maple syrup.

7 ▲ Set the pastry case (pie shell) on a baking sheet. Pour in the filling, then sprinkle the nuts over the top.

8 Bake until just set, about 35 minutes. Cool on a rack. Decorate with whipped cream, if you like.

Pecan Tart

SERVES 8

3 eggs
pinch of salt
200g/7oz/scant 1 cup soft dark brown sugar
120ml/4fl oz/$^1/_2$ cup golden (light corn) syrup
30ml/2 tbsp fresh lemon juice
75g/3oz/6 tbsp butter, melted
150g/5oz/1$^1/_4$ cups chopped pecan nuts
50g/2oz/$^1/_2$ cup pecan halves
FOR THE PASTRY
175g/6oz/1$^1/_2$ cups plain (all-purpose) flour
15ml/1 tbsp caster (superfine) sugar
5ml/1 tsp baking powder
2.5ml/$^1/_2$ tsp salt
75g/3oz/6 tbsp cold unsalted (sweet) butter, cut in pieces
1 egg yolk
45–60ml/3–4 tbsp whipping cream

1 For the pastry, sift the flour, sugar, baking powder and salt into a bowl. Add the butter and cut in with a pastry blender until the mixture resembles coarse breadcrumbs.

2 ▼ In a bowl, beat together the egg yolk and cream until blended.

~ COOK'S TIP ~

Serve this tart warm, accompanied by ice cream or whipped cream, if you like.

3 ▲ Pour the cream mixture into the flour mixture and stir with a fork.

4 Gather the pastry into a ball. On a lightly floured surface, roll out 3mm/$^1/_8$in thick and transfer to a 23cm/9in pie dish. Trim the overhang and flute the edge with your fingers. Chill for at least 20 minutes.

5 Preheat a baking sheet in the middle of a 200°C/400°F/Gas 6 oven.

6 In a bowl, lightly whisk the eggs and salt. Add the sugar, syrup, lemon juice and butter. Mix well and stir in the chopped nuts.

7 ▲ Pour into the pastry case (pie shell) and arrange the pecan halves in concentric circles on top.

8 Bake for 10 minutes. Reduce the heat to 170°C/325°F/Gas 3 and continue baking for 25 minutes.

Mince Pies

MAKES 36

175g/6oz/1¹/₂ cups finely chopped blanched almonds

150g/5oz/generous ¹/₂ cup ready-to-eat dried apricots, finely chopped

175g/6oz/generous 1 cup raisins

150g/5oz/²/₃ cup currants

150g/5oz/²/₃ cup glacé (candied) cherries, chopped

150g/5oz/³/₄ cup cut mixed (candied) peel, chopped

115g/4oz/1 cup finely chopped beef suet

grated rind and juice of 2 lemons

grated rind and juice of 1 orange

200g/7oz/scant 1 cup soft dark brown sugar

4 cooking apples, peeled, cored and chopped

10ml/2 tsp ground cinnamon

5ml/1 tsp freshly grated nutmeg

2.5ml/¹/₂ tsp ground cloves

250ml/8fl oz/1 cup brandy

225g/8oz/1 cup cream cheese

30ml/2 tbsp caster (superfine) sugar

icing (confectioners') sugar, for dusting

FOR THE PASTRY

425g/15oz/3¹/₂ cups plain (all-purpose) flour

150g/5oz/1¹/₄ cups icing (confectioners') sugar

350g/12oz/1¹/₂ cups cold butter, cut in pieces

grated rind and juice of 1 orange

milk, for glazing

1 Mix the nuts, dried and preserved fruit, suet, citrus rind and juice, brown sugar, apples and spices.

2 ▲ Stir in the brandy. Cover and leave in a cool place for 2 days.

3 For the pastry, sift the flour and icing sugar into a bowl. Cut in the butter until the mixture resembles coarse breadcrumbs.

4 ▲ Add the orange rind. Stir in just enough orange juice to bind. Gather into a ball, wrap in baking parchment and chill for at least 20 minutes.

5 Preheat the oven to 220°C/425°F/ Gas 7. Grease two or three bun trays. Beat together the cream cheese and sugar.

6 ▲ Roll out the pastry 5mm/¹/₄ in thick. With a fluted pastry cutter, stamp out 36 8cm/3in rounds.

~ COOK'S TIP ~

The mincemeat mixture may be packed into sterilized jars and sealed. It will keep refrigerated for several months. Add a few tablespoonfuls to give apple pies a lift, or make small mincemeat-filled parcels using filo pastry.

7 ▲ Transfer the rounds to the bun tray. Fill halfway with mincemeat. Top with a teaspoonful of the cream cheese mixture.

8 ▲ Roll out the remaining pastry and stamp out 36 5cm/2in rounds with a fluted cutter. Brush the edges of the pies with milk, then set the rounds on top. Cut a small steam vent in the top of each pie.

9 ▲ Brush lightly with milk. Bake until golden, 15–20 minutes. Leave to cool for 10 minutes before turning out. Dust with icing sugar, if you like.

Shoofly Pie

SERVES 8

115g/4oz/1 cup plain (all-purpose) flour

115g/4oz/1 cup soft dark brown sugar

1.5ml/¼ tsp each salt, ground ginger, cinnamon, mace and grated nutmeg

75g/3oz/6 tbsp cold butter, cut into pieces

2 eggs

120ml/4fl oz/½ cup molasses

120ml/4fl oz/½ cup boiling water

2.5ml/½ tsp bicarbonate of soda (baking soda)

FOR THE PASTRY

115g/4oz/½ cup cream cheese, at room temperature, cut into pieces

115g/4oz/½ cup cold butter, at room temperature, cut into pieces

115g/4oz/1 cup plain flour

1 For the pastry, put the cream cheese and butter in a mixing bowl. Sift over the flour.

2 ▲ Cut in with a pastry blender until the dough just holds together. Wrap in clear film (plastic wrap) and chill for at least 30 minutes.

3 Put a baking sheet in the centre of the oven and preheat the oven to 190°C/375°F/Gas 5.

4 In a bowl, mix the flour, sugar, salt and spices. Rub in the butter with your fingertips until the mixture resembles coarse crumbs. Set aside.

5 On a lightly floured surface, roll out the dough and line a 23cm/9in pie tin (pan). Trim the overhanging pastry and flute the rim.

6 ▲ Spoon a third of the crumbed mixture into the pastry case (pie shell).

7 ▲ To complete the filling, whisk the eggs with the molasses in a large bowl until combined.

8 Pour the boiling water into a small bowl. Stir in the bicarbonate of soda; the mixture will foam. Immediately whisk into the egg mixture. Pour carefully into the pastry case and sprinkle the remaining crumbed mixture evenly over the top.

9 Stand on the hot baking sheet and bake until browned, about 35 minutes. Leave to cool to room temperature, then serve.

Treacle Tart

SERVES 4–6

175ml/6fl oz/³/₄ cup golden (light corn) syrup
75g/3oz/1¹/₂ cups fresh white breadcrumbs
grated rind of 1 lemon
30ml/2 tbsp lemon juice
FOR THE PASTRY
175g/6oz/1¹/₂ cups plain (all-purpose) flour
2.5ml/¹/₂ tsp salt
75g/3oz/6 tbsp cold butter, cut in pieces
40g/1¹/₂oz/3 tbsp cold margarine, cut in pieces
45–60ml/3–4 tbsp iced water

1 For the pastry, combine the flour and salt in a bowl. Add the butter and margarine, and cut in with a pastry blender until the mixture resembles coarse breadcrumbs.

2 ▲ With a fork, stir in just enough water to bind the pastry. Gather into a ball, wrap in clear film (plastic wrap) and chill for at least 20 minutes.

3 On a lightly floured surface, roll out the pastry to a thickness of 3mm/¹/₈in. Transfer to an 20cm/8in pie dish and trim off the overhang. Chill for at least 20 minutes. Reserve the trimmings for the lattice top.

4 Preheat a baking sheet at the top of a 200°C/400°F/Gas 6 oven.

5 In a pan, warm the syrup until thin and runny.

6 ▲ Remove from the heat and stir in the breadcrumbs and lemon rind. Leave for 10 minutes so that the bread can absorb the syrup. Add more breadcrumbs if the mixture is thin. Stir in the lemon juice and spread evenly in the pastry case (pie shell).

7 Roll out the pastry trimmings and cut into 10–12 thin strips.

8 ▼ Lay half the strips on the filling, then lay the remaining strips at an angle over them to form a lattice.

9 Place on the hot sheet and bake for 10 minutes. Lower the heat to 190°C/375°F/Gas 5. Bake until golden, about 15 minutes more. Serve warm or cold.

Chess Pie

SERVES 8

2 eggs

45ml/3 tbsp whipping cream

115g/4oz/¹/₂ cup soft dark brown sugar

30ml/2 tbsp granulated sugar

30ml/2 tbsp plain (all-purpose) flour

15ml/1 tbsp whisky

40g/1¹/₂oz/3 tbsp butter, melted

50g/2oz/¹/₂ cup chopped walnuts

75g/3oz/¹/₂ cup pitted dates, chopped

whipped cream, for serving

FOR THE PASTRY

75g/3oz/6 tbsp cold butter

40g/1¹/₂oz/3 tbsp cold vegetable fat

175g/6oz/1¹/₂ cups plain flour

2.5ml/¹/₂ tsp salt

45–60ml/3–4 tbsp iced water

1 ▲ For the pastry, cut the butter and fat into small pieces.

2 Sift the flour and salt into a bowl. With a pastry blender, cut in the butter and fat until the mixture resembles coarse crumbs. Stir in just enough water to bind. Gather into a ball, wrap in baking parchment and chill for at least 20 minutes.

3 Place a baking sheet in the oven and preheat it to 190°C/375°F/Gas 5.

4 Roll out the dough thinly and line a 23cm/9in pie tin (pan). Trim the edge. Roll out the trimmings, cut thin strips and braid them. Brush the edge of the pastry case (pie shell) with water and fit the pastry braids around the rim.

5 ▲ In a mixing bowl, whisk together the eggs and cream.

6 Add both sugars and beat until well combined. Sift over 15ml/1 tbsp of the flour and stir in. Add the whisky, the melted butter and the walnuts. Stir to combine.

7 ▲ Mix the dates with the remaining flour and stir into the walnut mixture.

8 Pour into the pastry case and bake until the pastry is golden and the filling puffed up, about 35 minutes. Serve at room temperature, with whipped cream, if you like.

Coconut Cream Tart

SERVES 8

150g/5oz/scant 1½ cups desiccated (dry unsweetened) coconut

150g/5oz/¾ cup caster (superfine) sugar

60ml/4 tbsp cornflour (cornstarch)

pinch of salt

600ml/1 pint/2½ cups milk

50ml/2fl oz/¼ cup whipping cream

2 egg yolks

25g/1oz/2 tbsp unsalted (sweet) butter

10ml/2 tsp vanilla extract

FOR THE PASTRY

150g/5oz/1¼ cups plain (all-purpose) flour

1.5ml/¼ tsp salt

40g/1½oz/3 tbsp cold butter, cut in pieces

25g/1oz/2 tbsp cold white vegetable fat (shortening)

30–45ml/2–3 tbsp iced water

1 For the pastry, sift the flour and salt, then cut in the butter and fat until it resembles coarse breadcrumbs.

2 ▲ With a fork, stir in just enough water to bind the pastry. Gather into a ball, wrap in baking parchment and chill for 20 minutes.

3 Preheat the oven to 220°C/425°F/Gas 7. Roll out the pastry 3mm/⅛in thick. Line a 23cm/9in pie dish. Trim and flute the edges. Prick the base. Line with baking parchment and fill with baking beans. Bake for 10–12 minutes. Remove paper and beans, reduce heat to 180°C/350°F/Gas 4 and bake until brown, 10–15 minutes.

4 ▲ Spread 50g/2oz of the coconut on a baking sheet and toast in the oven until golden, 6–8 minutes, stirring often. Set aside for decorating.

5 Put the sugar, cornflour and salt in a pan. In a bowl, whisk the milk, cream and egg yolks. Add the egg mixture to the pan.

6 ▼ Cook over a low heat, stirring, until the mixture comes to the boil. Boil for 1 minute, then remove from the heat. Add the butter, vanilla and remaining coconut.

7 Pour into the prebaked pastry case (pie shell). When cool, sprinkle toasted coconut in a ring in the centre.

Black Bottom Pie

SERVES 8

10ml/2 tsp gelatine
45ml/3 tbsp cold water
2 eggs, separated
150g/5oz/1¼ cups caster (superfine) sugar
15g/½oz/2 tbsp cornflour (cornstarch)
2.5ml/½ tsp salt
475ml/16fl oz/2 cups milk
50g/2oz plain (semisweet) chocolate, finely chopped
30ml/2 tbsp rum
1.5ml/¼ tsp cream of tartar
chocolate curls, for decorating
FOR THE CRUST
175g/6oz/3 cups gingersnaps, crushed
65g/2½oz/5 tbsp butter, melted

1 Preheat the oven to 180°C/350°F/ Gas 4.

2 For the crust, mix the crushed gingersnaps and melted butter.

3 ▲ Press the mixture evenly over the bottom and side of a 23cm/9in pie plate. Bake for 6 minutes.

4 Sprinkle the gelatine over the water and leave to soften.

5 Beat the egg yolks in a large mixing bowl and set aside.

6 In a pan, combine half the sugar, the cornflour and salt. Gradually stir in the milk. Boil for 1 minute, stirring constantly.

7 ▲ Whisk the hot milk mixture into the yolks, then pour all back into the pan and return to the boil, whisking. Cook for 1 minute, still whisking. Remove from the heat.

8 ▲ Measure out 225g/8oz of the hot custard mixture and pour into a bowl. Add the chopped chocolate to the bowl, and stir until melted. Stir in half the rum and pour into the pastry case (pie shell).

9 ▲ Whisk the softened gelatine into the plain custard until it has dissolved, then stir in the remaining rum. Set the pan in cold water until it reaches room temperature.

10 ▲ With an electric mixer, beat the egg whites and cream of tartar until they hold stiff peaks. Add the remaining sugar gradually, beating or whisking thoroughly at each addition.

11 ▲ Fold the custard into the egg whites, then spoon over the chocolate mixture in the pastry case. Chill until set, about 2 hours.

12 Decorate the top with chocolate curls. Keep the pie chilled until ready to serve.

~ COOK'S TIP ~

To make chocolate curls, melt 225g/8oz plain chocolate over hot water, stir in 15ml/1 tbsp white vegetable fat (shortening) and mould in a small foil-lined loaf tin (pan). For large curls, soften the bar between your hands and scrape off curls from the wide side with a vegetable peeler; for small curls, grate from the narrow side using a box grater.

Velvety Mocha Tart

SERVES 8

10ml/2 tsp instant espresso coffee
30ml/2 tbsp hot water
350ml/12fl oz/1½ cups whipping cream
175g/6oz plain (semisweet) chocolate
25g/1oz dark (bittersweet) cooking chocolate
120ml/4fl oz/½ cup whipped cream, for decorating
chocolate-covered coffee beans, for decorating

FOR THE BASE

150g/5oz/2½ cups chocolate wafers, crushed
30ml/2 tbsp caster (superfine) sugar
65g/2½oz/5 tbsp butter, melted

1 ▲ For the base, mix the crushed chocolate wafers and sugar together, then stir in the melted butter.

2 Press the mixture evenly over the base and sides of a 23cm/9in pie dish. Chill until firm.

3 In a bowl, dissolve the coffee in the water and set aside.

4 Pour the cream into a mixing bowl. Set the bowl in hot water to warm the cream, bringing it closer to the temperature of the chocolate.

5 Melt both the chocolates in the top of a double boiler, or in a heatproof bowl set over a pan of hot water. Remove from the heat when nearly melted and stir to continue melting. Set the base of the pan in cool water to reduce the temperature. Be careful not to splash any water on the chocolate or it will become grainy.

6 ▲ With an electric mixer, whip the cream until it is lightly fluffy. Add the dissolved coffee and whip until the cream just holds its shape.

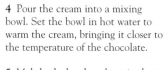

7 ▲ When the chocolate is at room temperature, fold it gently into the cream with a large metal spoon.

8 Pour into the chilled biscuit base and chill until firm. To serve, pipe a ring of whipped cream rosettes around the edge, then place a chocolate-covered coffee bean in the centre of each rosette.

Brandy Alexander Tart

SERVES 8

120ml/4fl oz/¹/2 cup cold water
15ml/1 tbsp powdered gelatine
115g/4oz/generous ¹/2 cup caster (superfine) sugar
3 eggs, separated
60ml/4 tbsp brandy
60ml/4 tbsp crème de cacao
pinch of salt
300ml/¹/2 pint/1¹/4 cups whipping cream
chocolate curls, for decorating
FOR THE BISCUIT CRUST
225g/8oz/4cups digestive biscuits (graham crackers), crumbed
65g/2¹/2oz/5 tbsp butter, melted
15ml/1 tbsp caster sugar

1 Preheat oven to 190°C/375°F/ Gas 5.

2 For the crust, mix the biscuit crumbs with the butter and sugar in a bowl.

3 ▲ Press the crumbs evenly on to the base and sides of a 23cm/9in tart tin (pan). Bake until just brown, about 10 minutes. Cool on a rack.

4 Place the water in the top of a double boiler set over hot water. Sprinkle over the powdered gelatine and leave to stand for 5 minutes to soften. Add half the sugar and the egg yolks. Whisk constantly over a very low heat until the gelatine dissolves and the mixture has thickened slightly. Do not allow the mixture to boil.

5 ▲ Remove from the heat and stir in the brandy and crème de cacao.

6 Set the pan over iced water and stir occasionally until it cools and thickens; it should not set firmly.

7 With an electric mixer, beat the egg whites and salt until they hold stiff peaks. Beat in the remaining sugar. Spoon a dollop of whites into the yolk mixture and fold in to lighten.

8 ▼ Pour the egg yolk mixture over the remaining whites and fold together.

9 Whip the cream until soft peaks form, then gently fold into the filling. Spoon into the baked biscuit case and chill until set, 3–4 hours. Decorate the top with chocolate curls before serving.

Candied Fruit Pie

SERVES 10

15ml/1 tbsp rum
50g/2oz/¹/4 cup mixed glacé (candied) fruit, chopped
450ml/³/4 pint/scant 2 cups milk
20ml/4 tsp gelatine
90g/3¹/2oz/¹/2 cup caster (superfine) sugar
2.5ml/¹/2 tsp salt
3 eggs, separated
250ml/8fl oz/1 cup whipping cream
chocolate curls, for decorating
FOR THE CRUST
175g/6oz/3 cups digestive biscuits (graham crackers), crushed
65g/2¹/2oz/5 tbsp butter, melted
15ml/1 tbsp sugar

1 For the crust, mix the crushed digestive biscuits, butter and sugar. Press evenly and firmly over the base and side of a 23cm/9in pie plate. Chill until firm.

2 ▲ In a bowl, stir together the rum and glacé fruit. Set aside.

3 Pour 120ml/4fl oz/¹/2 cup of the milk into a bowl. Sprinkle over the gelatine. Leave to soften for 5 minutes.

4 ▲ In the top of a double boiler, combine 50g/2oz/¹/4 cup of the sugar, the remaining milk and salt. Stir in the gelatine mixture. Cook over hot water, stirring, until the gelatine dissolves.

5 Whisk in the egg yolks and cook, stirring, until thick enough to coat a spoon. Do not boil. Pour the custard over the glacé fruit mixture. Set in a bowl of iced water to cool. Whip the cream lightly. Set aside.

6 With an electric mixer, beat the egg whites until they hold soft peaks. Add the remaining sugar and beat just enough to blend. Fold in a large dollop of the egg whites into the cooled gelatine mixture. Pour into the remaining egg whites and carefully fold together. Fold in the cream.

7 ▲ Pour into the biscuit base and chill until firm. Decorate the top with chocolate curls.

Chocolate Chiffon Pie

SERVES 8

200g/7oz plain (semisweet) chocolate

250ml/8fl oz/1 cup milk

15ml/1 tbsp gelatine

90g/3¹/₂oz/¹/₂ cup sugar

2 large (US extra-large) eggs, separated

5ml/1 tsp vanilla extract

350ml/12fl oz/1¹/₂ cups whipping cream

pinch of salt

whipped cream and chocolate curls,
    for decorating

FOR THE CRUST

200g/7oz/3¹/₂ cups digestive biscuits
    (graham crackers), crushed

75g/3oz/6 tbsp butter, melted

1 Place a baking sheet in the oven
and preheat to 180°C/350°F/Gas 4.

2 For the crust, mix the crushed
digestive biscuits and butter in a bowl.
Press evenly over the base and side
of a 23cm/9in pie plate. Bake for
8 minutes. Leave to cool.

3 Chop the chocolate, then grate in
a food processor or blender. Set aside.

4 Place the milk in the top of a
double boiler. Sprinkle over the
gelatine. Leave to stand for 5 minutes
to soften.

5 ▲ Set the top of a double boiler
over hot water. Add 40g/1¹/₂oz/3 tbsp
sugar, the chocolate and the egg
yolks. Stir until dissolved. Add the
vanilla extract.

6 ▲ Set the top of the double boiler
in a bowl of ice and stir until the
mixture reaches room temperature.
Remove from the ice and set aside.

7 Whip the cream lightly. Set aside.
With an electric mixer, beat the egg
whites and salt until they hold soft
peaks. Add the remaining sugar and
beat only enough to blend.

8 Fold a dollop of egg whites into
the chocolate mixture, then pour
back into the whites and fold in.

9 ▲ Fold in the whipped cream
and pour into the biscuit base. Put
in the freezer until just set, about 5
minutes. If the centre sinks, fill with
any remaining mixture. Chill for
3–4 hours. Decorate with whipped
cream and chocolate curls. Serve cold.

Chocolate Cheesecake Tart

SERVES 8

350g/12oz/1½ cups cream cheese

60ml/4 tbsp whipping cream

225g/8oz/generous 1 cup caster (superfine) sugar

50g/2oz/½ cup unsweetened cocoa powder

2.5ml/½ tsp ground cinnamon

3 eggs

whipped cream, for decorating

chocolate curls, for decorating

FOR THE BASE

75g/3oz/1½ cups digestive biscuits (graham crackers), crushed

40g/1½oz/¾ cup crushed amaretti biscuits (if unavailable, use extra crushed digestive biscuits)

75g/3oz/6 tbsp butter, melted

1 Preheat a baking sheet in the centre of a 180°C/350°F/Gas 4 oven.

2 For the base, mix the crushed biscuits and butter in a bowl.

3 ▲ With a spoon, press the mixture over the base and sides of a 23cm/9in pie dish. Bake for 8 minutes. Leave to cool. Keep the oven on.

4 With an electric mixer, beat the cheese and cream together until smooth. Beat in the sugar, cocoa and cinnamon until blended.

5 ▼ Add the eggs, one at a time, beating just enough to blend.

6 Pour into the biscuit base and bake on the hot sheet for 25–30 minutes. The filling will sink down as it cools. Decorate with whipped cream and chocolate curls.

Frozen Strawberry Tart

SERVES 8

225g/8oz/1 cup cream cheese

250ml/8fl oz/1 cup sour cream

500g/1¼lb/5 cups frozen strawberries, thawed and sliced

FOR THE BASE

115g/4oz/2 cups digestive biscuits (graham crackers), crushed

15ml/1 tbsp caster (superfine) sugar

70g/2½oz/5 tbsp butter, melted

~ VARIATION ~

For Frozen Raspberry Tart, use raspberries in place of the strawberries, and prepare the same way, or try other frozen fruit.

1 ▲ For the base, mix together the biscuits, sugar and butter.

2 Press the mixture evenly and firmly over the base and sides of a 23cm/9in pie dish. Freeze until firm.

3 ▼ Blend together the cream cheese and sour cream. Reserve 90ml/6 tbsp of the strawberries. Add the remainder to the cream cheese mixture.

4 Pour the filling into the biscuit base and freeze for 6–8 hours until firm. To serve, spoon some of the reserved berries and juice on top.

Chocolate Cheesecake Pie (top), Frozen Strawberry Tart

Kiwi Ricotta Cheese Tart

SERVES 8

75g/3oz/¹/₂ cup blanched almonds, ground

90g/3¹/₂oz/¹/₂ cup caster (superfine) sugar

900g/2lb/4 cups ricotta cheese

250ml/8fl oz/1 cup whipping cream

1 egg and 3 egg yolks

15ml/1 tbsp plain (all-purpose) flour

pinch of salt

30ml/2 tbsp rum

grated rind of 1 lemon

40ml/2¹/₂ tbsp lemon juice

30ml/2 tbsp honey

5 kiwi fruit

FOR THE PASTRY

150g/5oz/1¹/₄ cups plain (all-purpose) flour

15ml/1 tbsp caster (superfine) sugar

2.5ml/¹/₂ tsp salt

2.5ml/¹/₂ tsp baking powder

75g/3oz/6 tbsp butter

1 egg yolk

45–60ml/3–4 tbsp whipping cream

1 For the pastry, mix together the flour, sugar, salt and baking powder in a large bowl. Cut the butter into cubes and gradually rub it into the pastry mixture. Mix together the egg yolk and cream. Stir in just enough to bind the pastry.

2 ▲ Transfer to a lightly floured surface, flatten slightly, wrap and chill for 30 minutes. Preheat the oven to 220°C/425°F/Gas 7.

3 ▲ On a lightly floured surface, roll out the dough to 3mm/¹/₈in thickness. Transfer to a 23cm/9in springform tart tin (pan). Crimp the edge.

4 ▲ Prick the pastry with a fork. Line with baking parchment and fill with dried beans. Bake for 10 minutes. Remove the paper and beans and bake for 6–8 minutes more until golden. Leave to cool. Reduce the temperature to 180°C/350°F/Gas 4.

5 ▲ Mix the almonds with 15ml/ 1 tbsp of the sugar in a food processor or blender.

6 Beat the ricotta until creamy. Add the cream, egg, yolks, remaining sugar, flour, salt, rum, lemon rind and 30ml/ 2 tbsp of lemon juice. Combine.

7 ▲ Stir in the ground almonds until well blended.

8 Pour into a pastry case (pie shell) and bake for 1 hour. Chill, loosely covered for 2–3 hours. Turn out on to a plate.

9 Combine the honey and remaining lemon juice for the glaze.

10 ▲ Peel the kiwi fruits. Halve them lengthways, then slice. Arrange the slices in rows across the top of the tart. Just before serving, brush with the honey glaze.

Apple Strudel

SERVES 10–12

75g/3oz/generous ¹/₂ cup raisins

30ml/2 tbsp brandy

5 eating apples, such as Granny Smith or Cox's

3 large cooking apples

90g/3¹/₂oz/scant ¹/₂ cup soft dark brown sugar

5ml/1 tsp ground cinnamon

grated rind and juice of 1 lemon

25g/1oz/¹/₂ cup dry breadcrumbs

50g/2oz/¹/₂ cup chopped pecan nuts or walnuts

12 sheets frozen filo pastry, thawed if frozen

175g/6oz/³/₄ cup butter, melted

icing (confectioners') sugar, for dusting

1 Soak the raisins in the brandy for at least 15 minutes.

2 ▼ Peel, core and thinly slice the apples. In a bowl, combine the sugar, cinnamon and lemon rind. Stir in the apples and half the breadcrumbs.

3 Add the raisins, nuts and lemon juice, and stir until blended.

4 Preheat the oven to 190°C/375°F/ Gas 5. Grease two baking sheets.

5 ▲ Carefully unfold the filo sheets. Keep the unused sheets covered with baking parchment. Lift off one sheet, place on a clean surface and brush with melted butter. Lay a second sheet on top and brush with butter. Continue until you have a stack of six buttered sheets.

6 Sprinkle a few tablespoons of breadcrumbs over the last sheet and spoon half the apple mixture along the bottom edge of the strip.

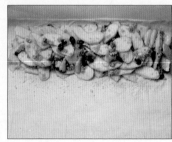

7 ▲ Starting at the apple-filled end, roll up the pastry, as for a Swiss roll tin (jelly roll pan). Place on a baking sheet, seam-side down, and carefully fold under the ends to seal. Repeat the procedure to make a second strudel. Brush both with butter.

8 Bake the strudels for 45 minutes. Leave to cool slightly. Using a small sieve (strainer), dust with a fine layer of icing sugar. Serve warm.

Cherry Strudel

SERVES 8

65g/2¹/₂oz/generous 1 cup fresh breadcrumbs
175g/6oz/³/₄ cup butter, melted
200g/7oz/1 cup caster (superfine) sugar
15ml/1 tbsp ground cinnamon
5ml/1 tsp grated lemon rind
450g/1lb sour cherries, pitted
8 sheets filo pastry, thawed if frozen
icing (confectioners') sugar, for dusting

1 In a frying pan, lightly fry the fresh breadcrumbs in 65g/2¹/₂oz of the melted butter until golden. Set aside to cool.

2 ▲ In a large mixing bowl, toss together the sugar, cinnamon and lemon rind.

3 Stir in the cherries.

4 Preheat the oven to 190°C/375°F/ Gas 5. Grease a baking sheet.

5 Carefully unfold the filo sheets. Keep the unused sheets covered with damp kitchen paper. Lift off one sheet, place on a flat surface lined with baking parchment. Brush the pastry with melted butter. Sprinkle about an eighth of the breadcrumbs evenly over the surface.

6 ▲ Lay a second sheet of filo on top, brush with butter and sprinkle with crumbs. Continue until you have a stack of eight buttered, crumbed sheets.

7 Spoon the cherry mixture along the bottom edge of the strip. Starting at the cherry-filled end, roll up the dough as for a Swiss roll tin (jelly roll pan). Use the paper to help flip the strudel on to the baking sheet, seam-side down.

8 ▼ Carefully fold under the ends to seal in the fruit. Brush the top with any remaining butter.

9 Bake the strudel for 45 minutes. Leave to cool slightly. Using a small sieve (strainer), dust with a fine layer of icing sugar.

Mushroom Quiche

SERVES 8

450g/1lb/6 cups mushrooms

30ml/2 tbsp olive oil

15ml/1 tbsp butter

1 clove garlic, finely chopped

15ml/1 tbsp lemon juice

30ml/2 tbsp finely chopped fresh parsley

3 eggs

350ml/12fl oz/1¹/₂ cups whipping cream

65g/2¹/₂oz/³/₄ cup freshly grated
Parmesan cheese

salt and ground black pepper

FOR THE CRUST

190g/6¹/₂oz/1²/₃ cups plain
(all-purpose) flour

2.5ml/¹/₂ tsp salt

75g/3oz cold butter, cut into pieces

50g/2oz/¹/₄ cup cold margarine, cut into
pieces

45–60ml/3–4 tbsp iced water

1 For the crust, sift the flour and salt. Rub in the butter and margarine until it resembles coarse breadcrumbs. Stir in enough water to bind.

2 Gather into a ball, wrap in clear film (plastic wrap) and chill for 20 minutes.

3 Preheat a baking sheet in a 190°C/ 375°F/Gas 5 oven.

4 Roll out the dough 3mm/¹/₈in thick. Transfer to a 23cm/9in quiche tin (pan) and trim. Prick the base all over with a fork. Line with baking parchment and fill with dried beans. Bake for 12 minutes. Remove the paper and beans and continue baking until golden, about 5 minutes more.

5 ▲ Wipe the mushrooms with damp kitchen paper to remove any dirt. Trim the ends of the stalks, place on a cutting board, and slice thinly.

6 Heat the oil and butter in a frying pan. Stir in the mushrooms, garlic and lemon juice. Season with salt and pepper. Cook until the mushrooms render their liquid, then raise the heat and cook until dry.

7 ▼ Stir in the parsley and add more salt and pepper if necessary.

8 Whisk the eggs and cream together, then stir in the mushrooms. Sprinkle the cheese over the base of the prebaked pastry case (pie shell) and pour the mushroom filling over the top.

9 Bake until puffed and brown, about 30 minutes. Serve the quiche warm.

Bacon and Cheese Quiche

SERVES 8

115g/4oz medium-thick bacon slices

3 eggs

350ml/12fl oz/1¹/₂ cups whipping cream

90g/3¹/₂oz Gruyère cheese, grated

pinch of freshly grated nutmeg

salt and ground black pepper

FOR THE CRUST

190g/6¹/₂oz/1²/₃ cups plain (all-purpose) flour

2.5ml/¹/₂ tsp salt

75g/3oz/6 tbsp cold butter, cut into pieces

40g/1¹/₂oz/3 tbsp cold margarine,
cut into pieces

45–60ml/3–4 tbsp iced water

1 Make the crust as per steps 1–4 above. Keep the oven at 190°C/375°F/Gas 5.

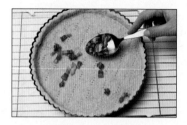

2 ▲ Fry the bacon until crisp. Drain, then crumble into small pieces. Sprinkle in the pastry case (pie shell).

3 ▲ Beat together the eggs, cream, cheese, nutmeg, salt and pepper. Pour over the bacon and bake until puffed and brown, about 30 minutes. Serve the quiche warm.

Mushroom Quiche (top), Bacon and Cheese Quiche

Cheese and Tomato Quiche

SERVES 6–8

10 medium tomatoes
1 × 50g/2oz can anchovy fillets, drained and finely chopped
120ml/4fl oz/¹/₂ cup whipping cream
200g/7oz/1³/₄ cups mature Cheddar cheese, grated
25g/1oz/¹/₂ cup wholemeal (whole-wheat) breadcrumbs
2.5ml/¹/₂ tsp dried thyme
salt and ground black pepper
FOR THE CRUST
215g/7¹/₂oz/scant 2 cups plain (all-purpose) flour
115g/4oz/¹/₂ cup cold butter, cut into pieces
1 egg yolk
30–45ml/2–3 tbsp iced water

1 Preheat oven to 200°C/400°F/ Gas 6.

2 For the crust, sift the flour and ¹/₂ tsp salt into a bowl. Rub in the butter with your fingertips until the mixture resembles coarse breadcrumbs.

3 ▲ With a fork, stir in the egg yolk and enough water to bind the dough.

4 Roll out the dough to about 3mm/¹/₈in thick and transfer to a 23cm/9in quiche tin (pan). Chill the dough until needed.

5 ▲ Score the bottoms of the tomatoes. Plunge in boiling water for 1 minute. Remove and peel off the skin with a knife. Cut in quarters and remove the seeds with a spoon.

6 ▲ In a bowl, mix the anchovies and cream. Stir in the cheese.

7 Sprinkle the breadcrumbs in the crust. Arrange the tomatoes on top. Season with thyme, salt and pepper.

8 ▲ Spoon the cheese mixture on top. Bake until golden, 25–30 minutes. Serve warm.

Onion and Anchovy Tart

SERVES 8

60ml/4 tbsp olive oil
900g/2lb onions, sliced
5ml/1 tsp dried thyme
2–3 tomatoes, sliced
24 small black olives, pitted
1 × 50g/2oz can anchovy fillets, drained and sliced
6 sun-dried tomatoes, cut into slivers
salt and ground black pepper

FOR THE CRUST

190g/6^1/2oz/1^2/3 cups plain (all-purpose) flour
2.5ml/^{1}/2 tsp salt
115g/4oz/^{1}/2 cup cold butter, cut into pieces
1 egg yolk
30–45ml/2–3 tbsp iced water

1 ▲ For the crust, sift the flour and salt into a bowl. Rub in the butter with your fingertips until the mixture resembles coarse breadcrumbs. Stir in the yolk and enough water to bind.

2 ▲ Roll out the dough to a thickness of about 3mm/^{1}/sin. Transfer to a 23cm/9in quiche tin (pan) and trim the edge. Chill in the refrigerator until needed.

3 ▲ Heat the oil in a frying pan. Add the onions, thyme and seasoning. Cook over low heat, covered, for 25 minutes. Uncover and continue cooking until soft. Cool. Preheat the oven to 200°C/400°F/Gas 6.

4 ▼ Spoon the onions into the pastry case (pie shell) and top with the tomato slices. Arrange the olives in rows. Make a lattice pattern, alternating lines of anchovies and sun-dried tomatoes. Bake until golden, 20–25 minutes.

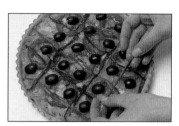

Ricotta and Basil Tart

SERVES 8–10

50g/2oz/2 cups basil leaves

25g/1oz/1 cup flat-leaf parsley

120ml/4fl oz/¹/₂ cup extra-virgin olive oil

2 eggs

1 egg yolk

800g/1³/₄lb/3¹/₂ cups ricotta cheese

90g/3¹/₂oz/scant 1 cup black olives, pitted

65g/2¹/₂oz/³/₄ cup freshly grated
  Parmesan cheese

salt and ground black pepper

FOR THE CRUST

190g/6¹/₂oz/1²/₃ cups plain
  (all-purpose) flour

2.5ml/¹/₂ tsp salt

75g/3oz/6 tbsp cold butter, cut into pieces

40g/1¹/₂oz/3 tbsp cold margarine,
  cut into pieces

45–60ml/3–4 tbsp iced water

1 ▲ For the crust, combine the flour and salt in a bowl. Add the butter and margarine.

2 Rub in with your fingertips until the mixture resembles coarse breadcrumbs. With a fork, stir in just enough water to bind the dough. Gather into a ball, wrap in clear film (plastic wrap), and chill for 20 minutes.

3 Preheat a baking sheet in a 190°C/375°F/Gas 5 oven.

4 Roll out the dough 3mm/¹/₈in thick and transfer to a 25cm/10in quiche tin (pan). Prick the base with a fork and line with baking parchment. Fill with dried beans and bake for 12 minutes. Remove the paper and beans and bake until golden, 3–5 minutes more. Lower the heat to 180°C/350°F/Gas 4.

5 ▲ In a food processor or blender, combine the basil, parsley and olive oil. Season well with salt and pepper and process until finely chopped.

6 In a bowl, whisk the eggs and yolk to blend. Gently fold in the ricotta.

7 ▲ Fold in the basil mixture and olives until well combined. Stir in the Parmesan and adjust the seasoning.

8 Pour into the prebaked pastry case (pie shell) and bake until set, about 30–35 minutes.

Pennsylvania Dutch Ham and Apple Pie

SERVES 6–8

5 tart cooking apples
60ml/4 tbsp soft light brown sugar
15ml/1 tbsp plain (all-purpose) flour
pinch of ground cloves
pinch of ground black pepper
175g/6oz sliced cooked ham
25g/1oz/2 tbsp butter or margarine
60ml/4 tbsp whipping cream
1 egg yolk
FOR THE PASTRY
225g/8oz/2 cups plain (all-purpose) flour
2.5ml/½ tsp salt
75g/3oz/6 tbsp cold butter, cut into pieces
50g/2oz/¼ cup cold margarine, cut into pieces
60–120ml/4–8 tbsp iced water

1 For the pastry, sift the flour and salt into a large bowl. Rub in the butter and margarine until the mixture resembles coarse crumbs. Stir in enough water to bind together, gather into two balls, and wrap in clear film (plastic wrap). Chill for 20 minutes. Preheat the oven to 220°C/425°F/Gas 7.

2 ▲ Quarter, core, peel and thinly slice the apples. Place in a bowl and toss with the sugar, flour, cloves and pepper to coat evenly. Set aside.

3 Roll out one dough ball thinly and line a 25cm/10in pie tin (pan), letting the excess pastry hang over the edge.

4 Arrange half the ham slices in the bottom of the pastry case. Top with a ring of spiced apple slices, then dot with half the butter or margarine.

5 ▲ Repeat the layers, finishing with apples. Dot with butter or margarine. Pour over 45ml/3 tbsp of the cream.

6 Roll out the remaining pastry to make a lid. Place it on top, fold the top edge under the bottom and press.

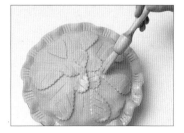

7 ▲ Roll out the pastry scraps and cut out decorative shapes. Arrange on top of the pie. Scallop the edge, using your fingers and a fork. Cut steam vents. Mix the egg yolk and remaining cream and brush on top to glaze.

8 Bake for 10 minutes. Reduce the heat to 180°C/350°F/Gas 4 and bake until golden, 30–35 minutes more. Serve hot.

CAKES & GATEAUX

AS DELICIOUS AS THEY ARE
BEAUTIFUL, THESE CAKES AND
GATEAUX ARE PERFECT TO SERVE
AT TEATIME OR FOR DESSERT.
DELIGHTFUL PARTY CAKES MAKE
SPECIAL OCCASIONS MEMORABLE.

Angel Cake

SERVES 12–14

130g/4¹/₂oz/generous 1 cup sifted plain (all-purpose) flour
30ml/2 tbsp cornflour (cornstarch)
300g/11oz/generous 1¹/₂ cups caster (superfine) sugar
275–300g/10–11oz egg whites (about 10–11 eggs)
6.5ml/1¹/₄ tsp cream of tartar
1.5ml/¹/₄ tsp salt
5ml/1 tsp vanilla extract
1.5ml/¹/₄ tsp almond extract
icing (confectioners') sugar, for dusting

1 Preheat the oven to 160°C/325°F/ Gas 3.

2 ▼ Sift the flours before measuring, then sift them four times with 90g/ 3¹/₂oz/¹/₂ cup of the sugar.

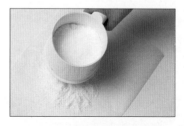

3 With an electric mixer, beat the egg whites until foamy. Sift over the cream of tartar and salt, and continue to beat until the whites hold soft peaks when the beaters are lifted.

4 ▲ Add the remaining sugar in three batches, beating well after each addition. Stir in the vanilla and almond extracts.

5 ▲ Add the flour mixture, in two batches, and fold in with a large metal spoon after each addition.

6 Transfer to an ungreased 25cm/ 10in tube tin (pan) and bake until just browned on top, about 1 hour.

7 ▲ Turn the tin upside down on to a cake rack and leave to cool for 1 hour. If the cake does not turn out, run a knife around the edge to loosen it. Invert on a serving plate.

8 When cool, lay a star-shaped template on top of the cake, sift over icing sugar and remove template.

Marbled Ring Cake

SERVES 16

115g/4oz plain (semisweet) chocolate

350g/12oz/3 cups plain (all-purpose) flour

5ml/1 tsp baking powder

450g/1lb/2 cups butter, at room temperature

725g/1lb 10oz/3¹/₂ cups caster (superfine) sugar

15ml/1 tbsp vanilla extract

10 eggs, at room temperature

icing (confectioners') sugar, for dusting

1 ▲ Preheat the oven to 180°C/350°F/ Gas 4. Line a 25 × 10cm/10 × 4in ring mould with baking parchment and grease the paper. Dust with flour.

2 ▲ Melt the chocolate in the top of a double boiler, or in a heatproof bowl set over a pan of hot water. Stir occasionally. Set aside.

3 In a bowl, sift together the flour and baking powder. In another bowl, cream the butter, sugar and vanilla with an electric mixer until light and fluffy. Add the eggs, two at a time, then gradually incorporate the flour mixture on low speed.

4 ▲ Spoon half of the mixture into the prepared tin (pan).

5 ▲ Stir the chocolate into the remaining mixture, then spoon into the tin. With a metal spatula, swirl the mixtures for a marbled effect.

6 Bake until a skewer inserted into the centre comes out clean, about 1 hour 45 minutes. Cover with foil halfway through baking. Leave to stand for 15 minutes, then turn out and transfer to a cooling rack. To serve, dust with icing sugar.

Coffee-iced Ring

SERVES 16

275g/10oz/2½ cups plain (all-purpose) flour

15ml/1 tbsp baking powder

5ml/1 tsp salt

350g/12oz/1¾ cup caster (superfine) sugar

120ml/4fl oz/½ cup vegetable oil

7 eggs, at room temperature, separated

175ml/6fl oz/¾ cup cold water

10ml/2 tsp vanilla extract

10ml/2 tsp grated lemon rind

2.5ml/½ tsp cream of tartar

FOR THE ICING

165g/5½oz unsalted (sweet) butter

575g/1lb 4oz/5 cups icing (confectioners') sugar

20ml/4 tsp instant coffee dissolved in 60ml/4 tbsp hot water

1 Preheat the oven to 170°C/325°F/ Gas 3.

2 ▼ Sift the flour, baking powder and salt into a bowl. Stir in 225g/8oz of the sugar. Make a well in the centre and add the oil, egg yolks, water, vanilla and lemon rind. Beat with a whisk or metal spoon until smooth.

3 With an electric mixer, beat the egg whites with the cream of tartar until they hold soft peaks. Add the remaining sugar and beat until the mixture holds stiff peaks.

4 ▲ Pour the flour mixture over the whites in three batches, folding well after each addition.

5 Transfer the mixture to a 25 × 10cm/ 10 × 4in ring mould and bake until the top springs back when touched lightly, about 1 hour.

6 ▲ When baked, remove from the oven and immediately hang the cake upside-down over the neck of a funnel or a narrow bottle. Leave to cool. To remove the cake, run a knife around the inside to loosen, then turn the tin over and tap the sides sharply. Invert the cake on to a serving plate.

7 For the icing, beat together the butter and icing sugar with an electric mixer until smooth. Add the coffee and beat until fluffy. With a metal spatula, spread over the sides and top of the cake.

Spice Cake with Cream Cheese Icing

SERVES 10–12

300ml/¹/₂ pint/1¹/₄ cups milk
30ml/2 tbsp golden (light corn) syrup
10ml/2 tsp vanilla extract
75g/3oz/¹/₂ cup walnuts, chopped
175g/6oz/³/₄ cup butter, at room temperature
300g/11oz/generous 1¹/₂ cups caster (superfine) sugar
1 egg, at room temperature
3 egg yolks, at room temperature
275g/10oz/2¹/₂ cups plain (all-purpose) flour
15ml/1 tbsp baking powder
5ml/1 tsp freshly grated nutmeg
5ml/1 tsp ground cinnamon
2.5ml/¹/₂ tsp ground cloves
1.5ml/¹/₄ tsp ground ginger
1.5ml/¹/₄ tsp ground allspice
FOR THE ICING
175g/6oz/³/₄ cup cream cheese
25g/1oz/2 tbsp unsalted (sweet) butter
200g/7oz/1³/₄ cups icing (confectioners') sugar
30ml/2 tbsp finely chopped stem ginger
30ml/2 tbsp syrup from stem ginger
stem ginger pieces, for decorating

1 Preheat the oven to 180°C/350°F/Gas 4. Line three 20cm/8in cake tins (pans) with baking parchment and grease. In a bowl, combine the milk, syrup, vanilla and walnuts.

2 ▼ With an electric mixer, cream the butter and sugar until light and fluffy. Beat in the egg and egg yolks. Add the milk mixture and stir well.

3 Sift together the flour, baking powder and spices three times.

4 ▲ Add the flour mixture to the egg mixture in four batches, and fold in carefully after each addition.

5 Divide the cake mixture between the tins. Bake until the cakes spring back when touched lightly, about 25 minutes. Leave to stand for 5 minutes, then turn out and cool on a rack.

6 ▼ For the icing, combine all the ingredients and beat with an electric mixer. Spread the icing between the layers and over the top. Decorate with pieces of stem ginger.

Caramel Layer Cake

SERVES 8–10

275g/10oz/2½ cups plain (all-purpose) flour

7.5ml/1½ tsp baking powder

175g/6oz/¾ cup butter, at room temperature

165g/5½oz/generous ¾ cup caster (superfine) sugar

4 eggs, at room temperature, beaten

5ml/1 tsp vanilla extract

120ml/4fl oz/½ cup milk

whipped cream, for decorating

caramel threads, for decorating (optional, see below)

FOR THE ICING

300g/11oz/scant 1⅓ cups soft dark brown sugar

250ml/8fl oz/1 cup milk

25g/1oz/2 tbsp unsalted (sweet) butter

45–75ml/3–5 tbsp whipping cream

1 Preheat the oven to 180°C/350°F/ Gas 4. Line two 20cm/8in cake tins (pans) with baking parchment; grease lightly.

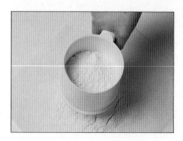

2 ▲ Sift the flour and baking powder together three times. Set aside.

~ COOK'S TIP ~

To make caramel threads, combine 65g/2½oz/5 tbsp sugar and 50ml/ 2fl oz/¼ cup water in a heavy pan. Boil until light brown. Dip the pan in cold water to halt cooking. Trail from a spoon on an oiled baking sheet.

3 With an electric mixer, cream the butter and caster sugar until light and fluffy.

4 ▲ Slowly mix in the beaten eggs. Add the vanilla. Fold in the flour mixture, alternating with the milk.

5 ▲ Divide the batter between the prepared tins and spread evenly, hollowing out the centres slightly.

6 Bake until the cakes pull away from the sides of the tin, about 30 minutes. Leave to stand for 5 minutes, then turn out and cool on a rack.

7 ▲ For the icing, combine the brown sugar and milk in a pan.

8 Bring to the boil, cover and cook for 3 minutes. Remove the lid and continue to boil, without stirring, until the mixture reaches 119°C/238°F (soft ball stage) on a sugar thermometer.

9 ▲ Immediately remove the pan from the heat and add the butter, but do not stir it in. Cool until lukewarm, then beat until the mixture is smooth and creamy.

10 Stir in enough cream to obtain a spreadable consistency. If necessary, chill to thicken more.

11 ▲ Spread a layer of icing on top of one cake. Sandwich with the second cake, then spread the top and sides with the rest of the icing and smooth the surface.

12 To decorate, pipe whipped cream rosettes around the edge. Place a mound of caramel threads, if using, in the centre before serving.

Lady Baltimore Cake

SERVES 8–10

275g/10oz/2½ cups plain (all-purpose) flour
12.5ml/2½ tsp baking powder
2.5ml/½ tsp salt
4 eggs
350g/12oz/1¾ cups caster (superfine) sugar
grated rind of 1 large orange
250ml/8fl oz/1 cup fresh orange juice
250ml/8fl oz/1 cup vegetable oil
18 pecan halves, for decorating
FOR THE FROSTING
2 egg whites
350g/12oz/1¾ cups caster sugar
75ml/5 tbsp cold water
1.5ml/¼ tsp cream of tartar
5ml/1 tsp vanilla extract
50g/2oz/⅓ cup pecan nuts, finely chopped
75g/3oz/⅔ cup raisins, chopped
3 dried figs, finely chopped

1 Preheat the oven to 180°C/350°F/ Gas 4. Grease two 23cm/9in round cake tins (pans) and line with baking parchment. Grease the paper. In a bowl, sift together the flour, baking powder and salt. Set aside.

2 ▲ With an electric mixer, beat the eggs and sugar until thick and lemon-coloured. Beat in the orange rind and juice, then the oil.

3 On low speed, beat in the flour mixture in three batches. Divide the cake mixture between the tins.

4 ▲ Bake until a skewer inserted into the centre comes out clean, about 30 minutes. Leave to stand for 15 minutes, then run a knife around the inside of the cakes and transfer them to racks to cool completely.

5 ▲ For the icing, combine the egg whites, sugar, water and cream of tartar in the top of a double boiler, or in a heatproof bowl set over boiling water. With an electric mixer, beat until glossy and thick. Off the heat, add the vanilla extract and continue beating until thick. Fold in the pecan nuts, raisins and figs.

6 Spread a layer of icing on top of one cake. Sandwich with the second cake, then spread the top and sides with the rest of the icing. Arrange the pecan halves on top.

Carrot Cake

SERVES 12

450g/1lb carrots, peeled

175g/6oz/1½ cups plain (all-purpose) flour

10ml/2 tsp baking powder

2.5ml/½ tsp bicarbonate of soda
(baking soda)

5ml/1 tsp salt

10ml/2 tsp ground cinnamon

4 eggs

10ml/2 tsp vanilla extract

115g/4oz/½ cup soft dark brown sugar

50g/2oz/¼ cup caster (superfine) sugar

300ml/½ pint/1¼ cups sunflower oil

115g/4oz/1 cup finely chopped walnuts

75g/3oz/⅔ cup raisins

walnut halves, for decorating (optional)

FOR THE ICING

75g/3oz/6 tbsp unsalted (sweet) butter

350g/12oz/3 cups icing (confectioners')
sugar

50ml/2fl oz/¼ cup maple syrup

1 Preheat the oven to 180°C/350°F/
Gas 4. Line a 28 × 20cm/11 × 8in tin
(pan) with baking parchment; grease.

2 ▲ Grate the carrots and set aside.

3 Sift the flour, baking powder,
bicarbonate of soda, salt and
cinnamon into a bowl. Set aside.

4 With an electric mixer, beat the
eggs until blended. Add the vanilla,
sugars and oil; beat to incorporate. Add
the dry ingredients, in three batches,
folding in well after each addition.

5 ▲ Add the carrots, walnuts and
raisins, and fold in thoroughly.

6 Pour the mixture into the prepared
tin and bake until the cake springs
back when touched lightly, 40–45
minutes. Leave for 10 minutes, then
turn out and transfer to a rack.

7 ▼ For the icing, cream the butter
with half the icing sugar until soft.
Add the syrup, then beat in the
remaining sugar until blended.

8 Spread the icing over the top of the
cake. Using the tip of a metal spatula,
make decorative ridges in the icing.
Cut into squares. Decorate with
walnut halves, if you like.

Cranberry Upside-down Cake

SERVES 8

350–400g/12–14oz/3–3¹/₂ cups
    fresh cranberries

50g/2oz/¹/₄ cup butter

150g/5oz/³/₄ cup caster (superfine) sugar

FOR THE CAKE MIXTURE

65g/2¹/₂oz/9 tbsp plain (all-purpose) flour

5ml/1 tsp baking powder

3 eggs

115g/4oz/generous ¹/₂ cup sugar

grated rind of 1 orange

40g/1¹/₂oz/3 tbsp butter, melted

1 Preheat the oven to 180°C/350°F/
Gas 4. Place a baking sheet on the
middle shelf of the oven.

2 Wash the cranberries and pat dry.
Thickly smear the butter on the
bottom and sides of a 23 × 5cm/
9 × 2in round cake tin (pan). Add the
sugar and swirl the tin to coat evenly.

3 ▲ Add the cranberries and spread
in an even layer over the bottom of
the tin.

4 For the cake mixture, sift the flour
and baking powder twice. Set aside.

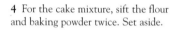

5 ▲ Combine the eggs, sugar and
orange rind in a heatproof bowl set
over a pan of hot but not boiling
water. With an electric mixer, beat
until the eggs leave a ribbon trail
when the beaters are lifted.

6 Add the flour mixture in three
batches, folding in well after each
addition. Gently fold in the melted
butter, then pour over the cranberries.

7 Bake for 40 minutes. Leave to cool
for 5 minutes, then run a knife
around the inside edge to loosen.

8 ▲ While the cake is still warm,
invert a plate on top of the tin.
Protecting your hands with oven
gloves, hold the plate and tin firmly
and turn them both over quickly. Lift
off the tin carefully.

Pineapple Upside-down Cake

SERVES 8

115g/4oz/¹/₂ cup butter

200g/7oz/scant 1 cup soft dark brown sugar

450g/1lb canned pineapple slices, drained

4 eggs, separated

grated rind of 1 lemon

pinch of salt

115g/4oz/generous ¹/₂ cup caster (superfine) sugar

75g/3oz/²/₃ cup plain (all-purpose) flour

5ml/1 tsp baking powder

1 Preheat the oven to 180°C/350°F/ Gas 4.

2 Melt the butter in a 25cm/10in ovenproof frying pan. Remove about 15ml/1 tbsp of the melted butter and set aside.

3 ▲ Add the brown sugar to the pan and stir until blended. Place the drained pineapple slices on top in one layer. Set aside.

~ VARIATION ~

For Apricot Upside-down Cake, replace the pineapple slices with 225g/8oz/1 cup ready-to-eat dried apricots. If they need softening, simmer them in about 120ml/4fl oz/¹/₂ cup orange juice until plump and soft. Drain the apricots and discard any remaining cooking liquid.

4 In a bowl, whisk together the egg yolks, reserved butter and lemon rind until well blended. Set aside.

5 ▼ With an electric mixer, beat the egg whites with the salt until stiff. Fold in the caster sugar, 25g/1oz/ 2 tbsp at a time. Fold in the egg yolk mixture.

6 Sift the flour and baking powder together. Carefully fold into the egg mixture in three batches.

7 ▲ Pour the mixture over the pineapple and smooth level.

8 Bake until a skewer inserted into the centre comes out clean, about 30 minutes.

9 While still hot, place a serving plate on top of the pan, bottom-side up. Holding them tightly together with oven gloves, quickly flip over. Serve hot or cold.

Lemon Coconut Layer Cake

SERVES 8–10

175g/6oz/1¹/2 cups plain (all-purpose) flour
pinch of salt
7 eggs
350g/12oz/scant 1³/4 cups caster (superfine) sugar
15ml/1 tbsp grated orange rind
grated rind of 2 lemons
juice of 1¹/2 lemon
65g/2¹/2oz/scant 1 cup desiccated (dry sweetened) coconut
15ml/1 tbsp cornflour (cornstarch)
120ml/4fl oz/¹/2 cup water
40g/1¹/2oz/3 tbsp butter
FOR THE ICING
75g/3oz/6 tbsp unsalted (sweet) butter
175g/6oz/1¹/2 cups icing (confectioners') sugar
grated rind of 1¹/2 lemons
30ml/2 tbsp lemon juice
200g/7oz/2¹/2 cups desiccated (dry sweetened) coconut

1 Preheat the oven to 180°C/350°F/ Gas 4. Line three 20cm/8in cake tins (pans) with baking parchment and grease. In a bowl, sift together the flour and salt and set aside.

2 ▲ Place six of the eggs in a large heatproof bowl set over hot water. With an electric mixer, beat until frothy. Gradually beat in 225g/8oz/ generous 1 cup caster sugar until the mixture doubles in volume and leaves a ribbon trail when the beaters are lifted, about 10 minutes.

3 ▲ Remove the bowl from the hot water. Fold in the orange rind, half the grated lemon rind and 15ml/1 tbsp of the lemon juice until blended. Fold in the coconut.

4 Sift over the flour mixture in three batches, gently folding in thoroughly after each addition.

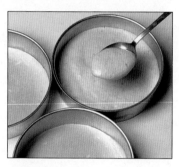

5 ▲ Divide the mixture between the prepared tins.

6 Bake until the cakes pull away from the sides of the tins, 20–25 minutes. Leave to stand for 3–5 minutes, then turn out to cool on a rack.

7 In a bowl, blend the cornflour with a little cold water to dissolve. Whisk in the remaining egg until just blended. Set aside.

8 ▲ In a pan, combine the remaining lemon rind and juice, the water, remaining sugar and butter.

9 Over medium heat, bring the mixture to the boil. Whisk in the eggs and cornflour mixture, and return to the boil. Whisk continuously until thick, about 5 minutes. Remove from the heat and pour into a bowl. Cover with clear film (plastic wrap); set aside.

10 ▲ For the frosting, cream the butter and icing sugar until smooth. Stir in the lemon rind and enough lemon juice to obtain a thick, spreadable consistency.

11 Sandwich the three cake layers with the lemon custard mixture. Spread the frosting over the top and sides. Cover the cake with the coconut, pressing it in gently.

Lemon Yogurt Ring

SERVES 12

225g/8oz/1 cup butter,
    at room temperature

300g/11oz/generous 1½ cups caster
    (superfine) sugar

4 eggs, at room temperature, separated

10ml/2 tsp grated lemon rind

85ml/3fl oz/generous ⅓ cup lemon juice

250ml/8fl oz/1 cup plain (natural) yogurt

275g/10oz/2½ cups plain
    (all-purpose) flour

10ml/2 tsp baking powder

5ml/1 tsp bicarbonate of soda
    (baking soda)

2.5ml/½ tsp salt

FOR THE GLAZE

115g/4oz/1 cup icing
    (confectioners') sugar

30ml/2 tbsp lemon juice

45–60ml/3–4 tbsp plain (natural) yogurt

1 Preheat oven to 180°C/350°F/Gas 4. Grease a 3 litre/5¼ pint/13¼ cup bundt or fluted tube tin (pan) and dust with flour.

2 With an electric mixer, cream the butter and caster sugar until light and fluffy. Add the egg yolks, one at a time, beating well after each addition.

3 ▲ Add the lemon rind, juice and yogurt, and stir to blend.

4 Sift together the flour, baking powder and bicarbonate of soda. In another bowl, beat the egg whites and salt until they hold stiff peaks.

5 ▲ Fold the dry ingredients into the butter mixture, then fold in a dollop of egg whites. Fold in the remaining whites until blended.

6 Pour into the tin and bake until a skewer inserted into the centre comes out clean, about 50 minutes. Leave to stand for 15 minutes, then turn out and cool on a rack.

7 For the glaze, sift the icing sugar into a bowl. Stir in the lemon juice and just enough yogurt to make a smooth glaze.

8 ▲ Set the cooled cake on the rack over a sheet of baking parchment or a baking sheet. Pour over the glaze and let it drip down the sides. Allow the glaze to set before serving.

Sour Cream Crumble Cake

SERVES 12–14

115g/4oz/¹/2 cup butter, at room temperature

130g/4¹/2oz/scant ³/4 cup caster (superfine) sugar

3 eggs, at room temperature

215g/7¹/2oz/scant 2 cups plain (all-purpose) flour

5ml/1 tsp bicarbonate of soda (baking soda)

5ml/1 tsp baking powder

250ml/8fl oz/1 cup sour cream

FOR THE TOPPING

225g/8oz/1 cup soft dark brown sugar

10ml/2 tsp ground cinnamon

115g/4oz/²/3 cup walnuts, finely chopped

50g/2oz/¹/4 cup cold butter, cut into pieces

1 Preheat the oven to 180°C/350°F/ Gas 4. Line the base of a 23cm/9in square cake tin (pan) with baking parchment and grease.

2 ▲ For the topping, place the brown sugar, cinnamon and walnuts in a bowl. Mix with your fingertips, then add the butter and continue working with your fingertips until the mixture resembles breadcrumbs.

3 To make the cake, cream the butter with an electric mixer until soft. Add the sugar and continue beating until the mixture is light and fluffy.

4 Add the eggs, one at a time, beating well after each addition.

5 In another bowl, sift the flour, bicarbonate of soda and baking powder together three times.

6 ▲ Fold the dry ingredients into the butter mixture in three batches, alternating with the sour cream. Fold until blended after each addition.

7 ▲ Pour half the batter into the prepared tin and sprinkle over half the walnut crumb topping mixture.

8 Pour the remaining batter on top and sprinkle over the remaining walnut crumb mixture.

9 Bake until browned, 60–70 minutes. Leave to stand for 5 minutes, then turn out and cool on a rack.

Plum Crumble Cake

SERVES 8–10

150g/5oz/10 tbsp butter or margarine, at room temperature

150g/5oz/³/4 cup caster (superfine) sugar

4 eggs, at room temperature

7.5ml/1¹/2 tsp vanilla extract

150g/5oz/1¹/4 cups plain flour

5ml/1 tsp baking powder

675g/1¹/2lb red plums, halved and stoned (pitted)

FOR THE TOPPING

115g/4oz/1 cup plain (all-purpose) flour

130g/4¹/2oz/generous ¹/2 cup soft light brown sugar

7.5ml/1¹/2 tsp ground cinnamon

75g/3oz/6 tbsp butter, cut in pieces

1 Preheat the oven to 180°C/350°F/ Gas 4.

2 For the topping, combine the flour, light brown sugar and cinnamon in a bowl. Add the butter and work the mixture with your fingertips until it resembles coarse breadcrumbs. Set aside.

3 ▲ Line a 25 × 5cm/10 × 2in tin (pan) with baking parchment and grease.

4 Cream the butter and sugar until light and fluffy.

5 ▲ Beat in the eggs, one at a time. Stir in the vanilla.

6 In a bowl, sift together the flour and baking powder, then fold into the butter mixture in three batches.

7 ▲ Pour the mixture into the tin. Arrange the plums on top.

8 ▲ Sprinkle the topping over the plums in an even layer.

9 Bake until a skewer inserted into the centre comes out clean, about 45 minutes. Leave to cool in the tin.

10 To serve, run a knife around the inside edge and invert on to a plate. Invert again on to a serving plate so that the topping is right-side up.

~ **VARIATION** ~

This cake can also be made with the same quantity of apricots, peeled, if preferred, or stoned cherries, or use a mixture of fruit, such as red or yellow plums, greengages and apricots.

Peach Torte

SERVES 8

115g/4oz/1 cup plain (all-purpose) flour
5ml/1 tsp baking powder
pinch of salt
115g/4oz/½ cup unsalted (sweet) butter, at room temperature
175g/6oz/scant 1 cup caster (superfine) sugar
2 eggs, at room temperature
6–7 peaches
sugar and lemon juice, for sprinkling
whipped cream, for serving (optional)

1 Preheat the oven to 180°C/350°F/ Gas 4. Grease a 25cm/10in springform cake tin (pan).

2 ▲ Sift together the flour, baking powder and salt. Set aside.

3 With an electric mixer, cream the butter and sugar until light and fluffy. Beat in the eggs, then fold in the dry ingredients until blended.

4 ▲ Spoon the mixture into the tin and smooth it to make an even layer over the bottom.

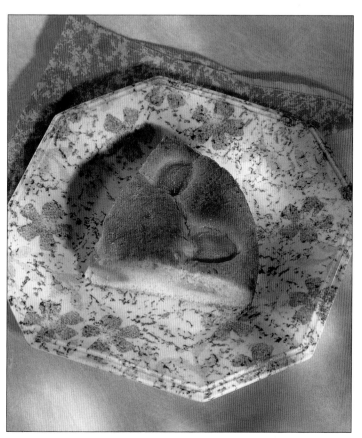

5 ▼ To skin the peaches, drop several at a time into a pan of gently boiling water. Boil for 10 seconds, then remove with a slotted spoon. Peel off the skin with the aid of a sharp knife. Cut the peaches in half and discard the stones (pits).

6 ▲ Arrange the peach halves on top of the mixture. Sprinkle lightly with sugar and lemon juice.

7 Bake until golden brown and set, 50–60 minutes. Serve warm, with whipped cream, if you like.

Apple Ring Cake

SERVES 12

7 eating apples, such as Cox's or
  Granny Smith

350ml/12fl oz/1¹/₂ cups vegetable oil

450g/1lb/2¹/₄ cups caster (superfine) sugar

3 eggs

425g/15oz/3¹/₂ cups plain (all-purpose) flour

5ml/1 tsp salt

5ml/1 tsp bicarbonate of soda (baking soda)

5ml/1 tsp ground cinnamon

5ml/1 tsp vanilla extract

115g/4oz/1 cup chopped walnuts

175g/6oz/generous 1 cup raisins

icing (confectioners') sugar, for dusting

1 Preheat the oven to 180°C/350°F/
Gas 4. Grease a 23cm/9in ring mould.

2 ▲ Quarter, peel, core and slice the
apples into a bowl. Set aside.

3 With an electric mixer, beat the oil
and sugar together until blended. Add
the eggs and continue beating until
the mixture is creamy.

4 Sift together the flour, salt,
bicarbonate of soda and cinnamon.

5 ▼ Fold the flour mixture into the
egg mixture with the vanilla. Stir in
the apples, walnuts and raisins.

6 Pour into the tin (pan) and bake until
the cake springs back when touched
lightly, about 1¹/₄ hours. Leave to stand
for 15 minutes, then turn out and
transfer to a cooling rack. Dust with
a layer of icing sugar before serving.

Orange Cake

SERVES 6

175g/6oz/1¹/₂ cups plain
  (all-purpose) flour

pinch of salt

7.5ml/1¹/₂ tsp baking powder

115g/4oz/¹/₂ cup butter or margarine

115g/4oz/generous ¹/₂ cup caster
  (superfine) sugar

grated rind of 1 large orange

2 eggs, at room temperature

30ml/2 tbsp milk

FOR THE SYRUP AND DECORATION

115g/4oz/generous ¹/₂ cup caster
  (superfine) sugar

250ml/8fl oz/1 cup fresh orange
  juice, strained

3 orange slices, for decorating

1 Preheat the oven to 180°C/350°F/
Gas 4. Line a 20cm/8in cake tin (pan)
with baking parchment and grease
the paper.

2 ▲ Sift the flour, salt and baking
powder on to baking parchment.

3 With an electric mixer, cream the
butter or margarine until soft. Add
the sugar and orange rind, and beat
until light and fluffy. Beat in the eggs,
one at a time. Fold in the flour in
three batches, then add the milk.

4 Spoon into the tin and bake until
the cake pulls away from the sides,
about 30 minutes. Remove from the
oven but leave in the tin.

5 Meanwhile, for the syrup, dissolve
the sugar in the orange juice over a
low heat. Add the orange slices and
simmer for 10 minutes. Remove and
drain. Leave the syrup to cool.

6 ▲ Prick the cake all over with a
fine skewer. Pour the syrup over the
hot cake. It may seem at first that
there is too much syrup for the cake
to absorb, but it will soak it all up.
Turn out when completely cooled and
decorate with small triangles of the
orange slices arranged on top.

Apple Ring Cake (top), Orange Cake

Orange and Walnut Roll

SERVES 8

4 eggs, separated

115g/4oz/generous 1/2 cup caster
(superfine) sugar

115g/4oz/1 cup very finely chopped walnuts

pinch of cream of tartar

pinch of salt

icing (confectioners') sugar, for dusting

FOR THE FILLING

300ml/1/2 pint/11/4 cups whipping cream

15ml/1 tbsp caster (superfine) sugar

grated rind of 1 orange

15ml/1 tbsp orange liqueur, such as
Grand Marnier

1 Preheat the oven to 180°C/350°F/
Gas 4. Line a 30 × 24cm/12 × 91/2in
Swiss roll tin (jelly roll pan) with
baking parchment and grease the paper.

2 With an electric mixer, beat the
egg yolks and sugar until thick.

3 ▲ Stir in the walnuts.

4 In another bowl, beat the egg
whites with the cream of tartar and
salt until they hold stiff peaks. Fold
gently but thoroughly into the
walnut mixture.

5 Pour the mixture into the prepared
tin and spread level with a spatula.
Bake for 15 minutes.

6 Run a knife along the inside edge
to loosen, then invert the cake on to
a sheet of baking parchment dusted
with icing sugar.

7 ▲ Peel off the baking parchment.
Roll up the cake while it is still warm
with the help of the sugared paper.
Set aside to cool.

8 For the filling, whip the cream
until it holds soft peaks. Stir together
the caster sugar and orange rind, then
fold into the whipped cream. Add
the liqueur.

9 ▲ Gently unroll the cake.
Spread the inside with a layer of
orange whipped cream, then re-roll.
Keep chilled until ready to serve.
Dust the top with icing sugar just
before serving.

Chocolate Roll

SERVES 10

225g/8oz plain (semisweet) chocolate
45ml/3 tbsp water
30ml/2 tbsp rum, brandy or strong coffee
7 eggs, separated
175g/6oz/scant 1 cup caster (superfine) sugar
pinch of salt
350ml/12fl oz/1½ cups whipping cream
icing (confectioners') sugar, for dusting

1 Preheat the oven to 180°C/350°F/ Gas 4. Line a 38 × 33cm/15 × 13in Swiss roll tin (jelly roll pan) with baking parchment and grease the paper.

2 ▲ Combine the chocolate, water and rum or other flavouring in the top of a double boiler, or in a heatproof bowl set over hot water. Heat until melted. Set aside.

3 With an electric mixer, beat the egg yolks and sugar until thick.

4 ▲ Stir in the melted chocolate.

5 In another bowl, beat the egg whites and salt until they hold stiff peaks. Fold a large dollop of the egg whites into the yolk mixture to lighten it, then carefully fold in the rest of the whites.

6 ▼ Pour the mixture into the pan; smooth evenly with a metal spatula.

7 Bake for 15 minutes. Remove from the oven, cover with baking parchment and a damp dish towel. Leave to stand for 1–2 hours.

8 With an electric mixer, whip the cream until stiff. Set aside.

9 Run a knife along the inside edge to loosen, then invert the cake on to a sheet of baking parchment that has been dusted with icing sugar.

10 Peel off the baking parchment. Spread with an even layer of whipped cream, then roll up the cake with the help of the sugared paper.

11 Chill for several hours. Before serving, dust with an even layer of icing sugar.

Chocolate Frosted Layer Cake

SERVES 8

225g/8oz/1 cup butter or margarine, at room temperature

300g/11oz/generous 1¹/₂ cups caster (superfine) sugar

4 eggs, at room temperature, separated

10ml/2 tsp vanilla extract

385g/13¹/₂oz/3¹/₃ cups plain (all-purpose) flour

10ml/2 tsp baking powder

pinch of salt

250ml/8fl oz/1 cup milk

FOR THE ICING

150g/5oz plain (semisweet) chocolate

120ml/4fl oz/¹/₂ cup sour cream

pinch of salt

1 Preheat the oven to 180°C/350°F/ Gas 4. Line two 20cm/8in round cake tins (pans) with baking parchment and grease. Dust with flour and shake to distribute. Tap to dislodge excess flour.

2 With an electric mixer, cream the butter or margarine until soft. Gradually add the sugar and continue beating until light and fluffy.

3 ▲ Lightly beat the egg yolks, then mix into the creamed butter and sugar with the vanilla.

4 Sift the flour with the baking powder three times. Set aside.

5 In another bowl, beat the egg whites with the salt until they hold stiff peaks. Set aside.

6 ▲ Gently fold the dry ingredients into the butter mixture in three batches, alternating with the milk.

7 Add a large dollop of the whites and fold in to lighten the mixture. Carefully fold in the remaining whites until just blended.

8 Divide the batter between the tins and bake until the cakes pull away from the sides of the tins, about 30 minutes. Leave to stand for 5 minutes. Turn out and cool on a rack.

9 ▲ For the icing, melt the chocolate in the top of a double boiler or a bowl set over hot water. When cool, stir in the sour cream and salt.

10 Sandwich the layers with icing, then spread on the top and side.

Devil's Food Cake with Orange Icing

SERVES 8–10

50g/2oz/¹/2 cup unsweetened cocoa powder

175ml/6fl oz/³/4 cup boiling water

175g/6oz/³/4 cup butter, at room temperature

350g/12oz/1¹/2 cups soft dark brown sugar

3 eggs, at room temperature

275g/10oz/2¹/2 cups plain (all-purpose) flour

7.5ml/1¹/2 tsp bicarbonate of soda
    (baking soda)

1.5ml/¹/4 tsp baking powder

120ml/4fl oz/¹/2 cup sour cream

orange rind strips, for decoration

FOR THE ICING

300g/11oz/generous 1¹/2 cups caster
    (superfine) sugar

2 egg whites

60ml/4 tbsp frozen orange juice concentrate

15ml/1 tbsp lemon juice

grated rind of 1 orange

1 Preheat the oven to 180°C/350°F/
Gas 4. Line two 23cm/9in cake tins
(pans) with baking parchment and
grease. In a bowl, mix the cocoa
and water until smooth. Set aside.

2 With an electric mixer, cream the
butter and sugar until light and fluffy.
Add the eggs, one at a time, beating
well after each addition.

3 ▲ When the cocoa mixture is
lukewarm, add to the butter mixture.

4 ▼ Sift together the flour, soda and
baking powder twice. Fold into the
cocoa mixture in three batches,
alternating with the sour cream.

5 Pour into the tins and bake until
the cakes pull away from the sides
of the tins, 30–35 minutes. Leave for
15 minutes. Turn out on to a rack.

6 Thinly slice the orange rind strips.
Blanch in boiling water for 1 minute.

7 ▲ For the icing, place all the
ingredients in the top of a double
boiler or in a bowl set over hot water.
With an electric mixer, beat until the
mixture holds soft peaks. Continue
beating off the heat until thick
enough to spread.

8 Sandwich the cake layers with
icing, then spread over the top
and side. Arrange the blanched
orange rind strips on top of the cake.

Best-ever Chocolate Sandwich

SERVES 12–14

115g/4oz/¹/₂ cup unsalted (sweet) butter
115g/4oz/1 cup plain (all-purpose) flour
50g/2oz/¹/₂ cup unsweetened cocoa powder
5ml/1 tsp baking powder
pinch of salt
6 eggs
225g/8oz/generous 1 cup caster (superfine) sugar
10ml/2 tsp vanilla extract
FOR THE ICING
225g/8oz plain (semisweet) chocolate,
75g/3oz/6 tbsp unsalted butter
3 eggs, separated
250ml/8fl oz/1 cup whipping cream
45ml/3 tbsp caster sugar

1 Preheat the oven to 180°C/350°F/ Gas 4. Line three 20 × 3cm/8 × 1¹/₂in round tins (pans) with baking parchment and grease.

2 ▲ Dust evenly with flour and spread with a brush. Set aside.

~ VARIATION ~

For a simpler icing, combine 250ml/ 8fl oz/1 cup whipping cream with 225g/8oz finely chopped plain chocolate in a pan. Stir over a low heat until the chocolate has melted. Cool and whisk to spreading consistency.

3 ▲ Melt the butter over a low heat. With a spoon, skim off any foam that rises to the surface. Set aside.

4 ▲ Sift the flour, cocoa, baking powder and salt together three times and set aside.

5 Place the eggs and sugar in a large heatproof bowl set over a pan of hot water. With an electric mixer, beat until the mixture doubles in volume and is thick enough to leave a ribbon trail when the beaters are lifted, about 10 minutes. Add the vanilla.

6 ▲ Sift over the dry ingredients in three batches, folding in carefully after each addition. Fold in the butter.

7 Divide the mixture between the tins and bake until the cakes pull away from the sides of the tin, about 25 minutes. Transfer to a rack.

8 For the icing, chop the chocolate and melt in the top of a double boiler, or in a heatproof bowl set over hot water.

9 ▲ Off the heat, stir in the butter and egg yolks. Return to a low heat and stir until thick. Remove from the heat and set aside.

10 Whip the cream until firm; set aside. In another bowl, beat the egg whites until stiff. Add the sugar and beat until glossy.

11 Fold the cream into the chocolate mixture, then carefully fold in the egg whites. Chill for 20 minutes to thicken the icing.

12 ▲ Sandwich the cake layers with icing, stacking them carefully. Spread the remaining icing evenly over the top and sides of the cake.

Rich Chocolate Nut Cake

SERVES 10

225g/8oz/1 cup butter

225g/8oz plain (semisweet) chocolate

115g/4oz/1 cup unsweetened cocoa powder

350g/12oz/1¾ cups caster (superfine) sugar

6 eggs

85ml/3fl oz/generous ⅓ cup brandy
    or cognac

225g/8oz/2 cups finely chopped hazelnuts

FOR THE GLAZE

50g/2oz/¼ cup butter

150g/5oz dark (bittersweet) chocolate

30ml/2 tbsp milk

5ml/1 tsp vanilla essence extract

1 Preheat the oven to 180°C/350°F/
Gas 4. Line a 23 × 5cm/9 × 2in round
tin (pan) with baking parchment; grease.

2 Melt the butter and chocolate
together in the top of a double boiler,
or in a heatproof bowl set over hot
water. Set aside to cool.

3 ▼ Sift the cocoa into a bowl. Add
the sugar and eggs, and stir until just
combined. Pour in the melted
chocolate mixture and brandy.

4 Fold in three-quarters of the nuts,
then pour the mixture into the
prepared tin.

5 ▲ Set the tin inside a roasting pan
containing 2.5cm/1in of hot water.
Bake until the cake is firm to the
touch, about 45 minutes. Leave to
stand for 15 minutes, then turn out
and transfer to a cooling rack.

6 Wrap the cake in baking
parchment and chill for 6 hours.

7 For the glaze, combine the butter,
chocolate, milk and vanilla in the top
of a double boiler or in a heatproof
bowl set over hot water, until melted.

8 Place a piece of baking parchment
under the cake, then drizzle spoonfuls
of glaze along the edge to drip down
and coat the sides. Pour the remaining
glaze on top of the cake.

9 ▲ Cover the sides of the cake with
the remaining nuts, gently pressing
them on with the palm of your hand.

Chocolate Layer Cake

SERVES 8–10

115g/4oz plain (semisweet) chocolate

175g/6oz/³/4 cup butter

450g/1lb/2¹/4 cups caster (superfine) sugar

3 eggs

5ml/1 tsp vanilla extract

175g/6oz/1¹/2 cups plain (all-purpose) flour

5ml/1 tsp baking powder

115g/4oz/1 cup chopped walnuts

FOR THE TOPPING

350ml/12fl oz/1¹/2 cups whipping cream

225g/8oz plain chocolate

15ml/1 tbsp vegetable oil

1 Preheat the oven to 180°C/350°F/ Gas 4. Line two 20cm/8in cake tins (pans), at least 4.5cm/1¹/2in deep, with baking parchment and grease.

2 Melt the chocolate and butter together in the top of a double boiler, or in a heatproof bowl set over a pan of hot water.

4 ▲ Sift over the flour and baking powder. Stir in the walnuts.

5 Divide the mixture between the prepared tins and spread level.

6 Bake until a skewer inserted into the centre comes out clean, about 30 minutes. Leave for 10 minutes, then turn out and transfer to a rack.

7 When the cakes are cool, whip the cream until firm. With a long serrated knife, carefully slice each cake in half horizontally.

8 Sandwich the layers with some of the whipped cream and spread the remainder over the top and sides of the cake. Chill until needed.

9 ▼ For the chocolate curls, melt the chocolate and oil in the top of a double boiler or a bowl set over hot water. Transfer to a non-porous surface. Spread to a 1cm/¹/2in thick rectangle. Just before the chocolate sets, hold the blade of a straight knife at an angle to the chocolate and scrape across the surface to make curls. Place on top of the cake.

3 ▲ Transfer to a mixing bowl and stir in the sugar. Add the eggs and vanilla, and mix until well blended.

~ VARIATION ~

To make Chocolate Ice Cream Layer Cake, sandwich the cake layers with softened vanilla ice cream. Freeze before serving.

Sachertorte

SERVES 8–10

115g/4oz plain (semisweet) chocolate

75g/3oz/6 tbsp unsalted (sweet) butter, at room temperature

50g/2oz/¼ cup caster (superfine) sugar

4 eggs, separated

1 extra egg white

1.5ml/¼ tsp salt

65g/2½oz/9 tbsp plain (all-purpose) flour, sifted

FOR THE TOPPING

75ml/5 tbsp apricot jam

250ml/8fl oz/1 cup plus 15ml/1 tbsp water

15g/½oz/1 tbsp unsalted butter

175g/6oz plain chocolate

75g/3oz/scant ½ cup caster sugar

ready-made chocolate decorating icing (optional)

1 Preheat the oven to 160°C/325°F/ Gas 3. Line a 23 × 5cm/9 × 2in cake tin (pan) with greaseproof paper and grease.

2 ▲ Melt the chocolate in the top of a double boiler, or in a heatproof bowl set over hot water. Set aside.

3 With an electric mixer, cream the butter and sugar until light and fluffy. Stir in the chocolate.

4 ▲ Beat in the yolks, one at a time.

5 In another bowl, beat the egg whites with the salt until stiff.

6 ▲ Fold a dollop of whites into the chocolate mixture to lighten it. Fold in the remaining whites in three batches, alternating with the sifted flour.

7 ▲ Pour into the tin and bake until a skewer comes out clean, about 45 minutes. Turn out on to a rack.

8 ▲ Meanwhile, melt the jam with 15ml/1 tbsp of the water over low heat, then strain for a smooth consistency.

9 For the frosting, melt the butter and chocolate in the top of a double boiler or a bowl set over hot water.

10 ▲ In a heavy pan, dissolve the sugar in the remaining water over low heat. Raise the heat and boil until it reaches 107°C/225°F (thread stage) on a sugar thermometer. Immediately plunge the bottom of the pan into cold water for 1 minute. Pour into the chocolate mixture and stir to blend. Leave to cool for a few minutes.

11 To assemble, brush the warm jam over the cake. Starting in the centre, pour over the frosting and work outward in a circular movement. Tilt the rack to spread; use a palette knife to smooth the side of the cake. Leave to set overnight. If you like, decorate with chocolate icing.

Raspberry and Hazelnut Meringue Cake

SERVES 8

150g/5oz/1¼ cups hazelnuts
4 egg whites
pinch of salt
200g/7oz/1 cup caster (superfine) sugar
2.5ml/½ tsp vanilla extract
FOR THE FILLING
300ml/½ pint/1¼ cups whipping cream
675g/1½lb raspberries

1 Preheat the oven to 180°C/350°F/ Gas 4. Line the base of two 20cm/8in cake tins (pans) with baking parchment and grease.

2 Spread the hazelnuts on a baking sheet and bake until lightly toasted, about 8 minutes. Cool slightly.

3 ▲ Rub the hazelnuts vigorously in a clean dishtowel to remove most of the skins.

4 Grind the nuts in a food processor, blender, or coffee grinder until they are the consistency of coarse sand.

5 Reduce oven to 150°C/300°F/Gas 2.

6 With an electric mixer, beat the egg whites and salt until they hold stiff peaks. Beat in 25g/1oz/2 tbsp of the sugar, then fold in the remaining sugar, a few tablespoons at a time, with a rubber scraper. Fold in the vanilla and the hazelnuts.

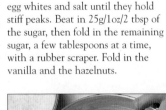

7 ▲ Divide the batter between the prepared tins and spread level.

8 Bake for 1¼ hours. If the meringues brown too quickly, protect with a sheet of foil. Leave to stand for 5 minutes, then carefully run a knife around the inside edge of the tins to loosen. Turn out on to a rack to cool.

9 For the filling, whip the cream until just firm.

10 ▲ Spread half the cream in an even layer on one meringue round and top with half the raspberries.

11 Top with the other meringue round. Spread the remaining cream on top and arrange the remaining raspberries over the cream. Chill for 1 hour for easy cutting.

Forgotten Gâteau

SERVES 6

6 egg whites, at room temperature

2.5ml/½ tsp cream of tartar

pinch of salt

300g/11oz/generous 1½ cups caster
(superfine) sugar

5ml/1 tsp vanilla extract

175ml/6fl oz/¾ cup whipping cream

FOR THE SAUCE

350g/12oz/2 cups fresh or thawed
frozen raspberries

30–45ml/2–3 tbsp icing (confectioners') sugar

1 Preheat the oven to 230°C/450°F/
Gas 8.

2 ▲ Grease a 1.5 litre/2½ pint/6¼ cup
ring mould. Beat the egg whites, cream
of tartar and salt until they hold soft
peaks. Add the sugar and beat until
glossy and stiff. Fold in the vanilla.

3 ▲ Spoon into the prepared mould
and smooth the top level.

4 Place in the oven, then turn the
oven off. Leave overnight; do not
open the oven door at any time.

5 ▼ To serve, gently loosen the edge
with a sharp knife and turn out on to
a serving plate. Whip the cream until
firm. Spread it over the top and upper
sides of the meringue and decorate
with any meringue crumbs.

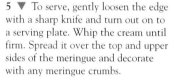

6 ▲ For the sauce, purée the fruit,
then strain. Sweeten to taste. Serve
with the gâteau.

~ COOK'S TIP ~

This recipe is not suitable for fan
assisted and solid fuel ovens.

Nut and Apple Gâteau

SERVES 8

115g/4oz/²⁄₃ cup pecan nuts or walnuts
50g/2oz/¹⁄₂ cup plain (all-purpose) flour
10ml/2 tsp baking powder
1.5ml/¹⁄₄ tsp salt
2 large cooking apples
3 eggs
225g/8oz/generous 1 cup caster (superfine) sugar
5ml/1 tsp vanilla extract
175ml/6fl oz/³⁄₄ cup whipping cream

1 Preheat the oven to 160°C/325°F/Gas 3. Line two 23cm/9in cake tins (pans) with baking parchment and grease the paper. Spread the nuts on a baking sheet and bake for 10 minutes.

2 Finely chop the nuts. Reserve 20g/³⁄₄oz/1¹⁄₂ tbsp and place the rest in a mixing bowl. Sift over the flour, baking powder and salt, and stir.

3 ▲ Quarter, core and peel the apples. Cut into 3mm/¹⁄₈in dice, then stir into the nut-flour mixture.

4 ▲ With an electric mixer, beat the eggs until frothy. Gradually add the sugar and vanilla, and beat until a ribbon forms, about 8 minutes. Gently fold in the flour mixture.

5 Pour into the tins and level the tops. Bake until a skewer inserted into the centre comes out clean, about 35 minutes. Leave to stand for 10 minutes.

6 ▲ To loosen, run a knife around the inside edge of each layer. Cool.

7 ▲ Whip the cream until firm. Spread half over the cake. Top with the second cake. Pipe whipped cream rosettes on top and sprinkle over the reserved nuts before serving.

Almond Cake

SERVES 4–6

225g/8oz/1¹/₃ cups blanched whole
   almonds, plus more for decorating

25g/1oz/2 tbsp butter

75g/3oz/6 tbsp icing (confectioners') sugar

3 eggs

2.5ml/¹/₂ tsp almond extract

25g/1oz/¹/₄ cup plain (all-purpose) flour

3 egg whites

15ml/1 tbsp caster (superfine) sugar

1 ▲ Preheat the oven to 160°C/325°F/
Gas 3. Line a 23cm/9in round cake tin
(pan) with baking parchment; grease.

2 ▲ Spread the almonds in a baking
tray and toast for 10 minutes. Cool, then
coarsely chop 185g/6¹/₂oz/generous 1 cup.

3 Melt the butter and set aside.
Increase oven temperature to
200°C/400°F/Gas 6.

4 Grind the chopped almonds with
half the icing sugar in a food processor,
blender or grinder. Transfer to a
mixing bowl.

5 ▲ Add the whole eggs and
remaining icing sugar. With an
electric mixer, beat until the mixture
forms a ribbon when the beaters are
lifted. Mix in the butter and almond
essence. Sift over the flour and fold
in gently.

6 With an electric mixer, beat the
egg whites until they hold soft peaks.
Add the caster sugar and beat until
stiff and glossy.

7 ▲ Fold the whites into the almond
mixture in four batches.

8 Spoon the mixture into the
prepared tin and bake in the centre
of the oven until golden brown, about
15–20 minutes. Decorate the top with
the remaining toasted whole almonds.
Serve warm.

Walnut Coffee Gâteau

SERVES 8–10

150g/5oz/1¼ cups walnuts
165g/5½oz/generous ¾ cup caster (superfine) sugar
5 eggs, separated
50g/2oz/1 cup dry breadcrumbs
15ml/1 tbsp unsweetened cocoa powder
15ml/1 tbsp instant coffee
30ml/2 tbsp rum or lemon juice
pinch of salt
90ml/6 tbsp redcurrant jelly
chopped walnuts, for decorating
FOR THE ICING
225g/8oz plain (semisweet) chocolate
750ml/1¼ pints/3 cups whipping cream

1 ▲ For the icing, combine the chocolate and cream in the top of a double boiler, or in a heatproof bowl set over simmering water. Stir until the chocolate melts. Leave to cool, then cover and chill overnight or until the mixture is firm.

2 Preheat the oven to 180°C/350°F/ Gas 4. Line a 23 × 5cm/9 × 2in cake tin (pan) with baking parchment and grease.

3 ▲ Grind the nuts with 40g/1½oz/ 3 tbsp of the sugar in a food processor, blender, or coffee grinder.

4 With an electric mixer, beat the egg yolks and remaining sugar until thick and lemon-coloured.

5 ▲ Fold in the walnuts. Stir in the breadcrumbs, cocoa, coffee and rum or lemon juice.

6 ▲ In another bowl, beat the egg whites with the salt until they hold stiff peaks. Fold carefully into the walnut mixture with a rubber scraper.

7 Pour the meringue batter into the prepared tin and bake until the top of the cake springs back when touched lightly, about 45 minutes. Let the cake stand for 5 minutes, then turn out and cool on a rack.

8 ▲ When cool, slice the cake in half horizontally.

9 With an electric mixer, beat the chocolate icing mixture on low speed until it becomes lighter, about 30 seconds. Do not overbeat or it may become grainy.

10 ▲ Warm the jelly in a pan until melted, then brush over the cut cake layer. Spread with some of the chocolate icing, then sandwich with the remaining cake layer. Brush the top of the cake with jelly, then cover the side and top with the remaining chocolate icing. Make a starburst pattern by pressing gently with a table knife in lines radiating from the centre. Arrange the chopped walnuts around the edge.

Light Fruit Cake

MAKES 2 LOAVES

225g/8oz/1 cup prunes

225g/8oz/1½ cups dates

225g/8oz/1 cup currants

225g/8oz/1⅓ cups sultanas (golden raisins)

250ml/8fl oz/1 cup dry white wine

250ml/8fl oz/1 cup rum

350g/12oz/3 cups plain (all-purpose) flour

10ml/2 tsp baking powder

5ml/1 tsp ground cinnamon

2.5ml/½ tsp freshly grated nutmeg

225g/8oz/1 cup butter, at room temperature

225g/8oz/generous 1 cup caster
(superfine) sugar

4 eggs, at room temperature,
lightly beaten

5ml/1 tsp vanilla extract

1 Pit the prunes and dates and chop finely. Place in a bowl with the currants and sultanas.

2 ▲ Stir in the wine and rum and leave to stand, covered, for 48 hours. Stir occasionally.

3 Preheat the oven to 150°C/300°F/ Gas 2 with a tray of hot water in the bottom. Line two 23 × 13cm/9 × 5in tins (pans) with baking parchment; grease.

4 Sift together the flour, baking powder, cinnamon, and nutmeg.

5 ▲ With an electric mixer, cream the butter and sugar together until light and fluffy.

6 Gradually add the eggs and vanilla. Fold in the flour mixture in three batches. Fold in the dried fruit mixture and its soaking liquid.

7 ▲ Divide the mixture between the tins and bake until a skewer inserted into the centre comes out clean, about 1½ hours.

8 Leave the cake to stand for 20 minutes, then turn out and transfer to a cooling rack. Wrap in foil and store in an airtight container. If possible, leave for at least 1 week before serving to allow the flavours to mellow.

Rich Fruit Cake

SERVES 12

150g/5oz/²/₃ cup currants
175g/6oz/generous 1 cup raisins
50g/2oz/¹/₃ cup sultanas (golden raisins)
50g/2oz/¹/₄ cup glacé (candied) cherries, halved
45ml/3 tbsp sweet sherry
175g/6oz/³/₄ cup butter
200g/7oz/scant 1 cup soft dark brown sugar
2 eggs, at room temperature
200g/7oz/1³/₄ cups plain (all-purpose) flour
10ml/2 tsp baking powder
10ml/2 tsp each ground ginger, allspice, and cinnamon
15ml/1 tbsp golden (light corn) syrup
15ml/1 tbsp milk
50g/2oz/¹/₃ cup cut mixed (candied) peel
115g/4oz/1 cup chopped walnuts
FOR THE DECORATION
225g/8oz/generous 1 cup caster (superfine) sugar
120ml/4fl oz/¹/₂ cup water
1 lemon, thinly sliced
¹/₂ orange, thinly sliced
120ml/4fl oz/¹/₂ cup orange marmalade
glacé cherries

1 One day before preparing, combine the currants, raisins, sultanas and cherries in a bowl. Stir in the sherry. Cover and leave overnight to soak.

2 Preheat the oven to 150°C/300°F/Gas 2. Line a 23 × 7.5cm/9 × 3in springform cake tin (pan) with baking parchment and grease. Place a tray of hot water on the bottom of the oven.

3 With an electric mixer, cream the butter and sugar until light and fluffy. Beat in the eggs, one at a time.

4 ▲ Sift the flour, baking powder and spices together three times. Fold into the butter mixture in three batches. Fold in the syrup, milk, dried fruit and liquid, mixed peel and nuts.

5 ▲ Spoon into the tin, spreading out so there is a slight depression in the centre of the mixture.

6 Bake until a skewer inserted into the centre comes out clean, 2¹/₂–3 hours. Cover with foil when the top is golden to prevent over-browning. Cool in the tin on a rack.

7 ▲ For the decoration, combine the sugar and water in a pan and bring to the boil. Add the lemon and orange slices and cook until crystallized, about 20 minutes. Work in batches, if necessary. Remove the fruit with a slotted spoon. Pour the remaining syrup over the cake and cool. Melt the marmalade over low heat, then brush over the top of the cake. Decorate with the crystallized citrus slices and cherries.

Whiskey Cake

MAKES 1 LOAF

175g/6oz/1¹/₂ cups chopped walnuts
75g/3oz/²/₃ cup raisins, chopped
75g/3oz/²/₃ cup currants
115g/4oz/1 cup plain (all-purpose) flour
5ml/1 tsp baking powder
1.5ml/¹/₄ tsp salt
115g/4oz/¹/₂ cup butter
225g/8oz/1 cup caster (superfine) sugar
3 eggs, at room temperature, separated
5ml/1 tsp freshly grated nutmeg
2.5ml/¹/₂ tsp ground cinnamon
85ml/3fl oz/generous ¹/₃ cup Irish whiskey
icing (confectioners') sugar, for dusting

1 ▼ Preheat the oven to 160°C/325°F/Gas 3. Line a 23 × 13cm/9 × 5in loaf tin (pan) with baking parchment. Grease the paper and sides of the pan.

2 ▲ Place the walnuts, raisins, and currants in a bowl. Sprinkle over 15g/¹/₂oz/2 tbsp of the flour, mix and set aside. Sift together the remaining flour, baking powder and salt.

3 ▲ Cream the butter and sugar until light and fluffy. Beat in the egg yolks.

4 Mix the nutmeg, cinnamon and whiskey. Fold into the butter mixture, alternating with the flour mixture.

5 ▲ In another bowl, beat the egg whites until stiff. Fold into the whiskey mixture until just blended. Fold in the walnut mixture.

6 Bake until a skewer inserted into the centre comes out clean, about 1 hour. Cool in the pan. Dust with icing sugar over a template.

Gingerbread

SERVES 8–10

15ml/1 tbsp vinegar
175ml/6fl oz/³/₄ cup milk
175g/6oz/1¹/₂ cups plain (all-purpose) flour
10ml/2 tsp baking powder
1.5ml/¹/₄ tsp bicarbonate of soda (baking soda)
2.5ml/¹/₂ tsp salt
10ml/2 tsp ground ginger
5ml/1 tsp ground cinnamon
1.5ml/¹/₄ tsp ground cloves
115g/4oz/¹/₂ cup butter, at room temperature
115g/4oz/generous ¹/₂ cup caster (superfine) sugar
1 egg, at room temperature
175ml/6fl oz/³/₄ cup black treacle (molasses)
whipped cream, for serving
chopped stem ginger, for decorating

1 ▲ Preheat the oven to 180°C/350°F/ Gas 4. Line an 20cm/8in square cake tin (pan) with baking parchment and grease the paper and the sides of the pan.

2 ▲ Add the vinegar to the milk and set aside. It will curdle.

3 In another mixing bowl, sift all the dry ingredients together three times and set aside.

4 With an electric mixer, cream the butter and sugar until light and fluffy. Beat in the egg until well combined.

5 ▼ Stir in the black treacle.

6 ▲ Fold in the dry ingredients in four batches, alternating with the milk. Mix only enough to blend.

7 Pour into the prepared tin and bake until firm, 45–50 minutes. Cut into squares and serve warm, with whipped cream. Decorate with the stem ginger.

Classic Cheesecake

SERVES 8

50g/2oz/1 cup digestive biscuits (graham crackers), crushed

900g/2lb/4 cups cream cheese, at room temperature

240g/8³/₄oz/scant 1¹/₄ cups caster (superfine) sugar

grated rind of 1 lemon

45ml/3 tbsp lemon juice

5ml/1 tsp vanilla extract

4 eggs, at room temperature

1 Preheat oven to 160°C/325°F/Gas 3. Grease a 20cm/8in springform cake tin (pan). Place on a round of foil 10–13cm/4–5in larger than the diameter of the tin. Press it up the sides to seal tightly.

2 Sprinkle the biscuits in the base of the tin. Press to form an even layer.

3 With an electric mixer, beat the cream cheese until smooth. Add the sugar, lemon rind and juice, and vanilla, and beat until blended. Beat in the eggs, one at a time. Beat just enough to blend thoroughly.

4 ▲ Pour into the prepared tin. Set the tin in a roasting pan and pour enough hot water in the roasting pan to come 2.5cm/1in up the side of the cake tin. Place in the oven.

5 Bake until the top of the cake is golden brown, about 1¹/₂ hours. Leave to cool in the tin.

6 ▼ Run a knife around the edge to loosen, then remove the rim of the tin. Chill for at least 4 hours before serving.

Chocolate Cheesecake

SERVES 10–12

275g/10oz plain (semisweet) chocolate

1.2kg/2¹/₂lb/5 cups cream cheese, at room temperature

200g/7oz/1 cup caster (superfine) sugar

10ml/2 tsp vanilla extract

4 eggs, at room temperature

175ml/6fl oz/³/₄ cup sour cream

15ml/1 tbsp unsweetened cocoa powder

FOR THE BASE

200g/7oz/3¹/₂ cups chocolate biscuits (cookies), crushed

75g/3oz/6 tbsp butter, melted

2.5ml/¹/₂ tsp ground cinnamon

1 Preheat oven to 180°C/350°F/Gas 4. Grease a 23 × 7.5cm/9 × 3in springform cake tin (pan).

2 ▲ For the base, mix the biscuits with the butter and cinnamon. Press on to the base of the tin.

3 Melt the chocolate in the top of a double boiler, or in a heatproof bowl set over hot water. Set aside.

4 Beat the cream cheese until smooth, then beat in the sugar and vanilla. Add the eggs, one at a time.

5 Stir the sour cream into the cocoa powder to form a paste. Add to the cream cheese mixture. Stir in the melted chocolate.

6 ▼ Pour into the crust. Bake for 1 hour. Cool in the tin; remove the rim. Chill before serving.

Classic Cheesecake (top), Chocolate Cheesecake

Lemon Mousse Cheesecake

SERVES 10–12

1.2kg/2¹/₂lb/5 cups cream cheese, at room temperature

350g/12oz/1³/₄ cups caster (superfine) sugar

40g/1¹/₂oz/¹/₃ cup plain (all-purpose) flour

4 eggs, at room temperature, separated

120ml/4fl oz/¹/₂ cup fresh lemon juice

grated rind of 2 lemons

115g/4oz/2 cups digestive biscuits (graham crackers), crushed

1 Preheat the oven to 160°C/325°F/ Gas 3. Line a 25 × 5cm/10 × 2in round cake tin (pan) with baking parchment and grease the paper.

2 With an electric mixer, beat the cream cheese until smooth. Gradually add 275g/10oz/1¹/₂ cups of the sugar, and beat until light. Beat in the flour.

3 ▲ Add the egg yolks, and lemon juice and rind, and beat until smooth and well blended.

4 In another bowl, beat the egg whites until they hold soft peaks. Add the remaining sugar and beat until stiff and glossy.

5 ▲ Add the egg whites to the cheese mixture and gently fold in.

6 Pour the mixture into the prepared tin, then place the tin in a roasting pan. Place in the oven and pour hot water in the pan to come 2.5cm/1in up the side of the tin.

7 Bake until golden, 60–65 minutes. Cool in the tin on a rack. Cover and chill for at least 4 hours.

8 To turn out, run a knife around the inside edge. Place a flat plate, bottom-side up, over the tin and invert on to the plate. Smooth the top with a metal spatula.

9 ▲ Sprinkle the biscuits over the top in an even layer, pressing down slightly to make a top crust.

10 To serve, cut slices with a sharp knife dipped in hot water.

Marbled Cheesecake

SERVES 10

50g/2oz/¹/₂ cup unsweetened cocoa powder
75ml/5 tbsp hot water
900g/2lb/4 cups cream cheese, at room temperature
200g/7oz/1 cup caster (superfine) sugar
4 eggs
5ml/1 tsp vanilla extract
65g/2¹/₂oz/1¹/₄ cups digestive biscuits (graham crackers), crushed

1 Preheat the oven to 180°C/350°F/ Gas 4. Line an 20 × 8cm/8 × 3in cake tin (pan) with baking parchment; grease.

2 Sift the cocoa powder into a bowl. Pour over the hot water and stir to dissolve. Set aside.

3 With an electric mixer, beat the cheese until smooth and creamy. Add the sugar and beat to incorporate. Beat in the eggs, one at a time. Do not overmix.

4 Divide the mixture evenly between two bowls. Stir the chocolate mixture into one, then add the vanilla to the remaining mixture.

5 ▲ Pour a cupful of the plain mixture into the centre of the tin; it will spread out into an even layer. Slowly pour over a cupful of chocolate mixture in the centre.

6 ▲ Repeat alternating cupfuls of the batters in a circular pattern until both are used up.

7 Set the tin in a roasting pan and pour in hot water to come 4cm/1¹/₂in up the sides of the cake tin.

8 Bake until the top of the cake is golden, about 1¹/₂ hours. It will rise during baking but will sink later. Leave to cool in the tin on a rack.

9 To turn out, run a knife around the inside edge. Place a flat plate, bottom-side up, over the tin and invert on to the plate.

10 ▼ Sprinkle the crushed biscuits evenly over the base, gently place another plate over them, and invert again. Cover and chill for at least 3 hours, or overnight. To serve, cut slices with a sharp knife dipped in hot water.

Heart Cake

MAKES 1 CAKE

225g/8oz/1 cup butter or margarine

225g/8oz/generous 1 cup caster (superfine) sugar

4 eggs, at room temperature

175g/6oz/1½ cups plain (all-purpose) flour

5ml/1 tsp baking powder

2.5ml/½ tsp bicarbonate of soda (baking soda)

30ml/2 tbsp milk

5ml/1 tsp vanilla extract

FOR ICING AND DECORATING

3 egg whites

350g/12oz/1¾ cups caster sugar

30ml/2 tbsp cold water

30ml/2 tbsp fresh lemon juice

1.5ml/¼ tsp cream of tartar

pink food colouring

75–115g/3–4oz/6–8 tbsp icing (confectioners') sugar

1 Preheat the oven to 180°C/350°F/ Gas 4. Line a 20cm/8in heart-shaped tin (pan) with baking parchment; grease.

2 ▲ With an electric mixer, cream the butter or margarine and sugar until light and fluffy. Add the eggs, one at a time, beating thoroughly after each addition.

3 Sift the flour, baking powder and baking soda together. Fold the dry ingredients into the butter mixture in three batches, alternating with the milk. Stir in the vanilla.

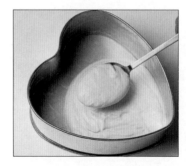

4 ▲ Spoon the mixture into the prepared tin and bake until a skewer inserted into the centre comes out clean, 35–40 minutes. Leave the cake to stand in the tin for 5 minutes, then turn out and transfer to a rack to cool completely.

5 For the icing, combine two of the egg whites, the caster sugar, water, lemon juice and cream of tartar in the top of a double boiler or in a bowl set over simmering water. With an electric mixer, beat until thick and holding soft peaks, about 7 minutes. Remove from the heat and continue beating until the mixture is thick enough to spread. Tint the icing with the pink food colouring.

6 ▲ Put the cake on a board, about 30cm/12in square, covered in foil or in paper suitable for contact with food. Spread the icing evenly on the cake. Smooth the top and sides. Leave to set for 3–4 hours, or overnight.

7 ▲ For the paper piping (pastry) bags, fold a 28 × 20cm/11 × 8in sheet of baking parchment in half diagonally, then cut into two pieces along the fold mark. Roll over the short side, so that it meets the right-angled corner and forms a cone. To form the piping bag, hold the cone in place with one hand, wrap the point of the long side of the triangle around the cone, and tuck inside, folding over twice to secure. Snip a hole in the pointed end and slip in a small metal piping nozzle to extend about 5mm/¼in.

8 For the piped decorations, place 15ml/1 tbsp of the remaining egg white in a bowl and whisk until frothy. Gradually beat in enough icing sugar to make a stiff mixture suitable for piping.

9 ▲ Spoon into a paper piping bag to half-fill. Fold over the top and squeeze to pipe decorations on the top and sides of the cake.

Iced Fancies

MAKES 16

115g/4oz/1/2 cup butter, at room temperature

225g/8oz/generous 1 cup caster
(superfine) sugar

2 eggs, at room temperature

175g/6oz/11/2 cups plain (all-purpose) flour

1.5ml/1/4 tsp salt

7.5ml/11/2 tsp baking powder

120ml/4fl oz/1/2 cup plus 15ml/1 tbsp milk

5ml/1 tsp vanilla extract

FOR ICING AND DECORATING

2 large egg whites

400g/14oz/31/2 cups sifted icing
(confectioners') sugar

1–2 drops glycerine

juice of 1 lemon

food colourings

hundreds and thousands, for decorating

crystallized lemon and orange slices

1 Preheat oven to 190°C/375°F/Gas 5.

2 ▲ Line 16 bun-tray cups with
fluted paper baking cases, or grease.

~ COOK'S TIP ~

Ready-made cake decorating
products are widely available, and
may be used, if you prefer, instead
of the recipes given for icing
and decorating. Coloured icing in
ready-to-pipe tubes is useful.

3 With an electric mixer, cream the
butter and sugar until light and fluffy.
Add the eggs, one at a time, beating
well after each addition.

4 Sift together the flour, salt and
baking powder. Stir into the butter
mixture, alternating with the milk.
Stir in the vanilla.

5 ▲ Fill the cups half-full and bake
until the tops spring back when
touched lightly, about 20 minutes.
Let the cakes stand in the tray for
5 minutes, then turn out and transfer
to a rack to cool completely.

6 For the icing, beat the egg whites
until stiff but not dry. Gradually add
the sugar, glycerine and lemon juice,
and continue beating for 1 minute.
The consistency should be spreadable.
If necessary, thin with a little water or
add more sifted icing sugar to thicken.

7 ▲ Divide the icing between several
bowls and tint with food colourings.
Spread different coloured icings over
the cooled cakes.

8 ▲ Decorate the cakes as you like,
with sugar decorations such as
hundreds and thousands.

9 ▲ Other decorations include
crystallized orange and lemon slices.
Cut into small pieces and arrange on
top of the cakes. Alternatively, use
other suitable sweets (candies).

10 ▲ To make freehand iced
decorations, fill paper piping (pastry)
bags with different coloured icings.
Pipe on faces, or make other designs.

Snake Cake

SERVES 10–12

225g/8oz/1 cup butter or margarine, at room temperature
grated rind and juice of 1 small orange
225g/8oz/generous 1 cup caster (superfine) sugar
4 eggs, at room temperature, separated
175g/6oz/1¹/₂ cups plain (all-purpose) flour
5ml/1 tsp baking powder
pinch of salt
FOR THE ICING AND DECORATING
25g/1oz/2 tbsp butter, at room temperature
350g/12oz/3 cups icing (confectioners') sugar
150g/5oz plain (semisweet) chocolate
pinch of salt
120ml/4fl oz/¹/₂ cup sour cream
1 egg white
green and blue food colourings

1 Preheat the oven to 190°C/375°F/ Gas 5. Grease two 21cm/8¹/₂in ring tins (pans) and dust them with flour.

2 Cream the butter or margarine, orange rind and sugar until light. Beat in the egg yolks, one at a time.

3 Sift the flour and baking powder. Fold into the butter mixture, alternating with the orange juice.

4 ▲ In another bowl, beat the egg whites and salt until stiff.

5 Fold a large dollop of the egg whites into the creamed butter mixture to lighten it, then gently fold in the remaining whites.

6 Divide the mixture between the prepared tins and bake until a skewer inserted into the centre comes out clean, about 25 minutes. Leave to stand for 5 minutes, then turn out on to a wire rack to cool.

7 Prepare a board, 60 × 20cm/ 24 × 8in, covered in paper suitable for contact with food, or in foil.

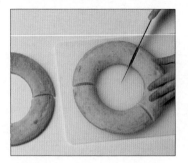

8 ▲ Cut the cakes into three even pieces. Trim to level the flat side, if necessary, and shape the head by cutting off wedges from the front. Shape the tail in the same way.

9 ▲ For the buttercream, mix the butter with 40g/1¹/₂oz/scant ¹/₂ cup of the icing sugar. Use to join the cake sections and arrange on the board.

10 ▲ For the chocolate icing, melt the chocolate. Stir in the salt and sour cream. When cool, spread over the cake and smooth the surface.

11 ▲ For the decoration, beat the egg white until frothy. Add enough of the remaining icing sugar to obtain a thick mixture. Divide among several bowls and add food colourings.

12 ▲ Fill paper piping (pastry) bags with icing, and pipe decorations along the top of the cake.

Sun Cake

Serves 10–12

115g/4oz/1/2 cup unsalted (sweet) butter
6 eggs
225g/8oz/generous 1 cup caster (superfine) sugar
115g/4oz/1 cup plain (all-purpose) flour
2.5ml/1/2 tsp salt
5ml/1 tsp vanilla extract
For icing and decorating
25g/1oz/2 tbsp unsalted butter, at room temperature
450 g/1lb/4 cups sifted icing (confectioners') sugar
120ml/4fl oz/1/2 cup apricot jam
30ml/2 tbsp water
2 large egg whites
1–2 drops glycerine
juice of 1 lemon
yellow and orange food colourings

1 Preheat the oven to 180°C/350°F/ Gas 4. Line two 20 × 5cm/8 × 2in round cake tins (pans), then grease and flour.

2 In a pan, melt the butter over very low heat. Skim off any foam that rises to the surface, then set aside.

3 ▲ Place a heatproof bowl over a pan of hot water. Add the eggs and sugar. Beat with an electric mixer until the mixture doubles in volume and is thick enough to leave a ribbon trail when the beaters are lifted, 8–10 minutes.

4 Sift the flour and salt together three times. Sift over the egg mixture in three batches, folding in well after each addition. Fold in the melted butter and vanilla.

5 Divide the mixture between the tins. Level the surfaces and bake until the cakes shrink slightly from the sides of the tins, 25–30 minutes. Leave to stand for 5 minutes, then turn out and transfer to a cooling rack.

6 Prepare a board, 40cm/16in square, covered in paper suitable for contact with food, or in foil.

7 ▲ For the sunbeams, cut one of the cakes into eight equal wedges. Cut away a rounded piece from the base of each so that they fit neatly up against the sides of the whole cake.

8 ▲ For the butter icing, mix the butter and 25g/1oz/1/4 cup of the icing sugar. Use to attach the sunbeams.

9 ▲ Melt the jam with the water and brush over the cake. Place on the board and straighten, if necessary.

10 ▲ For the icing, beat the egg whites until stiff but not dry. Gradually add 400 g/14oz/3 1/2 cups icing sugar, the glycerine and lemon juice, and continue beating for 1 minute. If necessary, thin with water or add a little more sugar. Tint with yellow food colouring and spread over the cake.

11 ▲ Divide the remaining icing in half and tint with more food colouring to obtain bright yellow and orange. Pipe decorative zigzags on the sunbeams and a face in the middle.

Jack-O'-Lantern Cake

SERVES 8–10

175g/6oz/1½ cups plain (all-purpose) flour

12.5ml/2½ tsp baking powder

pinch of salt

115g/4oz/½ cup butter,
   at room temperature

225g/8oz/generous 1 cup caster
   (superfine) sugar

3 egg yolks, at room temperature,
   well beaten

5ml/1 tsp grated lemon rind

175ml/6fl oz/¾ cup milk

FOR THE CAKE COVERING

500–675g/1¼lb–1½lb/5–6 cups icing
   (confectioners') sugar

2 egg whites

30ml/2 tbsp liquid glucose

orange and black food colourings

1 Preheat the oven to 190°C/375°F/
Gas 5. Line a 20cm/8in round cake
tin (pan) with baking parchment
and grease.

2 Sift together the flour, baking
powder and salt. Set aside.

3 With an electric mixer, cream the
butter and sugar until light and fluffy.
Gradually beat in the egg yolks, then
add the lemon rind. Fold in the flour
mixture in three batches, alternating
with the milk.

4 Spoon the mixture into the
prepared tin. Bake until a skewer
inserted into the centre comes out
clean, about 35 minutes. Leave to
stand, then turn out on to a rack.

~ COOK'S TIP ~

If you prefer, use ready-made
roll-out cake covering,
available at cake decorating
suppliers. Knead in food
colouring, if required.

5 For the icing, sift 500g/1¼lb/5 cups
of the icing sugar into a bowl. Make a
well in the centre, add 1 egg white,
the glucose and orange food
colouring. Stir until a dough forms.

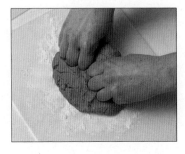

6 ▲ Transfer to a clean work
surface dusted with icing sugar and
knead briefly.

7 ▲ Carefully roll out the orange
cake covering to a thin sheet.

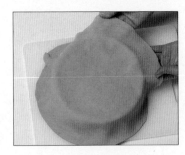

8 ▲ Place the sheet on top of the
cooled cake and smooth the sides.
Trim the excess icing and reserve.

9 ▲ From the trimmings, cut shapes
for the top. Tint the remaining cake
covering trimmings with black food
colouring. Roll out thinly and cut
shapes for the face.

10 ▲ Brush the undersides with
water and arrange the face on top
of the cake.

11 ▲ Place 15ml/1 tbsp of the
remaining egg white in a bowl and
stir in enough icing sugar to make
a thick icing. Tint with black food
colouring, fill a paper piping (pastry)
bag and complete the decoration.

Stars and Stripes Cake

SERVES 20

225g/8oz/1 cup butter or margarine,
   at room temperature

225g/8oz/1 cup soft dark brown sugar

225g/8oz/generous 1 cup granulated sugar

5 eggs, at room temperature

275g/10oz/2½ cups plain (all-purpose) flour

10ml/2 tsp baking powder

5ml/1 tsp bicarbonate of soda
   (baking soda)

5ml/1 tsp ground cinnamon

5ml/1 tsp ground ginger

2.5ml/½ tsp ground allspice

1.5ml/¼ tsp ground cloves

1.5ml/¼ tsp salt

350ml/12fl oz/1½ cups buttermilk

75g/3oz/½ cup raisins

FOR THE CAKE COVERING

25g/1oz/2 tbsp butter

1–1.25kg/2¼lb–2lb 10oz/9–10 cups icing
   (confectioners') sugar

3 egg whites

60ml/4 tbsp liquid glucose

red and blue food colourings

1 Preheat the oven to 180°C/350°F/
Gas 4. Line a 30 × 23cm/12 × 9in
baking tin (pan) with baking
parchment and lightly grease.

2 With an electric mixer, cream the
butter or margarine and sugars until
light and fluffy. Gradually beat in the
eggs, one at a time, beating well after
each addition.

3 Sift together the flour, baking
powder, bicarbonate of soda, spices
and salt. Fold into the butter mixture
in three batches, alternating with the
buttermilk. Stir in the raisins.

4 Pour the mixture into the prepared
tin and bake until the cake springs back
when touched lightly, about 35 minutes.
Leave to stand for 10 minutes, then
turn out on to a wire rack.

5 Make buttercream for assembling the
cake by mixing the butter with 40g/
1½oz/scant ½ cup of the icing sugar.

6 ▲ When the cake is cool, cut a
curved shape from the top.

7 ▲ Attach it to the bottom of the
cake with the buttercream.

8 Prepare a board, about 40 × 30cm/
16 × 12in, covered in paper suitable
for contact with food, or in foil.
Transfer the cake to the board.

9 For the cake covering, sift 1kg/
2¼lb/9 cups of the icing sugar into a
bowl. Add two of the egg whites and
the liquid glucose. Stir until the
mixture forms a dough.

10 Cover and set aside half of the
covering. On a clean work surface
lightly dusted with icing sugar, roll
out the remaining covering to a
sheet. Carefully transfer to the cake.
Smooth the sides and trim any excess
from the bottom edges.

11 ▲ Tint one-quarter of the
remaining covering blue and tint the
remainder red. Roll out the blue to a
thin sheet and cut out the background
for the stars. Place on the cake.

12 ▲ Roll out the red covering, cut
out stripes and place on the cake.

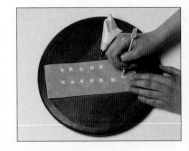

13 ▲ For the stars, mix 15ml/1 tbsp
of the egg white with just enough
icing sugar to thicken. Pipe small
stars on to a sheet of baking
parchment and leave to set. When
dry, peel them off and place on the
blue background.

INDEX

~

NOTES

NOTES

NOTES

NOTES

NOTES

NOTES

NOTES

NOTES